RELIGION OF FEAR

RELIGION OF FEAR

*The True Story of the Church
of God of the Union Assembly*

David Cady

The University of Tennessee Press
Knoxville

Library of Congress Cataloging-in-Publication Data
Names: Cady, David, author.
Title: Religion of fear : the true story of the Church of God of the Union Assembly
/ David Cady.
Description: First edition. | Knoxville : University of Tennessee Press,
[2019] | Includes bibliographical references and index. |
Identifiers: LCCN 2018043529 (print) | LCCN 2018053078 (ebook) |
ISBN 9781621905097 (kindle) | ISBN 9781621905103 (pdf) |
ISBN 9781621905080 (hardcover)
Subjects: LCSH: Church of God of Union Assembly—History. |
Holiness churches—United States. | Pratt, Charles Thomas, 1879–1966. |
Pratt, Jesse Franklin, 1946–2005.
Classification: LCC BX7062.A4 (ebook) | LCC BX7062.A4 C33 2019 (print) |
DDC 289.9/40973—dc23
LC record available at https://lccn.loc.gov/2018043529

"A closed society which exerts power and influence over its followers, The Church of God of Union Assembly has been dominated by the general overseer who tightens control by preaching fear of God's wrath. The faithful are controlled by detailed church rules . . . on penalty of being 'dismissed.' And one of the rules commands members to stay away from any dismissed member."

MOODY CONNELL
"Faithful Follow Rules of Church," *The Daily Citizen-News*,
July 2, 1980, 1

"One cannot and must not try to erase the past merely because it does not fit the present."

GOLDA MEIR
Prime Minister of Israel (1969–1974)

"It may be too late for justice but never too late for the truth."

AUTHOR UNKNOWN

CONTENTS

Index of Individuals xiii

Foreword xvii
  Dr. Ralph W. Hood Jr.

Acknowledgments xxi

Introduction: The Beginning of the End xxiii

Prologue: The Devil in Chains 1

Part I. Building a Dynasty, 1897–1945

1. In the Beginning 7
2. Creation 19
3. Camp of the Saints 25
4. Bringing in the Sheaves 33
5. Love Thy Neighbor 41
6. Thou Shall Not Covet Thy Neighbor's Wife 53

Part II. Betrayal, 1945–1974

7. An Attitude Change 69
8. Thou Shall Not Bear False Witness 73
9. Thou Shall Not Commit Adultery 83
10. Honor Thy Father and Thy Mother 101
11. Building Fear 115
12. The Boss 127
13. The Root of All Evil 137
14. The Wages of Sin Is Death 143
15. A Prudent Wife 155

Part III. A Dutiful Son, 1974–1996

16. A New Level of Hell 175
17. Dying in the Faith 189
18. And Ye Shall Know the Truth 203
19. And the Truth Shall Make You Free 225

Epilogue 231

Notes 235

Bibliography 259

Index 269

ILLUSTRATIONS

Charles Thomas Pratt Family Tree	xi
The Early Pratt Family	3
Margaret Elizabeth Pratt, ca. 1900	8
C. T. Pratt's Second Church, 1919	17
Crown Cotton Mill	28
The Young Preacher, C. T. Pratt	30
Johnny Burnette and Jesse F. Pratt	44
Assistant Moderator W. P. Foster with Moderator C. T. Pratt, ca. 1940	50
Picnic Lunch Called "Homecoming," ca. 1946	54
Inside Drawing of the Union Assembly Church	55
The Bill of Sale of C. T. Pratt's Chenille Company	57
The Harmonetts, Including Irene Pratt	60
Rev. Clinton Bell, 1959	88
Dorothy Pitner at Age Ten	90
C. T. Pratt and Minnie Doing Their Radio Program, Late 1950s	95
The Church of God of the Union Assembly in Kokomo, Indiana	96
Clinton Bell and Johnny Burnett as Patrolmen in Union City	99
Dennis Smith, H. D. "Cash" Carmical, and Ollen Brewer	107
Eight of C. T. Pratt's Children	125
Portrait of Irene and Jesse	128
Margie Lewis Haney	136
Jesse and Irene Pratt	140
US Army Photograph of Jesse F. Pratt Jr.	145
Paul Hughes with Jesse Pratt	147
The Union Assembly's Maternity Center, Spring Place, Georgia	159
Wayman Pratt, Jesse Pratt, and Estle Pratt	168
Robert Anderson at Age Seventeen	185
Marie Hoskins at Age Sixteen	185
Jesse Junior and "Mother" Irene	188
Charles Roberts with His Father, William "Junior" Roberts	192
Marie Hoskins with Her Mother, Donna, 1973	200
Jesse Pratt Jr. with Second Wife, Wanda Poole	226
Jesse Jr.'s Tombstone in Dalton	232

CHARLES THOMAS PRATT OF
WAYNE COUNTY, KENTUCKY, FAMILY TREE

George W. Pratt (1844-1921) *married* Margaret Lair (1841-1918)

Charles T. Pratt (1879-1966) *married* Minnie Broyles (1889-1971)

Edmond	Lloyd	Flora	Estle	Alma	Jesse	Martha	Leola	Herbert	Wayman
b.1906	*b.1908*	*b.1911*	*b.1912*	*b.1914*	*b. 1917*	*b. 1921*	*b.1923*	*b. 1928*	*b. 1931*

Jesse Franklin Pratt

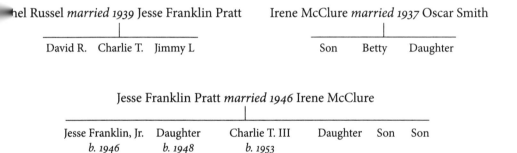

hel Russel *married 1939* Jesse Franklin Pratt   Irene McClure *married 1937* Oscar Smith

David R.	Charlie T.	Jimmy L		Son	Betty	Daughter

Jesse Franklin Pratt *married 1946* Irene McClure

Jesse Franklin, Jr.	Daughter	Charlie T. III	Daughter	Son	Son
b. 1946	*b. 1948*	*b. 1953*			

INDEX OF INDIVIDUALS

The Family

CHARLES THOMAS PRATT

(born in 1879): Also called Charlie and C. T., founder of the Union Assembly of the Church of God. Name later changed to the Church of God Union Assembly (CGUA). Served as moderator and general overseer.

MARY "MINNIE" BROYLES PRATT

(born 1889): Wife of Charlie and secretary/treasurer of the Union Assembly Church.

OFFSPRING OF CHARLIE (C. T.) AND MINNIE PRATT (IN ORDER OF BIRTH)

EDMOND L. (ED) PRATT

(born 1906): Preacher for the Union Assembly.

LLOYD B. PRATT

(born 1908): Twin to Lewis Pratt who died at four months.

FLORA E. PRATT HUGHES

(born 1911): Midwife of the Union Assembly Church.

ELMER "ESTLE" PRATT

(born 1912): Preacher and member of the Supreme Council.

CORA "ALMA" PRATT EDWARDS

(born 1914): Midwife for the Union Assembly Church.

JESSE FRANKLIN PRATT

(born 1917): Became general overseer after his father in 1961.

MARTHA PRATT VAN METER

(born 1921): Called Tiny, she was a midwife of the Union Assembly church.

ELVA "LEOLA" PRATT CRIDER

(born 1923): Midwife of the Union Assembly church.

HERBERT H. PRATT

(born 1928): Minister and manager of the ranch in Arizona.

WAYMAN P. PRATT

(born 1931): Minister and assistant general overseer.

PAUL L. HUGHES

(born 1931): Minister, on Supreme Council. Son of Flora Pratt Hughes. Grandson of C. T. and Minnie.

JESSE FRANKLIN PRATT JR.

(born 1946): Became the Church's general overseer. Son of Jesse F. Pratt and Irene.

CHARLIE THOMAS PRATT III

> (born 1953): Became general overseer. Son of Jesse F. Pratt and Irene.

CHARLES THOMAS 'TOM' PRATT

> (born 1929): Became pastor in Kokomo, Indiana, and Hamilton, Ohio. Son of Lloyd Pratt.

SPOUSES OF THE CHILDREN OF C. T. AND MINNIE PRATT

ETHEL B. RUSSELL PRATT

> (born 1922): First wife of Jesse F. Pratt Sr.; Children of Ethel and Jesse were David Ronald, Charlie T. II, Jimmy L.

IRENE MCCLURE PRATT

> (born 1918): Divorced Oscar Smith to marry Jesse F. Pratt Sr.; Children were Jesse F. Junior, Charlie T. III plus two more sons and two daughters.

WESLEY CRIDER

> Second husband to Leola Pratt (they married twice); member of the Supreme Council.

WANDA JEAN POOLE

> (born 1951): Jesse Pratt Junior's second wife. They had five children together.

Important Ministers and Members of the Union Assembly

CLINTON BELL

> Minister of the Union Assembly Church in Kokomo, Indiana, and at other CGUA churches. A member of the Supreme Council.

JOHNNY BURNETT

> A one-armed pilot for the church and a minister of one of the Union Assembly churches in TN. Wife was sister to Irene. On the Supreme Council

J. WILLIE BURNETT

> Minister and founding father of the Union Assembly with C. T. Pratt. Life-long member of the Supreme Council, but was removed by Jesse Sr. in 1945.

CHARLIE CARMICAL

> (born 1942): Son to Hugh "Cash" Carmical. Old friend of the author's.

HUGH "CASH" CARMICAL

> Became the pastor of the Knoxville Union Assembly Church in the late 1940s. Moved to Dalton to become Assistant general overseer under C. T. Pratt.

DAN HELMICK

> Pastor in Kentucky. Sent to pastor the Union Assembly Church in Hamilton, Ohio.

CHARLES ROBERTS

> (born 1954): Son of William (Junior) Roberts—Union Assembly pastor at Center (Cartersville), and Trion, Georgia. Grandson of Otha Pitner—Union Assembly pastor in Hamilton, Ohio, and in North Carolina.

Charles had great insight into the Union Assembly and was interviewed by the author hundreds of times. He was put on trial by the CGUA in 1995 and expelled from the church.

DENNIS SMITH

Minister and on the Supreme Council. Married to one of Irene's sisters.

DON WEST

A minister and editor of the Church paper, *The Southerner,* he was forced to leave Atlanta and then Dalton because of his Communist and union affiliations.

FOREWORD

David Cady has written an important and highly readable book. At times it reads like a novel, full of intrigue and suspense. Yet it is not a novel. Neither is it the work of a historian nor that of a psychologist, although both history and psychology are implicit when not explicit throughout the story David tells. Even the word story is misleading, for David's book is definitely not a work of fiction. David's considerable talent is directed at letting others tell their stories, their experiences of being involved in and leaving what was once a powerful emerging religion rooted in the Pratt family. The religion exists today, attenuated in the power it wields and heavily modified in its beliefs and less able to enforce behaviors among those who continue to believe in what are now less restrictive dogmas. To those well versed in the study of religion, this is the story of the founding of one of the many variants of Church of God associated with the holiness and Pentecostal traditions that began emerging in America in the nineteenth century.

David's story is of the rise of a particular tradition, the Union Assembly of the Church of God, granted a charter in 1920 in the Superior Court of Bartow County, Georgia, to Charles Pratt. Charles was a charismatic figure who began a three-generation Pratt lineage of religious influence that, for some, became a religion of fear. David wisely avoids what neither historians nor scholars of religion have been able to achieve—a consensus about what constitutes a religion, a sect, or, most problematic of all, a cult. David lets the people tell their own stories. Most are disaffiliated with the church that many say quickly evolved into a cult. While David rightly notes that "cult" is a legitimate term among those who study religious groups centered around a charismatic figure, he also rightly notes that in the popular culture it is often associated with denigrating the religious claims of the group and portraying members as being manipulated or even "brainwashed" by devious if not deluded motivations of the leader. Such popular views have given rise to a genre of what psychologists who study religion have described as atrocity tales. Most forms of religion have them. They are common among Mormons, Seventh-day Adventists, Catholics, Jehovah's Witnesses, and Christian Scientists, to name but a few. Such atrocity stories often depend on exclusive reliance upon former believers who have left a religion, often for reasons of perceived abuses, ranging from the physical to the psychological. Their narratives need not be doubted, and David is careful to document claims of abuse in diverse ways by former members of Pratt's church who have not only trusted him, but pleaded with him to let their stories be heard. However, it is important to remember that David does not have access to the narratives of believers who stayed within the tradition and who likely found solace and comfort in a tradition that persists, in radically different form, today. Religions more in tension with their host cultures, especially small religious sects and cults, often have former members anxious to establish the validity of the atrocities committed in the name of the religion they abandoned. However, of course, there are members who continue to believe and see the atrocities as exceptions (for instance, many Catholics, horrified as they may be by particular instances, believe that cases of pedophilia among priests are isolated events) or endorse the alternative vision of a world others find difficult to accept (as with Christian Science). As Pratt's new religion was growing, its reliance upon faith rather than medicine to heal was common in an age in which effective medicine was in its infancy, when influenza was a modern plague and available medicines at best were weak alternatives to prayer. Likewise, Pratt's vision of a communal society (forget the dreaded phrase "communism") was once a popular ideal, and numerous groups supported and tried to practice what others now see as utopian efforts to transform society under a shared religious vision associated then as now with versions of democratic socialism.

However, despite the fact that David's work cannot help us understand the true believers who supported stages of the Union Assembly of the Church of God's transformations, he does reveal a dark side, undoubtedly real as narrated by those willing and anxious for David to tell their stories. Many were abused, and the atrocities of that abuse are self-evident in the words of those willing to talk to David. We need not attempt another amateur diagnosis of any of the Pratts to understand the abuse and atrocities imposed on at least some members of their church. Neither need we doubt David's chronicling of acts of deceit, financial deception, and the wealth amassed by the various generations of the Pratts who ruled their church with an iron hand. Neither do we need to use pseudo-scientific terms, such as "brainwashing," to understand the powerful coercive techniques employed to keep members from leaving (or, likely for David's confidants, escaping) what many thought had become a cult, a term fraught with confusion even among scholars of religion. It is not only cults and sects that skillfully use techniques of coercive persuasion; many mainstream religious groups do as well, all the more when they advocate beliefs or behaviors that stand in opposition to the larger host culture or when members appear to defy internal norms established by their practices. Attempts to isolate believers, to control access to alternative sources of information, and to shun those who would leave the fold are common in many traditions, some of which appeal to the larger culture that rejects them (e.g., Amish communities) and are hard on those who know that if they leave their loved ones likely will shun them. As harsh as this reality is, those who stay do so in support of beliefs and practices that force the reader to question atrocity less and then to ask who suffers. The Amish mother who shuns her daughter who has left the tradition could certainly be an atrocity tale for her daughter, but it would be half the story, which does not convey the whole truth about Amish community life.

It would be a mistake to take what is a remarkable book like this as definitive of any one understanding on what remains a religion, and, as David forthrightly acknowledges, is surely less a religion of fear now than it once was. David's documentation of its rapid growth, its amazing expansion, and the height of its wealth and power now diminished is a good read. It is also a powerful reminder that, whatever the ultimate truth claims of any religion, they are filtered through fallible humans, whose motivations are complex. David's book is more than a great telling of atrocity tales. It is a necessary source for religious scholars and historians to do justice to the narratives of those undoubtedly violated by a religion that scholars have little knowledge of, and David's book is a remarkable part of a larger story that religious scholars, and historians, and psychologists should address. They have a great start with David's extensive documentation of sources scholars are sure to find invaluable.

Ralph W. Hood Jr., PhD
Professor of Psychology & LeRoy A. Martin
Distinguished Professor of Religious Studies &
UT Alumni Association Distinguished Service Professor

ACKNOWLEDGMENTS

I would like to extend my sincere thanks to those who helped me create *Religion of Fear*. Without their help and support, I might not have made it.

To those willing to be interviewed, I appreciate your sacrifice and time. I want to give special thanks to Charles Roberts, who kept me on track and provided me with guidance about what to believe and not believe from others' stories. To my lifetime friend Buddy Coiffure (a pseudonym to protect his identity), who also corroborated interviews, I want to say thank you. Among the group from Kokomo, I want to acknowledge former Union Assembly members Brenda Moore, Don Pitner, and especially Dorothy Bliss, who died just before getting to read her heartfelt experiences as a member of the Church in this book. I deeply appreciate former CGUA member Johnnie Haney Butler, who gave me her unpublished memoir and allowed me to ask her questions until a month before her death in 2017. I want to thank her sister, Martha Sue Johnson, for her moving interviews. I want to express my gratitude to Teresa Howard Coker, who gave me lots of interviews and was brave enough to come out and admit to her friends that she allowed me to interview her even though some of her friends in the Church unfriended her on Facebook for doing so. I am so grateful for Marie Hoskins Anderson and her husband Robert Anderson for coming to Dalton from Knoxville to give me a four-hour interview about their lives as members of the Church, and for their follow-up interviews in the weeks to come. I want to thank the three former Union Assembly members who now live in Hamilton, Ohio, for their hundreds of emails. I want to thank former US Congressman Harlan Erwin Mitchell, now deceased, for his interview. I want to thank the Pratt family members who talked with me anonymously and sent me great pictures of their family. Thank you to Tammy Magill, who contacted me from San Diego and gave me useful information. I must acknowledge Charlie Carmical. I know he got tired of seeing me come in his furniture store to ask him questions about his father and C. T. Pratt, but he was incredibly generous with his information. There were many others interviewed whose names do not appear here, but I really appreciated your information.

Thanks to Willis Treadwell of Forwell Studio, Inc. for helping me find and reproduce many pictures in this book. To Yong Son Painter of Fast Foto for helping me reproduce and restore many photos in this book.

Thanks especially to my wife, Cindy, who wasn't so excited about me writing this story in the beginning but finally became my strongest supporter. Once she got on board with this project, I relied heavily on her advice. During the few interviews she witnessed, Cindy asked better questions than I did.

Thanks to the early readers who lent a discerning eye to this manuscript: Bette Chesser, Brian Suits, Woody Glenn, and my lawyer and friend, Tracy Ward. Tracy also spent hours searching for documents that proved very useful for this work.

Thanks to my son, Craig Cady, who helped me record interviews and then guided me to seek out Dr. Ralph W. Hood, professor of psychology and religion at the University of Tennessee at Chattanooga. Dr. Hood, who read my manuscript and saw enough potential in it to take it to Scot Danforth, the director of the University of Tennessee Press in Knoxville, deserves special thanks. Without Dr. Hood's unwavering assistance, continuing encouragement, and resolute dedication, my story might still be in a manuscript box in my basement.

To my publisher and editor, Scot Danforth, who spent so much time and effort with this project and made it read so much better. I know that I drove Scot crazy with my repeated stories. Also, many thanks go to Dr. W. Paul Williamson, Dr. Christopher Silver, and Dr. Donald Davis who critiqued this manuscript and gave boundless advice that improved it immensely. Thanks to Glenna Schroeder-Lein for her diligent work in creating the index.

Finally, to the members of the Church of God of the Union Assembly and the members of the Pratt family, I need to add that this story told herein is not without controversy—some of it is unquestionably explosive. I realize that many people represented in this story still have living relatives who may have deep feelings about these events and my interpretations of them. For the record, I would like to say that I strived to be fair to everyone involved—to find confirmation for each event I describe. Many stories were withheld because I failed to confirm the information. Some members may feel I have misrepresented them or their families by sharing these stories told to me by former and present members of the Church. Nevertheless, historians have to tell it like they see it. If I have made mistakes, please understand they were honest ones.

INTRODUCTION

The Beginning of the End

In October 1983, as the United States mourns 216 Marines killed in a Beirut truck bombing, the Church of God of the Union Assembly became nationally known. *The New York Times*, *The Chicago Sun Times*, and all the major news agencies in the United States came to Knoxville, Tennessee, and began asking questions about the religious practices of this church, which was fighting in the courts to allow a twelve-year-old preacher's daughter the right to refuse life-saving treatment for cancer. This preacher's daughter, Pamela Hamilton, had been taught by her church leaders that death and deliverance are better settled by God and not doctors or medication, and if she took medicine, she would go to hell.

It started in early July when Pamela complained about a pain in her left leg. After a month of suffering, her father, Larry Hamilton, pastor of the LaFollette Church of God of the Union Assembly, finally took her to a chiropractor, since visits to a chiropractor were allowed by her church. The practitioner, determining that Pamela's leg was broken, sent her to an orthopedic surgeon, who set the fracture and also took tissue samples of her leg—all allowed by her church. They discovered that she had Ewing's sarcoma, a rare bone cancer, in her thigh. When her parents refused to allow treatment for Pamela's condition because taking medication was against their religion, the Tennessee Department of Human Services sued for custody in Campbell County, Juvenile Court. Pamela's parents hired attorney James Alexander Hamilton Bell to represent them in the battle to keep Pamela from receiving medication. After two months of legal battle, the case finally went to court in mid-September in Knoxville, but by then Pamela's tumor had spread to cover her left leg from the hip to the knee.

By the beginning of October, Pamela's case received national attention and so did the Church of God of the Union Assembly. The reporters who came to Tennessee covering this trial started an investigation of the Union Assembly Church and word spread that this religious group could possibly be a cult. It had only been five years since the Jonestown Massacre had shocked the world, when on November 18, 1978, 912 people committed mass suicide in a religious cult led by Jim Jones. Since then there had been movies and TV documentaries relating the story behind Jim Jones's cult, so the world had become fascinated with this self-destructive type of human behavior. After Pamela's story became public, many news agencies sent reporters to Knoxville to examine this Holiness religious group and its eccentric beliefs. These journalists quickly learned that the Union Assembly Church was much larger than first reported and had unconventional religious beliefs that were similar to cults.

Rick Soll, a journalist from the *Chicago Sun-Times*, investigated the Hamilton case and the church that was stopping her treatment. On October 7, 1983, he wrote two articles that were widely reprinted. In one article, Soll reported the situation facing Pamela's struggle, and the other he wrote about his investigation into this church:

> Fundamentalist Fear: Former Church Members Paint Picture of Intimidation
>
> KNOXVILLE, Tenn. (IPS).—Cotton Smith was a big guy with a wrecking ball head and eyes the size of Cheerios.
>
> He had just caught a reporter inside the Knoxville Church of God of the Union Assembly.
>
> Smith's face clouded over when the newsman mentioned that, customarily, churches are open to all.
>
> "Ours ain't," he growled.
>
> Smith's church— like Pamela Hamilton's church—is closed to outsiders.
>
> But later, six former members of the Church of God of the Union Assembly revealed disturbing details that shed new light on cancer-stricken Pamela's faith.
>
> The former members, who included two former pastors, painted for the *Chicago Sun-Times* a portrait of a religious organization of 4,000 in 17 states that controls its membership by intimidation, humiliation, ostracism, and strict enforcement of rules governing everything from marriage to the style of a woman's hair.
>
> For example, said former members, they had to ask church elders for permission to leave town on Sunday.
>
> "The idea was that if you were gone on Sunday, you wouldn't be there to make your weekly cash donation," said Manuel Smith, a former pastor of the Hamiltons' congregation. "Permission was granted as long as you made your donation before you left. If you didn't, they forced you to beg forgiveness from the entire congregation the next week."
>
> In the late 1960s, Smith said, members were urged repeatedly to sell their homes and give the proceeds to the church. In return, he said they were told they would be moved to a church-owned site in Arizona, where leaders once planned to locate the entire membership.
>
> "I was born into that church," said Smith, 58. "I might have stayed in it all my life."
>
> But on a rainy Saturday night in 1979, sitting at home with a jumpy wife and ashtrays full of cigarette butts, Smith got the picture.

It was on his television screen.

"We were watching that movie they made about a crazy cult. And when it was over, we turn and look at each other. We was wide-eyed, kind of shaky. I says to her, 'My God, do you believe it?' See, a lot of them things in that movie—well, we had the same things going on in our church. Looking at that movie was like looking at ourselves."

Today, the former members say, Pratt's grandchildren run the church like "military dictators" from their headquarters in Dalton, Georgia. Smith hasn't been allowed to see his mother, who has high blood pressure, since he left the church.

"I worry about her," he said. "If I drive down to Dalton to see her, my brother gives me 10 minutes, and she won't say a word to me. He won't let me give her no medicine for her illness. She's there suffering but too afraid to go against the church."

Another former member, who asked not to be identified, is afraid her "escape" from the church would deprive her forever of seeing her mother. Last Christmas, she said her sister's husband left the church as well, causing a split in their marriage.

On Christmas, she said, his children visited him and the church found out.

"During services, the kids had to ask the whole congregation's forgiveness for violating church rules and visiting their dad," she said.

The rules are as comprehensive as they are strict, said Estelle Paul, 68, another former member who left the church. His wife is threatening to leave him because of his decision.

"They can tell you who to marry, to sell your house, to empty your pockets and hand it over to the leader right then and there," Paul said. "Any argument and you're out."

Efforts to contact church officials were unsuccessful.

At the top, there is the overseer. His name is Jesse Pratt Junior, grandson of founder Charles Thomas Pratt and son of Jesse Pratt Sr., whose picture hangs in every church in the Pratt domain.

"What happens," said Manuel Smith's wife, Mae, is that right off you all have to salute the picture, and you do it several more times during the service, too. It was as if you worshiped the Pratts."

Another former member put it this way: "The leaders—you were taught to ask them for help, for forgiveness. You don't ask God—you got a go through them."

It was the leaders of the church who nurtured the faith of Pamela Hamilton.

During the court hearing to decide the issue of her medical care, Pamela had told the judge she was ready to die anytime "the Lord gets ready for me."

At the same hearing, Pamela's court-appointed guardian testified that he felt the girl was dominated by her father, and that, concerning her survival, she "had no independent thought on the matter."

Dr. Frank Haraf, Pamela's cancer specialist, said the ten weeks spent in the legal battle over high principles reduced Pamela's chance of survival from 75 percent to 25 percent. The tumor had grown from the size of a baseball to the size of a watermelon.

What Pamela Hamilton thinks is not known. Behind all the battles and bitterness, there still remained only this: an eighty-six-pound girl in a private room at East Tennessee Children's Hospital—a child taught to believe her prayers were strong enough to beat cancer, and if not, that would be okay, too.[1]

In most cases, members of this sect never mentioned the Church of God of the Union Assembly by name. They always referred to it simply the Church.[2] I was tempted to use all caps throughout the book, but my editor persuaded me that this would be a little wearying for the reader, so we settled on referring to the group as the Church.

RELIGION OF FEAR

The Devil in Chains

The following story evolved according to Minnie Pratt's book about her early life, from the Minutes of the Church of God Mountain Assembly, from the Minutes of the Church of God of the Union Assembly, and from the history of this year.

On April 6, 1917, the United States Congress voted to enter the war that had raged in Europe for three years. Millions of young men from all over the world had already lost their lives in The Great War—The War to End all Wars—and, twenty-one years later when Germany attacked Poland in 1939, its new name became, World War I. In 1917 President Woodrow Wilson would sign the declaration of war into law and in a speech say: "It is a fearful thing to lead this great peaceful people into war, the most terrible of all wars. But the right is more precious than the peace, and we shall fight for the things that we have always carried nearest our hearts—for democracy . . . for the rights and liberties of small nations . . ."[1]

Nine days later on a Sunday evening, April 15, 1917, in the farming town of Middlesboro, Kentucky, only a few miles from the Tennessee state line, an ordained Holiness minister stood at a podium blaring out his sermon to a small group of members. Seated in the front row, across the aisle from the minister's wife and children, were a group of other ministers from other Church of God of the Mountain Assembly churches. These men—all men—who had made a special trip to be present that night, sat with grim faces full of disbelief as they glared up and listened to their fellow preacher who was denouncing their newly adopted doctrines on the connotation of the Millennium. They believed in the imminent physical return of Jesus Christ in the future.[2]

Outside the wooden structure, lightning flashed, illuminating the room, and thunder rumbled down the valley nestled between the majestic Cumberland Mountains. Rain, splattering off the tin roof, tried to drown out the words of this thirty-seven-year-old, thin, wiry man, but his voice held strong with determination as perspiration drenched his shirt and poured from his face and leaked onto the floor.[3]

As Charlie Thomas Pratt shouted and screamed his words, the other ministers began to yell "No!" as he tried to explain why they were wrong, and he was right. His loud voice boomed like the thunder as he refused to abandon his views while trying to explain what God had shown him in a dream. Rain pelted the windows and water ran down the panes just like the tears that ran down the cheeks of this preacher's wife, Minnie Pratt. Minnie, already big with another child growing in her, sat on the front row with all five of their children and looked up at her tall husband as he continued to roar out why they would all go to hell if they didn't listen to him. "It's God's way," he scolded them. His tattered suit jacket lay in a chair beside the rostrum.

Charlie beat on the rostrum and in his booming voice shouted at the congregation that the people name everything wrong "the devil," but everything wrong isn't the devil—everything wrong is of the devil. Pratt quoted John 8:44 to show them that there was a difference between the devil and the children of the devil.[4] The other Mountain Assembly ministers squirmed in their seats, and one started to speak, but Charlie belted out, "In a vision, God showed me Satan bound in chains; therefore the millennial reign of Christ has already begun; it is not in the future as you say."[5] He pointed to the group of ministers with a quivering finger. "Read your Bible. The children of the devil were to be here until the end of the world. Matthew the thirteenth chapter, verses 37 through 42."[6]

One minister who had been seated on the front row stood and took one step forward, but Charlie stopped him by holding out his upturned palm on an extended arm. "Wait, Brother, there is proof." Charlie had an open Bible in his other hand, but everyone knew he could not read a word from it. He had memorized all that he quoted from the Bible. Minnie would read to him from it, every night after the children went to bed.

Charlie glared at the old man standing and said in a voice now rasping with fatigue, "He, who was He? He was Jesus who answered and said unto them, he that soweth the good seed is the Son of Man. Jesus was talking about himself there in Matthew. The field is the world; the good seed are the children of the kingdom; but the tares are the children of the wicked one—the devil was who Jesus was talking about because in verse 39 He said, the enemy that sowed them is the devil: the harvest is the end of the world; and the reapers are the angels."[7]

The ministers from the Church of God of the Mountain Assembly who were still standing commanded Charlie Pratt to stop preaching this doctrine, which was not in line with the dogma of the Mountain Assembly Church, and confess his sins of blasphemy.

Charlie countered with this response: "The Son of Man shall send forth his angels, and all things that offend them shall be cast into a furnace of fire. There shall be wailing and gnashing of teeth, and it will be you."

One leader told Charlie he would be cast out of the Mountain Assembly Church if he did not stop this and confess to the general moderator that he was preaching the wrong doctrine.[8]

Charlie said, "I don't owe him a confession and you haven't put a padlock on my mouth."[9]

Under total control, Charlie turned, picked up his coat, and took long quick strides off the platform to Minnie and wrapped his coat around her shoulders. The gathering grew quiet as the thunder's rumbling shook the building. Only the rain splattering on the roof created any sound. Brother Charlie, taking Minnie by the hand, turned his back on his church family and led his pregnant wife and five children out the Mountain Assembly door into the rain. The seven of them—eight if you count unborn Jesse in Minnie's womb—walked in the lightning and pouring rain two miles down the railroad track to the home of a friend by the name of Bledsoe, who would give them shelter, for they had no home.[10] As bad as everything seemed, Charlie must have known that this event was a major turning point in his life, and it was. However, it would also change thousands and thousands of other lives.

The early Pratt family. *From left*: Lloyd, C. T. holding Flora, Minnie holding Estle, and Edmond, ca. 1912. Courtesy of an anonymous family member.

PART I

Building a Dynasty, 1879–1945

"I don't care who knows all about me, or what they write as long as its [it's] the truth. Men ought to love truth better than anything else—even better than their life."

C. T. PRATT
"Charlie Pratt Sayings," *The Southerner:
Voice of the People*, Jan. 1956, 2

1

In the Beginning

"The one who is writing this to you now, was raised up at
the feet of a widowed mother with six small children without
raiment. Many times I have gone to bed hungry."

CHARLIE T. PRATT
"Three Classes of People," (Dalton, GA) *The Southerner,
A Voice of the People,* July 1955, 3

1

Charles Thomas Pratt, a.k.a. Charlie, C. T., grew up and spent his early life in southern Kentucky not far from the Kentucky and Tennessee state line. Even though
almost everyone—even family members—thought his name was Charlie and never
Charles, the U.S. censuses of 1880, 1910, and 1930 records his name as Charles
Thomas. He was born in Wayne County, Kentucky, six miles from Monticello, in
1879. Even today, Monticello is considered a small town because its population was
only 6,188 in the 2010 U.S. census. Once a farming community, Monticello is today
known for its houseboat manufacturers. In the 2010 census, the racial makeup of
the city was 94.63% white, 2.43% African American, with the rest consisting of
people with other ethnic heritages.

Charlie always claimed to have been the youngest of six children born to George
Washington Pratt and Margaret Elizabeth Lair. However, United States census

records from 1870 through 1880 indicate that he was the fifth child born into the family. The 1880 census records show that Margaret and George had one daughter born after Charlie.[1] Margaret was two years older than her husband and 39 when Charlie was born. Charlie had three older brothers and one older sister.

His father, George Washington Pratt, born in 1844, was a Civil war veteran.[2] George W. Pratt enlisted in the Confederate Army, Company H, Sixth Kentucky Cavalry in Livingston, Tennessee, on February 24, 1863.[3] He was captured in Saline-ville, Ohio, on July 20, 1863, but released in a prisoner exchange soon thereafter.[4] He may have seen action in many places, including the Battle of Chickamauga, September 19–20, 1863, the Battle of Chattanooga, November 23–25, 1863, and the Atlanta Campaign, May 5–September 3, 1864. George was stationed in and near Dalton, Georgia, during the winter of 1863–64. After Atlanta fell to Sherman in September, the Kentucky Sixth Calvary fought back through Dalton and finally participated in the battle of Nashville at the end of the war. He was mustered out at Edgefield, Tennessee, on July 14, 1865.[5]

Even though Charlie T. Pratt claimed that his mother was widowed when he was three, records show his father, George W. Pratt, still lived with Margaret in 1888.[6] According to U.S. Census records, George left Margaret and their six children soon after September 13, 1888, because their last child, Virginia, was born on

Margaret Elizabeth Pratt, Charlie's mother, ca. 1900. Courtesy of an anonymous family member.

that date. It was reported by Charlie's grandson, Jesse Junior, in 1990, that George W. Pratt was a drunkard who had left Margaret Elizabeth when Charlie was three. This has not been established by research, however. According to the 1900 census and marriage records, George married Polly Young on February 4, 1889, and had two more children by her.[7] Grandson Jesse Junior reported that Margaret provided for her family by washing over a scrub board for other people, and that she earned money by knitting and quilting.[8]

Charlie's father was the son of Charles Pratt—Charlie's namesake. George Pratt's grandfather was Stephen Pratt of Virginia, who was a Revolutionary War Veteran and was listed in the 1840 United States census as a Revolutionary War pensioner. Stephen Pratt had moved his family to Wayne County, Kentucky, between 1810 and 1820. This move may have occurred because during the early part of the nineteenth century some land grants were given out to Revolutionary War veterans, and many of these were in the southern part of the United States.[9]

2

The first decade of the twentieth century revealed many signs of changes that were about to transpire in America and across the world. By 1900 mass production of automobiles had begun. The Studebaker brothers, having become the world's leading manufacturers of horse-drawn vehicles, made a transition to electric cars in 1902 and gasoline engines in 1904.[10] On December 17, 1903, Orville and Wilbur Wright achieved the first heavier-than-air flight in an aircraft. This first airplane was built by the brothers and flown at Kitty Hawk, North Carolina. Out of four flights, the longest lasted almost a minute and covered 850 feet.[11] On March 27, 1904, Mrs. Mary Harris "Mother" Jones, the fervent labor leader, was ordered out of Colorado for stirring up strikes in the coal mines.[12] Although Charlie claimed to have been a coal miner, no record of this exists. When Minnie wrote their life story, published by the Church press in 1955, she never mentioned that Charlie was a coal miner even though she listed numerous other places where he had worked.

In 1903, thirteen-year-old Mary Minnie Broyles from Whitley County, Kentucky, near Williamsburg met and fell in love with Charlie. She spelled his name Charley. Wayne County, Kentucky, where Charlie lived, was the adjoining county west of Whitley. Minnie had become a Christian two years before, when she was eleven. Minnie was the oldest of four children of Lewis and Martha (Tiny) Broyles. Minnie's father, Lewis Broyles, was born in Tennessee in 1865 to William Broyles and Lucinda Broyles.[13] Minnie and her parents regularly attended the Methodist church in Williamsburg. Charlie Pratt's mother was a God-fearing Methodist, but in his youth Charlie avoided all churches. Minnie said, "I had wonderful parents who taught me to live right, but I sometimes strayed away from the narrow path."[14]

Minnie's parents tried to prevent her from seeing this twenty-three-year-old man because of his bad reputation for drinking hard liquor, carousing, and fighting.

On Tuesday April 8, 1904, Minnie's parent's worst nightmare happened. On that day, Charlie T. Pratt, by now age twenty-four, married Minnie at the age of fourteen without her parents' blessings. Minnie gave her age as 15 on the Marriage Bond.[15]

Many years later, Minnie reflected on these times and Charlie's attributes. She said that Charley drank but did not spend all of his money on drink. Minnie explained that Charley always made sure the family had plenty to eat and a fire to sit beside. Even though she was raised by non-drinking parents, she said she never complained to her husband about his drinking. Nevertheless, she went on to say that Charley was a "high tempered man especially when he was drinking." She said that he never tried to hide his drinking, but everybody knew when he was drunk.[16]

A Tuesday marriage suggests they were not married in a church but eloped. They didn't stray too far from her parents, however, for they resided in Southern Kentucky near Williamsburg, some 78 miles north of Knoxville, Tennessee. At the turn of the century, this part of Kentucky was rural, with narrow dirt roads connecting small communities. Williamsburg is nestled between the Cumberland River and the Daniel Boone National Forest and is often referred to as "Gateway to the Cumberlands."[17] People traveled from place to place by walking, riding a horse or mule, by carriage, and, if longer distances were required, riding the train. Few people had a horse or a mule, much less the newly invented automobile. The land was used for farming and growing timber. Early in their married life, Charlie tried his hand in all areas of work, including farming, timbering, as well as opening a restaurant for a short period.

At six feet, three inches tall, Charlie created a majestic presence who towered over most men of his generation. His brother, Edmond, was even taller at, six feet, six inches tall. Charlie was lanky with little musculature. His hair was dark and short on the sides and this allowed his ears, which stood out from his head, to appear even bigger than they actually were. He had a booming voice that would play a huge part in his future and dominated most conversations. Charlie was in constant motion and always ready to interact with anyone close by. He was a restless, moody man, who was extremely intelligent even though he never learned to read or write.

Minnie, on the other hand, said she was the opposite of Charlie. She was short and petite as a young woman. She had dark hair and light skin, which glowed with health. According to her own writings, she seemed to give little regard for material things, but she believed in cleanliness as the Bible taught. She had been raised as a Christian and had a cool head, which made her a good match for a man like Charlie. She had been educated and learned to read and write, even in a time when school attendance was, in many places, not obligatory. During the late nineteenth and early twentieth centuries, in rural communities, most children only attended as far as the sixth, seventh, or eighth grades.[18]

Minnie had perseverance and incredible patience while standing beside Charlie through their years of hardship. She pushed him to become a Christian, but he was a stubborn man. The road to Christian piety was not smooth. Charlie would revert back to his drinking and rough living again and again even after converting to the faith, but Minnie was there to bring him back to the Lord. Without this strong woman and wife, Charlie T. Pratt would not have experienced the success that finally came to him years later. She was his glue and the glue for the Pratt family until late in her life.

In 1905, two years after marrying Minnie, Charlie Pratt was 'saved' and became a Christian. At the same time, he felt the calling to be a preacher. During this year he and Minnie were members of the Methodist Church and continued following that denomination for about five years. Their life was happy in Williamsburg, Kentucky, for about eight months before Charlie acquired a timbering job near Pineville, Kentucky, about fifty miles to the east. He left his wife at home and moved to Pineville. He worked there during the Christmas holidays and started drinking again. He soon found a place to rent and sent for Minnie.

In her own words, Minnie recalled, "When I got off the train in Pineville, Kentucky, the first thing I saw he was smoking a big pipe. I knew right then he wasn't living right. I began to cry right there in that big crowd; it almost broke my heart."[19] Charlie responded gently, "Don't cry," Later, in February of 1906 they bought a restaurant in Corbin, Kentucky, thirty-nine miles west of Pineville. It was a saloon town and, according to Minnie, Charlie continued drinking. Within a few months, they lost the restaurant and moved back near the home of her parents in Williamsburg, Kentucky. Charlie's drinking habit grew worse.[20]

On Sunday October 28, 1906, when Minnie was a month shy of being seventeen their first child was born and they named him Edmond after Charlie's older brother. Charlie continued to drink and changed jobs frequently as they moved back and forth from Tennessee to Kentucky with each job. It was on Saturday, March 28, 1908, when Minnie gave birth to two twin boys they named Lloyd (some census records have Lloyd's name spelled Loyd) and Lewis. About the same time, Minnie attended a revival meeting in a shed or tent and talked Charlie into going. While there, he rededicated his life to Christ and felt the Lord calling him to preach again. But, as before, Charlie fought against this calling.[21]

When the twin boys were about four months old, and Charlie was away from home working with a bridge crew, one of the boys, Lewis, became sick and lifeless. It was about two in the afternoon when a neighbor named Johnson walked to where Charlie worked to let him know that his child was deathly ill. Imagine the stress Charlie must have felt as he hurried back toward home on foot. A fast-pace walk is about four miles per hour, but he might have run some of the way because he was young. Nevertheless, it took Charlie until ten that night to arrive home, and his baby son died about six the next morning. They buried him the next day. Charlie blamed himself for the child's death. He thought it was because he had fought against his calling to do the work of God. He told Minnie the night after the burial that he would not turn his back on God again. Charlie started preparing to preach in the Methodist Church, and he worked with diligence for a while, but Charlie could not abandon his sins completely, and it wasn't long before he wandered from God's beckoning.[22]

3

Each Sunday Minnie walked four miles with her two boys, Edmond and Lloyd, to the Methodist Church in Williamsburg. Charlie went for a while, but he became indifferent and seldom went to church with his family. Before the year ended, the family began a series of moves that took them from one town to another as Charlie worked different timber jobs. Minnie continued going to a Methodist church. In time, Charlie stopped going to church altogether, even after Minnie's pleading.

Charlie became sick with some unknown illness in 1908. Instead of recovering, Charlie's illness kept worsening until he became so sick he could no longer work or even walk fifty yards without resting. He developed depression and prepared to die.[23]

In November of 1908 Republican William Howard Taft defeated Democrat William Jennings Bryan in an Electoral College landslide, 314–169. About that same time, Charlie caught a break when he acquired a position as an overseer on a timber job. He was given a horse and saddle so he could travel through the woods making sure the hired men were working properly. He was paid sixty-five dollars a month, which were high wages during this time in the southern United States. But Charlie was still ill and growing weaker, and the medicine he took seemed to be making him worse.

Even though we do not know what type of medicine Charlie was taking, it is not surprising that during the early part of the twentieth century that the medicine appeared to be making him worse. Medicines, which poorly trained doctors gave for illnesses, often made the patient worse if it didn't kill them outright, as quinine, digitalis, and opium were often prescribed indiscriminately. Supreme Court Justice Oliver Wendell Holmes's father who was a physician and who lived well into the twentieth century, once declared, "I firmly believe that if the whole *material medica* (pharmacology), as now used, should be sunk to the bottom of the sea, it would be all the better for mankind—and all the worse for the fishes."[24] Medicine had remained virtually unchanged from the time of Hippocrates more than two thousand years earlier until just before World War I, when science and medicine began to make significant advances. As late as 1900, only one medical school in America required a student to have a college degree.[25]

It is no wonder then that in 1908, while on his horse riding from job site to job site, Charlie took out his medicine, but, instead of taking it, threw it deep into the woods. Charlie said, "Lord, live or die, I will never take another dose of medicine."[26] And as far as anyone knows, he lived up to his word.

At some point during 1909, Charlie went back to church and began training to become a minister in the Methodist Church. They asked him to become a trial minister and attend a conference to be ordained. Charlie had a major obstacle to overcome before becoming an ordained Methodist minister: he could not read, which meant could not read a word aloud. Minnie read to him, and he tried memorizing the verses from the Bible. Charlie had great recall, but remembering every book, every chapter, and every verse from a work as long and complex as the Bible must have caused him to hesitate. Whatever the reason, Charlie gave the Methodists this excuse. "I'm leaving because I've got to stay with the Bible, and I can't find the Methodist Church written anywhere in the Bible." Instead, he joined the Holiness Church of God of the Mountain Assembly and was ordained immediately on a Monday night, October 18, 1910.[27] It is feasible to think that Charlie's decision to stop taking medicine had been planted in his mind from his visits to the new Holiness Church gaining a foot-hold in the area. One of their beliefs was in divine healing, which is trusting that the body can be healed by the power of God through the prayer of faith and the "laying on of hands."[28]

It was two years before Minnie joined the Church of God of the Mountain Assembly, but she stopped taking medicine the night he was ordained.

The new Church of God, organized in 1905, had its origins in the United Baptist Church. It was overwhelmingly labeled fundamentalist and southern in origin.[29] It was also called a Holiness group because its members believed in a life of holiness and being cleansed of sin. It was not until 1911 that they added "Mountain Assembly" to the name, thus becoming the Church of God of the Mountain Assembly. Scholar Ernest Sandeen points out that "fundamentalist groups had their roots in Millenarianism and this is the defining characteristic of fundamentalism. They believed in the Dispensationalist theory that said Christ would return to earth and reign for one thousand years on an earthly throne."[30] George Marsden argues that "fundamentalism's base was much wider and included the Evangelical and Holiness movements of the late nineteenth century."[31]

The Church of God of the Mountain Assembly was located primarily in rural settings throughout the South. Some scholars group the Holinesses and Pentecostals together because their beliefs are almost identical. However, Pentecostalism is a fairly modern movement within Christianity that can be traced back to the Holiness movement within the Methodist Church.[32]

When Charlie and Minnie made friends with a couple by the name of Guyton in Quicksand, Kentucky, neither realized what a change this would make in their lives. Sam Jones Guyton, who was from Bartow County in North Georgia, had moved his family to Quicksand during the first decade of the twentieth century so he could take a job on the railroad. Sam and his wife became close friends with Charlie and Minnie, and they also became followers of Charlie's preaching. Sam started pressuring Charlie into leaving Kentucky and moving his family to Georgia, where they could establish a church in Sam's hometown.[33] Just after Minnie and Charlie's baby girl, Flora, was born on Sunday, January 8, 1911, they went on a trip to Georgia. This trip made all the difference in the Pratts' lives and the lives of thousands of other people who would fall under the spell of Charlie Pratt.

4

In 1911, Charlie, Minnie, and their three children traveled with the Guyton family to Cass Station—renamed Cassville years later. Cassville is a small community in Bartow County in Georgia. Presently it lies on Highway 41 and Interstate 75 between Adairsville and Cartersville. During the 1920s the dirt road which ran through Cass Station, Cassville, would become known as the "Dixie Highway;" the nation's first planned interstate roadway. Cassville is 234 miles south of Williamsburg, Kentucky, and 41 miles north of Atlanta, Georgia. In Cassville, Charlie conducted a revival and saved forty-four souls. While there, he organized a church at Cass Station. The families attending his meetings in different homes wanted to build a church structure and make Charlie the pastor. Enthused about this proposal, Charlie took his family back to Williamsburg to prepare to move to Georgia, but Minnie reported in her book that they did not have enough money to make the move back to Georgia. However, with Charlie's mood swings, he may have cooled off about the proposal and would not make a decision. While living with Minnie's parents, Charlie borrowed money and bought a half interest in a livery stable to try to get them on their feet and back to his church in Georgia.

It is certainly possible that Charlie had a problem living with Minnie's parents. They did not approve of him, thinking that Minnie was too good for this uneducated "Holy Roller" drunkard. They didn't agree with Charlie's religious beliefs, and he didn't agree with theirs. So being as hot-tempered as Charlie could be at times, and realizing that two roosters in one henhouse didn't work well, he stayed away from home as much as he could. It was not long until Charlie backslid and started drinking heavily.[34] For her part, Minnie never gave up on Charlie. A lesser-willed woman may have turned him out, but when he didn't come home one Friday night, Minnie went to the livery stable where she found Charlie drinking. She cried and begged him to come home, but he told her to go on home, that this was between him and God.[35] The next day, on Saturday, Minnie's sister, Gracie Lee, brought her sick baby to her parents' home where Minnie and her family were still staying. Minnie thought the baby was almost dead with pneumonia. Again, Charlie did not come home that night. Minnie cried and prayed all of the night for the baby and for her husband. After Charlie failed to come home on Sunday night, Minnie went back to the stable again. She begged and cried until one of Charlie's drinking friends said, "For God's sake, Charlie, go home with her." Reluctantly, Charlie did.[36]

About two o'clock that morning Charlie awoke Minnie, who was in bed next to him, and told her that he had to decide to either preach or he was going to hell. He said it was his last chance. Minnie told him he needed to become a preacher. Charlie explained to Minnie how hard it would be on her and the family, and that they would have many lonesome hours and may go hungry. She said, "Charley, I would rather wash over the wash tub and eat corn bread than for you to fail God and go to hell."[37]

That very night in 1912 Charlie made the decision to serve God. He got up and prayed for the sick baby of Minnie's sister. In the morning he prayed again, and within hours the child was eating and alert.

Soon, Charlie started preaching in Mountain Assembly churches throughout Kentucky and Tennessee, but Sam Guyton kept urging Charlie to come back to Georgia. Nevertheless, Charlie had a major problem. Charlie had borrowed money on a note for the livery stable, and he still needed to pay that loan back. Charlie and Minnie wanted to leave Kentucky and move to Georgia with the Guytons, so they prayed for God's guidance. Within days Charlie made his decision. With Minnie's approval, Charlie decided to just walk away from the loan.[38]

In 1912—the same year that the *Titanic* sank killing 1,595—the Pratts left Kentucky and moved back to Bartow County near an area called Center, Georgia, which was located close to where White is today. With the help of Charlie's followers, a new church was built in Cassville, near Cass Station, Georgia. The land for the church was donated by a relative of Sam Guyton, Jim Knight, who attended the services but never officially joined.[39] While the church was being built the Pratt family moved onto a farm near Cass Station. However, the farm was on rocky ground and made just enough money to feed Charlie's growing family. On Saturday, September 12, 1912, Minnie gave birth to another boy, Elmer Estle.

That same year, the Bartow County Sheriff came after Charlie with a warrant. The young pastor was arrested and spent eight days in the Cartersville jail before being sent back to Williamsburg, Kentucky. A man from Williamsburg by the name of Jack Ross had accused Charlie of walking away from a note on the livery stable. After a speedy trial, the judge dismissed the charges for lack of evidence.[40]

Charlie hurried back to his wife in Georgia, and on July 25, 1914, another girl, Cora Alma, was born to Charlie and Minnie. Some non-church members around Cass Station objected to this Holiness group being in their area, but these protesters could not stop Charlie and his movement. His congregation grew.

Charlie, still a member of the Mountain Assembly but living in Georgia, received news that on October 3, 1914, the Mountain Assembly Church had adopted a 'five-point" creed that included the doctrines of justification, sanctification, and baptism of the Holy Ghost. Church members believed in physical healing of the body and the power of Christ to destroy Satan's work.[41] They also decided that only the King James translation of the Bible could be used by members and that only the New Testament could be used in Sunday school classes.

Growing in his confidence as an evangelist, in February 1915, Charlie left another man as pastor of the Cass Station Church and moved his family to Knoxville, Tennessee, where he established a new church with 28 members. Knoxville, only 70 miles from the Kentucky border, is situated in the Great Appalachian Valley—also known as the Tennessee Valley—almost halfway between the Great Smoky Mountains to the east and the Cumberland Plateau to the west. The surrounding area is characterized by long, narrow ridges flanked by broad valleys. The Tennessee River slices through the downtown area. On February 1, 1915, Pratt established his church in Knoxville. When the Pratts moved to Knoxville, it was a rapidly growing city known as a major distribution and manufacturing center. Money was plentiful there, and Charlie believed there were lots of sinners in Knoxville who needed saving. Minutes from the Church of God Mountain Assembly reported this newly founded church met in general assembly in Knoxville on Christmas Day 1916 to agree on the church doctrine and called it The Union Assembly Church of God.[42] However, Charlie was still considered part of the Church of God of the Mountain Assembly, but his doctrine began to differ slightly with the Mountain Assembly, and a clash between the two became inevitable.[43]

Meanwhile, trouble erupted back in Georgia and caused Charlie's return. At Cass Station, the owner of the land where the church was built was dismissed, even though he had never joined. The congregation had never filed for a deed, so Mr. Knight gave the land and building to the Church of God of Cleveland, Tennessee. Charlie went down and knocked the lock off the door and held a service that night. The Church of God in Cleveland filed an injunction against him, and a trial was held in Dalton, Georgia. Little did Charlie realize how this small cotton-milling town of Dalton would become the center of his entire future. After several months of delays, Judge Tarver of Dalton ruled in favor of Charlie's Church of God and gave them rightful ownership of the land and property.[44]

In 1917, the Church of God of the Mountain Assembly adopted two new articles of faith, one condemning war and another confirming the millennial reign of Christ.[45] The Mountain Assembly Church was incorporated in 1917. That same year Charlie T. Pratt broke away from this group and eventually formed his own Church of God.[46]

5

The records of the Church of God of the Mountain Assembly show that, in October of 1917, six months after the United States entered World War I, Charlie was expelled from that church.[47] Minnie wrote that when they left the Mountain Assembly they had all five of their children with them.[48] She gave birth to her sixth child, Jesse Franklin, on Tuesday October 23, 1917, in Lindale, Georgia, so she was probably pregnant with Jesse at the time of Charlie's dismissal.

According to the literature, his dismissal seemed to have started over differences in the principles of millennialism. Like many other Christian groups, members of the Church of God of the Mountain Assembly were believers in millennialism, the belief that the second coming of Christ is inevitable—and near at hand. Upon the second coming, the faithful believe Christ will defeat evil on the earth and will reign

Pratt's second church in Bartow County, Georgia, 1919. Photo owned by the author.

eternally. There are many different versions of millennialism among Christians, but Charlie held fast to a view that is called full-preterism (from the Latin Praeter, a prefix indicating that something is "past" or "beyond"), or amillennialism. This is the belief that all the prophecies found in Revelation were entirely fulfilled in AD 70 and that we are now living in the eternal state.[49]

The key to Charlie Pratt's new crusade was established, and he would say these words time after time throughout the rest of his life: "Everything belongs to God, so why worry about earthly wealth? Give it all to God. Don't hold anything back and your rewards in heaven will be abundant."[50] Minnie was destined to be the linchpin to this new movement because all of the money given to God by their followers would go through her hands. And for the next 44 years, she, along with advice of her husband, would decide how this money would be allocated.

The family moved back to Kentucky in 1917, and Charlie tried to convert the Mountain Assembly followers to his preterist beliefs. Not long after arriving, Charlie preached a sermon at Middlesboro that caused his expulsion from the Church of God of the Mountain Assembly. As lightning flashed and thunder cracked outside, he condemned the beliefs of the Mountain Assembly by simultaneously extolling the millennial reign of Christ.[51]

During that sermon, Pratt claimed to have seen a vision of Satan in chains and began teaching that the millennial reign had already begun. Because these beliefs were viewed as heretical by the Mountain Assembly, Charlie was kicked out of that church forever.[52] Charlie was not alone, however, because he had laid the groundwork for this breakaway in advance by forming a group of followers who wanted him as their leader. Several of the ministers and a few members of the Church of God of the Mountain Assembly broke away with Charlie, and thus the Union Assembly of the Church of God, began to take form. But it was not an easy journey for the Pratt family—not in the beginning. Within months they were on their way back to Georgia.

2

Creation

"Woe unto the man whom everybody speaks well of—
I know that's not been me."

C. T. PRATT
"Charlie Pratt Sayings," *The Southerner*, 2

1

1918 was a pivotal year for the United States' position in the world and also one for
C. T. Pratt—as Charlie was now being called. The Armistice was signed by Germany
on November 11, ending the Great World War. More than ten million people had
died in the war—including six million civilians. In the United States and around
the world, a virulent flu was also killing millions. The Bureau of Public Health in
the United States reported that American deaths from influenza far exceeded those
among troops abroad, and that more servicemen died from influenza than from
wounds suffered in battle. During September and October of 1918, nearly 80,000
influenza deaths occurred in 46 cities in the U.S. According to the bureau, during
the two weeks ending on October 26, 40,000 deaths were recorded.[1]

Ministers were preaching all over the southern United States as well as across
the globe that the influenza pandemic was the pestilence predicted by Jesus in

Matthew 24:7, and that it fulfilled the prophecy of Amos 8:3, "there shall be many dead bodies in every place." C. T. Pratt, always the evangelist, used these "hard times" to build his membership in his new churches across the South, and, by being a professed healer for God, his church membership grew so fast he could not serve as the pastor to all of his parishioners. He appointed new preachers but demanded that they follow the doctrines prescribed by him. One of his doctrines prohibited any minister or member of his church to seek healing from a doctor or take any form of medicine. He believed in only God's healing power and prayer was the only way it could be achieved. If a person died, then C. T. preached that they had not trusted God to heal them.

When the flu pandemic of 1918–19 was at its height, patients had just as good a chance of recovery if they did nothing rather than taking medication and being under the care of physicians. The medical profession had no clue as how to cure this killer flu, so they tried almost everything. Some physicians even injected people with the typhoid vaccine in hopes of boosting the immune system. Others poured every known vaccine into their patients on the same theory. Quinine, which worked on malaria, was often prescribed by physicians. Some medical doctors convinced themselves that their treatment could cure their patients regardless of the actual results.[2]

A Montana doctor reported in the *New York Medical Journal* of his experimental treatment: "The results have been favorable," even though two out of the six patients he treated died. Two University of Pittsburgh researchers reasoned just as poorly when they reported that only twenty patients out of forty-seven died who took their treatment. They actually did not include seven of those deaths, arguing that the patients received the treatment too late. One physician gave hydrogen peroxide intravenously to twenty-five flu-stricken patents with severe pulmonary distress in hopes that it would get oxygen into the blood. He claimed success when thirteen recovered, but twelve died—almost half.[3]

Other outlandish treatments were tried and even heralded. In Italy a doctor gave injections of mercuric chloride—a poison—to his patients. Another insisted that his patients take enemas of warm milk mixed with creosote, used to preserve wood on utility poles, every twelve hours for every year of age to prevent pneumonia from developing as a result of the flu. In France methylene blue, a dye used to stain bacteria for viewing under the microscope, was injected despite being extremely toxic to the human body. Some physicians in Europe injected metallic solutions into the patient's muscles. One doctor who tried the metallic solution intravenously said that the treatment was "a little brutal."[4]

Almost everyone and every business took advantage of the panic by claiming to have a cure for the influenza. A shoe store advertised that "one way to keep the flu away is to keep your feet dry." Balms and salves were sold in abundance as were gas masks—all guaranteed to prevent or cure the flu.[5] What all of these tactics played on was *fear.* C. T. Pratt believed that prayers and the "laying on of hands" healed the sick just as well as the majority of doctors practicing in the South, so it is no wonder that this was a prosperous time for Brother Pratt's recruiting. Nonetheless, during this year, Brother Pratt started making enemies, and would continue to do so in the many months to come.

2

Staying in the vicinity of his original church at Cass Station, Charlie—preferring to be called "C. T." by now—continued to preach and convert new members to his church, but he also had to make a living for his growing family. Pratt sharecropped at a farm about a mile outside of Kingston, Georgia, which is located almost halfway between Cartersville and Rome, Georgia. The land was initially not cleared so the family had to remove tons of rocks and boulders before planting a cotton crop. That summer they were only able to make 3 bales of cotton because of the bad soil, and also because it was the year of the boll weevil. They only grew enough food to keep from starving.[6]

One night in October of 1918, Charlie had preached a moving sermon during a revival at the Cass Station church. He always stood at the exit door to shake hands with each member as they left the small building that could hold about fifty people comfortably. (That building is still standing today.) After all the members had wandered off to travel home, C. T. took Minnie with their six children and started walking to their buggy. The youngest child, Jesse, was only a year old and in his mother's arms. She was also leading the youngest daughters by her hand.

They had not reached the buggy when a rock flew out of the dark and struck C. T. in the head. Three men stepped out and continued to hurl stones at the preacher and his family. When they ran out of rocks, the men started beating C. T. about the face with their fists. Blood oozed from the cuts on his head and face. Minnie put Jesse down and grabbed one of the men and pushed him between the buggy wheels. She held him there as C. T. fought off his attackers. When the men fled back into the woods, C. T. began to preach, saying they could never run him off. They were here to stay. C. T. and Minnie never learned who the attackers were, but the next day C. T., with a face black and blue, baptized fifteen men.[7]

After the baptism, the family rode in their wagon eighteen miles westward down Cass White Road to start a revival at Aragon, Georgia. Nonmembers in and around Aragon formed a mob to run the Holiness group out of town, but after C. T. and his believers refused to budge, the mob left, and a new church in Aragon was eventually organized from that revival. The next church they formed would seem insignificant at first, but it would play a huge part—the principal part—in the new Church of God being assembled by Charlie and Minnie Pratt.

How did Brother Pratt stir up such antagonism within the community? The simplest answer stems from prejudices people sometimes feel against anyone who is different from themselves. The Holiness tradition is different from other Christian traditions in only a few ways, but these variances tended to encourage bigotry. For instance, Charlie Pratt's church, like other Holiness groups, practiced *glossolalia* ("speaking in tongues") along with "baptism of the Holy Spirit" with their emphasis on a post-conversion encounter with God. Unlike many other branches of Christianity, they believed in other supernatural gifts such as prophecy and the ability to heal. Moreover, women associated with Pratt's churches dressed plainly and wore no makeup or jewelry. They did not participate in anything they considered "worldly," such as going to social events outside the Church. These minor stylistic differences, unusual practices, and certain beliefs were sometimes enough to arouse the suspicions of their neighbors, even ones who also considered themselves Christian.[8]

3

In 1919 the United States understood its future economic growth depended on the development of road and highway construction. The automobile business was booming and proving to be a cheaper transportation method; moreover, it was creating new channels of employment which boosted the economy.[9] Also in June of that year Germany signed the Treaty of Versailles to formally end The Great War. But the Germans were humiliated by the Allies, and many leaders said they would not have come to Versailles if they had known in advance how they were going to be treated. Protesters in Germany spilled into the streets and set fire to French military insignia. The treaty would prove to be an economic disaster for Germany and would become a major factor in starting another world war some twenty years and three months later.

In that summer of 1919, C. T. Pratt borrowed money for a forty-mile trip from Cartersville to a cotton milling town in North Georgia called Dalton. Minnie objected to Charlie's journey by saying, "Charley, it looks like the Lord would provide train fare for you if he wanted you to keep going up there." C. T. told Minnie that he had to go because he felt the Lord drawing him there. Quickly, Pratt established a new Church of God in Dalton with thirteen members, but they had no building, so they met in a house belonging to one of the new members.[10]

Seeing promise in Dalton, Pratt went back there in July and organized a revival meeting under a canvas tent. In the daytime, usually on Saturdays when people were in town shopping, Charlie and Minnie stood on street corners in Dalton. Minnie read scriptures for C. T. as he preached about the verses she read. At night under the tent she stood next to him on the platform reading selected verses from the Bible, and then he would interpret the Bible's words for the poor lost souls present—most of whom could not read. In only one week while in Dalton, Pratt saved 150 people and baptized 75 who joined the movement. In less than a month a church was built, and they moved out of the tent.[11] Brother Pratt kept traveling from one of his newly established churches to another, but this thriving mill town of Dalton, only thirty miles south of the Tennessee border, kept drawing him back.

Pratt and seven of his church leaders applied for a church charter in November of 1919 in Bartow County, Georgia.[12] On May 18, 1920, a charter was granted to C. T. Pratt, on behalf of the church, by the Superior Court of Bartow County, Georgia, under the name of the Union Assembly of the Church of God, Inc. A church covenant was drawn up and went into effect on October 9, 1921.[13] Members who were active in support of the Union Assembly of the Church of God from its beginning included J. Willie "J. W." Burnett, Tom Bohannon, Joe Vaughn, Claud Jones, Alec Ledford, and T. R. Bell.[14]

On Monday June 5, 1922, Minnie had her seventh child. She named this daughter Martha after her own mother, and, like Minnie's mother, this child would be called Tiny. That same year C. T. Pratt moved his family to Dalton, and made the town the headquarters of his growing number of churches. Pratt continued traveling around the South forming new ones. In 1923 he formed a new church above Knoxville in Claxton, Tennessee, before he went to Lynch, Kentucky, to form churches. Like a man possessed with a spirit, C. T. wasted no time in moving to Cumberland, Kentucky, trying to convert new members—then back to Middlesboro, Kentucky, trying to start a new church there before making the move back to Dalton.[15]

During the 1920s and early 1930s, Pratt worked and traveled endlessly building his parishioners into a formidable force. While his family lived in Dalton, C. T. and his fellow ministers journeyed into new states, such as Ohio, Indiana, Arkansas, and Texas preaching their beliefs and building new Union Assembly churches and converting new members.[16] In 1923, another daughter, Elva Leola, was born, and then in 1926 yet another girl was born and they named her Lula Mitchell, but in 1927 Lula died while C. T. was in Harlan, Kentucky, conducting a revival. In 1929, just before the Great Depression, a son was born to C. T. and Minnie. They named him Herbert Hoover. Then in 1931, with the world starving and in turmoil, their last child was born—a son they named Wayman Paul.

In 1936 Pratt, who was conducting a revival in Elizabethton, Tennessee, sent a message home to Minnie instructing his grown sons, Ed and Jesse, to haul gravel to make concrete cornerstones for a new church in Dalton.[17] As reported in later interviews, he would eventually call this community in Whitfield County, Georgia, the "New Jerusalem" and the "Camp of the Saints" because he believed that in the final days Jesus would come back to this town and only the members of the Union Assembly Church would survive.[18]

Camp of the Saints

"There are thousand(s) of acres of land laying idle,
uncultivated, and some of the land owners had rather see
it lay out and grow up than to give the poor man a chance
to make his own support."

C. T. PRATT
"Three Classes of People," *The Southerner*, 3

1

The environs surrounding Dalton, Georgia, the county seat of Whitfield County,
were once home to thousands of Cherokee Indians until they were removed to
lands west of the Mississippi River. President Andrew Jackson had pushed through
Congress the Indian Removal Act of 1830, which meant death or dislocation for
these Native Americans. These proud Cherokee were considered the most civilized
of all Indians in the East because they had tried to fully adopt the culture of the
white man. A few were landowners who owned their own slaves, but that was their
downfall because the white people who poured into the area wanted the Indian
lands, which the white settlers thought were their divine destiny to take. In 1832, with
the aid of a state-sponsored land lottery, they began seizing Cherokees lands. Some
white settlers who moved in from Tennessee and the Carolinas even homesteaded

on parcels of land still occupied by Cherokee families. Finally in 1838 the Cherokees, who were the final Native Americans to be resettled, were sent west in what later became known as the "Trail of Tears." Although Whitfield County is surrounded by majestic mountains, which adds to the magnificence to its landscape, most of the Whitfield County environs lies between these mountains, in long narrow valleys and the occasional wide plain. During the nineteenth and early twentieth centuries, the land on these plains, as well as the soil on the hills, was fertile and very productive for crops and orchards. The county contains numerous springs, branches, creeks, and the Connasauga River to make the whole county well-watered.[1]

It wasn't until 1851 that Whitfield County was formed by splitting Murray County in half, and the new county seat's name was changed from Cross Plains to Dalton in honor of Captain Edward White's mother, Mary Dalton.[2] Much of the land of Dalton was owned by a syndicate headed by Captain White from Massachusetts who laid out the principal streets. At that time, there was no town of any size between Knoxville, Tennessee, and Augusta, Georgia. Ross' Landing, later named Chattanooga, and Marthasville, later to be named Atlanta, were towns comprised of only a single town square, a few brick storefronts, and a collection of log cabins. Dalton seemed destined to become the next metropolis.[3]

By the turn of the century, industrialization had changed the demographics of the southern United States. What was formerly a region comprised of unincorporated rural villages, was now home to numerous townships and small cities. Not all people had moved off farms, but the tenant farmers now had a choice in occupation, while the majority of the land owners stayed on the farm. A former farm laborer himself, C. T. Pratt realized that there were other ways of making money for himself and his family. He made up his mind that he would work full-time saving souls and teaching them to give all they had to the Lord, and he became excellent at his job.[4]

What put Dalton ahead of the other nearby settlements in the early nineteenth century was the railway systems that traversed it while crossing one another diagonally at its heart. These railroads were the *Southern* and the *Louisville and Nashville*—the latter leased from the *Western Atlantic*.[5] The main source of income for the white and black people of Whitfield County after they took the land from the Cherokees was farming, and agriculture continued to be the most important economic driver until the latter part of the nineteenth century when industrialization crept into Dalton in the form of cotton milling. In 1870, the population of Dalton was listed as 1,800, but only ten years later, in 1880, it had increased to 2,516—a 72 percent growth. The citizenry began to make Dalton into a small city, constructing a waterworks, macadam streets, and creating a public school system. In 1882 small industrial operations sprung up around Dalton, including a flour mill, an axe-handle plant, a hub-and-spoke factory, a small furniture factory, a cotton press, two gins, a number of sawmills, and a small tannery. One of Georgia's first meat-packing plants opened in Dalton and shipped sausage and cured meats throughout the region.[6] To industrial speculators, Dalton looked like a promising community, so on January 24, 1885, Crown Cotton Mill opened in North Dalton, creating new opportunities for its citizenry. What attracted Charlie Pratt to this area as well as other developing towns such as Chattanooga and Knoxville, Tennessee?

2

In 1880, cotton mills were springing up in towns throughout the hill country of the South where farming had before created economic isolation. With this new textile industry, the financial nucleus changed from a "Plantation Belt" economy to one driven by urban industrial centers.

By the middle of the 1920s, southern cotton mills were even exceeding the production of their New England counterparts. This new lifestyle created a vital adjustment in the people of the South, both socially as well as economically. These new mill workers were mostly southern whites, who had come from nearby farms and never worked for wages or in a factory. After the Great War ended in 1918, the long-established farm economy collapsed, causing entire families of farmers to migrate toward the mills and move into the company-owned mill villages. Living in company-owned settlements offered a change in lifestyle for many of the area's poor whites.[7]

Even though these economical and lifestyle changes were happening through-out the southern United States, cotton mills in Dalton, Georgia, at the end of the nineteenth century provides an excellent case study. When Crown Cotton Mill opened on January 24, 1885, it presented an exciting spectacle for people living in a small town. All other buildings in Dalton were small in comparison. The men who took control of Crown believed they were helping Dalton in two critical ways. First, they believed they were generating urban growth by attracting a large population of laborers who in turn would create a steady market for local merchants.[8] Second, they believed Dalton's industrial elite would become civic leaders who would control the destiny of the city.[9]

This action created three classes of white people to populate Dalton, classes that lasted well into the twentieth century. The Dalton industrial elite stood apart from the plain laborers who worked for Crown and other businesses. These economi-cally powerful individuals helped shape the culture of Dalton along with a business class, who ran shops, stores, and other smaller enterprises in the city. Although members of the business class were called "uptown" by the mill workers, they were considered bourgeoisie middle-class by the wealthiest Daltonians. Most uptown people of Dalton went to elaborate churches and lived in fine houses. They belonged to exclusive clubs. Uptown people were Daltonians who were not poor farmers, cotton-mill workers, or blacks.[10] African Americans who lived in Dalton were seldom hired by Crown in any quantity from the day it opened in 1885 until it shut down in 1969. Although black Daltonians made up 30 percent of the population

Crown Cotton Mill. Photo owned by the author.

in 1890, this number dropped to only 10 percent by 1930. With few opportunities for work, African Americans had little choice but to move.[11]

With a stroke of brilliance, C. T. Pratt foresaw his opportunity to build a mighty congregation in this growing community as these poorly educated white workers moved off the farms to work in the mills. He quickly set up a tent and started bringing in new members for his church. He sent his partners, ordained ministers, to other industrially expanding cities, such as Chattanooga and Knoxville, Tennessee, to convert souls to his brand of religion, giving birth to a unique religious dynasty.

3

During the first thirty years of the operation of Crown Cotton Mill, the major labor force was comprised of children under twelve and women. Large poor families arriving in Dalton put their children to work as early as eight of age, even though the legal age to work was ten. Very few men as old as thirty worked during this time. The fathers of these working children were called "Drones" or "Vampire fathers" and were considered useless by the uptown residents. In 1899 the local press reported, "Lillie Staten, a twelve-year-old employed at the Crown Cotton Mill, got her hair caught in a steel spinning frame yesterday and her scalp was literally torn from her head . . . President Hamilton had to take the machine apart to get the scalp from the rollers around which it had become tightly wound."[12] It was not until late 1899 that the mill began hiring men in a larger capacity, and by 1900 half of the work force constituted men or boys, but only one in ten were heads of households. By 1912, three out of ten workers at Crown were heads of households. The number of children in the work force fell from 66 percent to 44 percent during this time period. Crown also had a large turnover in labor through the 1920s, creating instability and a problem for management.[13]

By the end of World War I, Crown had grown rapidly to a payroll of nearly one thousand workers and enlarged the size of the mill village to house hundreds of families. By 1920 corporate paternalism, reflected in mill-sponsored athletic teams and company bands, had been adopted by Crown to keep experienced workers on the job. Crown added other nonwage economic benefits for the same reason.[14]

C. T. most likely noticed that the company's success also carried seeds of instability, as the new families moved off the farms into Dalton. The mill hands working at Crown increased nearly 500 percent between 1890 and 1920.[15] The population of Dalton increased from 2,500 in 1890 to 10,000 by 1924.[16] The average income at the mill increased from $3.13 per week in 1890 to $14.99 per week in 1927, but because of inflation, the real earning power was not that great of an increase. In inflation-adjusted dollars, the workers' income went from $3.13 in 1890 to only $7.78 per week by 1927.[17]

C. T. Pratt, the clever Holiness evangelist, saw a large growing niche for his ministry. The uptown elite, who were members of one of three mainline Protestant denominations, had built elaborate antebellum church houses. Practically all of Crown's leaders worshiped at the extravagant First Presbyterian Church. The First Baptist Church was also a grand brick edifice that boasted a steeple as high as the Presbyterians. First Methodist remodeled its church to compete with the other two. By the turn of the century all three had built parsonages for their full-time pastors, who were all well-educated men of the cloth.[18] In 1921 when C. T. established his church in Dalton, other churches became available for the mill-hands and their families. Some of these small churches in and around Dalton were Hamilton Street Methodist (established in 1888), South Dalton Baptist (1915), Mount Rachel Baptist (1892), East Side Baptist (1927), Crown View Baptist (1913), Morris Street Methodist Episcopal (1927), and a few others.[19]

4

What kind of preacher was C. T. Pratt? Charlie Carmical, seventy-three at the time I interviewed him, had grown up in the Church of God of the Union Assembly, and left with his family in 1957 at the age of thirteen. Charlie's father, Hugh "Cash" Carmical, was second-in-command of all the Union Assembly churches behind C. T. during the 1950s. Charlie was named after Charles T. (C. T.) Pratt.

Charlie Carmical said, "C. T. could sing. He was a good singer. Preacher Pratt sang everything acapella. At the end of his sermon he would sing: "Bring Back to Me My Wandering Boy."

Carmical sang the song and then continued: "He would be preaching about anything and this would fit in. He'd stand on one foot, and shout, 'God will never take me, for I will never die.' Then he'd do the buck dance. He'd put on a show. It didn't make any difference. He was a showman, my daddy was a showman, I'm not a showman . . . I wouldn't take that chance. Have you ever seen someone take a chance and totally flop? If you're a showman, you don't mind taking a chance and flopping—that's just another day in showmanship."

Carmical then held up a finger on his right hand and put the finger from his other hand on it. "C. T.'s charisma came from one: personal appeal." Charlie moved his finger to another finger on the upturned hand, "Two: his charisma also came from his showmanship that was in him." Moving one finger to another, "Three: his

The young preacher, C. T. Pratt, with his Bible. Courtesy of an anonymous family member.

knowledge of the Bible in the oral tradition, and four: fear, and the ability to cast fear and evil in a black and white narrative."

Later during the interview Carmical said, "The perception of Christianity back then is not what we have today. In the South back then, Christianity was king—the most important thing in the South. Now football is king in the South. People today can't relate to the way Christianity was in its day. What Pratt offered these people—his people—was HOPE. His ideology, his religion offered HOPE! All they had to do was to believe when they died, they'd go to heaven or be resurrected when Christ came. That's the best program you could ask for. If you got one to beat it let me know, and I'll join it."[20]

4

Bringing in the Sheaves

"There are three classes of people: a low class, a middle class
and a high class. We want to work to bring the low class up to
the standard of the middle class and the high class down with
the middle class so that all can have a decent living."

C. T. PRATT
"Three Classes of People," *The Southerner,* 3

1

Possibly the reason C. T. Pratt was so attracted to Dalton, and made it the headquarters for his Holiness churches, was its place on the Dixie Highway. Besides
Dalton, the Union Assembly's largest congregations were in Cassville, Chattanooga,
and Knoxville, all towns on the newly developed highway system. Although the
interstate highway did not officially open until 1925, its planning and construction
started as early as 1915. Dalton business leaders made full use of the road's potential
for tourism and trade, as did C. T. Pratt, who traveled the highway often during
recruitment and business forays. Another likely reason Pratt chose Dalton was its
large, non-unionized workforce. In 1924, the city advertised that it had 2,500 "All
American" factory workers, meaning they were mostly white Americans.[1] Although
the city frequently advertised that its labor force was sympathetic to unionization

or agitations, C. T. Pratt was a strong believer in labor unions, and saw this as an opening for his growing church community.

Although Dalton was not unionized, the people who lived in the different mill villages in Dalton stood together and took care of one another. Any welfare that a cotton miller received came from other cotton mill workers. This was just the way of life in the 1920s and 1930s. The heart of the community, either in the mill village or on the farm, was the church. Social events and gatherings were organized by the small churches that had been established around town. Other than Sunday worship, religious activities included special "singing conventions," ice-cream socials, and picnics, the latter also referred to as "homecomings." Churchgoers professed to believe in sobriety as did the cotton mill owners themselves, and proper behavior by the people was influenced by Protestant mores.[2]

In fact, people of today would have difficulty understanding how important a church was to a person and his family during the 1920s and 1930s. The churches provided entertainment, camaraderie, recreational activities, and a distraction from the monotony and boredom of millwork. While radios were becoming more available, there were no televisions, iPads, iPhones, Netflix, or Facebook accounts. Pursuits we now take for granted as mass entertainment were much less common in everyday life. Football, for example, which came to be so important in the South, was not yet popular. Movie going was also not yet a widespread form of entertainment. The church was everything, and if a person didn't go regularly, he was considered a heathen and could be marked for social ostracism.

The services at many mill churches were full of fire and spirit with lots of "pew jumping" and shouting among the inspired.[3] Sometimes the whole church congregation would start shouting, raising their voices in spontaneous, glorifying praise. At one of the local Baptist churches, a Mr. Morgan, who liked to jump the pews and shout, climbed in a tree at the church and did his shouting from there. Once at Crown, some church members brought their enthusiasm from church to the job and started a spontaneous meeting with lots of testifying, shouting, and leaping around inside the workplace. When the superintendent, Frank Springer, was called to calm the situation, he saw it was no use trying and ordered the machines shut down until the men and women were finished and returned to their job.[4] ("Shouting" might involve speaking in tongues, testifying, or loud preaching, which is very different from mere "hollering" sessions.)

C. T. Pratt, who understood the worshiping preferences of the local population, offered a different kind of church for the common mill workers—a church that would never have drawn the interest of the mill owners and local business men. As historian Douglas Flamming notes, there was scarcely any interaction between mill churches and "uptown" churches, especially the Presbyterian congregation to which a large majority of Crown's managers belonged.[5]

Pratt's fundamentalist church thrived among the poor people of the Southern Appalachians, especially in mill towns. He attracted humble people with little formal education who were brought up on the King James Version of the Bible. He developed his religious movement by reminding the people how they were not welcomed by the "high-toned" services at the "big-wigged" churches. He also provided a social life for his people, which became an escape from the drabness of everyday life that could be found in the mills and mill villages. He wanted them to feel uncomfortable with these uptown people and their pastors where religion seemed cold and less heartfelt. He kept telling them that the Union Assembly of the Church of God, as it was called then, was looked on with contempt by the mill owners and business men, who regarded his members as uncultured lint-heads.[6]

He also created a distinctive identity among his members, which separated them from other church-goers. This led to strict conformity among his followers, which encouraged further obedience. The Holiness religion, as Preacher Pratt presented it, was an absolute rejection of the mainline Baptist, Presbyterian, and Methodist churches. This "old-time religion" endorsed speaking in tongues, faith healing, and the rejection of worldly affairs.

Of course, Pratt's church was not the only Holiness-Pentecostal church in the Upper South, but it did grow to have one of the largest memberships. The Church of God opened new paths of faith for poor whites. By 1945, C. T. had established churches in Dalton, GA, Rome, GA, Trion, GA, Cedartown, GA, Aragon, GA, Center, GA, Summerville, GA, Knoxville, TN, Luttrell, TN, Chattanooga, TN, Elizabethton, TN, Dooley Chapel, TN, Hamilton, OH, Cincinnati, OH, Middleton, OH, Ft. Payne, AL, Middlesboro, KY, Williamsburg, KY, Everts, KY, Teetersville, KY, and Malta, TX—all answering to him or his leadership.[7]

It is uncertain how many cotton mill workers left the mainline churches for the Holiness congregations, but a great number did, even though townspeople referred to them derisively as Holy Rollers.[8] Perhaps these economically disadvantaged spiritual seekers found, as historian Robert Mapes Anderson has written, that "in the unrestrained atmosphere of Pentecostal worship, the distinctions and prejudices encountered in the larger culture were often swept away, giving birth to a new sense of community and a new sense of status."[9]

2

Without question, much of the growth of the Union Assembly was simply due to C. T. Pratt himself. According to older members, who witnessed his sermons and daily activities first-hand, C. T. Pratt was also a master of manipulation. He knew just what people needed and how to give it to them. He gave them a community, a group to belong to that gave them comfort as they faced the prejudices they encountered in the larger culture outside the church. He gave them something special to belong to—something that they could be proud to be part of—a new awareness of importance.

The uniqueness of the Union Assembly of the Church of God demonstrated its independence from any other religious group. Indeed, according to the *Official*

History of Whitfield County, Georgia (1936), the Union Assembly of the Church of God was the most influential of Dalton's Holiness congregations because it embraced the notion of collective social justice, and thus would play a major role in future labor disputes in Dalton.[10] However, when outsiders tried to associate the "Union" in the church's name to labor unions, C. T. replied that "Union" in its title referred to the union of its twenty four different churches established by Mr. Pratt and his ministers and not to labor unions.[11]

It was no secret what Brother Pratt did to win mill workers to his camp, and it was not just one thing in particular that drew the poor to him. One topic that he kept expounding on at each service was basic: "It is us against them—the rich against the poor," but he didn't always use those words—he also created metaphors that developed his message. In his own words, C. T. said, "As I am writing I can see a crowd of people who are helpless widow women and orphan children shivering with cold, and the high class sitting in their luxuries seeing these poor unfortunate people seeking something to eat even from the garbage can, and will not help them unless they are forced to do so."[12]

It was stated that to add to his flock of parishioners, Pratt would spend all day on Saturdays standing on a street corners preaching to the people who shopped from store to store. He put on a show and people stopped to watch. Some observers found themselves mesmerized by Pratt's words and then visited his church on Sunday. Pratt preached on the street in other towns such as Chattanooga and Knoxville, Tennessee. Knoxville even had a town square specifically designated for street ministers. There, each man took his turn preaching God's word to the people who gathered in town on Saturday to do their weekly shopping.

Reverend Pratt used Bible verses as well as any highly educated clergyman to illustrate his point of view. He told his people that he could tell them what the Bible meant, and all they needed to do was listen to his interpretations. It was reported that one of C. T.'s most often quoted scriptures was James 5: 1–4, which belittles wealth and tells how the wealthy will cry for mercy in the final days of judgment. He would then preach about those verses, saying, "The reason the moth has eaten their clothes, there are thousands of dollars worth of fine garments laying back not used, the poor people going ragged without clothes. . . Lots of this wealth has come from the blood of innocent men. Oh, what an awful day that we are living in now! So many people living in luxury with more heaped up than they can ever use, while millions are going hungry and shivering with cold."[13]

Over time, Brother Pratt also effectively established himself as an *authority figure* among his followers. Once his leadership went unquestioned by his followers, they were willing to do almost *anything* he asked of them. Why? If they disobeyed him they felt as if they would be left out of the group, which is something no one wanted. Also, C. T. maintained his authority through trust. How? He did it with the power of suggestion and creating illusions they wanted to believe. When Pratt made a statement which was suggestive toward an action such as "Blessed are the poor—give all you have to God!" then his 'authority' in their life was unquestionable. He also used part truth here because everyone knew the first part of his statement came from the Bible, therefore it was natural for his members to believe that they needed to give all they had to God to be part of the church group.

3

It is important to note that C. T. Pratt's religion was similar to other Holiness faiths except in minor details. He offered these poor mill workers hope for a better day and life everlasting. He was an apocalyptic preacher, who continued to remind his people that the end was near and would happen during his lifetime. When Brother Pratt foretold that he would never die, most people did not understand what he meant. According to several former members, Pratt believed Jesus had been reigning at the right hand of God since his ascension into heaven and would never return to earth until all enemies were destroyed. Pratt had faith that he would be here when Jesus came down from heaven, and Jesus would not come back to earth until death was destroyed. Therefore, Charlie Thomas Pratt would never die. He was sure all the wicked would be destroyed before Christ returned.

"The people call everything wrong the devil. Everything wrong is of the devil, but everything wrong isn't the devil—St. John, 8 chapter—44 verse will show you that there is a difference between the devil and the children of the devil. (The children of the devil were to be here until the end of the world)—We will refer you to Matthew 13 chapter—37 to 42 verses: There wasn't but one man to be bound and that was the chief head of evil which is the devil. Ezek., 29 chapter—3 verse will show you that he is a man, and the man is the devil that created evil and gave the human family an evil nature, brought on us by Adam because he broke the commandments of God and ate of the tree. . . . The devil has never been in the heaven where God is, and never will be, because there is a gulf fixed between heaven and hell."[14]

In other words, according to Pratt, man himself is evil and of the Devil, and the only salvation for a person is to be a Christian by joining his church. He told the people that they could only go to heaven by belonging to the Union Assembly because it was the only way to get the Devil out of one's own life. Pratt also preached that worldly things are of the Devil and that his members need to avoid all worldly temptations or go to hell.

C. T. also taught that women should be submissive to their husbands and listen only to men for interpretation of the Bible because he argued that the Bible showed a man that women were easily deceived, and were not able to bear the hardships of a minister.[15] Moreover, women and girls of the Church were required to refrain from being fashionable outside the home. Women had to wear a dress or skirt that was below the knees and not tight but full. She was required at all times to keep her arms covered with sleeves, and the neckline of her garment had to cover her up to her neck. A woman was not permitted to wear slacks, shorts, or a bathing suit. If she did go swimming she had to use a safety pin to fasten the dress together between her knees. Men and women were not permitted to swim together. Once a woman reached puberty, she was required to wear stockings. She was not permitted to wear makeup or jewelry, although a married woman could wear a wedding band. Women were not permitted to cut or color their hair, or do anything except tie it up in a modest fashion. The painting of nails with fingernail polish was forbidden. C. T. called these adornments being "worldly."

Members of the Church were not allowed to attend movies, read novels, play board games, or read newspapers—later, when televisions were first sold, they were not allowed to own or watch one. It is no wonder that these members knew very little of the events in the outside world taking place around them. They were not allowed to attend other churches or social events unless sanctioned by the Church. They were not allowed to marry a person outside the Church. If a member did fall in love and wanted to marry someone who was not a member, that outside person had to join the Church and belong for six months before marriage was permitted. If a member left the Church then no member could have contact with that person, even if it was a relative. In some cases it was not uncommon for a member to go years without seeing or speaking with his or her own parent or child.[16]

Members of the Church were also forbidden to take any type of medicine or see a medical doctor. They were allowed to see chiropractors and dentists. If a person became sick then the group would pray for God to heal that person. Pregnant women were not permitted to use doctors to deliver their babies; untrained midwives were used to do this. C. T.'s daughter, Flora Hughes, delivered more than half of the church's children while he presided over the Church. His other daughter, Tiny Van Meter, delivered Union Assembly babies when she was in Tennessee.

About divorce, C. T. stated in the church laws in the 1928 Minutes of the Union Assembly of the Church of God that a minister could not remain a minister if he divorced his wife and remarried.[17] This rule was changed in the 1945 Minutes of the Union Assembly of the Church of God just before an event occurred that rocked the foundation of the Church.

4

On October 24, 1929—Black Thursday—frightened investors sold their stocks for whatever price they could get and the stock market on Wall Street crashed. The losses were in the billions of dollars and thousands of accounts were wiped out. The primary villain was rumor—on and off the exchange. The shock on Wall Street spread to other exchanges and markets until a panic took hold of the nation, and later the world. A few analysts had been warning that the euphoric buying spree at the stock exchange had to stop at some point. They said prices had been pushed too high, some selling at 15 to 150 times their worth. Even though it was yet to be named, the Great Depression had started.[18]

The Great Depression did not leave any town or individual untouched by its enormity, and it hit the southern states with a force that left people with little hope for recovery, but it did not come on all at once as people are led to believe. The Depression started small and grew over time to the horrific event that it later became. For a while in the beginning, the people of Crown Cotton Mill and the other industries in Dalton enjoyed a period of remarkable cohesiveness. Then the mill village paternalism started to fall apart because of economic collapse, which revealed its internal flaws and the brittle foundation it had rested on before the Depression began.[19]

The power of the system was always in the hands of the management, which left few options for the millhands when the economic downturn began. In April 1930 the level of unemployment was not alarming in Georgia or Dalton, but ultimately, the Great Depression overwhelmed the textile industry and devastated both Crown Cotton Mill and the whole region of North Georgia. A few of Dalton's manufacturing plants dissolved in the economic crisis and never reopened.[20] Ford Motor Company's orders for automobile fabrics and Dalton's bedspread companies kept Crown from going totally under, but the mill ran only two or three days a week, until the mid-1930s when the old mill shut down completely. During all of the 1930s, the company made zero profit. Because mill officials saw labor costs as one of the major culprits in the mill's loss of profit, they went to faster labor-saving machines. All of this was passed down to the employees who had little choice except to unite.[21]

By the time Franklin Roosevelt took office in March of 1933, the third year of the Great Depression, 15 million Americans were unemployed, approaching a third of the country's working force.[22] In Dalton, a community chest was organized by local philanthropic organizations to help the unemployed and needy people in the community, but by 1933 this relief effort was overburdened. Churches such as the Union Assembly of the Church of God created their own relief efforts as C. T. Pratt had people pool their resources so he could contribute to the those without jobs. He stopped charging rent to some of the people who lived in his apartments and homes. It is not known how he acquired many of these homes, but interviews suggest that they came from members who gave the Church their property—some even before they died. This would become common practice after the Second World War.[23]

A "Share-the-Work" plan was implemented statewide and used in Dalton. All mills, including Crown, ran their factories at full capacity several days a week and not just a few hours every day. The mills in Dalton tried to make sure that one member of a family stayed on the job, so younger men and most women who had husbands were laid off. What transpired were employment clashes between the workers. The "Share-the-Work" system created countless opportunities for abuse. At Crown Cotton Mill the management was able to dictate various policies to their workers and even the families who lived in the mill village. People were discharged for doing things that before the Depression had been overlooked. One worker was fired when a mill official saw two chickens in his front yard, and they were not even his chickens; they were his neighbors'.[24] This type of action was referred to in the mill villages as "favoritism." The Depression made it difficult to contest company policies. Supervisors could and did tell employees: "Well, if you don't do as I say, get through that hole in the wall [door]. There are men outside the front door waiting for this job."[25] These attitudes caused Crown's mill hands to successfully organize a union in the fall of 1933. They joined the Local 1893 of the United Textile Workers Union of America (UTW).

By 1930 some of C. T. and Minnie's grown children had married and left the family dwelling even though Minnie was yet to have her youngest child, Wayman (spelled Waymund or Waymond in some records). Their oldest daughter, Flora, who was nineteen, had married Winston "Tobe" Hughes who was twelve years her senior. In the 1930 census Flora and Tobe lived in the city of Dalton, with Ulyess and Beulah Kennemer (spellings in census records). Flora, who would become the midwife of the Church, had just had her oldest son John E. Hughes.[26] The 1930 census also showed that C. T., who was then fifty, and Minnie, who was then forty, lived in Murray County, Georgia, on Green Road with their children listed as Edmond (24), Estle E. (17), Jesse F. (11), Tiny (7), Leola (5), and Herbert H. (1). They also were housing two boarders Clarence Beards and Paul Dean—both from Kentucky. C. T. and Minnie's second son, Lloyd (spelled Loyd in census records), had married a woman from Georgia by the name of Katie and they had a four-year-old daughter named Juanita and a two-year-old son named Charles T. They also lived in Murray County, Georgia.[27] During the latter part of the 1930's, Estle, who had already been ordained, married a woman named Floyd Howard, and in 1938 they had a daughter they named Minnie. Floyd's brother, Dayton, lived with them.[28]

There is not abundant information about how the Church and the Pratt family handled the Great Depression. C. T. and Minnie continued to build church membership in Dalton, in other churches scattered across the South, and into the Midwestern portion of the United States. It was reported that the members took care of one another and did the best they could to get through the decade of "hard time." That is not to say that there is little information about the Pratt family during the Depression; however, C. T. and Minnie's offspring were growing up and starting a life of their own. All of them stayed in the Church—five of their sons became ministers. The girls stayed involved and even some of their husbands became ministers for the Church.

5

Love Thy Neighbor

"There ought to be a law passed forbidding any man to put anyone out of his house when he hasn't any job and can't pay."

C. T. PRATT
"Three Classes of People," *The Southerner*, 3

1

C. T. Pratt had served as moderator for all the Union Assembly Churches since their creation in 1921, but in 1943, as scores of the young male Union Assembly members were serving in World War II, Pratt was also elected by the body of elders as the Assembly treasurer. This gave C. T. Pratt the power and authority to transact any business he saw necessary for the benefit of the Assembly, such as buying and selling property. The Board of Elders who gave Brother Pratt this power were J. W. Burnett, Clinton Bell, E. E. Pratt, W. T. Howard, Jesse F. Pratt, W. P. Foster, G. E. Wiggs, J. H. Burnett, L. B. Pratt, L. L. Coker, Tom Bohannon, and Frank McCollum.[1]

At this 1943 assembly, four men were ordained to preach. They were Junior Howard, Clarence Roberts, Wesley Bonner, and Lonnie Starnes. Fifty-two Church of God Ministers were present for this ordination ceremony, and four will be players again in this narrative. They were Jim Brewer, Clinton Bell, Otha Pitner, and Dennis Smith.[2] Also at this meeting the Supreme Council voted on and passed a church rule which stated that no minister of the Church of God of the Union Assembly shall marry any couple who are not members of the Church, and a rule was made by the committee to forbid any Christian boy or girl that belongs to the Church to have a love affair with sinner boys or girls who are not members of the Church.[3]

Out of all these poor millhands and farmers, how did C. T. Pratt obtain the money he needed to build this dynasty? He made sure to build his membership first, but by 1940 after the church membership had grown to approximately four thousand, Pratt knew that he needed money to keep the Church thriving. Pratt explained his view on tithing to his people by asking them how much of the money and the world's goods belong to God. He taught that if all is not God's, there is nothing that belongs to Him. He said it was false teaching to say that 10 percent belongs to God. His reasoning was that if God only owns 10 percent, then 90 percent belongs to the devil. He told his members that everything either belongs to God or the devil.[4] C. T. Pratt backed everything up with Bible scripture. High tithing was encouraged by referring to Psalms 50:9, Isaiah 50:1, First Corinthians 6:20—"For ye are bought with a price, therefore glorify God in your body, and in your spirit which are God's." C. T. Pratt convinced his people that everything they had belonged to God and they should give it all to the Lord—which meant give it all to the Church.

According to church literature, Pratt preached that nowhere in the New Testament did Jesus or any of his disciples give a commandment to pay tithes because it would not be grace. He stated that grace is favor and a law is force and not favor. Brother Pratt created guilt, and he was good at it. He went back and forth quoting scriptures from the Old Testament to the New, but he continually said that Jesus changed the law of the Old Testament. He would use particular Bible verses to create guilt—he established guilt—he used guilt like a double-edged sword. Often, Pratt recited Psalms 37:21, which states, "The wicked borroweth and payeth not again, but the righteous showeth mercy and giveth." Then Pratt explained the verse to mean that his people were under the grace covenant, the covenant of love, and they should show mercy and give it all to God. But he reminded them that if they were under the carnal covenant (flesh, bodily, material, and not spiritual) they should pay tithes (10 percent). In the *Minutes of the 24th Annual Meeting of the Union Assembly of the Church of* God (1945) Pratt is quoted as saying: "To prove that we are under the giving-commandment I will refer them to 2 Corinthians 9:7—"Every man according as he purposes in his heart, so let him give, not grudgingly; or of necessity for God loveth a cheerful giver. And not a compelled payer."[5] The problem lies in the fact that Pratt had added the last sentence—"*And not a compelled payer*"—which is not found in 2 Corinthians or anywhere in the Bible. By adding this statement where he did, Pratt made it sound as if the words came from the Bible. (According to the minutes of the CGUA and informants, C. T. preached against tithing because he believed they needed to give all they had to the church and not just 10 percent because if they gave only 10 percent to God then the devil got the other 90 percent.)

It was stated by several older members interviewed that by the mid-forties, the members were not encouraged to read the Bible because they were told they didn't understand its meaning. Only Brother C. T. Pratt and his ministers knew what the Bible meant and the members were told the meanings; therefore, all the members needed to do was come to the services and listen to the explanation. Those interviewed said that C. T. Pratt also told his ministers what the Bible meant, so all understanding came from him. If a minister departed from Pratt's teaching, he was removed. Some interviewed said that Jesse talked his aging father into this practice.[6]

For a long time, C. T. did not abuse his power. He gave to people who needed his help. He cared for his people like a king looked after the subjects under his dominion. He was considered a kind man by his membership, a con man by nonmembers. He was a smart man in one respect—he knew how to build church membership, but his establishment grew beyond Pratt's ability to control it, especially in matters related to fiscal management, and he became overwhelmed by the enormity of his creation. According to the older former members I interviewed, by the mid-1940s Brother Pratt had already started losing control, and there were people ready to pounce on his world and take away his power, but he wouldn't give up easily.

2

Even though Jesse Franklin Pratt does not appear in the 1940 census, there is much written about him, and other records about his life have been recovered. Jesse was born in Lindale, Georgia, on October 23, 1917. He was the fourth son of C. T. and Minnie but, unlike his three older brothers, he would play a major role in the church's future. He served for a trial period as minister of the Union Assembly of the Church of God in either 1933 or 1934, which would put him at either sixteen or seventeen-years-old. Jesse was formally ordained in Old Salem, Texas, on July 24, 1937, at age nineteen. It was said of him by his son Jesse Junior: "He was called a 'walking Bible' by many of his peers because he knew so much about the scriptures."[7] Unlike C. T., Jesse had enough schooling to read even though it was reported that he did not reach high school before quitting. The census records of 1930 indicate that all the Pratt children, including Jesse, age eleven, were not enrolled in school. Tiny, Leola, and Herbert were too young, but Jesse had evidently quit, which would put the fourth grade as his highest level of formal education. (Some people interviewed corroborated that Jesse claimed to have only gone through the fourth grade.) Many interviewees observed that Jesse was much like his father in his emotional range: he could appear to be extremely caring and outgoing, but he could also withdraw completely and react with severe, unreasoning anger at times. Former members interviewed said Jesse's changing demeanor was much worse than his father's. "Jesse could be the kindest most caring person one day and the meanest most hateful person the next. A rage would take over him. You could see it in his face and no one within his range was safe."[8]

Just before Jesse turned twenty in 1937 he was sent to Cincinnati, Ohio, to preach for the Union Assembly of the Church of God located there. Sometime between 1937 and 1939, Jesse met a woman named Ethel Russell. Eight days after Germany attacked Poland and five days after France and England declared war on Germany to begin World War II, twenty-one-years-old Jesse F. Pratt married Ethel Russell, age seventeen, in Whitfield County, Georgia, on a Friday, September 8, 1939. They were joined in marriage by one of Jesse's best friends and a minister of the Church, Reverend Johnny H. Burnett.[9] It was reported that Johnny had lost his right arm

Pilots for the Church of God of the Union Assembly: Johnny Burnett and Jesse F. Pratt.
Courtesy of Haynes Townsend.

in a mining accident, but he was still an accomplished pilot. He stood about five-foot-nine or -ten and was modestly built—neither skinny nor heavy. He had jet black curly hair and a broad smile. It was reported that C. T. loved him like one of his own sons. Johnny along with his older brother, J. Willie Burnett, were both charter members and preachers at the Church.

Ethel R. Pratt, during an interview recorded in 2014, was described by an 81-year-old former church member from Powell, Tennessee.

I asked, "Do you remember what Ethel Russell Pratt looked like?"

The woman said, "I only saw her one time. The fact is they had come to church (Luttrell, Tennessee) that one time . . . Jesse came up there to preach and she didn't come in the building. She sat in the car. The way I remember her, she was small statured, not tiny-tiny, but small statured. And I believe she had dark hair. They are so closed-mouth about everything and undercover for so long, people are afraid to talk about it."[10]

Twenty-one-year-old Jesse Pratt, standing a little over six feet tall, was not as tall as his father. Jesse was slimly built when he married Ethel. He had dark hair, but not black. Like his father, his ears stood away from his head. Jesse had a broad white smile, but one front tooth looked slightly uneven. Jesse learned to fly and received his pilot's license at an early age. C. T. bought several airplanes for the Church, and Jesse and Johnny Burnett were the official church pilots.[11] However, to get a pilot's license, an applicant had to undergo a regular medical physical examination by a licensed doctor, so the rule prohibiting church members from seeing doctors had to be disregarded. As reported by one of his sons, sometime between 1945 and 1946, Jesse would lose his left eye while chopping cordwood. A stick flew into Jesse's left eye and became imbedded. Jesse removed the piece of wood himself, but this left him blind in his left eye for the rest of his life.[12] Jesse never tried to cover the affliction with a patch or a glass eye. The damaged eye pointed outward which made people feel they were in the presence of someone special.

2

In 1939, under order of their Union, the mill-hands at Crown went on strike. This strike left the paternalism and the mill village in shambles with families in turmoil just trying to find enough money to stay alive. Even as the Crown Mill strike continued during September 1939, Adolf Hitler's Germany invaded Poland, and the European conflict set in motion forces that would impact the American South and virtually every part of the world.[13] The war changed the Dixie's cotton-mill families radically as it eventually meant the end of the Great Depression and boosted the southern workers' income immensely. Thousands of married women went into the textile workforce and stayed there even after the war, permanently changing the nature of the family economy. When the federal government enforced a truce between managers and unions, it empowered the growth of organized labor across the entire United States.[14]

As 1939 moved into 1940, the world was in a turmoil that it had never seen before. Warsaw had already surrendered, and Poland had crumbled as the Russians, briefly allied with Nazi Germany under the terms of the Molotov-Ribbentrop Pact, also attacked from the east while the Germans invaded from the west. Japan launched a drive on the Chinese, killing millions. Most able-bodied Americans went back to work as the United States ended its embargo against the sale of ammunition and other implements of war to nations at war with Germany. Pratt's members were again making money and, most likely, giving much of it to the church.

In 1940 Estle Pratt, C. T.'s third son, had steady work as a machine operator in a bedspread company.[15] By 1940, his second son, Lloyd, and wife, Katie, spelled Kate in 1940 census, had five children, Frances (13), Charles T. (11), Lillian M. (9), Faye (6), and Betty J. (5). Lloyd was also ordained to preach and worked full-time in Crown Cotton Mills as a cleaner. They had lived in Arkansas in 1935 but moved back to Dalton after the war started.[16] Also by 1940 C. T.'s daughter Flora and her husband, Winston "Tobe" Hughes, had moved from Murray County to Whitfield County, Georgia, and lived within the city limits of Dalton. Tobe worked in the mills and barbered hair on the side. Living with them were their children, Paul (8), Minnie Kate (6), George (5), and Jessie (2).[17]

An interesting story about C. T.'s showmanship surfaced during interviews for this book. It was reported by two people—one woman who is in her eighties now and Grady Lance. It was during summer of 1940 when C. T. was at the height of his power. C. T. had a platform built under the surface of a lake by Grady Lance's family who were not affiliated with the Church. They built it in South Whitfield County near an area called Redwine's Cove. The lake was called the "Touch Hole" because kids swimming there were unable to touch the bottom. The family of Grady Lance built the platform just below the surface of the water a few feet out into the lake using a frame covered with chicken wire. On a hot July Sunday C. T. told his members during church services that he could walk on water and for them to meet him at the "Touch Hole" at two o'clock and he'd show them. According to reports, C. T. had the members stand on the opposite bank of the lake. When he started walking across the surface of the water—on the chicken wire members could not see—everyone started "oohing and hawing," holding their hands up, shouting, dancing around, and some praying. When Brother Pratt accidently stepped off the platform, he disappeared under the water and about drowned before they could get him to dry land.[18] C. T. was always the showman.

In Dalton, once World War II began, some of the chenille companies, such as Cabin Craft, started making parachutes and other war materials as the economy soared. The demand for Dalton's goods grew rapidly.[19] According to interviews money flowed into the church faster than C. T. and Minnie could count it. Minnie presided as the church secretary, and C. T. was treasurer in name only because Minnie kept up with the money coming in and out to help those still in need.[20] By 1944 there were thousands of Union Assembly members spread across eleven states.[21] Jesse Pratt and Johnny Burnett were using the church airplanes to fly the tithing collections from these different churches into Dalton each week.[22]

As far away as the churches were from C. T. in Dalton, Brother Pratt maintained total control over them. He decided who would preach and what they would preach. C. T. used only his most trusted men to be head ministers at the other Union Assembly Churches. By 1940 this number of churches reached into the twenties. These head-ministers had been with C. T. since the Church's founding.

In time some of these churches were pastored by C. T.'s family members—either sons or sons-in-law. Four times a year the ministers of all the Union Assembly churches would meet in Dalton with C. T. and report the happenings at their particular church. C. T. would go over the church doctrine and make sure each minister was following these beliefs. He also encouraged them to raise more money by creating competition between the churches to see who was gathering the most money. Once a year all the members in all the Union Assembly Churches were told to come to the church in Dalton for a church-wide assembly. Sickness was not an excuse for not being present. During the annual meeting, members enjoyed gospel singing, spirited preaching, good food, foot washing, healing prayers, and of course they were reminded of church rules. Former members said everyone looked forward to the annual meeting in Dalton; it was the highlight of their year. When the annual assembly ended, the members were already marking next year's meeting on their calendars.[23]

Along with the money that flowed into the Church came power and influence. This power was embellished by Brother Pratt. Church membership grew so rapidly that they became a voice in the politics of Whitfield County and, in some cases, the state of Georgia. Brother Pratt encouraged his members to register to vote, which created a substantial voting bloc. During the 1940s, anybody running for an office in the county had to 'court' Pratt in order to secure votes from church membership. And if they got Brother Pratt's vote they got all his followers' votes. Just before the election, C. T. would invite the candidate of his choice to visit the Church during a Sunday meeting, and at the end of the sermon C. T. would introduce the man— always a man—as his friend and tell the members he planned on voting for him. Then C. T. would raise his arm and ask for a show of hands for all those who were going to vote for this friend of his. Everyone in the room would raise their hands and then vote for Brother Pratt's choice.[24]

3

Jesse Pratt, C. T.'s forth son, who was only twenty-three in 1940, had already made a name for himself as a dynamic preacher and student of the Bible. Jesse and his young wife, Ethel, were model representatives of the Church. It was reported that Ethel took very good care of herself and kept her nice figure even after giving birth to two children. Ethel kept her dark hair neat and long—never cutting it—putting it up in a wave or bun. Even though the women of the Church were not allowed to wear makeup or jewelry, it was reported that Ethel was so radiant that she appeared to be wearing makeup on occasions, but this was never substantiated. As far as could be determined, Ethel acted like the majority of other women in the Church—she knew her place. On November 12, 1940, Ethel Pratt gave birth to a son she and Jesse named David Ronald. Ethel had her and Jesse's second son in 1942. They named him Charles Thomas II after the child's grandfather, the Reverend C. T. Pratt.

Jesse tried his hand as a house painter, but was semi-successful because he spent much of his time traveling from one church to another across the South and the Midwest. He became the pastor (in Church parlance, pastors were called laborers) of one of their churches in Detroit, and on July 3, 1941, at the yearly assembly meeting he was elected along with eleven other fellow laborers to a committee that was called the twelve elders of the Union Assembly Church. It was later renamed the Supreme Council.[25]

In July 1942 attorneys Mitchell and Mitchell filed an application with Whitfield County, Georgia, for the incorporation of the Union Assembly of the Church of God. Minnie Pratt was listed as secretary on the application. The charter members, called "the Twelve Elders," were listed as C. T. Pratt of Dalton, Georgia; J. W. Burnett of Attalla, Alabama; J. H. Burnett of Middleton, Ohio; G. E. Wiggs of Knoxville, Tennessee; L. B. Pratt of Tunnel Hill, Georgia; Jesse F. Pratt of Hamilton, Ohio; E. E. Pratt of Dalton, Georgia; W. T. Howard of Dalton, Georgia; Tom Bohannon of Knoxville, Tennessee; L. L. Coker of Chattanooga, Tennessee; W. P. Foster of Dalton, Georgia; and Clinton Bell of Dalton, Georgia[26] These men were the head-ministers at their respective churches.

After the Japanese attacked Pearl Harbor on December 7, 1941, war came to the United States and raged throughout the world. C. T. Pratt along with his sons continued preaching the gospel, which brought in new members—the majority of these new members were women because their husbands were fighting in Europe or in the Pacific Theater. None of the Pratt boys served in the U.S. Army during the war, or at least no record of them was found. The Church had a doctrine that they would not serve in combat because they did not believe in killing. They were allowed to serve in other capacities as long as they were not asked to carry arms, but none of the Pratt boys were called, or, if they were called, they were not listed as serving. However, it was stated in several interviews that some young Union Assembly men actually fought in combat.

4

Just after the close of World War II after Japan's unconditional surrender, the Union Assembly of the Church of God had their annual assembly meeting in Dalton on October 18, 19, and 20, 1945. It was the Church's twenty-fourth annual meeting. It was reported in the Union Assembly minutes that they received an offering of $462.54 on the 19th to pay for rooms rented for visitors. That amount of money seems modest; however, in 2017 dollars that would be over $7,000. At the next meeting on October 20, 1945, the reported offering given was $3,028.03. That would be valued at over $40,000 today.

By the end of the decade, C. T. Pratt and the Church had started acquiring property in Whitfield County and in the surrounding North Georgia counties. The deed books in the Whitfield County Clerk of Superior Court disclosed that the Union Assembly had obtained five deeds totaling 18 lots inside the county alone.[27] Some of these lots were signed over to the Church by widows; however some were purchased by assuming a loan against the property. They had also bought and were given farms in Tennessee, Kentucky, Alabama, and West Texas. For example, on March 25, 1952, the Union Assembly purchased 764 acres of farming land in Whitfield and Murray Counties, Georgia from Hugh Maddron for $14,000.[28] That would be worth nearly $130,000 today. From 1953 through 2014 the Union Assembly bought or was given 197 deeds to property that totaled 5,536.11 acres and 959 lots in subdivisions and city lots. The largest purchase of land by the Union Assembly was in 1956, when it spent $288,637.21 on mostly farms.[29]

To buy this much property, many dollar bills had to be collected from all these church members. The Church would send entire families to live on and contribute volunteer labor to these farms. The children were expected to work alongside their parents. One member reported he picked cotton on one of their farms in West Texas when he was a small child, and he remembered getting in the cotton wagons to pull the cotton over his head to keep from freezing to death.[30] All the money made on this farm was pooled together and given back as needed to all the other Union Assembly churches. The Pratts, though, kept their share, and Minnie was in charge of distributing all the funds. C. T. Pratt encouraged communal living because he was planning for the end of time. Pratt preached that only the Church of God of the Union Assembly members would be left, and Jesus would live in the "Camp of the Saints" in Dalton, Georgia. He planned to move all Union Assembly members from all the other Churches to Dalton by 1961. He told his people that all should "share and share alike" or "spread the wealth." Pratt's governance wasn't really communism or socialistic, at least as far as political theory goes. It was more like an authoritarian dictatorship in which one person or one group of people collect and benefit from earnings of all, and that person decides what is given out to other earners.

In addition to acquiring property, the Church wielded economic power in other ways. In the late 1940s and early 1950s, for example, C. T. and the Church started buying Studebaker trucks from a dealership in Dalton that was owned by Claude Poston. C. T. had what he called "goodwill" offerings at church. During this period he used these special offerings to buy Studebaker 2R Series Trucks from Claude. C. T. would come buy them so often that Poston Motors bought forty to fifty a year. When they were sold—all to the Church—Claude would order 40 to 50 more. This went on for years until about 1954, when Studebaker had financial troubles and merged with fellow company Packard to become the Studebaker-Packard Company.

Claude Poston's son Jack estimated his dad may have sold C. T. and the Church about 500 trucks. He said that at one point during this period, Studebaker sent a representative to Poston Motors to see how it was selling so many trucks.[31]

5

While C. T. and his church had long enjoyed good relations with their home base in Dalton—indeed, they had wielded considerable power over local elections—suspicions about the Church among community leaders were growing, and things were about to change. On October 6, 1956, the chief of police of the city of Dalton, Louis Vinning, levied a tax lien, issued by the city council, against C. T. Pratt and the Church of God of the Union Assembly, Inc. Dalton authorities contended that the corporation was indebted to the city in an amount stated in the execution for back taxes. The amount owed was over one million dollars. City officials argued that all the farms, apartments, and various business owned by the Union Assembly Church were not exempt from being taxed because the church did not fit under the Federal statute passed in 1955 that provided exemption for non-profit corpora-

Assistant Moderator W. P. Foster with Moderator C. T. Pratt, ca. 1940.
Courtesy of Haynes Townsend.

tions because Pratt was receiving personal profit from his church affiliates. C. T. Pratt petitioned and sued the city of Dalton, arguing that the Church was, in fact, a non-profit corporation. The Whitfield County Superior Court dismissed C. T.'s case on grounds of general demurrer and ordered the taxes paid.

C. T. Pratt hired famed attorney Bobby Lee Cook—later rumored to be the model for the lead character on the long-running *Matlock* television series, starring Andy Griffith—from Summerville, Georgia, and promptly appealed the court's ruling, which sent the case to the Supreme Court of Georgia. Carlton McCamy was the attorney who represented the city of Dalton. Attorney Cook argued that the Church of God of the Union Assembly, Inc., received no dividends, income, or profits, from the church properties and businesses, and that no personal gains were received by any person, including C. T. Pratt. On March 11, 1957, the Georgia Supreme Court reversed the ruling and the Church did not have to pay the back taxes.[32] But they had to start paying taxes on the Church's business-owned property. While Dalton was unsuccessful in collecting taxes on the Church, soon the Internal Revenue Service (IRS) would take an interest in affairs of the Church.

6

Thou Shall Not Covet
Thy Neighbor's Wife

"We ought to get the spirit in us that would do nothing
to wound the feelings of a brother or sister."

C. T. PRATT
"Charlie Pratt Sayings," *The Southerner,* 2

1

In 1943 the building on Glenwood Avenue that housed the Union Assembly of
the Church of God burned to the ground. C. T. and many of his members were in
Williamsburg, Kentucky, for a ministers' meeting. Upon return, they immediately
purchased property on Spencer Street, which was one block east of Glenwood. Until
a new church was built, they had their services in the Odd Fellows Hall.[1] The lot
for the new church on Spencer Street was located in an area of Dalton called Fort
Hill after a fort was built at the top of the hill during the Civil War. Some residents
in the area of Fort Hill went to the Dalton City Council and had the area rezoned
so that the Church would not be allowed a building permit. These residents and
the City Council didn't realize the growth of C. T. Pratt's political power, however.
C. T., using the Mitchell and Mitchell law firm, went before the judge and got a court

Picnic lunch called "Homecoming," ca. 1946. C. T. Pratt is at front right.
Courtesy of Nell Belcher.

order that forced the City to give the Church a permit.[2] Soon a new Church was built, but it quickly became overcrowded during the war years as workers moved into Dalton and joined the Church. Also the Church lacked sufficient parking, since many members now traveled to church in cars. In 1947 the Church bought the old Ford dealership building on 41 Highway in South Dalton. The property also included ample land across the street which provided abundant parking, so the Church could grow and accommodate more people.[3]

The interiors of all the Assembly Churches were designed the same. The men and older boys sat on risers situated on the side and behind the rostrum, which was on a platform about one foot above the floor. Also, on this stand would be the Supreme Council of twelve selected men who would sit on two benches facing each other and between them would be the rostrum where preaching took place. Behind the Supreme Council would be the organ on one side and the piano behind the other. Behind the organ or piano were the Board of Elders. In later years a small band was situated directly behind the rostrum and in front of a set of risers for the

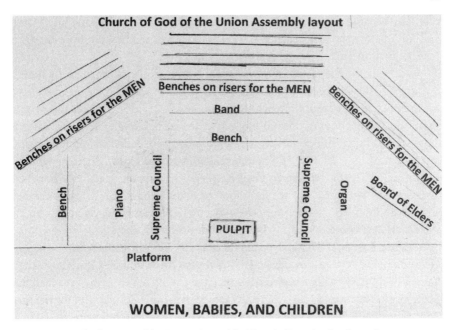

Inside drawing of the Union Assembly Church. Drawing by the author.

men. The women, babies, and children sat on benches at ground level looking up at everyone else.[4]

By the early 1940s C. T.'s son, Jesse, had moved back to Dalton. Jesse and Johnny Burnett became the Union Assembly pilots. They would visit the satellite churches organized by C. T., who maintained control as the organization's moderator (later the title was changed to general overseer). They would fly to these churches in order to bring back the offerings that had been collected during the Sunday services. Minnie would then send back to these satellite churches the money they needed to survive.[5] According to Dr. Paul Williamson, this was a common practice with the Holiness churches at the time.[6]

Besides being an ordained minister for the Church, Jesse continued his work as a house painter to bring in extra money. It was also common knowledge, and still is today, that Jesse took up the hobby of quick-draw with pistols. He would wear them in holsters on a belt around his waist as was seen in Western movies of that era. Jesse collected these pistols and practiced until he acquired a reputation as a quick-draw expert. During this time period, Jesse and a friend who went by the nickname of "Doc Holiday" practiced quick-draw on one another and shot rats in an alley behind the Crescent Theater on Hamilton Street—Dalton's main thoroughfare running north to south through town. Jesse and Doc also carried long bullwhips like the 1940s cowboy screen actor Lash LaRue.[7] It was rumored that Jesse became so good at quick-draw that he could drop a coin, pull his pistol, and hit it before the coin reached the ground. He learned how to shoot between his legs, behind his back, and hit about anything he chose.[8]

Jesse's quick-draw talents were observed by numerous individuals, including a young Charlie Carmical, who recalled a scene he witnessed as a small boy. Jesse apparently had an outbuilding behind his home where he kept crates full of ammunition. On the door of the building was a life-size painting of a man in western clothes including pistols in holsters. Jesse, who had two loaded pistols at his sides, put his back to the drawing and marched about ten paces away. There he whirled around as he drew his guns and quickly emptied them into the head of the drawing. Then Jesse would repeat this act and shoot the drawing in the chest. Carmical said all twelve shots were grouped very close together. "He was good, real good, and it was scary." Jesse probably had to buy lots of doors for his shed.[9]

On June 6, 1944, D-Day arrived in France as an Allied invasion of Europe began. On September 17, 1944, 103 days later, Ethel gave birth to Jesse's third son. They named him Jimmy. This was two days after the United States Army breached the main Siegfried line east of Aachen and crossed over onto German soil for the first time. Some of the men who went to Union Assembly churches were fighting in Europe and in the Pacific Theater while their wives worked in factories in Dalton and other cities where the satellite churches were located. But some of the males who worked at Crown Cotton Mill received exemptions as those jobs became important to the war effort. The money came rolling in, and the Church grew.

2

On August 10, 1945, Japan offered to surrender to the Allies and on September 2, 1945, the imperial government signed an unconditional surrender officially ending World War II. The industrial boom in the United States during the war years came to a sudden halt in some areas, but the textile labor shortage of mid-1945 presented new and better job opportunities for the employees of Dalton after the war. Once life returned to "normal" and the service men returned home after the war, the unions that had formed in Dalton plants during the war grew weaker because the South had an anti-labor press, which started hammering away against the unions. In September of 1945 the *Textile Labor* (newspaper) printed: "With the end of the war, our union faces a crucial test. An era has ended—an era has begun."[10] However, at war's end, only 20 percent of the South's textile workers were members of unions and this ran far below the national average.[11]

When wages declined in the south and in Dalton after the war, the Union Assembly of the Church of God saw fewer "good will offerings" coming in, and, as one former minister stated, "C. T. Pratt had grown an appetite for acquiring lots of other people's money."[12] He quickly came up with a plan. He would just demand that the people give more money to the Church and would get involved with the development of a strong union force in the South. He would also create his own

The bill of sale indicating C. T. Pratt had sold his chenille company
to Harry Saul. Saul's son, Julian, confirmed that the bill is in his
father's handwriting. Courtesy of Julian Saul.

brand of socialism or communism within his church domain. C. T., having been given total financial control of the Church had even started forming businesses of his own. The C. T. Pratt Chenille Company, for example, was opened on Martha Sue Drive east of Dalton. There, he hired church members to be employees as they manufactured chenille bedspreads and women's housecoats. W. P. Foster, also a member of the Church, started Pat Craft Chenille Company where he hired only church members, usually women. These women would make thirty dollars a week, and one dollar of that went directly from their checks to the Church.[13]

On May 15, 1946, Pratt sold C. T. Pratt Chenille Company to Harry Saul for $1,750. Harry would rename it Queen Chenille, and it later became a huge company when Dalton's carpet industry started. Eventually Queen Carpet merged with Shaw

Industries, one of the largest carpet manufacturers in the world.[14] W. P. Foster hired a man outside the Church by the name of I. V. Chandler, who was an educator at Valley Point School. Chandler kept books for Pat Craft Chenille. It wasn't long before Chandler bought this company from Foster. One other chenille company was sold to W. R. Evans by the Church.[15] All three businesses would later become prosperous and wealthy companies in the carpet industry.

Any smart person, man or woman, could envision the wealth and strength growing in the Church. A person with keen forethought could foresee what power lay ahead for the Church and the members of the Pratt family. If a shrewd and manipulative person gained access to this enterprise, they could not only enjoy its clout and riches but, with a sufficient amount of deception, take total control. In 1945, two people, one man and one woman, were waiting in the wings to do just that. Only one would survive the battle, however.

3

Despite the Union Assembly's growth, the Church soon faced a crisis involving favorite son Jesse and some fundamental dogma in the Church. C. T. and all the ordained ministers for the Union Assembly of the Church of God preached that divorce was a sin. The *Minutes of the 24th Annual Meeting of the Union Assembly of the Church of God* held on October 18, 19, and 20, 1945, in Dalton, Georgia, read: "Any minister of the Church of God of the Union Assembly that has been married and his wife has left him without a lawful cause is free to marry if he desires. If any minister has left his wife without a lawful excuse, he is forbidden to marry. He must remain single or be reconciled to his wife."[16] This decree was soon taken out of the Church's General Rules after the event of 1946.[17]

During March of 1944, Ethel and Jesse Pratt learned they would be having their third child in the fall. Jesse was still going on revival trips with C. T. or other preachers to the other churches. At some point during this time a young twenty-six-year-old mother of two started coming along to play the piano at the revivals.[18] Her name was Irene Smith, formerly Irene McClure, and she was married to Oscar Smith, who owned his own restaurant in Dalton near East Morris Street. Irene was small and petite with an attractive smile that made anyone who beheld it feel warm.[19] She was a lifetime member of the Church. Her parents, Murray and Naomi McClure, had come to the Dalton area from Etowah County, Alabama, in the 1930s. Murray McClure's family had six daughters and two sons.[20]

In 1937 Irene had married Oscar and they had their first child, William, in 1938 when Irene was twenty-years-old. They soon had a daughter, named Betty, and on April 19, 1944, Irene gave birth to another daughter she and Oscar named Janet. Oscar's restaurant did well, as it was located only several blocks away from downtown Dalton. Irene had her hands full with the three children and traveling on revivals with C. T. and his crew. Not long after Irene gave birth to Janet, Jesse's wife, Ethel, gave birth to their son Jimmy. At this time Jesse started accompanying his dad to the revivals and doing his share of the preaching. Jesse also sang along with Irene's piano while he played a steel guitar.[21]

Sometime during late October, November, or early December of 1945, a few months after the most devastating war in history ended, twenty-nine-year-old Jesse Pratt moved to Reno, Nevada, in Washoe County. He left his wife, Ethel, and their three young sons at home in Dalton. But he took with him his piano player, the wife of Oscar Smith, twenty-eight-year-old Irene Smith—formerly Irene McClure. Irene left two of her three young children at home with Oscar in Dalton. It was reported that she took her youngest daughter, eighteen-month-old Janet, with them.[22] Both Jesse and Irene set up permanent residence in Washoe County. In 1931, Nevada had made it simple: six weeks' residency anywhere in the state (reduced from three months residency); a short list of nine legal grounds that required little or no proof (the most popular was mental cruelty); and an average of six minutes in court before the judge to get the divorce decree.[23]

Irene McClure Smith was described during an interview with the 81-year-old former member who earlier described Jesse's wife Ethel. I asked, "Do you remember what Irene McClure Smith looked like when she was young?"

The woman said, "She was smaller—she didn't gain weight until her later years. She was small. All them McClures were small. I knew all her sisters and her brother. She was attractive . . . She was very attractive. [Supreme Council member] Johnny Burnett's wife was a sister to her—Edna Burnett was a sister to her."

I said, "One of her sisters married Dennis Smith." (Smith was also one of the Supreme Council members.)

The woman said, "That was Ruth. Now, Ruth was very attractive, and she was of normal size stature."

I asked, "Irene played the piano, didn't she?"

The woman answered, "Yeah, Irene played the piano. They [McClures] were all musically inclined."[24]

There are few people who are alive today left to provide exact information of what happened after the divorce. After over twenty-five interviews, one with a ninety-year-old woman who is now deceased, the outcome of this event is clear. Court records show that on February 26, 1946, Jesse F. Pratt married Irene Smith in Reno, Washoe County, Nevada.[25]

What happened next was agreed upon by all witnesses interviewed even though some of the people interviewed only obtained their information from their parents, who were no longer living. At some point during the end of February, through March, or the beginning of April, Jesse and Irene arrived back in Dalton as man and wife. Most likely this happened during the first of March because they were married on February 26, 1946. The first Sunday back in Dalton, Jesse and Irene came to church and marched down the aisle. Present in Church that Sunday were Irene's former husband, Oscar, and two of her older children whom she had not seen in months. Also present was Jesse's former wife, Ethel, and all three of his children whom Jesse had not seen in months.[26] According to one witness, Jesse's father, C. T., was so furious that he ran Jesse off for a few weeks, forcing him to live in the woods on the east side of Dalton. His meals were apparently prepared by Nell Belcher who took him in for meals. Jesse would always speak kindly of Nell in later years.[27] The previous marriages of Jesse and Irene became a banned topic in the Church and its members as the years passed.[28]

Since divorce was forbidden by the Church, some members questioned C. T. and the other ministers whether the rules should be enforced. Some, but only a few people, left the Church over this incident. In a sermon by Jesse, he told the congregation that God had ordered him to marry Irene. Some members questioned why C. T. was allowing Jesse to change the church rules. Nonetheless, in just a short time the divorce rule was altered to reflect the new reality—they completely dropped the rule about divorce.

Jesse left his children with Ethel, who stayed in the Church for a while. It was reported that C. T. and Minnie helped Ethel some with the children, especially with young Jimmy who, as reported in interviews, seemed to take the divorce of

The Harmonetts, one of several musical groups associated with the Church,
included Ruth Smith, Betty Pratt, Mildred Wilson, Tiny Van Meter, and Irene Pratt
on piano. Courtesy of an anonymous family member.

his parents harder than the older ones.[29] The Church gave Irene's three children to her, but Oscar went to court, contested, and received custody of his children. At first Irene would not obey the court order, but a court bailiff came into the Church one Sunday and took the kids from her and gave them to Oscar. Oscar was immediately thrown out of the Church.[30] On December 19, 1946, Irene and Jesse had their first child together. They named him Jesse Junior after his daddy. Just after Junior's birth, Jesse and Irene's marriage had been accepted by people in the Church, and Jesse wanted to return to preaching, so C. T. and the assembly sent Brother Jesse to pastor the Church of God in Detroit, Michigan, and later to their affiliate in Hamilton, Ohio.[31] Nevertheless, J. Willie Burnett contested the new divorce rule and was thrown out of the Church. Irene's brother, Buddy, would also leave with Burnett and form their own Holiness Church. The McClure sisters were getting well established in with the leadership of the Church, but Irene, who was once outside looking in, now was close to becoming the so-called "queen bee."

By making the change to the divorce law and removing some of his father's closest allies, Jesse had made his first move in taking over the church from his dad. He also introduced more changes to the doctrine of the Church which will be discussed later.

Jesse and Irene would stay in Hamilton, Ohio, for nine years and have two more children—one son and one daughter. The son would be named Hughie Arlan—the name Arlan came from Nell Belcher's husband's name and the name Hughie came from a new rising star in the Church, Hughie D. "Cash" Carmical.[32]

4

Another important player in the Pratt story was Hugh D. Carmical. In the 1940 census he was listed as H. D. Carmical and was married to Lillian, and he had a stepdaughter Virginia Jo Cline, who was then four. They lived in Hamilton County, Tennessee, in the town of Chattanooga. Hugh's mother, Clara F., had introduced Hugh to the Union Assembly of the Church of God when he was a young boy. When World War II broke out, Carmical enlisted in the U.S. Army and served in the state of Washington but never went overseas. While in the service in Washington, Hugh felt the calling to become a minister.[33]

In 1946, Hughie (Hugh) D. Carmical came home to Chattanooga, Tennessee from military service. He and his wife Lillian. Everyone called Lillian Bill—already had two sons who were born during the war years before Hugh left for service. After the war another sons would be born. Hugh's heritage was Scottish and he looked every bit the type with his dark blond hair and blue eyes. He stood six feet, four inches tall and was well built when he returned from the war. He had a booming vibrato voice that served him well as a preacher. His father had been a Holiness pastor before his untimely death during the 1920s. Hugh's mother had joined the Union Assembly Church of God in Chattanooga, and that is where Hugh wanted to preach. He went on trial to be ordained in 1946 and was ordained in 1947. In

1948 he and his family moved to Knoxville where he became assistant pastor along with Reverend George E. Wiggs. Brother Carmical proved to be such a dynamic and loved pastor that it didn't take long before he took over as head minister in the Knoxville church. Brother Wiggs moved to another church.[34]

Hugh's energetic personality and gift of charisma immediately started bringing in new members, causing the Knoxville Church's membership to grow. Hugh and another man by the name of A. K. Guyton bought over a thousand flattop houses in Oak Ridge after World War II and the Korean War—these were modest modular homes, easy to move, that the Department of Defense had built to house workers involved with the Manhattan Project—and had them moved to Knoxville, where they designed subdivisions. They then had roofs put on these homes and sold some and rented the rest of them to members of the Church in Knoxville. Hugh's son, Charlie, stated that the money came pouring into the Knoxville Church, and that much of that money went to Minnie Pratt, who retained a big part of it. Charlie stated in an interview that they started receiving so much money from all the Union Assembly churches that C. T. could barely comprehend the magnitude of his dynasty.[35]

A former minister's son and friend to the author later told the following anecdote about the extent to which the Pratt family was awash in cash: "Dad came back from visiting Old Man Pratt—that's what dad called C. T.—this was in the mid-fifties. Dad said that Old Man Pratt took him into his kitchen and started opening up cabinets and they's all stacked full of money. They'd taken all the dishes out, he said. Dad told my mommy, that Old Man Pratt said, 'What am I going to do with all this money?' I swear this is the honest truth of what I overheard."[36]

As Hugh Carmical's own son related, everything his daddy touched seemed to turn to money—he even sold jewelry out of the trunk of his Cadillac Coupe De Ville. Soon he was selling anything he could find to go into the trunk of his car. "Most of this money went to the Church," said Charlie. Hugh started an auction business that turned into a furniture store in Knoxville. Carmical started advertising his business on Knoxville's radio stations and would introduce himself by saying, "This is 'Cash' Carmical from the Knoxville Auction." Hugh would only take cash money for the goods he sold, and it wasn't long before his real name was never used.[37] He was referred to as either Brother Carmical, or Cash Carmical, and even his own children in later years referred to their daddy as Cash.

Admiration for Carmical grew among his parishioners along with his own wealth. Cash Carmical was also becoming a star in eyes of the Union Assembly leadership. As mentioned earlier, Carmical added new churches around the Knoxville area which added to his worth in the Church organization. Apparently, C. T. and Minnie in Dalton noticed this and became concerned about the possibility of internal competition creating a problem at the home churches. The situation became a double-edged sword for Brother Pratt. If he sent Hugh to another church,

C. T. risked losing Hugh's financial contribution, but if Pratt let Hugh continue to succeed he might possibly take over the entire organization. Carmical was that dynamic.[38]

Brother Pratt appealed to working-class individuals who made seventy-five cents per hour and lived in the mill village. Cash attracted a higher-end clientele in Knoxville—not the very rich, but more middle-class businessmen. In Dalton during the early and mid-fifties, the chenille business dropped off, and the carpet industry was just getting started, so the working-class people were still poor.[39] And C. T. took all the money he could from his people. Several of those interviewed said that a man might have only ten dollars to his name, but C. T. could get this ten out of him and the man and his family might go hungry for the rest of the week. But in Knoxville, Brother Carmical kept the money coming in—and in large amounts.

Carmical's activities churned out so much money a competition developed between the different Union Assembly churches to see who could raise the most money. When Brother Carmical started bringing in more money from the Knoxville Church than the Dalton Church, C. T. pressed his membership to give more and more. On one occasion in 1955, Brother Pratt created a goal of $5,000 just for Sunday school. One of the assistant pastors counted the money and reported back to the assembly that it was $5,005. He told Brother C. T. Pratt in front of the congregation, "Well, God must have been in this." C. T. then told the congregation that he wanted $5,000 more given that morning at the Sunday service. After all the members came forward and put money on the Bible, there was nothing close to the five grand. Brother Pratt was not happy, so he reversed his pockets, pulled his billfold out and turned it upside down. Then he pointed his finger at the members, and said, "I have nothing left to give. I gave it all to the Lord, and if you hold back on God and don't give all you got, somebody here is going to drop dead before we leave this morning." The people flew out of their seats like bees out of a hive and rushed up to the Bible and gave all the money they had. After it was counted, they had raised the extra $5,000. That totaled $10,000 in one day. It has been stated that some gave their entire paycheck for a week's work that Sunday. It was reported that Woodrow Whaley told his wife as they were leaving the service that morning that he had given all he had which was ten dollars, and he wanted to know how much she had given. Woodrow's wife told him that she felt her heart fluttering and thought she was going to have a heart attack, so she had put her entire week's check in the offering.[40]

Fifty-seven-year-old Robert Anderson, who went to the Union Assembly Church in Maryville, Tennessee, where his dad, Andy, was the pastor had this to say about how much money the Church expected from its members. "I remember when I was a little boy; sometimes our electricity would be turned off because Dad couldn't pay the electric bill because he'd given everything he had to the Church. That's just the way they made everyone feel—like if you didn't give everything you had to the Church you were going to hell. Dad would borrow the money from someone at work to get the electricity turned back on. He'd pay the man back on Friday, but then, about two weeks later it all would happen again."[41]

5

C. T. was no fool. He saw that Carmical was a rising star in the Church and pro-moted him ahead of some of the founders and even Pratt's children. Carmical would preach on Saturdays in Knoxville's town square along with other pastors from other denominations. Hugh Carmical's dynamic speaking and preaching ability grew huge crowds of people in Knoxville who wanted to listen to his message. Carmical had another outstanding ability—he could raise and make money for the Church and a lot of it.[42] As a result, in just a few years, C. T. promoted Hugh Carmical to assistant moderator of all the churches. Brother Carmical's major obstacles, however, would appear like snakes striking out of tall grass and test his resolve—chiefly because he was not a member of the Pratt family.

During the 1950s a new method of collection became standard in all of Pratt's established churches. At first a Bible was placed on a table in front of the rostrum and members were asked to come forward and put their "free-will-offering" on the Bible. One of the twelve Supreme Council members would count the money. All the time the minister of the different churches watched to see who put in what.

If Brother C. T. didn't think the people had given enough he would preach about how they should not hold back on the Lord, and how they needed to give all they had to God. After this ranting about holding back on God, he would have the people come forward and place more money on the Bible. It was not long before the money was falling off the table and onto the floor, so someone came up with the idea of putting the Bible in a guitar case. Before the people left, someone appointed by C. T. would take the guitar case out so the money could be counted. The money counter would give a report on the amount received, and, if C. T. was satisfied, the service was dismissed. No one was free to leave the church until the dismissal. The doors were usually kept locked until then.[43] Charles Roberts said that on some occasions they would still pass one of the foot-washing tubs used in the Church's practice of washing one another's feet during some services.[44] Most nonmembers rumored that the collection was taken up in a washtub, but a foot-washing tub is much smaller than a washtub.

Several older former members said that occasionally Pratt would get the free-will offering started by opening a leather purse he carried and counting out about ten silver dollars. C. T. then would place the coins on the Bible and showed his purse to be empty. While he was doing this he would say, "God told me to give all I got to him, so I'm gonna give all I got." He would reverse his pockets and tell the people that he gave all he had to the Lord. The members would then say, "Aaaaah." Then he'd look at them with those piercing light blue eyes, point his finger at them, and in a booming voice, say, "I think you need to give all you got to God, it belongs to him anyway." Of course this money including his silver dollars went back into Brother Pratt's pockets to be brought out at another meeting.[45]

One seventy-one-year-old former member whose father was a minister in the '50s, stated that "Old Man Pratt would go to the bank and get hundred-dollar bills, and before the service, he'd give them to a few trusted members like my daddy and tell them to put it on the Bible. When Dad and the others did this, Old Man Pratt would go grab that hundred-dollar bill, wave it in the air, and say, 'look what Brother 'So-n-So' gave to the Lord. We need more like him.' He created guilt. He was a natural born con-man."[46]

With this money, C. T. bought farms in Whitfield County and Murray County, Georgia. By the early '50s, the dynasty had been fully formed and was growing rapidly. But at this point forward, C. T. Pratt was putting much of the money raised back into the Union Assembly Church and its property. Although Pratt drove fine cars such as Cadillacs, he never lived in a home that was extravagant, but his family never went without whatever they wanted, either. Outsiders—what the Union Assembly call nonmembers—had trouble believing that a human being in his right mind would give everything he had to a church, or another group, or another person when it took food out of their children's mouths. Why do normal people put up with these transgressions? Why did they stay? Why would a person give this church family their home and follow them blindly into personal devastation? The Church's methology had already started changing and changing for the worst according to informants. A power struggle had started and C. T. may or may not have realized that a takeover of the Church had begun.[47]

PART II

Betrayal, 1945–1974

"If you want to have life everlasting, you had better show
mercy to the needy. There is but one thing that will keep
you out of torment. Every time you see some one in need
you had better help them if you can."

C. T. PRATT,
"Three classes of people," *The Southerner*, 2

7

An Attitude Change

"The Book says: 'Blessed is he that considers the poor.'
That has been a guide to my life."

C. T. PRATT,
"Three Classes of People," *The Southerner*, 3

1

According to at least one witness, sometime during the early 1950s Jesse had started preaching behind his daddy's back, trying to set the table for a takeover of the Church.[1] It was reported that he went to all of the Union Assembly churches around the South, telling their members that his father was growing old and losing his mind. Jesse would not come out and directly say this about his father, but Jesse would make innuendoes about his poor aging father who he said was losing his mind and how everyone should pray for Brother C. T. Pratt. Beginning in 1946 and 1947, Jesse started spreading his own form of fear to his membership. If any members questioned Jesse, he would make life hell for them by telling them that they were going to die of some horrible disease like cancer or be in an accident that would leave them mangled or in pieces.[2] He painted a good horror story and scared his members to the point of sheer terror.

This is also about the time that Jesse started showing selected members that he disapproved of their action by rebuking or reproving them physically. He would grab unfortunate parishioners by the head with both his large hands and shake them violently until they couldn't stand. The amount of shaking depended on how angry Jesse was at the time or the perceived transgressions executed by the wayward member. It was stated in interviews that members grew fearful of Jesse and started doing whatever he asked of them. He convinced them that he had the power of God on his side, and all he had to do was tell God to strike them dead and they were goners. Undoubtedly, Jesse's skills with pistols also created fear within the membership.[3]

Several informants stated that Jesse started using his conniving power early by eliminating two men who had opposed him and whom he knew were against his "double" marriage. J. W. Burnett, also called Willie Burnett, and a brother to Johnny Burnett, had permanent membership on the Supreme Council of the Church and had a direct track to C. T.'s ear. Jesse knew that J. Willie had been calling for a vote to expel Jesse from the Church since he and Irene had run away to be married, so Jesse planted the seeds of shame and sin on Brother Burnett until the membership believed these rumors and spread the word themselves about J. Willie. The implications got so bad that a special meeting of the Supreme Council was called and Brother Burnett, who had a lifetime membership, was voted off. Of course, J. Willie didn't know anything about this meeting until afterwards.

It is not known what transgressions Jesse accused Burnett of, but according to a few older members, the claims could have been any type of lie Jesse wanted to fabricate about J. Willie. Jesse never accused Burnett to his face, nor gave him an opportunity to defend himself. After being removed from the Supreme Council, J. Willie stayed with the Church for a while, but eventually had to quit after being openly shunned by the members.[4]

In an interview published in the *Dalton Daily Citizen-News* in 1980, J. Willie Burnett said that he sought to bring the matter of Jesse's divorce from Ethel and marriage to Irene before the Supreme Council, but was removed from the council that he had organized. He said, "I pioneered the work of the Church of God of the Union Assembly in Ohio and Alabama," adding that he began preaching when he was 13 years old and was "practically raised by Brother Pratt." Talking about C. T., Willie said, "For many years I was with him day and night. Brother Pratt was one of the greatest men I ever knew." In the same article, Reverend Burnett said, "In breaking off a relationship with the church years ago I was warned a vision had been observed in which I would die tragically on Thanksgiving Day." Usually Jesse was the one who had these warning-visions of members dying tragically.[5]

Others indicated that without his father's knowledge Jesse worked to get another permanent member of the Supreme Council removed. That man's name was Tom Bohannon. Tom opposed Jesse and was not afraid of him. Like Brother Burnett, Brother Bohannon had been with C. T. for a very long time, almost since the beginning of the Union Assembly, and he was a threat to Jesse's power. Tom was also voted off the council in a secret meeting after Jesse fabricated lies about him, but Brother Bohannon did not stay with the Church. He and his family stopped attending immediately.[6] So another church forefather and a close associate of C. T. had departed.

Jesse may have only had a fourth-grade education, but he quickly learned how to control people with fear and by eliminating his adversaries. Nonetheless, during the decade of the '50s C. T. still controlled his church and had a majority of the power, but it had already started slipping away.

All former members who were interviewed stated that the Church of God of the Union Assembly was "a cult." However, most of those interviewed grew up in the Church at the end of C. T.'s ministry and at the beginning of Jesse's power. Members and true believers deny that it was ever cult like. By examining the characteristics of a cult one can try to evaluate if the Church of God of the Union Assembly was ever a true cult.

In *Combating Cult Mind Control*, author Steve Hassan states that "when a group is becoming 'cult like' it does so harmlessly. Nobody starts out to form a cult. Instead, unconsciously certain individuals start to behave in a particular manner and they support one another. The leadership starts to create an idealistically perfect religious atmosphere and those who want and need that sort of religious group will support it and making it even more powerful. The faithful will set the leader up on a pedestal and declare him to be brilliant and the leader (who needs and likes the hero worship) will encourage the adulation. Those who object or suspect what is happening will be automatically excluded."[7]

In the late 1950s, Brother Pratt turned eighty years old and was starting to show outward signs of his advancing age. As we have seen, even by the 1950s, C. T.'s own son, Jesse F. Pratt, had started making subtle changes in the Church's direction, which slowly ate into his own father's control and shifted that power toward the son. Nevertheless, during the decade of the 1950s, Brother C. T. proved to be a powerful man and the Church's dominant leader. Most of the former members interviewed who remember C. T., believe he did not turn the Union Assembly into a cult. But they had a very different opinion about his son, Jesse.

As stated by scholars Hood, Hill, and Spilka, a cult is "the sociological equivalent of psychopathology in the popular mind. . . Its leader is likely to be a solitary, powerful, charismatic figure. . . . Cults are often defined and identified by the name of their leader, at least in popular media. Hence we have the 'Manson cult,' the 'Jim Jones' cult, and the 'Moonies.'"[8] Likewise, outsiders call the Union Assembly Church the "Pratt Church" and the members were and are called "Pratts."

According to Hood, Hill and Spilka, initially, "Charismatic domination is established through the extraordinary qualities (real or supposed) of the leader. . . . Law is not the source of authority; on the contrary, he [or she] proclaims new laws on the basis of revelation, oracular utterance, and inspiration. Given the charismatic nature of cult leadership combined with the fact that cults (like sects) are in opposition to salient [main] cultural values, there is often some confusion as to whether or not cults are truly 'religions.'"[9] C. T. Pratt made his own church laws which the membership was to follow. He was prophetic and made oracular utterances by prophesying and predicting the date and time of Jesus's return to earth. However, C. T. did not punish his members. He might preach directly to them at times, and they would follow the Church laws out of love and respect. Nonetheless, when Jesse gained ample control over the Church in the 1950s, the former members interviewed believed the Union Assembly had turned into a cult.

When C. T. Pratt broke away from the Church of God of the Mountain Assembly, he created a religious sect—not a cult. Sects are religious protest movements that has separated from an established church; a nonconformist church. On the other hand, as Hood, Hill, and Spilka point out, "cults lack prior ties with religious bodies and tend to emerge afresh, often under the direction of a single charismatic leader. Cults are novel forms of religion, which, not surprisingly, are likely to emerge in tension both with established religious groups (such as churches and sects) and with the host culture."[10]

According to statements, by the end of the 1940s and early 1950s church membership consisted of people whose parents were members of the Church of God of the Union Assembly when they were born. These life-long members knew nothing else about religion and what was expected of them except through the teachings of the Church. C. T. Pratt and his children were gods to these people—royalty to these people—the only way to heaven for these people—EVERYTHING to these life-long members. They were born willing to do ANYTHING for the Pratt family, and they did—almost all of them.

A former Church of God of the Union Assembly member, whose father was also on the Supreme Council, told me this story about the very real life consequences of the Church's shunning practices started by Jesse: "I'm not going to paint you a picture that's not there, but when I was about fourteen, I had already decided mentally that this is not for me, and if this is God's plan, then I would be honored just to go on to hell. . . . And I think that once you get tied up in that, you don't ever get loose from it mentally. But I've come to a decision that I'm tougher than they are, and they are not going to destroy me. When I left, it got so bitter that I went to Florida and worked for a company for seven years, and I never seen my parents. I wasn't allowed to."[11]

8

Thou Shall Not Bear False Witness

"It is a sad thing to see people believing so many lies."

C. T. PRATT
"Charlie Pratt Saying," 2

"Messengers of Satan are men who tell lies on men
like my Daddy and Don West."

JESSE PRATT
"Jesse Pratt Says," *The Southerner:*
Voice of the People, Jan. 1956, 4

1

Henry Wallace was Franklin Roosevelt's Vice President during his third term from 1941 to 1945. However, Harry Truman won the Democratic nomination for Vice President in the 1944 election, which kept Wallace from becoming the United States president by 82 days. A month before Roosevelt died, he consoled Wallace by appointing him Secretary of Commerce. Soon thereafter in a speech, Wallace, always outspoken, infuriated conservatives, moderates, and the U.S. Allies of WWII. In a speech on April 12, 1946, Wallace distanced himself from the former U.S. wartime Allies by stating that "aside from our common language and common literary tradition, we have no more in common with Imperialistic England than with Communist Russia."[1] In September 1946, Truman fired Wallace.

Wallace ran for president himself in 1948 as a third-party candidate and the leader of the Progressive Party. His platform outraged the Southern states when he advocated for universal government health insurance, an end to the emerging Cold War, full voting rights for black Americans, and an end to segregation. While campaigning in the South, he refused to appear before segregated audiences or to eat or stay in segregated establishments. However, Wallace's refusal to disavow publicly the endorsement of his candidacy by the U.S. Communist Party cost him the backing of the majority of liberals and independent socialists. When Wallace campaigned throughout the segregated South he did so with an African American secretary. During the Southern tour, a salvo of eggs and tomatoes were often thrown at Wallace and hit him and his campaign members on numerous occasions.[2]

In Georgia, C. T. Pratt became co-chair of Georgia's Wallace Committee, along with pro-labor activist Don West. In a speech in Atlanta, West compared Pratt and Henry Wallace to Jesus Christ. When Wallace came to Dalton before the election, he was received with open arms by C. T. Pratt and the Union Assembly of the Church of God. He was guest speaker at the Church's annual assembly meeting with five thousand members of Pratt's churches. Wallace preached on universal brotherhood by telling the crowd to "take up the mighty sword of moral conviction" and "cut down the evil forces of hate and exploitation." He attacked the Jim Crow society of segregation and the poll tax.[3] While at the meeting the Church took up a collection in washtubs and bestowed a sizeable amount of money on Wallace for him to use in his campaign. The Church also formed a parade down the main street of Dalton. In the parade, the Union Assembly ministers wore white suits and marched along with Wallace and his entourage.[4]

In response to these endorsements, Ralph McGill, a liberal columnist for the *Atlanta Constitution*, attacked Don West by featuring the words of the original poem "Listen, I Am a Communist" by West, which McGill offered as his subject's own confession:

> I am a Communist
> A Red
> A Bolshevik!
> Do you, toilers of the South
> Know Me?

McGill ended his argument by asking if Georgia's Wallace party was "Communist-directed or not?"[5]

On Election Day, Wallace lost the Presidential election handily, receiving only 2.4 percent of the popular vote, but that helped incumbent Harry Truman beat Dixiecrat Presidential candidate Strom Thurmond, who won the popular vote in Georgia but lost the electoral vote. Strom Thurmond actually carried several states in the Deep South and received 39 electoral votes while Wallace received none. By backing Wallace, C. T. Pratt put himself on the side of progressivism and communism, and that would haunt him for almost a decade.

2

On October 18, 1950, the name of the Church was officially changed from the Union Assembly of the Church of God, Incorporated, to the Church of God of the Union Assembly, Incorporated. When the 1950 application for the charter to change the name of the Church was applied for, it was signed by the members of the Supreme Council plus C. T. Pratt, Moderator. These others signing it were: G. E. Wiggs, Arlan Belcher, L. L. Coker, H. D. Carmical, Clifton Allen, Jesse F. Pratt, E. E. Pratt, M. O. Brewer, Clinton M. Bell, Johnny H. Burnett, Frank McCollum, W. T. Howard, and Rufus Allen.[6]

H. D. "Cash" Carmical was brought to Dalton from Knoxville in 1951 to become the assistant moderator. C. T. must have thought that this move would solve his dilemma concerning the growing popularity of Brother Carmical, or he genuinely needed him in Dalton. Several interviews supported both ideas. Carmical continued to bring in money while in Dalton. He created Dalton Auction, which turned into a furniture store at an old Packard car dealership on the 41 highway. He purchased this business plus property from the Church, and after he had it remodeled, according to his son Charlie, C. T. came in upon completion and told Brother Carmical that he had not spent this much money on the store when it belonged to God. Carmical turned around and gave the deed to the property back to the Church. Brother Carmical would buy this business from the Church three times before it became his.[7]

Locally, the Union Assembly continued to be an important political force. In 1952, for example, Hayes P. McArthur ran against incumbent Louie Vinning for Sheriff of Whitfield County. It was reported that C. T. told members of his congregation to vote for Hayes McArthur. They did so and McArthur beat Vinning. However, Louie Vinning later became the Chief of Police for Dalton as well as a powerful political figure. He was no match for the Church of God of the Union Assembly, which continued to endorse candidates and political causes to its own advantage.

By 1952, the Church's congregation had outgrown the structure on 41 Highway. They moved east of Dalton (one mile outside the city limits of Dalton) onto a large tract of land on the Chatsworth Highway—Highway 52. A new church building was constructed on Goodwill Drive. In fact, the Church bought (or was given) so much land that a village was formed called "Union City." There, C. T. continued to expand the church-owned businesses. The Church owned and operated Whitfield Milling Company, which produced flour. There was also the Union Super Market, which one observer called "a large modern and first-class food store." The Church ran a cannery that preserved vegetables grown on Church farms. They owned the Union Slaughterhouse and a dairy that was run by W. P. Foster and Mr. Ledford. They claimed to give free milk to poor families and widows. They owned the Union Dry Cleaners. The Church also built a complex of apartments behind the main church building on Goodwill Drive where members could rent after giving most of their check to the Church. The Pratt family owned the A & W Root Beer Stand on Highway 52; across town on South 41 Highway, they owned the Dalton Tourist Court and two restaurants.[8] (The Church also owned the historic Prater's Mill and often gave free cornmeal to its members after Sunday services.)

It was once said that Preacher Pratt and the Church must have owned a quarter of the property in Whitfield County. The Church was definitely the single largest private land owner in Whitfield and neighboring Murray County by 1961. In fact C. T. and Minnie lived in Murray County for a short time.[9] The deed records at the Whitfield County Clerk of Superior Court disclosed that the Union Assembly acquired 5 deeds—all lots—between 1943 through 1949. None were transferred to the Church during 1950, but, starting in 1951 and going only through 1958, 83 more deeds were transferred to the Union Assembly, which included over 300 lots and almost 4,000 acres of farm land. Former members interviewed stated that widows were talked into giving their land to the Church, and, in return, they could reside rent-free in these or other apartments owned by C. T. Pratt and the Union Assembly. Interviews reveal, however, that some of these widows were eventually asked to pay rent if they lived too long.[10]

3

In 1954, with the Cold War raging, Senator Joseph R. McCarthy accused countless prominent people in the United States of being Communists during congressional hearings in the nation's capital. These hearings were also televised, causing Americans to become paranoid about communism to the point of being obsessed about its supposed takeover of the world. However, the Union Assembly rules forbade the owning and watching of television and actively discouraged engagement with the outside world, so few members knew about a Cold War.

In October 1954, Reverend Pratt brought forty-six-year-old Don West, the pro-labor radical and co-chair of Wallace's 1948 Georgia campaign, into Dalton to start a monthly newspaper funded by the Union Assembly. It was called *The Southerner: A Voice of the People* and hit the newsstands in March 1955.[11] At that time C. T. Pratt was still a relatively healthy seventy-five-year-old man who said he had not gone to a medical doctor in fifty years. By 1955, the Dalton Church of God of the Union Assembly claimed 500 members with another ten thousand scattered around the South and Midwest. The Union Assembly had added churches in St. Petersburg, FL, Corinth, MS, Fort Smith, AR, Rock Hill, SC, Kokomo, IN, Icard, NC, Wilkesboro, NC, Texarkana, TX, Gadsden, AL, and Scottsboro, AL. The circulation of *The Southerner* was about fifty thousand and regularly featured editorials written by West and other labor activists.[12] Besides publishing *The Southerner*, Pratt and West planned for a new church college in Dalton that would provide educational opportunity for the deprived youth of mill and farm workers' children. Plans were for Don West to become the president of Charlie Pratt College, named in honor of its founder, the peoples' preacher.[13]

Don West was a tall thin man whom some called handsome with his dark hair and tanned skin. Born in 1906 in Gilmer County, Georgia, in the middle of the Appalachian mountains, by 1955, forty-seven-year-old Don West was a highly educated man. He had worked his way through college and earned a Bachelor of Divinity degree in 1932 from Vanderbilt University as well as a Master's Degree from Oglethorpe University in 1944. He had also been a former public school superintendent in nearby Hall County, Georgia. He helped establish the Highlander Folk School in the mountains of East Tennessee and became a leader of various liberal and radical causes—including organized labor and civil rights for southern blacks. It is not clear if West was ever an official member of the Communist Party even though he worked closely with Communist party members. During the 1940s, West completed his doctoral degree in English at Oglethorpe University in Atlanta and taught English there until Ralph McGill and the *Atlanta Constitution* put pressure on the university to fire West because of his co-chairmanship of Henry A. Wallace's 1948 presidential campaign.[14]

Don West and C. T. Pratt shared the opinion that Jesus was a true social revolutionary who had believed in the rights of the poor. West was drawn to Pratt's preaching of the gospel and unionism as central doctrines of his church, and because Pratt ministered to hard-pressed mill workers who thought labor activism was a religious duty.[15] According to one historian, it was because of West and Pratt—not the leaders in the Textile Workers Union of America (TWUA) state office—that the chenille labor campaign of 1955 was sparked.[16]

After several issues of *The Southerner*, it was clear what stories the newspaper would pursue, and the wealthy whites in Dalton saw it as Protestantism gone afoul. Pratt and West identified the world as being engrossed in a struggle between rich and poor with God on the side of the exploited. Through the newspaper, they said, "God was going to bring the proud and mighty low and lift up the weak and lowly."[17] One editorial in *The Southerner* of April 1955 stated: "We believe in the principles of organized labor because we believe in the life and teaching of Jesus Christ . . ." and went on to say: "You can't be a Christian and a scab. The two just don't go together."[18] C. T. Pratt knew this kind of talk could get a person branded as a Communist, so he wrote in *The Southerner* in May 1955: "Anybody who ever stood up for the poor people has been called a communist. I've been called a communist. I'm not a communist, but I've always stood up for the laboring people." In the same issue a minister from Tennessee said: "If you are afraid of being called a communist, don't preach God's Bible."[19]

During the Union Assembly Labor Day rally in 1955, C. T.'s son, Jesse Pratt, said that he would rather be called a communist than a Catholic.[20] Former members interviewed believed this remark by Jesse cost the Church dearly in 1961 when

John F. Kennedy became president. In that same year the IRS audited the Church and levied a huge fine with back taxes. The audit may have been entirely coincidental, however, as there has been no independent confirmation that the Kennedy administration specifically targeted the Union Assembly as a result of its presidential election activities.

Don West probably lost some support from the TWUA International office when he suggested that Catholic McCarthyites was equivalent to Judas and called both "children of the devil" who blamed the righteous.[21] However, West's overall labor organizing campaign, as well as his past links with communism, were what the TWUA continued to denounce. Nonetheless, in the spring of 1955, Crown Cotton Mill's Local 185 union in Dalton allied themselves with Don West and *The Southerner*. In Dalton, local industrial leaders organized their own resistance to political radicalism and labor activism. Henry Ball of the Tufted Textile Manufacturer's Association asked Congressman Henderson Lanham for assistance in accessing the House Un-American Activities Committee files on West and *The Southerner*. Lanham sent a lengthy file detailing West's association with Communists and radical causes to David S. Burgess of the Georgia State Industrial Union Council, who in turn, informed Charlie Gillman, Region 5 director of the Congress of Industrial Organizations (CIO). Burgess and Gillman advised the labor unions of Whitfield County through James O'Shea, manager of TWUA's Northwest Georgia Joint Board, that the CIO would be damaged if textile locals did not end their entanglement with West and *The Southerner*. The Dalton union leaders were the last to learn of Don West's past connections to communists.[22]

In July 1955 two Dalton companies, Lawtex and Belcraft, moved to undermine TWUA organizing when they circulated questionnaires to their employees that included, along with other questions, a query about their church affiliation. In a short time, over two dozen employees who had listed the Church of God of the Union Assembly as their church found themselves without jobs. The final number of Union Assembly employees who lost their jobs was listed as fifty-six by Don West—10 percent of the Church's 's congregation in Dalton, but Lawtex and Belcraft reported only twenty-six were laid off due to cutbacks. West contacted the TWUA and asked for a Senate investigation into the firings, but the TWUA national office openly apologized for West's involvement in Dalton's labor affairs. Reverend Pratt was condemned by the state and nationwide offices of the TWUA, saying he was a corrupt millionaire. They accused him of robbing his congregation while evading taxes through his church.[23] When news leaked out about West's previous involvement with Communism, he and Pratt lost allies from the chenille workers union, and a campaign was launched by the manufacturers and the local press to get West out of town and Pratt under control. At closer examination it may be more complicated than that.

4

Mark Pace, the editor of the *Dalton Citizen and News*, was the main figure in expos-
ing Don West's affiliations with communism. Pace started with a bang on August 27,
1955, with a full-page report on Don West taken from "THE FILES OF THE COM-
MITTEE ON UN-AMERICAN ACTIVITIES, U.S. HOUSE OF REPRESENTATIVES."
Pace had become familiar with West during the Henry Wallace presidential campaign of 1948 when West came to the Union Assembly's rally. Pace also knew of
West's prior communist connections.[24] When Don West came back to Dalton in
1955 to start *The Southerner*, he visited Pace to inform him of their plans. West later
wrote that Pace was "sort of pitiful . . . a weak little fellow who has a string around
his neck."[25] Pace in turn contacted Congressman Henderson Lanham, from whom
he received the report on West from the House Un-American Activities file. West
also claimed that Pace felt threatened by him, not only a publishing competitor, but
as an intellectual inferior. Donald Davis, who once taught at Dalton State College,
stated: "I also interviewed Pace and found him to be an anti-union apologist for
the mill owners and Dalton elite, who were his biggest advertisers. In all newspaper
articles about Don West, he always capitalized the words communist and communism—for obvious reasons."[26]

Mark Pace continued to punch away at West when he printed the poem, "Listen, I'm a Communist," on the front page. West fought back by saying the poem
should have been titled "Listen, I'm an Agitator," (as later versions were), so Pace
printed that version as well. But West's redemption was short-lived, for Pace found
the original version of the poem under West's name in a 1934 issue of the *Daily
Worker*, a communist newspaper. As a result, the *Dalton Citizen* labeled West a
liar and reprinted part of the communist poem. West continued to send rebuttals
to Pace's articles, and Pace would print them word-for-word, hoping that "if given
enough rope, West would hang himself." West, on the other hand, tried to deflect
the attention away from the communism issue by saying "the real issue is wages
and working conditions and organization of the unorganized." Pace continued to
hammer away at West: "As far as we are concerned, the only issue right now is Don
West and his background. The fact that union organization movements are going
on simultaneously with this series of West articles, editorials, etc., is something entirely out of our control." Even if this was true, Pace was hiding the point that West
and *The Southerner* were essential mobilizers for the chenille union campaign. By
attacking West's affiliations with communism, Pace was also attacking the union.[27]

In early September 1955, the building where *The Southerner* was produced was
vandalized and equipment destroyed in an effort to intimidate Pratt and his church.
Within days, talk of mob action spread, along with the rumors of the formation
of a lynching party for the "Damned Communist." West became so worried about
the lynch-mob attitude in town that he went to Pratt for protection, and C. T. gave
West a .38 caliber revolver for his car and a shotgun for protection at home.

West contacted the TWUA for its support, but the TWUA tried to remain aloof after the volatile Pratt called for a mass meeting where he encouraged the organization of chenille workers as well as made openly hostile anti-Catholic and anti-Semitic remarks.[28] Pace warned against mob violence in his weekly column, "Pipe Smoke." In it, Pace stated that the *Citizen* newspaper condemned such action. Pace specified that "mob actions can be dangerous from either end—the attacked as well as the attackers." Then Pace continued, "We say leave it to the law and to legal channels, including the Whitfield County grand jury, if it is interested."[29] The October grand jury would definitely be interested.

In mid-September, Lawtex workers went on strike, and the situation soon turned hostile. Fifty workers banded together to form the TWUA Local 10, which gave them support from the national office while on strike. On September 29 violence erupted near the plant gate, but no one was hurt. Georgia governor Marvin Griffin quickly sent a contingent of state troopers as well as agents from the Georgia Bureau of Investigation to Dalton. On October 11 they accompanied antiunion workers called "scabs" into Lawtex Mill.[30]

Meanwhile, the October session of the Whitfield County grand jury took up the issue of communism to explore the charges made by Mark Pace. Edgar C. Bundy of the Illinois American Legion's Americanism Committee came to Dalton to forewarn of the threat created by Don West. For two weeks, Bundy fueled the flames of public opinion by being widely quoted in the newspaper and on Dalton radio about the dangers of communism. Allston Calhoun Jr., who claimed to be a "professional anticommunist" from South Carolina, came to Dalton and linked communism, unionism, and non-mainline religions together as a threat to the working man. On the heels of this bombardment against West, West himself was called to appear before the grand jury in October 1955.[31] Solicitor Erwin Mitchell, a WWII fighter pilot combat veteran, asked West about his past record and his current activities in Dalton, but West took his Fifth Amendment rights and refused to answer any questions.[32]

The bewildered citizens of Dalton had grown tired of the continuous controversy in their community. In 1955, ordinary citizens of Dalton did not see themselves as communist supporters, but middle-class homeowners.[33] On December 15, 1955, 682 workers at Belcraft voted down the union by casting only 57 votes for the union with 625 against. This signaled the end of the chenille campaign and an end to Dalton's established unions. But it did not end the campaign against West by Mark Pace, who continued to hammer away with damaging articles in late December and early January. West and Pratt continued to voice contrasting opinions in *The Southerner*, but their campaign for unions in northwest Georgia held little public sway.[34]

By January, 1956, C. T. Pratt himself had grown tired of the battle between Pace and West and the negative publicity that was no doubt having an impact on his Church. In 2011, only a few months before he passed away, Erwin Mitchell told me how C. T. Pratt ultimately responded to the West controversy that continued to play on in the Dalton press, a story never before recorded or published. In Mitchell's own words:

> When I was the solicitor [what is now called the district attorney] we had Don West before the Grand Jury, because many people in the community were upset saying that Preacher Pratt had this communist brought in. We had him brought in to the Grand Jury in October 1955 and tried to question him but he claimed his Fifth Amendment rights and waived them on everything asked of him.
>
> Some time later, [January 13, 1956] . . . and the community was in a flurry, and I assume probably the local pressure was on Preacher Pratt about having this communist. Anyway, I got a call from C. T. Pratt at two-thirty in the morning, and he told me he wanted me to come to his church at eight o'clock that night. And I wasn't the only one who got a call. The mayor got a call, the sheriff [H. P. McArthur] and Mark Pace [editor of the Dalton Newspaper] got a call.

Mitchell added that he arrived at the church early but didn't go inside until the appointed time. He was welcomed at the entrance door to the new church off of the Chatsworth Highway in the area now dubbed Union City. Once inside the building, Mitchell saw several hundred women in the audience and another 200 men stationed behind the rostrum with C. T. Pratt. The room fell silent as Mitchell was escorted to the front row to be seated beside Mark Pace and Sheriff H. P. McArthur.[35] Then C. T. Pratt stood and strode to the podium. He was dressed in an expensive suit and tie. His long white hair was combed back but not covering his ears. Mitchell thought he looked very distinguished. All the men behind Brother Pratt were also dressed in suits and ties. Mitchell recognized C. T.'s son Jesse as well as Cash Carmical in the front of the group.

C. T. looked directly at Mitchell and Pace and said, "On Tuesday morning about two o'clock, I awoke to hear the Lord talking about Communism. Mr. Mitchell, I want you to administer a loyalty oath to all my ministers that they are not communist and have not been communist since joining the Church of God of the Union Assembly."

Mitchell saw through this statement and said, "Are there any of the ministers here that had invoked the Fifth Amendment in refusing to testify before a grand jury or the House Committee on Un-American Activities?"

From behind the speakers' rostrum someone said, "Yes, I have." It was Don West.

Mitchell then turned to the Reverend C. T. Pratt and said, "I will be glad to administer the oath to everyone except Don West."

In a strong voice, Brother Pratt made a declaration. "If any of my ministers won't swear before a grand jury or any other jury that he is not a communist, I don't want him in this church. We want to know if any of you are communists."

Then Pratt called Don West forward and said, "You shall appear before the grand jury and testify by answering whether you have been a communist since joining the Church of God in 1952."

Solicitor Mitchell said to Reverend Pratt, "There are questions concerning West's activities before 1952 that should be answered, and I promise that he will be the first witness to appear before the Whitfield grand jury Monday morning."

Pratt turned to West and said, "You will answer all questions asked of you at the grand jury meeting Monday or any other day or leave this church."

Erwin Mitchell then administered the loyalty oath to the other ministers by having them swear that they had never been a member of the Communist party. Don West told Brother C. T. Pratt that he would not testify. Pratt then told West that he was expelled from the Union Assembly church. West left the building. After this, Mitchell, Pace, and Sheriff H. P. McArthur left the church.[36]

West, who had been renting a room at Cash Carmical's home on 41 Highway, packed up his belongings and left Dalton that very night for Blairsville in Union County, Georgia, where his mother lived. As he drove over Fort Mountain on a narrow, winding road, he noticed that a car was closely following his. West realized that only a week earlier someone had forced union organizers into a ditch. He reached for the .38 revolver on the seat beside him and emptied it into the front tires of the trailing automobile, stopping it.[37]

That year, 1956, Mark Pace won the Whitfield County "Man of the Year" award. Don West was gone so *The Southerner* stopped its presses and shut down for good. Nonetheless, C. T. Pratt, at age seventy-six, let the incident run like water off a duck's back. He moved onward with his loyal followers as if nothing out of the ordinary had happened—but the end of his dynasty was at hand and was rushing forward unimpeded.

9

Thou Shall Not Commit Adultery

"He admitted in conversation that he was guilty of 'relations
with girls' of the church . . . 'You know how it is with a
minister,' Bell said regarding his female associates, 'they just
push themselves off on you.'"

FRED ODIET
"Pastor Says He Regrets His Actions," *Kokomo Tribune,*
Dec. 19, 1959

1

Clinton M. Bell was born in Whitfield County, Georgia June 2, 1919. He was just a little over a year younger than Jesse Pratt. Bell probably grew up in the Union Assembly Church and may have been related to T. R. Bell who was one of the original organizers of the Union Assembly in 1921. However, that is not a certainty. Clinton was ordained by the Church in 1941. In 1942 the Church listed Bell as a member of the twelve-man Supreme Council of the Union Assembly of the Church of God. In 1942, his address was listed as Dantzler Avenue, Dalton, Georgia. In 1950 he was still listed as being on the Union Assembly's Supreme Council of twelve men. That same year Clinton moved to Kokomo, Indiana, with his second wife, Jackie, whom he had married four years earlier, in 1946. According to the *Kokomo Tribune* his first wife had divorced him earlier because she had filed complaints against Bell for having sexual relationships with other women and young girls. The Union Assembly had defrocked Bell in 1944 or 1945 after these complaints came to light, but reinstated him in 1946 after he married Jackie.[1]

In late 1959, *The Kokomo Tribune* described Bell "as a handsome smooth-talking person with a liking for 'free spending and good things.' About six feet tall, he is sturdily built, weighs about 190 pounds, has ruddy complexion and light hair." A picture in that same paper shows the Reverend Clinton Bell with a broad smile, a round face with a double chin, and a long nose shaped much like actor Liam Neeson's, except flatter at the tip. In another picture of Bell, taken January 1960, he is shown from the mid-thigh up—he had his hands in his pockets as he listened to Deputy Sheriff Pete Dieterly read a warrant for his arrest. Bell was heavy with his large girth and double chin. His hair was long and combed back—somewhat unruly as if he had been running his hands through it, but his hair was not below his ears. Brother Bell was not smiling in this picture.[2]

Several informants reported that Bell had been sent to the Kokomo Church of God of the Union Assembly to remove him from the bad publicity he had received at his other church somewhere in Tennessee before being defrocked. By this point C. T. routinely moved his ministers around when they strayed from Church doctrine; he would still use them if they remained loyal to him and could make money for the Church. However, almost all former members interviewed said that by this time Jesse had control of his father and the Church as a whole. In Kokomo, Bell tried to build his congregation up with fiery sermons, promising hell-fire-and-damnation to sinners, but he did well just to hold on to the members he inherited from the previous minister. According to former members who went there while he was the pastor, Brother Bell didn't talk much about love, forgiveness, or even Jesus—it was mostly a lot of screaming about the sins that would send his people to hell. Bell's sermons were apparently like that of other Union Assembly ministers at the time—it was all about fear, money and more fear, which brought more money.[3]

Former members from the Kokomo church pointed out that Bell also opened his own furniture/convenience store, called Bell Bargain Fair or Bargain Barn, which sold everything from furniture to hound dogs in Kokomo at 208 Jefferson Street. Bell then opened two restaurants, one near his Bargain Fair where he had members—mostly women—working for him for small wages, which they were expected to give back to the Church.[4] Bell also owned a drug store, plus a swap shop where he had a regular radio spot called the "Swap Shop Show" for conducting his business and advertising. It was broadcast daily and opened with these lines: "Bell's Bargain Fair is on the air with low, low prices of today—from hunting boots to living room suits, you get them all at Bell's Bargain Fair."[5]

Don Pitner reported how Bell crafted a scam that enabled him to get more money from his members. He would have them go to Lincoln Finance in Kokomo and sign a note for a thousand dollars. The money would go directly to Bell, and he applied the money to furniture that these members had picked out. Supposedly, the members would then make payments on the thousand dollars, and when it was paid off he would give them their furniture. The problem was no one ever got their furniture. He would get the money and the members would make payment after payment.[6] As one member reported succinctly in an interview, "Bell got the money, we got the shaft."[7]

In 1958, Brother Bell preached to his members about C. T. Pratt's prediction that the end of the world was coming in September 1961. Bell said Brother C. T. Pratt was going to set one foot on land and one foot on water and to declare time to be no more. Bell had everybody scared to death. He told people they needed to sell their homes and move in with other families to save money so they could give everything they had to the Church.[8] After this prediction of the Apocalypse, Brenda Moore observed that as many as three or four families lived together in a single house that was not big enough for a single family. Added Don Pitner in an interview: "Bell had everyone who worked turn their paychecks over to him and he would give them back what they needed to live on, but it became just enough to survive on. He left Church on Sundays with a guitar case full of money. Then Bell had his members come to Bell's Bargain Fair so he could hand out bologna, dried beans, and a fruit-filled pound cake."

Dorothy Bliss backed up this claim. "He'd give us that stuff, and I don't know how many pounds of fruit cakes I ate. Today, I can't stand a fruit cake, and that's all we had to live on."[9]

Like all the Supreme Council members of the Church, Bell drove a new Cadillac; either a Coupe DeVille or an Eldorado. He had a big fine home just outside of Kokomo with three other vehicles to drive. The members of the Church drove older used cars, if they had a car at all. It was unheard of for an ordinary member to have more than one car, and when they did, they bought it at a used car lot where Bell worked and got commissions on his members who bought cars there. According to former members, Bell had all his assets listed under his own name and that of the Church of God of the Union Assembly of Kokomo for tax purposes. These properties included Bell's Bargain Fair, a drug store, and two restaurants. Some of the money he received went directly to the moderator, Brother C. T. Pratt. How much he kept for himself is unknown, but it was hard to fool the Pratt family and slip money away from them without getting caught. But with Bell's lifestyle, lots of money came his way either back from Minnie or he kept his share.[10] Bell also spent time as a Deputy Sheriff. It is not known how long Bell did this but it gave him a little clout in Howard County, Indiana.[11]

Don Pitner explained the following story. It was backed up by Charles Roberts and other former members. Not all the ministers for the Church made out like bandits and grew rich. In fact, most of the ministers who were not part of the Supreme Council or related to the Pratts were expected to contribute more money than an average member. During the 1950's at one of the quarterly ministers meeting in Dalton, C. T. told his ministers that each one of them had to give one thousand dollars to the Church. All of these ministers had to pledge this and then follow through within weeks or be expelled from the Church. Each one of the thirty-plus churches had three or four ordained ministers. Over a hundred ministers were listed in the 1945 Church minutes. Almost all of these ministers had to borrow the $1,000 and pay it back monthly to a bank or a finance firm. $1,000 in 1955 is worth a little over $10,000 today. It was a struggle to survive for ninety percent of these ministers (200 by 1955), who had jobs other than being ministers.[12] The only ministers who were financially secure were members of the Pratt family and the twelve members of the Supreme Council—most of whom were members of the Pratt family. Another problem for these working ministers was that Brother Pratt expected all members to have large families, all of whom had to be fed and clothed. Their wives and children went without much of the time.[13]

2

In 1952, forty-seven-year-old Otha Pitner and his forty-three-year-old wife, Stella Mae, moved from Hamilton, Ohio, to Kokomo. Having been married in 1925, they brought with them seven of their twelve children—another would be born the next year, making a total of thirteen. Otha and Stella's first five children had been girls, and they did not made the trip to Kokomo because they had already become married on their own and had moved out of the Pitner house. The oldest girl, Esther Mae, married William (Junior) Roberts, lived in Dalton, and belonged to C. T.'s church. The next oldest girl, Betty Lou, had married a man by the name of Marshall, and they lived in Wainwright, Ohio. They did not attend the Union Assembly, and neither did the Pitner's third daughter, Elsie Jean, who had married a man by the name of Alexander. The fourth girl, Barbara Lou, married Ronnie George and they, too, did not belong to the Church. The fifth girl, Gladys age fifteen, married a man by the name of Hannah, and they attended the Union Assembly Church. Otha would not have anything to do with his three daughters who left the Church and would not allow his wife to see her daughters, call them, or even write them.[14]

Otha and Stella had lived in Knoxville during the 1940s, where they had initially joined the Union Assembly of the Church of God. After being ordained, Otha took his family to the Union Assembly Church in Hamilton before moving to Kokomo.[15] Otha was a carpenter by trade and built houses and other types of buildings. He was very strict with his children and wife, making sure they lived by the standards of the Church. He kept telling them that he would never get a church of his own if they didn't adhere to the guidelines set forth by Brother Bell and the Pratts. The wife and daughters could not cut their hair. Dorothy said:

> I could sit on my own hair while in my teens. We could not wear makeup or jewelry, except married women could wear wedding rings. Our dresses had to come below the knee, and the girls had to wear full stockings even in the summer no matter how hot the weather. If we went swimming, we

could not wear bathing suits or shorts. We had to fasten the skirt between our legs with a safety pin to hold the dress together not allowing it to come open while under water, and we were never permitted to swim in the company of boys or men. The boys were not allowed to play sports or join clubs—church was everything to both boys and girls—the only activity we could attend. We were not allowed to attend movies or watch TV. We did have radios, but they were for the news and to listen to Union Assembly preachers and singers."[16]

When Otha's daughter Dorothy became old enough to read the Bible, she would read it to him and he would tell her what it meant. She, like all the other girls and women, was not allowed to have a Bible. All the women were trained to be underlings, and the boys did not learn to respect women, even their own mother or sisters. Therefore, a vicious cycle kept perpetuating itself—men treating the women not much better than slaves. Otha had two three-inch wide, three-foot long leather razor straps that he used to beat the girls. On the end of these straps was a metal buckle that Otha used when he whipped his sons.[17]

Soon after the Pitners arrived in Kokomo in 1952, Otha built an addition onto the side of Clinton Bell's Bargain Fair Furniture Store according to Bell's specifications. Dorothy said during an interview: "The room was not much bigger than a bedroom—had no windows—was soundproof—had only one door in and out, and Bell had the only key. Bell called this special room his "training closet." The members of the Church in Kokomo called it "the darkroom." Bell claimed he needed it to take wayward members inside for counseling and therapy about their sins and how to live a righteous life trusting the Lord. It seemed strange that the members who needed his therapy were all women and young teenage girls. It didn't matter to Bell if the women were married or not and if the girls were under sixteen—some as young as twelve or thirteen. If Bell caught one of the females not wearing stockings, or breaking any other church rule, she was ordered by him or even their own father or husband to meet at the 'training closet' for counseling about her sinful ways."[18]

According to Dorothy, by 1958 rumors spread as thick as pollen in the spring concerning Bell's activities in his "training closet." Rumors were being whispered among the girls that Bell was engaging in sexual acts in the room with some of the females, but no one had outright admitted it. Bell also had young girls sent, usually by their parents, to live in his home to be maids for him and his family while he counseled them. There were only insinuations about Bell's sexual activities to this point, but the proverbial cat was about out of the bag. Bell had gone too far and, because young girls will divulge their secrets, the majority of the membership had heard the rumors.[19]

On January 15, 2014, I interviewed former Union Assembly member of the Kokomo Church, Dorothy Pitner Bliss. She had just recovered from stage IV breast cancer but was very intelligent and spoke clearly over the phone. I had never spoken to Dorothy before but was given her name by a family member. I called Dorothy at

Rev. Clinton Bell, 1959. UPI Telephoto
(file). Courtesy of Historic Images.

her home in Kokomo, Indiana, and identified myself. I told her I was researching for a book on the Church of God of the Union Assembly. Dorothy was sixty-nine at the time. After more explanation about me and my plans for a book on the Union Assembly we began.

After asking her about Clinton Bell, and the stories I had heard about him, including accusations that he had sex with underage girls, Dorothy replied:

"I had this eerie feeling every time I was around Clinton Bell, okay, I think it was something . . . something that we're given—that sixth sense that tells you something's not right, okay? In the meantime, I had gone on vacation with one of my sisters and her children, and I had worn a bathing suit and a pair of shorts while we were gone. So when I'd gotten back home I had this sunburn and Dad saw it and he told me that I had to get up in front of the church and ask for their forgiveness, or he was going to have to take some measures. So I went to church on Sunday morning." The sunburn over her legs and back proved that Dorothy had broken a church rule which forbid members from wearing bathing suits.

"When was this?" I interrupted.

"It was 1959, '54, it was 1955, I think it was—no it was '58 because I was thirteen at the time. That Sunday all the ministers were there and my own father called me a whore right there in front of all the people. I didn't budge because I knew I wasn't that, so when we go home that Sunday, Dad said, 'You didn't do what I asked you to do. Now tonight if you don't get up there and ask for forgiveness, you're going in there—that special room with Clinton Bell.'"

I said, "I heard that he had a special 'darkroom' he used to take members for counseling. What was it?"

"Just girls and women—Bell called it a training closet. It was on Washington and Jefferson Street. They . . . Bell had this room—my daddy built this room on the side of this furniture store. Bell sold furniture out of the store. It [training closet] was completely windowless, sound proof, and there was only one door in and out of there and Clinton had the key. He didn't take me there, but they said he took women there. I believe my dad knew all about it. I really do."

"So, it wasn't called a 'darkroom?'"

"Yeah, it was called that too."

"Let's go back to the time your dad said he was going to take you in Clinton's special room."

"Well, you know, there was something in my psyche that told me . . . there ain't no way . . . there was just something there. Shirley told me . . . there was just something there. The girls whispered about a lot of stuff. You couldn't figure out what was going on, but you knew it had to do with Bell. So I just got up out of church that night and went to the basement . . ." There was a long pause before she continued. "After that, I ran away from home and went to my older sister's home in Ohio." Dorothy voice had started to break here and she seemed to be crying.

I waited, as I wanted to hear what happened in the basement. I thought I heard her crying. When I felt like she was not going to tell me, I said, "I'm sorry for causing this to be brought up in your mind again."

Dorothy appeared to pull herself together—and continued, "It was just the way Clinton talked to me, you know. When you went down to the basement, it was unfinished—it was a dirt floor—dirt and gravel, and they had these wooden walkways . . . Yeah, it is still so apparent in my mind."

I waited again but kept my silence until she said in a stronger voice—almost a mad voice now, "Anyway, there was this walkway, and only one person could get across it except . . . there was one going to the men's room and one going to the women's room. Well, I was going into the ladies room and here comes Clinton Bell, and instead of turning sideways or backing up to let me through he rubbed against me, and that really—you know—I don't know . . ."

Charles Roberts had told me that Dorothy had hit Clinton once so I said, "What happened? I heard you hit Clinton?"

"Did I hit Clinton? NO! I ran away from home and went to my sister's house in Ohio and stayed gone for six months, and nobody ever looked for me. That right there should have told them something."[20]

Dorothy and I talked seven or eight more times. She sent me a large envelope full of newspaper articles from the *Kokomo Tribune* about the Clinton Bell case of 1959–1960 that proved very useful. The last time I talked to Dorothy was January 5, 2015, while she was visiting her sister in Port Orange, Florida. The last thing

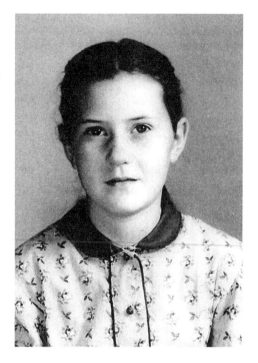

Dorothy Pitner at age ten in a school photo. Courtesy of Brenda Moore.

Dorothy said to me over the phone was, "A book about this group has been a long time coming. I hope I live long enough to read your book."

Truthfully, I was stunned. No one had ever said anything like this to me. I told her I hoped I lived long enough to finish it. She laughed. We said good bye.

Two months later I got a call from her sister, March 7, 2015. She told me Dorothy had died of cancer that day. I didn't know her cancer had returned. She never mentioned it or complained. I went down to my workroom in our basement and worked on this book until my eyes would no longer focus.

3

After Dorothy's encounter with Bell in the basement of the church, she ran away from home to live with her married sister, Jean Alexander, in Ohio. After Dorothy ran away, two of her brothers, Otha Junior and Richard, went to see their married sister, Gladys, at her home and tried to get information about Dorothy. There a fight broke out between her husband, Brooks, and the brothers. The brothers broke their brother-in-law's ribs. Otha Junior and Richard were arrested, but a family was torn further apart as would other Union Assembly families in the near and distant future. Later, Gladys and Brooks had to move in with her parents and siblings because Bell ordered them to do this to save money so they would have more to give the Church. Brooks lost his job but still the family had to come up with a pledged amount each week. The family went hungry for a while until Brooks got another job. Brenda Moore told this in an interview in 2015 about families having to live together in the '50s: "I was about nine then. We had to do it, because Bell and them had us scared to death. I stayed scared to death all the time because of the way they preached about hell and such."[21]

Otha waited six months before he called his daughter Jean to look for Dorothy. He told Jean that if Dorothy would come home, she could finish school. Dorothy was going into her sophomore year in high school, so she took the train and went back home to her parents. She missed her mother terribly. Once home, Dorothy was guarded night and day. She was not allowed to go to the bathroom alone. Otha nailed her bedroom windows shut, and she was made to go back to the Church.[22] It wasn't long before Clinton Bell regretted this, because one night at Church, Dorothy stood with a blank expression on her face and said slowly as if in a trance, "This man you're worshiping—you don't know what he's doing. This man you think is the man of God is doing all kind of things."[23] Dorothy was beaten with a razor strap that night by her father. Only a short time after this, Bell left town with a young girl who was not his wife.

4

Dorothy had three older brothers, two younger brothers, and two younger sisters at home. Eighteen-year-old Donald, who was five-years older than Dorothy, was tall and lanky but looked like he could take care of himself. He had dark wavy hair that he kept combed back. During three interviews in February 2014, Don told the following story: In 1958 Don got into trouble with his father because he would not stop seeing a certain fifteen-year-old girl named Mary who was also a member of the Church. Single members could only date other single members. Reverend Bell told Don's father that Don was messing around with this underage girl. Otha ordered Don to stop, but when he didn't, the pastor decided that Don had to move in with him. Bell was going to straighten Don out. At the time, Don didn't know why his dad and Bell didn't want him to see this particular girl. He would not learn the reason for another year. Don's primary job for Brother Bell became chauffeuring his pastor around. Don would take Bell to the furniture store, leave him there, and come back to pick him up later.

A few weeks after Don moved in with the Bells, the pastor had Don drive him to Dalton—the Church's national headquarters. They left in Bell's new green Cadillac Eldorado about mid-day and two hours later arrived at Sam's Subway, which was located on Meridian Street in Indianapolis. Bell said he wanted a corned beef sandwich. He told Don to stay in the car and he'd bring him a sandwich back. Don waited and waited but Bell didn't return, so after waiting over an hour, Don went to find Bell. Sam's Subway had a bar at ground level, and Don looked inside to see Bell pouring whiskey out of a bottle into a shot glass and downing it several times.

Don wondered what in the world was going on, but Bell was already so drunk he didn't even recognize Don when he came inside to get him.

It wasn't even dark yet when Bell stumbled back across the street to the Eldorado where he immediately passed out. Don drove out of Indianapolis and headed toward Dalton. About six hours later, when they arrived in Chattanooga, Don noticed that the Cadillac was almost out of gas. Don stopped at a gas station and looked at his pastor, who was slobbering all over himself and said, "Brother Bell, we need some gas."

Bell came out of his stupor and mumbled, "Where we at?"

"We're in Chattanooga about thirty-five miles from Dalton."

Bell sat up and said, "We can't go into Dalton tonight." Then Bell popped a few breath mints called "Sen-Sen" into his mouth. Sen-Sen was a breath mint originally called a "breath perfume" that resembled Vigroids—a liquorish sweet. Bell soon consumed the entire box of mints.

That night Bell had Don drive him down on Ninth Street in Chattanooga—now called Martin Luther King Boulevard—where they found a man selling barbequed ribs. Bell, still drunk, bought some and got the sauce all over his clothes, face, even on his shoes. They spent the rest of the night sleeping in the car. By the next morning Bell had sobered up, so Don drove him on to Dalton. They drove straight to C. T. Pratt's house, and Bell went to the door. Don followed. Once inside, Clinton Bell handed Brother Pratt a thousand dollars in cash. In ten minutes they were back in the Cadillac headed toward Kokomo. Once they returned home, Don went to see his dad and told him that Clinton Bell was nothing but a drunk. Otha refused to believe the story and physically threw his own son out of the house for saying such a thing.

Later one afternoon, after the drive to Dalton, Don dropped Bell off at his "training closet" connected to the furniture store. About two hours later Don was on his way back to pick up Bell as instructed when Earl Wayne (not his real name), who was a member of Bell's church stopped Don and wanted to know where he was going. After Don told him, Earl said he'd go get Bell, so Don drove back to his pastor's house. By the time Don got back to Brother Bell's house, Bell was calling him on the phone and wanted to know why he had not picked him up. Bell's words were slurred because he was so drunk. Don told him that Brother Wayne was going to pick him up. "No!" Bell screamed, "You come back and pick me up." Don drove back to the furniture store; Bell was so drunk that Don had to help him inside the Cadillac. This was on a Sunday, so Bell called the church and reported that he would not be there that night because he had the flu. Don tried to tell his daddy about Bell's drinking again, but Otha said, "Ah, he don't do anything like that." But he didn't throw his son out this time.

Don then went to see three prominent men in the Church—Earl Jenkins, Oky Gilsby, and Marshall Dukes—and told them about Bell's drunkenness. They said they believed every word about Bell but didn't know what to do about it. Don talked to his younger brother Richard and they decided to blackmail Bell. They didn't know anything about blackmail, but they wanted to get even with Clinton Bell. Don confronted Bell and told him that he was going to tell everybody about his drinking and messing around in his "training closet" with girls. Clinton Bell gave Don five hundred dollars, so Don gave his brother Richard half of it. Furthermore, Bell offered to give Don a 1940 panel truck if he would stay quiet.

Not long after this, Bell arranged for Don and his sweetheart to be married by telling Otha that it was the Lord's wishes that the young couple get married. Within a few weeks, Don and sixteen-year-old Mary were married. Immediately she became pregnant, but not long before the child was to be born, Mary noticed that the unborn fetus had stopped moving. Don drove her all the way to Dalton to let C. T. Pratt's daughter Flora Hughes, an unlicensed midwife, deliver the child. The child was born dead. In fact, it had been dead for a couple of weeks because Mary told her sister-in-law, Brenda Pitner Moore, later that the baby was decayed. She told Brenda that the baby's eyes were decayed as was its tiny face. Flora kept Mary there a few extra days trying to keep the sixteen-year-old girl alive. Don never saw the baby and was not told what happened to it. When they returned to Kokomo, Mary was still frail and close to death, as well as being extremely depressed. The midwife sent Don a bill for $200 for their services. Because the child had been born so early, Don became convinced that Bell must have fathered his wife's child.[24]

That same day, Don took a pistol and went down the highway looking for Bell but ran into his father headed in the opposite direction. Otha stopped his son and wanted to know what he was doing. Don said, "Dad, you don't believe a damn thing I tell you."

Otha said, "I do now, son." Together they went to see Clinton Bell but Bell lied and acted as if nothing had happened. Bell said Don misinterpreted everything.

On the way back home, Don said to his father, "That guy is rotten as hell."[25]

In December of 1959, just after Dorothy Pitner got up in church to accuse Bell of misconduct, Jesse Pratt came to Kokomo for a revival. Bell talked to Don and Richard and told them that if they would not mention anything about his drinking and the training closet to Brother Jesse, he would give the boys more money. At the start of the revival, Bell got up in front of the congregation and bragged on Don and Richard. Bell told everyone what fine Christian boys they were. It made Don sick to hear all of Bell's compliments, so he turned to his brother and said, "I'm going to tell on that sonofabitch after church."

Don waited outside until Jesse got into his Cadillac as Bell got in on the passenger's side. It was winter and freezing out, and Brother Jesse was sweaty from his fiery preaching, so he was cold and had the windows on his big Cadillac rolled up to stay warm. Don walked up to Jesse's window and knocked on the glass. Jesse didn't roll the window down but just looked at this young kid. Don said in loud voice, "Brother Jesse, I need to talk to you." Don looked at Bell whose face had turned white.

Jesse rolled down the window and said, "Brother Don, if you got anything to say, you gotta say it to your pastor."

Don bent over, pointed his finger at Bell, and said, "It's about that sorry sonofabitch right there that I want to tell you about. I want to tell you what he's been doing."

Jesse had a shocked expression on his face as he looked at Don and then at Bell who was squirming and sweating.

Bell started to speak but Jesse held his hand up to the pastor and turned back to Don and said, "Well, if you're going to say something say it in front of the man you're accusing."

Don who was still bent over and looking in the window of the big automobile said, "He's a drunk. I lived at his house for a while, and I can tell you, he's a drunk—gets drunk all the time—misses church 'cause he's too drunk to walk. And he's got this special room at the furniture store—a darkroom—where he takes women and young girls to do God-knows-what in there with them."

A crowd of people had already moved around the car and were listening.

Bell broke in and said, "The boy's a liar. I may have had a drink or two, but . . ." Jesse interrupted Bell, held the palm of his hand toward the pastor, and said, "Wait a minute, Brother Bell, and we'll talk." Jesse turned back to Don and said, "That's a strong statement to say about a man if it ain't true—especially when he's right here listening. Does anybody else know about this?"

"Yeah," said Don pointing to the people standing around the car, "about everybody in the church knows. Talk to Brother Earl Wayne—I bet he knows plenty. I bet his daughter Cheryl knows even more." Don leaned his head back in Jesse's car and said, "Bell trapped my sister in the basement and accosted her and she ran away from home because my daddy was going to make her go in that 'treatment room . . . or darkroom' with him."

Jesse said as the Cadillac's window started moving up, "Let me and Brother Bell talk for a while." That night Clinton Bell left his wife and two children—a boy and a girl, picked up Earl Wayne's twenty-two-year-old unmarried daughter, Cheryl (not her real name), and left town.[26] Clinton Bell would be back.

5

On December 8, 1959, Bell left Kokomo with Cheryl Wayne, fourteen-year-old Dorothy Pitner complained to authorities that her father had mistreated her and that she had run away from home three times in the past six months. She told them about her recent beating with a razor strap and about her encounter with Clinton Bell. She also reported the names of other girls who had been alone with Bell. This led to an investigation of the pastor, and shortly afterwards a seventeen-year-old girl filed a complaint against him to the Howard County authorities. Immediately, three other underage girls, one only fifteen, filed complaints against their pastor. The girls gave sworn affidavits telling the authorities that Bell had sexually assaulted them while they were in his "training closet."[27] Also, complaints were filed against Bell for his "handling of money turned over to him by members of his congregation.[28] Prosecutor L. Owen Bolinger reported that several people had talked to him and alleged that the minister "skipped town with money belonging to them." Bolinger further stated in the *Kokomo Tribune* that he had received complaints that the minister had taken an undetermined amount of money with him that belonged to the church and to individual members of the congregation. One church member said several thousand dollars might be missing.[29]

Bolinger also reported he had received another complaint from two merchants who had given Bell permission to sell their furniture through his auction/furniture store, with the understanding that Bell was to use the sales money to pay off mortgages on the merchandise. As noted earlier, Bell did not pay off the mortgages on the merchandise—merchandise the members had borrowed money against. Bolinger also highlighted a report that Bell had an agreement with the operator of a used car lot in Kokomo whereby the minister was to receive $25 for each customer that he brought to the dealer. Bolinger said, "The dealer admitted having such an arrangement with Bell, and acknowledged that the minister had brought several customers to his place—all members of Bell's church."[30]

C. T. Pratt and Minnie doing their radio program (late 1950s).
Courtesy of Nell Belcher.

The Church of God of the Union Assembly in Kokomo, Indiana, during 1950–70.
Courtesy of Brenda Moore.

On December 18, 1959, C. T. Pratt talked Bell into returning and giving himself up to the authorities. After the girls' sworn affidavits against Bell were filed in Howard Superior Court by Prosecutor Bolinger, a $7,500 bond was set by Judge Davidson. When Bell returned on a Saturday about 1:15 p.m., he called the authorities and said, "Come and get me." When brought into custody, Bell was unshaven and had a furrowed brow from lack of sleep. Bell said he and Cheryl Wayne had been caught in a snow storm in New Mexico and had had trouble getting back. He said to reporter Fred Odiet from the *Kokomo Tribune*, "I just came back to make everything right with everyone I've mistreated." When asked what happened to the girl, Bell said, "I left her with her father this afternoon. I had a scare last week before leaving when an agent for the FBI walked into the car sales place, but that the federal officer was only checking on a stolen car."

Bell confessed to the reporter, "If I'd only listened to our moderator, Brother Pratt. It is not the policy of our church to uphold or cover up the things I've done. Our church is a straight organization and believes in upholding the law and order. I'm very sorry about this whole thing. And I intend from here on and the rest of my life to make up to the people that I've mistreated." Bell was fingerprinted and photographed before being released.[31]

It was stated that all of the Church of God of the Union Assembly Supreme Council members arrived in Kokomo to join Jesse and C. T., who were trying to keep the situation from escalating and spreading, which would cause even more bad publicity for the Church. The moderator, C. T. Pratt, had already taken over operation of Bell's property and started paying off the debts Bell allegedly left behind. C. T. also paid off a $4,000 debt on Bell's 1959 Cadillac, which had been financed through a loan company in Kokomo.[32]

Don Pitner said that a mandatory meeting was called by C. T. Pratt to take place a few nights after Bell's return at the Kokomo Church. At the meeting, Clinton Bell sat in a chair on the platform facing the congregation. C. T. Pratt gave a fiery sermon in which the sins of sex out of wedlock and adultery were the main topics. He had the women crying when he talked about how they would go to hell if they didn't confess their sins and be forgiven. By the time Brother Pratt got everyone worked up, he hit the congregation with a bomb that equaled the magnitude of the explosion over Hiroshima in 1945. He said, "I want every woman and girl who had sexual encounters with Brother Clinton Bell to come forward and ASK HIM TO FORGIVE YOU. I don't want any of you to go to hell, so come forward and do this and you will be forgiven. The Lord will take care of Clinton Bell." To the surprise of almost everyone there, except maybe Bell, more than half of the women and young girls—over fifty were reported—left their seats and came forward to face Bell and ask for HIS forgiveness. Men screamed while some fell over in their seats or onto the floor. A few men walked out when their wife or daughter or both asked for forgiveness. In a few instances Bell had made a family affair out of his adultery by accosting both mother and daughter.[33]

A furious Don Pitner was stupefied that Brother Pratt had commanded that the *women* confess and ask Bell for forgiveness. But when Don's young wife went forward, too, asking Bell for forgiveness, he wished he'd killed Bell earlier when he had had a chance. Don reported that he thought the first baby his wife had might have been fathered by Clinton and that is why Clinton pushed them to get married. Don was bitter for a long time, and the thought of Bell with his wife would not leave his mind, even though they stayed together long enough to have three children. Eventually, their marriage ended in divorce, and Don blamed himself. He said he'd had a good wife but never treated her right after that.[34] Don said that was when he started drinking and became an alcoholic.[35]

Some of the men whose wives had sex with Bell divorced them, and some families were destroyed, but C. T. Pratt held the Church together by threatening everyone with hell and damnation. It worked to some extent.[36]

The next day after the mandatory meeting, Ken Atwell reported in the *Kokomo Tribune*: "The moderator also said, according to Deputy Dieterly, that he had held a meeting at the church after arriving in Kokomo, and that the names of 'about a dozen young girls and women who had had something to do with Brother Bell' had been given to him. Pratt also said he told the young girls and women 'that you will be forgiven, but the Lord will take care of Clinton Bell.'"[37]

On December 30, just after Bell had returned, Dorothy Pitner's case had gone before Judge Merton Stanley. The *Kokomo Tribune* reported that "the girl told him she didn't want to go to church because she was afraid of Bell." She told him the former pastor had accosted her in the church located at 2115 Apperson Way N. on several occasions. Prosecutor Frank L. Oliver also said, "The interview brought out the names of several young women of the church who the girl said had had 'relations' with Bell."[38]

During the hearing, one of Dorothy's older sisters whom Dorothy had been living with claimed the girl's trouble stemmed from the Church of God of the Union Assembly, of which her father was an elder. Her father, Otha, under questioning by Oliver, testified he whipped the girl with a razor strap on one occasion, but said it wasn't because of the Church. The girl had sassed her mother, he said. Dorothy's older sister who was married and did not attend the Church said Dorothy had bruise marks when she came to her home after the whipping. The father denied he had struck the girl any place but on the back. When the judge asked where he thought Dorothy should live, her father said, "In a good Christian home but they would have to belong to the Church of God of the Union Assembly." Otha suggested his home or at his daughter's home in Dalton, Georgia. With that, Dorothy said nothing but broke into tears when the church was mentioned. Dorothy's mother agreed with the father and did not want Dorothy living with either of her three married sisters who were not members of the Union Assembly Church.[39]

On January 7, 1960, Judge Merton Stanley of the Howard County Juvenile Court ordered the girl, Dorothy, a ward of the court, to live with her married sister in Ohio, and ordered the father who claimed to be a minister of the Union Assembly Church to pay eight dollars a week into the Howard County Clerk's office for support of the child.[40]

6

On Tuesday January 5, 1960, the Howard County Grand Jury met, and Don Pitner testified against Clinton Bell. Don told the jury what had happened while he lived with Bell, about his "seduction room," as it was now being called, and about what happened at church with the women and young girls admitting what had happened.[41] Bell appeared before the grand jury that day but did not testify. Meanwhile, the four girls who had testified and given affidavits against Bell did not show up to testify before the grand jury. A deputy sheriff was sent to get the girls, but their parents said they had left town and did not know when they would return.[42]

Leaders of the Union Assembly Church stated they had ousted Bell from the pulpit, but if they did, it was only for a short time because Bell was soon preaching at another Union Assembly Church. By mid-January 1960 he had left town. Jesse F. Pratt reported to the press that Bell had gone to Dalton to attend a church convention, but members of the congregation told an AP reporter that Bell told them he was going on a vacation.[43]

On March 24, 1960, the trial of Clinton Bell was set for May 16, to be held in Cass County Circuit Court in Logansport, Indiana. Judge Norman Keisling would preside. Bell requested a jury trial, and it was expected to last three days. In the trial at Logansport, L. Owen Bolinger was pressing an assault and battery charge against Bell, who now had Edgar W. Bayliff as his attorney. Bell had spent much of his time in Dalton at the Union Assembly headquarters. His wife and children had left town and were also reported living in Dalton.[44] The parents of the girls who were to testify took their daughters out of town. It was reported by former members interviewed that the girls who gave the affidavits were in Dalton until after the trial.[45]

On Monday May 16, 1960, all charges were dropped against Clinton Bell on legal technicalities by Judge Keisling. Even though Bell had admitted to the press that he was guilty of sexual charges, including acts performed upon minors, and sworn affidavits were filed that accused him of these charges, he was released because his attorney contended that the charges were misdemeanors and that Bell's appearance before the Howard County Grand Jury on January 5 was enough to grant him immunity.[46] Of course what happened at the Church's mandatory meeting in December of 1959 when approximately 50 women and young girls, some as young as twelve and thirteen, admitted to being forced to have sexual relations with Clinton was never brought up in court.[47] When shattering events like this happen, people remember, and through the years the story has stayed alive among members and former members of the Church. However, the events of what happened

Clinton Bell and Johnny Burnett as patrolmen in Union City.
Courtesy of an anonymous family member.

in the Clinton Bell case from the *Kokomo Tribune* are still in print on microfilm in the Kokomo-Howard County Public Library across the street from the *Kokomo Tribune*.

Around 1963, Clinton Bell went on a revival trip to the Union Assembly Church in Luttrell, Tennessee. On a Sunday night after preaching, Bell asked a young boy by the name of Kale if he wanted him to take him to eat at the church restaurant run by Reverend Johnny Burnett's sister and then take him home. Kale had two unmarried sisters who had been at church that night and Bell had been keeping his eye on them. When Bell brought Kale home, he told him to go in the house and tell those two girls that the Lord had given Bell a message for them, so they needed to come out to the car so he could tell them what God wanted. The girls would not go outside and the oldest girl said to her brother, "Go tell Bell if he has a message from the Lord to give to me and my sister, he needs to come inside and say it in front of our mother."[40]

As Bell grew older, he moved back to Dalton where he spent the last years of his life with a crippling disease which left him without the power to speak.[49] On January 7, 1989, at the age of 69, Clinton Bell died and was buried in Dalton's West Hill Cemetery. It was reported that Clinton left behind a fine respectable family—some still living in Georgia, some in Kokomo.

10

Honor Thy Father and Thy Mother

"The time is coming and it can't be stopped when the low will
be exalted and the high is going to be abased. The word of God
has foretold these days and it can't be changed."

C. T. PRATT,
"Three Classes of People," *The Southerner,* 3

1

Charlie Thomas "C. T." Pratt turned seventy-eight on August 11, 1957—two months
before Russia successfully launched the first satellite, Sputnik, into orbit. To his
membership, C. T. Pratt seemed almost as vibrant as he had in his younger years,
but those closest to him could detect that his mental and physical health were in a
fast decline. It was reported that he didn't preach as often as he had, and when he
did, the sermons were shorter or longer and were not as coherent as in the past.
Cash Carmical did much of the preaching. Jesse, who was now the pastor of the
Atlanta Church of God of the Union Assembly, had moved to Dalton in 1955 to
help his daddy manage the expanding church businesses in Union City and other
places in the area. Jesse drove to Atlanta to conduct its Sunday services.[1] The very
popular Hugh "Cash" Carmical was the assistant moderator and was set to take

over as moderator if C. T. died.[2] But particular events were waiting on the horizon that would change significantly who would be in control of the Church.

In the later 1950s, a banker in Dalton held much of the liquid assets of the Church. He called C. T., Jesse, and Cash Carmical in for a meeting and wanted C. T. to decide who would be in charge of the Church's money in the bank if he died. C. T. named the assistant moderator, Cash Carmical. Cash's son and several others interviewed believed this spelled the end for Carmical because this showed Jesse that he had not won his own father's approval in becoming the next moderator. Even after all the scheming he had done to take over the Union Assembly at the time of his father's death, this act by C. T. made Jesse rightfully worry that whoever controlled the money controlled the church.[3] Remember that informants interviewed stated that Jesse did much of his plotting to take control of the Church behind his father's back.

As noted in Chapter 6, during the late 1940s, Jesse changed the Church's practice of "rebuking" or "reproving" by physically shaking the members who had transgressed. At the 24th (1945) Annual Meeting of the Union Assembly of the Church of God, C. T. Pratt taught that all ministers of the Union Assembly were to respect one another's feelings, and if any minister should preach anything contrary to the doctrine, he must be told of his mistake outside of the church first, then if he refused to admit his error and did the same thing again, he should be rebuked openly before others so all may be clear about doctrinal matters.[4] According to this church rule, C. T. meant for only ministers to be rebuked and he only rebuked them verbally. However, Jesse soon changed his rebuking to include members of the congregation as well as ministers. Jesse also increased the ferocity of his rebuking.

As a result, some interviewees revealed that some of C. T.'s charter ministers who had helped found the Union Assembly asked Brother Pratt to get control of Jesse. They warned the 78-year-old leader that Jesse was making unwelcome changes to church rules. C. T. Pratt reportedly answered: "Jesse is just so wild, I can't control him anymore." But he promised to try.[5]

One person interviewed said Jesse had experimented with his method of rebuking at his church in Hamilton, Ohio, and at other Union Assembly churches during revivals. Jesse would call a member forward who had been caught going against the rules of the Church. In some cases, another member would tell on the person, and Jesse would then say God told him in a vision the member's wrongdoing. During the "rebuking," Jesse would grab the wrongdoer by the head and start shaking him or her and pulling them from side to side. At times, the transgressor who was being rebuked would fall over chairs, fall in the floor, be slammed against a pew bench, or sustain an injury such as bruises over their body or, in some incidents, sustain neck injuries. It was not uncommon for the rebuking to last up to an hour. During the punishment, Jesse or another minister would shout phrases at the person, telling him that he were going to burn in hell or prophesy another horrific event that would happen in the near future to that person. Female transgressors received the same treatment. Most of the time a rebuked women's hair would fall out of its bun, and some, especially young girls, urinated on themselves or all over the floor as they were being dragged around by the head in the floor.[6] Some reported that Jesse and other ministers who rebuked physically always tried to get their victims to confess more sins. Sometimes other men, usually ministers, would stand around the sufferer shouting and screaming insults and warnings at them. These ministers would yell for the transgressor not only to ask for God's forgiveness but beg for the forgiveness of the Church and the congregation. Of course, they came up with a Bible verse for their reasoning. It was Matthew 18:18 which states: "Verily I say unto you, whatsoever ye shall bind on earth shall be bound in heaven: and whatsoever ye shall loose on earth shall be loosed in heaven." The ministers' interpretation of that verse was this: If the church does not forgive you, then you are not forgiven in heaven.[7] The author actually verified that Jesse Senior gave this interpretation while listening to one of Jesse's sermons on YouTube.[8] In this way the Union Assembly leaders kept the congregation tied to the Church if the members wanted to go to heaven and stay out of hell.

One of the most pitiful cases of rebuking happened at a revival in Trion, Georgia, in the late 1960s, when a young girl—we will call her Pam—had a seizure. It was known by the membership that Pam had suffered from epilepsy most of her life. While Jesse was preaching that night, Pam had a seizure, and Jesse had the girl, who was still convulsing, brought down to the pew in the front, where he grabbed her by the head, started slinging the slobbering child around, and screamed for the devil to come out of the poor sick girl. It wasn't long until about fifty men gathered around Pam stomping their feet and screaming for the devil to come out. Finally, after thirty to sixty minutes of this treatment, black bile came flowing from Pam's mouth and nose. Jesse announced that it was the devil escaping through the child's mouth. Jesse took full credit for this miracle over Satan. Later, people present reported that it looked as if the young girl had actually thrown up blood and not a devil. However, when Pam continued to have seizures, Jesse blamed it on Pam herself, saying that Satan kept coming back into the child because she was not keeping the faith.[9]

Several men interviewed said that in the 1960s at a minister's meeting, Jesse was berating the minister, Shady Owens, for something he had done, which was usually disagreeing with church rules and this of course upset Jesse. The majority of times when Jesse's scolding started, it led to that person being rebuked violently. Everyone there was expecting the reproving to happen soon. Brother Owens could have been anticipating it, too, because when Jesse approached him on the podium, Shady passed out and fell onto the floor. Danny Bailey, the man sitting next to him, tried to lift the unconscious Brother Owens. Bailey soon realized, however, that the older minister being berated by Jesse had died. Owens was moved to the church's kitchen where an ambulance was called. Owens was taken to the Dalton Hospital where he was pronounced dead. Jesse continued the sermon, but it did not last long after all the commotion. Owens, only in his fifties, had been the minister from the Union Assembly church in Maryville, Tennessee. According to Robert Anderson, a former member in the Maryville Church, soon after this tragedy Jesse and a large group from Dalton came to the Maryville church, where Jesse appointed his own fifteen-year-old son, Charlie T. Pratt III, to replace Shady Owens as the Maryville minister.[10]

Apparently, at least two other men died while attending services at the Dalton Union Assembly Church. Brother L. B. White died after preaching a sermon in the presence of Jesse. A man by the last name of Dyer died during one service preached by Jesse, and a Willie Howard died in another, but, according to some reports, was brought back to life by Jesse. When asked if Brother Howard had really died, Charles Roberts thought he had because the man had urinated all over himself. "People die all the time in hospitals and are brought back to life, so I guess it can happen in church," said Roberts.[11]

None of the former members interviewed stated that C. T. Pratt never physically rebuked a single one of his followers. Forcible rebuking was solely created by his son, Jesse, and in a short time other ministers and family members took up the practice. Most of the membership by then had come from life-long followers of the Church. It was their home. Their religion was everything to them, and most members were so programmed through religious socialization into the ways of the Church of God of the Union Assembly that they allowed the abuse. Reverend J. Willie Burnett, the co-founder of the Union Assembly Church, said in an interview in 1980 that he opposed the rebuking of church members, which he described as "a physical shaking of that individual."[12]

Several informants reported that Jesse seemed mad at the world on occasion and sweet as an angel at other times. They also talked about how Jesse had these extremes of emotions throughout his adult life.[13] As one long-time member reported, "Jesse would get mad at himself and take it out on his people. It was like he was possessed by evil spirits. In his own mind, he would blame others for his own problems. He never accepted responsibility. He even blamed the people for his divorce and fall from grace."[14] Four members claimed that Jesse was bipolar. When asked how he/she knew, one person said, "Because I'm bipolar." One former member said this when asked if he/she thought Jesse had been bipolar: "Well, that's a good excuse for his evil behavior, I guess."[15] In truth, no one will ever know if Jesse or Jesse Junior were really bipolar, but their extreme emotions are amply documented by informants. Former member Charles Roberts, for instance, urged: "You can't be around somebody like that who is happy-go-luck one minute and unhappy another and not think they are insane. One night after church, Jesse hauled off and kicked the fire out of James Robertson for eating Jesse's cookie. Another time, Jesse kicked a kid in the ribs for eating his cookies. We were scared to go to church and scared not to go to church. If you didn't go, they'd turn you out, and if you went they might turn you out, too."[16]

2

On a Thursday night in 1958, Jesse came to Dalton to preach the evening service. This was a low-attendance night. C. T. did not come that night, and it is not known if Minnie attended. Irene was there. Cash was there, but his family was not, as they stayed at home on 716 South Thornton Avenue where the 41 Highway made a severe set of turns known as the "S-curve." This service occurred a few weeks after the Dalton banker was told by C. T. Pratt that Cash Carmical would be taking over the Union Assembly if C. T. either died or became incapacitated.

During one of Jesse's sermons, Cash Carmical was located on the platform to the left of Jesse, who faced the women. While preaching, Jesse would turn to preach to the men who were on his side and to his rear. Carmical, sitting in the section designated for the twelve supreme council members, was close to Jesse. Jesse rushed up to Carmical, slapped him in the side of the head, grabbed his head, and started rebuking the assistant moderator. He shook Cash's head violently and screamed insults at him, saying that Carmical had stolen money that belonged to the Church. Cash had been in charge of taking the money from the collections and having it deposited in the bank. He also was in charge of the houses owned by the Church that had either been bought from or taken from members.[17] An eyewitness of the event said, "If members liked you, then he [Jesse] tried to run you off. That's what happened to Cash Carmical. Jesse was jealous of Cash—liked to have broken Cash's neck shaking him around—rebuking him—ran him off."[18]

How far in advance did Jesse and possibly Irene plan this? Did he know in advance that Cash would not go against the family, or that the family would stick together against him? As many reported, C. T. may have already lost control of his son by this time. Also, the brothers stood with Jesse, and Minnie stood with Jesse.

Carmical went home that night after the rebuking and talked to his family about the situation. According to his son, his daddy told them that he was going to talk to C. T., and he did. Cash told his family that C. T. wanted him to go back to church and C. T. would have Jesse apologize. Carmical's son, Charlie, said, "I prayed he'd go back because I trusted my daddy. I was surprised he went back to church that night, but I was pretty sure daddy had his mind made up because he knew the future and what was probably going to happen. He came home from that meeting and said, 'I'm never going back.' I saw going to Pratt's church as a blessing not as a curse."[19] In 2016, Charlie recalled additional details regarding the incident and the Church's shift toward physical rebuking: "During this time and leading up to my daddy leaving, I can remember my mother and daddy talking a lot about the changes in the Church. I can remember my mother telling Cash that what the Church was doing wasn't right—taking money and homes away from their members—she didn't like it, and I don't think—no I'm sure—Cash didn't care for it either. My daddy didn't like the physical rebuking. He told us in the car one night coming home from a meeting after Jesse physically rebuked an old woman because she'd been reported to have been dipping snuff—Even one of Jesse's kids grabbed the woman by the head and shook her—anyway my daddy said, 'I'll never rebuke anybody like that, and I better never see you boys doing that either.' My mother was fed up with it all by now. 'Brother Pratt has lost control of that church,' she would say.

> "I think Daddy found himself in a bind. The house we lived in was owned by the Church. Dad's furniture store belonged to them because he'd given it back to them twice. Our car probably belonged to them, too. I believe that's why it took Cash so long to finally leave—even though he'd been thinking about it for quite a while."

Others who were there that night said that Jesse did not apologize when Carmichal reappeared. Jesse actually started to rebuke Cash again, but was stopped by the bigger stronger man, who resigned then turned and walked out. Because of Carmical's leaving, a split in the Church took place.[20]

Not surprisingly, Cash Carmical and his family were promptly excommunicated from the Union Assembly Church. Interviewees reported that the following Monday, Jesse and a group of men from the Church marched back and forth in front of the entrance to Carmical's Dalton Auction Furniture store with guns in hand. They would not allow anyone to enter, because the Church owned the building and Cash owned the business. Jesse, wearing twin pistols on each hip, along with his men who were mostly Jesse's cousins or members of the elite circle, blocked the entrance. Carmical had a few of his own friends there, some with guns, which created a stand-off that lasted all morning. In the afternoon Cash's wife Lillian Carmical—everyone called her Bill—came and asked Jesse to come inside the office with Cash. There Lillian worked out a deal with Jesse to allow Cash to buy the building back again—for a third time. Jesse agreed to all terms and left the premises.[21] On Tuesday February 25, 1958, Hugh D. "Cash" Carmical paid for all rights to the property and the Dalton Auction Company.[22]

Carmical started his own church, and some Union Assembly members left to follow him. However, the Union Assembly did not slow down, only suffered a brief bump in the road. C. T. was still able to hold the church together, even at his advanced age. Cash's business took off, and he built the furniture store—Dalton Auction Company—into one of the finest in North Georgia. His son Charlie still runs the business today.

Jesse was quickly elected assistant moderator to take the place of the departed Carmical. Another minister was appointed to the Atlanta church, and Jesse stayed in the Dalton church to conduct services with his father. Irene and her children moved to the front pew with her mother-in-law, Minnie, who still controlled the money. Jesse preached against Hugh Carmical and told the members that Cash had been stealing money from the Church.[23] Former members interviewed agreed that Jesse had the same power of persuasion as his father except Jesse added more fear tactics to control his flock.[24] Jesse and Irene's second son had been named Hughie

Left to right: Dennis Smith, H. D. "Cash" Carmical, and Ollen Brewer.
Courtesy of Charlie Carmical.

Arlan Pratt, but his name was changed to Charlie Thomas Pratt III. The Church claimed Carmical and Rev. Arlan Belcher, who had sided with Carmical, were kicked out.[25] Arlan Belcher would come back to the Union Assembly Church at a later date.

Later that year, in July 1958, Carmical took C. T. Pratt, Jesse F. Pratt, and five other named persons to court for stealing his property and interfering with his business. Carmical also brought litigation against the Church of God of the Union Assembly for conducting a business, which was contrary to the law under which the church was incorporated in 1950 and contrary to its charter, since operating a business implied buying and selling various articles of merchandise in auction.

The original Church of God incorporation stated that the purpose of the church was "to promote the interest of religion and the cause of Christ on earth."

A jury was selected and a trial began. Carmical, as the plaintiff, used the Pittman, Kinney and Pope Law firm. C. T., Jesse, and the five other men, as defendants, used Carlton McCamy, of Hardin, McCamy and Minor. Carmical accused the defendants of stealing his tent and various articles of merchandise from a leased building near Athens, Georgia, and then auctioning the merchandise. Carmical accused them of "harassing" him by stealing his property and physically interfering with his legal right to conduct his auction sales in an orderly and peaceful manner.

Jesse admitted that they had taken possession of Carmical's merchandise and sold some of it, but he stated that they were willing to return the part not sold and pay him for the part they had sold. Jesse denied that the tent belonged to the plaintiff, arguing that it was the private property of C. T. Pratt. After hearing the case, the jury found in favor of Carmical and ordered the defendants to pay $400 for the tent and $390.20 for the value of merchandise, which they had disposed of by sale. The jury also found in favor of a permanent injunction to prevent further acts of interference by the defendants with the conduct of the plaintiff's auction business. The Pratts moved for a new trial. It went before the Supreme Court of Georgia on September 5, 1958, and the jury verdict was upheld by the state court.[26]

3

There remained but two major obstacles in Jesse and Irene's way to keep them from taking over total control of the Church—his father, C. T. Pratt, and his mother, Minnie Pratt. Former members who were old enough to remember claimed that when Jesse came back to Dalton in the mid-1950s to be his father's assistant things changed for the worse. One former member said even more about the changes, "It [the Church] was all about religion until Cash Carmical, Jesse, and G. E. Wiggs got involved. Once those three got around C. T., the old man changed and, M–O–N E–Y, money became the objective of the Church."[27]

During the latter part of the 1950s and early 1960s, C. T. Pratt became obsessed with his belief that the end of time was coming very soon. He had never planned to die but be on earth when Jesus returned to reign on his throne. Witnesses said that Brother Pratt claimed God had sent him visions, signs, and even told him to get his people prepared. He ordered his people to sell everything and move to Dalton, where Jesus would set up his kingdom. He had families move in together and give all they had to the Church. According to numerous interviewees, most members had barely enough to sustain themselves.[28]

C. T. and Jesse preached that a "man of sin" would soon rule the world and when he tried to destroy the "Camp of Saints," the end of the world would come about. God would rescue the Camp of Saints and, in preparation, about three thousand members from several cities moved into North Georgia. They were told to sell their homes if they had one, pay their bills, and give the rest of the money to the Church. Hundreds of thousands of dollars came in. At first these people were given homes to live in when they arrived in Dalton. Others moved onto the farms to work for no wages.[29] Interviewees stated that no one wanted to be left behind or thrown into the fires of hell.

It was reported that Brother Pratt said the end of time would come in September of 1961.[30] Of course when September turned into November, and 1961 turned into 1962 without the world coming to an end, those interviewed said people who had given away all they had realized they had lost their homes and all their money. An example of how devastating this loss was can be found in the court case of *Chester F. Isaacs of Hamilton, Ohio v. the Church of God of the Union Assembly*. Chester Isaacs was just one of several members who sued the Church of God of the Union Assembly for the return of their money and property. On January 20, 1962, Isaacs filed a suit in the Superior Court of Whitfield County against the Church and its governing body, arguing they used a fraudulent scheme to take his possessions for their own personal ventures and enterprises. Isaacs told the court that during the latter part of 1955, the Supreme Council of the Church of God of the Union Assembly adopted and preached to ALL members that, in order to be "saved," it was necessary for them to sell all their worldly possessions and lay the proceeds from such sales at the feet of the moderator of the Church, C. T. Pratt, whom they represented to be an Apostle. Isaacs and all the members were told to come together in Union City in Dalton, Georgia, where all property of the Church would be owned in common and distributed among the believers according to their needs.

Chester Isaacs testified that he liquidated his property and possessions in Hamilton, Ohio, and moved to Dalton. On May 28, 1956, Isaacs delivered to C. T. Pratt his personal property, with a value of $9,772.85, and a check for $25,000, which was paid from Isaacs' account. Isaacs was promised by Pratt that the $25,000 would be made as a down payment on the Archer Farm in Whitfield County, Georgia, and when the farm was purchased and the seller vacated the property, Isaacs would be permitted to live on the Archer Farm for the rest of his life. After the Archer Farm was purchased by C. T. Pratt and the Church, they refused to let Isaacs and his family live on it as they promised. Chester Isaacs stated that he had given to C. T. Pratt the total sum of $34,672.85, which comprised all of his worldly assets. Today that sum of money would be in hundreds of thousands if not half a million dollars. After going all the way to the State Supreme Court of Georgia, Isaacs lost on the grounds that the statute of limitations prevented the lawsuit from succeeding.[31]

Chester Isaacs lost all his assets, everything he had, but he was not the only one to lose all they had to this church and the Pratt family. In the early 1960s, Louis Taylor and his wife, Viola, had a 130-acre farm in Rock Springs, Georgia, which is about 20 miles west of Dalton. Louis and Viola had fourteen children and most of them still lived with them on the farm. Brother Jesse told them they needed to sell their farm and give all the money to the Church. In return, they could live rent-free at one of the Church-owned homes on Cleveland Highway, just a few miles north of Dalton. Louis and Viola gave a few acres to one of the deacons and sold the remaining property. They then gave the Church all of the money obtained from the sale of the property and moved into the house just outside of Dalton. Two months later, the supposedly rent-free home where the Taylors lived was sold, and they were evicted from the property. Louis and Viola Taylor took their children and moved into a small apartment owned by the Church—and they had to pay rent to the Church of God of the Union Assembly.[32]

One member wrote, "My family was among those that sold their home and gave the proceeds to the Pratt family. My Dad worked at one of the church-owned businesses (in Dalton) for slave wages. In the end, Dad lost everything to that family. The Pratts treated the church members as their 'subjects' and kept them in line through fear. If Dante was writing *The Inferno* today, he'd have to create a new level of hell for the Pratts."[33]

Bobby Barton told the story of how a man who worked with his father at American Tread in Dalton lost everything he had to the Union Assembly. This happened in the late 1950s, when ministers from the Church came and took a milk cow away from a father of four children because they said he wasn't contributing enough money. Weeks later, these ministers talked the man into signing his small farm over to the Church with the promise that he and his family could live there forever. Within a month the poor man was kicked off his farm and had to rent an apartment belonging to the Union Assembly.[34]

About this time, two groups or categories of members formed inside the Church—an elite group and a common group. The elite group included all family members, church ministers, and the well-to-do who were close to the Pratt family. The common group included the ones who gave all they had to the Church and received very little in return. Soon a split between the two groups formed inside the Church, but it would be a long time before this split led to actual changes in the Church of God of the Union Assembly.[35]

After the removal of Carmical, and with C. T. Pratt showing signs of failing health, the power of the Union Assembly Church started to shift. After Jesse moved his family back to Dalton permanently, he became the minister whom members started going to with their mental, material, social, spiritual, and other needs.

Former Union Assembly member, Libby Neighbors, described her family's misery during the late 1950s and early '60s when the Pratts had her family move from Hamilton, Ohio to Dalton to prepare for the second coming of Christ: "We was so poor, so poor," Libby said.

> We did live in one of their houses, but we was so poor. We had to wear dresses—our panties fell off. As we walked to the blackboard [in school] our panties fell off. All the children laughed at us. It was awful. We walked right out [of the school], me and my sister, both. I quit school in the eighth grade. I lied about my age. I went to work when I was thirteen. The Church wanted us to quit and go to work. It was terrible for a family to live the way we had to live. My daddy had to walk from Cohutta all the way to Dalton to work. [A distance of about 12 miles] Sometimes, somebody would pick him up. He was just so pitiful. And he'd come home so tired, and then one of them Pratts jumped on him for having a dirty house. Mama then sent us outside to clean up. She died when I was twelve. She wasn't able to do any work. She had bone cancer. She sent us out to clean the yard. Oh, we cleaned up the yard; we slung everything up under the house. We were kids, we didn't know no better.

"Did your dad work for one of the Pratt companies?"

Libby said, "Yes, I don't know which one. He'd walk to Dalton [Georgia] and they'd put him to work. They would take him out of town for a week to work and then they'd bring him back just in time for church on Saturday night and take him straight to the Church. Dad and other men went to Atlanta and all around and they'd paint houses, hang wallpaper mostly, and such. My daddy worked all week out of town for the Pratts."

I asked, "Who paid your dad, the Pratts?"

Libby said, "No, no, the people that they painted for would pay them, and then someone from the Church would go get 'em and bring them home on Saturday night just in time for Saturday night service. They'd take him straight to the Church. They'd tell them they's going to die and go straight to hell if they didn't give them all their money they'd made working that week and they [the men] did. I don't care what they say, they really said it. They [Pratts] would scream and shake them men's heads until they emptied all their pockets out—scared them to death."[36]

I asked. "He didn't come home with any money?"

"He didn't have a dime left from a whole week of work. It was terrible the way they did him."

"And you and his family too. How did you survive?"

"My sister Patsy and my brother, Paul, worked and made a little money to buy food with. We depended on people to give us clothes. I went to work when I's thirteen."

I asked, "Did you work for the cannery owned by the Pratts?"

"No," answered Libby, "but my oldest sister did. I worked for those people at the root beer stand they [the Pratts] owned. It was Jesse and Irene that had it. I worked from the time I was thirteen—I turned fourteen a week after starting work there. I stayed there until I was sixteen, and then I went to work for a restaurant down on 41 Highway after that."[37]

"What was your sister's name?"

"Barbara Saunders. She lived in Ohio, see, we came from Ohio. See, he [C. T.] said we had to come down here so we could go to heaven. So, my daddy followed him. They [the Pratts] just up and sold the house we's living in."[38]

"Did she move down here with you and the family?"

"No, she was already married and had three kids. She didn't come until later. I was already working for that restaurant on the 41 Highway when she came down."

"That would put Barbara at about twenty six."

"I was sixteen or seventeen then."

I asked, "Do you know anything about C. T. coming in the cannery and asking some women to take their clothes off?"

"Yes," answered Libby, "my oldest sister, Barbara worked there and she come to me crying one day and told me what happened. They all worked in the cannery, and he, C. T., told them he wanted to prove to them that he could look at all of them without their shirts on and not lust after them. Well, they [the women] all got scared, but they done what he told them because they was scared not to do it. She [Barbara] came to me that day crying and crying and asked me if I could get her a job at the restaurant on 41 Highway where I worked. She did go to work there but kept on crying and crying. I told her, 'Why don't you go home? This ain't no life for you. You need to be with your husband and kids back in Ohio.' I gave her my check that week and . . . and with her own check, she went home [to Ohio], and she never came back."

"Why did Barbara move down here to Dalton and away from her husband and kids?"

"Because the Pratts told her she had to leave her husband if he couldn't join the Church. And he wouldn't join the Church, and they wanted his home and everything. That's why they did people like that. They thought he'd move here with her. They'd have a home to sell and put the money in their pockets, but he stayed up in Ohio, and she went back to her husband and kids after what happened at the cannery."[39]

4

C. T. Pratt started doing some uncharacteristic things in 1960 and 1961. Being eighty-one years of age may have had much to do with it. Some relatives and present church members said "the old man" had had a stroke—some referred to them as mini-strokes. Some said he had Alzheimer's disease or some other form of dementia. He never went to a doctor, so no one knows for sure why he seemed to lose his mind to the point of doing these unusual acts. According to some interviews, even Jesse told people that his father was not capable of running the organization.

C. T. Pratt predicted that Christ would return to rule from Dalton, Georgia during September of 1961, so he and his people, unlike the rest of the people in America, were not worried about a nuclear war with Russia causing the destruction of the world. The members laughed about all the crazy people across the United States building bomb shelters. They didn't worry about such stuff for Brother Pratt had told them what was about to happen, and they believed him.[40] According to those interviewed, in 1961 C. T. Pratt appeared to lose his mind when he said he had to find a virgin bride for Christ.[41] Some interviewed stated that C. T. said he was going to father the child. Former members interviewed said that other than search his businesses for women, Brother Pratt invited women to his residence and told them to take off their clothes and march around in front of him while he inspected their qualifications. To make them feel comfortable, or to maintain her sanity, Minnie Pratt read verses from the Bible while the nude women were being scrutinized.[42] On one occasion he asked one of the women who worked in the Church office to undress, and she said, "Brother Pratt, I only take my clothes off in front of my husband."[43] Could C. T. Pratt have been encouraged by someone close to him to look for a virgin to carry his seed? One can only speculate why he engaged in this behavior.

The news of C. T.'s strange behavior went straight to his son, Jesse. After some husbands and fathers went to Jesse complaining about his father's acts, Jesse called a special session of the Supreme Council—and excluded his father, the moderator.

Interviewees, including family members, reported that Jesse had been laying the groundwork for his father's demise for about a year by 1961. He did this by preaching against his father's teaching and telling everyone that C. T. had lost his mind and was incapable of serving as their leader. Jesse worked against his father from the pulpit and during casual meetings with members. He had prepared the Supreme Council members for this very day; therefore, everything had been planned and put in place for Jesse's takeover. For years, Jesse had handpicked the new Supreme Council members who were easily controlled by Jesse.[44]

When Christ failed to appear in September of 1961, the Supreme Council—under the control of Jesse—decided to defrock C. T. Pratt and remove the founder from the Church he created. Reports are not clear how the Supreme Council also removed Minnie. Of course, the reason she had to go is obvious—she controlled the money.[45] The Supreme Council then elected C. T.'s son, Jesse F. Pratt, to take over his father's position and become the National Moderator of the Church of God of the Union Assembly. If Jesse's brothers rejected this, it was not recorded. Were they already under the control of their brother?[46]

Former members said by being defrocked and removed from the Church, C. T. and Minnie were not allowed to attend any services, meetings, or events carried out by the Church of God of the Union Assembly—the church they had founded. Some of those interviewed said that, on several occasions, C. T. tried to attend Sunday services, but Jesse would escort him out the door and lock it. If C. T. came in another door, Jesse would chase his father out another. Jesse informed his mother that they could no longer attend the Church and she needed to keep her husband away. It was stated that Minnie broke down in tears at times. Also, members were told to shun C. T. and Minnie, just as they would any other person kicked out of the Church. Not all family members obeyed this rule, and some were rebuked by Jesse.[47] The Union Assembly checkbook found its way into Irene's hands.[48]

According to several eyewitnesses, the family was split apart for a while as was the Church membership. Jesse's actions had negative consequences; attendance dropped at the Dalton Church from averaging over a thousand every Sunday morning to a few hundred souls.[49] With the attendance dropping so did the incoming money. Jesse started selling off businesses and liquidating assets to pay debts. He actually sold the large tabernacle in Union City and had to hold meetings in an abandoned supermarket building. This lasted about three years.[50]

Once C. T. and Minnie lost power and Jesse took over, a former minister and deacon took his teenage son to visit the "Old Man," which was what this former minister called C. T. Pratt. At that time, C. T. lived on Pine Hill Road in East Dalton within Union City. The house had a chain link fence running completely around it. While there, C. T. said, "I've learned more behind this fence than any other time in my life." C. T. told them that Jesse had confined him to this home and banned him from the Church. C. T. held his hand in the air about waist high and said, "If Jesse can build a church, then I can build one here in the air." The former pastor's young son, now a man of 71, said in an interview, "It was only years later when I understood what C. T. meant—that a church was not made of material such as wood and bricks but made of PEOPLE. C. T. meant that he brought people into the church while Jesse ran them off."[51]

Another member, Charles Roberts, had this to say about C. T. Pratt: "C. T. was a fine man—a good living man. He created that church. He was one of the best preachers that I've ever heard. He couldn't sing very well, but when he sang at the end of one of his sermons, they'd come running to the altar. I thought they did him wrong. He should have been taken down, but not the way it was done. I think later they were sorry for the way they did him."[52] Added George Hobbs, C. T. Pratt's great-grandson: "My [great] grandfather was a good man. We believe he had mini-strokes or some form of dementia during his final years. I didn't like what some of the family did to him, but he was a good man."[53]

The takeover by Jesse was complete, and a new era of the Church of God of the Union Assembly began. According to members interviewed, these church goers were not prepared for the hell they were about to live through under Jesse, as he made this Holiness group a religion of fear.

11

Building Fear

"People ask me for forgiveness, but I never had anything
against anybody. I'm sorry for people who do evil."

C. T. PRATT
"Charlie Pratt Sayings," *The Southern*, 1

1

Jesse Franklin Pratt turned forty-four in October 1961 when he took over as National Moderator of the Church of God of the Union Assembly. The majority of people who left the Church after C. T. had been dismissed started trickling back into the flock. Even former Supreme Council member J. Willie Burnett came back in 1961. In his own words from Dalton's *Daily Citizen-News:* "I came back to the church. Everyone was coming back, but a year later they went back to the money thing." Soon Reverend Burnett stopped going again.[1]

During 1961 Jesse made another change. He told members that they could own a television. However, they were encouraged to buy them from the Church's furniture store. He also told them to watch only wholesome family shows.[2] By the end of the decade, Jesse had 54 churches in sixteen states that were under his control, and the Church had survived the rupture that occurred after C. T. and Minnie were discarded. By some measures, the Church was thriving. Although total church membership may have reached as high as 15,000, the majority of former members estimated the total membership to be between five and ten thousand.

Although it is difficult for present-day generations to imagine how Jesse Pratt could grow his church given the strict rules and his past behavior, a former member responded by stating: "You give me your son who is six months old now, and let me keep him for eleven years, and when I bring him back I can have him thinking that a red car is really a green car, and you will have a tough time trying to change his mind."[3] So when the members came back, Jesse took them in and treated them with kindness and gave them his love for a while. Added Charles Roberts, "These people didn't understand—he needed them as much, if not more, than they needed him. He probably had forgotten how to paint houses and earn a living by doing an honest day's work. Why work when you have others to work for you?"[4]

As mentioned earlier, C. T. Pratt was given authority to transact business for the Church at the 1943 Assembly, but Jesse officially gained total control of the Church of God of the Union Assembly and its membership on September 4, 1961. On that date he had the Supreme Council and Board of Elders issue a decree that transferred all power to the Overseer or National Moderator. Who was that man? Jesse Pratt. This transfer included giving over "full authority to purchase property in the name of the church—real, personal, and otherwise," and without "confirmation of their body or any other organ of the church." This decision gave the authority to the overseer (Jesse) to "employ and discharge employees for and on behalf of the Church, its businesses, and enterprises," and to "apply for loans on behalf of the Church."[5] Jesse made himself a dictator of the Church, but wanted them to believe he was actually their God.

To solidify his control, Jesse had a church rule modified to place more restrictions on his people. When his father was moderator, rule ten explained that all members were forbidden to attend meetings that were held by a dismissed preacher or a dismissed member that has been dismissed from the Church of God of the Union Assembly.[6] He used Romans 16:17 which states: "God said mark them that cause division and offenses contrary to the doctrine and avoid them." However, there is no evidence that Jesse recited Romans 16:18, which warns the people "to stay away from those who do not serve our Lord Jesus Christ, but their own belly." Nevertheless, do not all Christian religions serve Jesus Christ?[7]

Jesse made a subtle change in this rule, but that change was significant in moving the members totally under his control. Jesse's new rule stated that all members were forbidden to attend meetings that were being held by a dismissed preacher *or even to associate with him.* Jesse added these last five words which made a slight but substantial change. Instead of not going to their meetings, the members were now told not to associate with preachers who left the Church. There was more. Jesse then made a new rule found in the Union Assembly Church Rules, which commanded all members to *stay away from any dismissed member who is against the Church.*[8] By using the technique of coercive persuasion, this slight change in the wording of the church rule enabled Jesse to create a closed community whose members were answerable only to himself and the Church. The new rule told the people of the Union Assembly Church that they are *commanded* to stay away from any dismissed member. Of course, if they were dismissed members then they were considered to be against the Church of God of the Union Assembly. This change split countless families apart for the next thirty-five years.

As stated by those interviewed, Jesse also sent his loyal family members to pastor in all but a few of the Union Assembly Churches. Even though they answered directly to Jesse, some of these family ministers created their own forms of coercion for members. Jesse put pressure on all church ministers to raise money—money to be sent back to him in Dalton. Failure could mean defrocking for even family pastors. An example of the hell created can be seen in an email received by the author in 2014 and confirmed in another email from another person in 2015:

> In the 1960s, Jesse's brother, Tom Pratt, was pastor at our church. [It was actually Jesse's first cousin, son of Lloyd Pratt.] He treated those members there terribly, making them work ungodly hours and then turning over most of their wages to him. My precious Mother worked for him in some business he owned—grocery store—and he forced her to work—get this—from 7 AM TO 11 PM at night. Tom Pratt was an evil man, and he also "loved the women" as most Pratts you will see later did, too. But there was so much FEAR that was infused in that church through Jesse, Sr., that everyone was so afraid and fearful of "the family of God" and no one would ever stand up for themselves or revolt. We just thought that was the way it was supposed to be. Jesse could have easily told those people to drink the Kool Aid and all of them would have.[9]

On March 16, 2014, after receiving a phone call from Brenda Moore who lived in Kokomo, Indiana, I was told another story about Tom Pratt, after a small baby had died during a Sunday service.

"Okay, now tell me more about that baby who died in church. Did you say it was 1962?"

Brenda said, "Yeah, [Clinton] Bell was already gone. It was a Pratt preaching up here at the time—Tom Pratt."

I said, "You said the baby was small, and the mother was holding it, and it was crying and having trouble breathing, right?"

"Yeah, I am sure the baby had pneumonia. The mother, Betty, took the baby down in the basement. The restrooms and stuff were downstairs. Then all of a sudden the mother started screaming, 'Oh, my God, it's dead, it's dead.' Some of the women stood up to go down, but Tom Pratt, who was preaching, told the women to sit down. My mother went down anyway."

"Why did Tom Pratt not want anyone to go see about the baby?"

"He kept preaching. The sermon went on for two more hours. Then he sent somebody to go get the baby. When they brought the baby up, it had turned blue-black. Tom had them hold the baby and he prayed over it to try to bring it back to life."

I said, "Of course, it didn't."

"Nope, they buried it a few days later—sad, so sad."[10]

A third interview, with Robert Anderson and his wife, Marie, from Knoxville, Tennessee, documents not only a rebuking performed by Tom Pratt, but its impact on other church members

Robert looked down at Marie and said, "Tell them the story about your dad." In a clear voice, Marie said, "There was a bunch of church members—I don't know how many—but them and my mother and daddy were to work at the restaurant in Hamilton, Ohio. They (the Union Assembly) would have everyone sign their checks and turn them back into them (the Church) at the end of the week. So my daddy started working a moonlight job just to take care of us. And they found out about it, and they rebuked him in church and literally threw him out the front door."

I asked, "What pastor did this?"

Marie said, "Tom Pratt. And my daddy started walking home, and he said, 'I don't know how many church members passed me that didn't even stop to pick me up, and here it was pitch dark and I had to walk all the way home.' Dad told me years later that those people who didn't pick him up apologized to him."

Robert said, "If they threw you out the door, anybody who went to church there had to withdraw any fellowship with you."[11]

2

In 1962, when the Church was having its services in the old supermarket building and times were so hard, Jesse had to raise $61,000 a month to meet the debts of the church., It is unlikely that Jesse went back to painting houses, so there were but two ways he could have raised this amount of money—selling off property and businesses owned by the Church, or get the money from the poor members. Jesse did both. Some of the businesses owned by the Union Assembly Church he sold included the cannery, slaughterhouse, and dry cleaners—everything except a big chunk of the land. But by 1964 Jesse and the Church were able to borrow enough money to build a new church across Whitfield County off 41 Highway. The new church building was large enough to hold 3,500 people, even though the Dalton membership was close to 1,000 at that time. Jesse designed the building himself, and members constructed it.[12] The Church of God of the Union Assembly's main headquarters is still located here today.

A former member of the Union Assembly Church, Johnnie Haney Butler, described her first visit to the new church building in Dalton during the 1960s:

It was all bricked, white brick, and there were three giant doors on the front. As you came through the front door, there was a place on both sides for coats and hats. The floor was carpeted. The wall just past the coat room was painted with a giant sunset, with a clock in the middle of the sun. Upon entry into the main room there were three sets of benches with lots of rows. There was a set of benches in the middle of the room and a set on either side of those. The rostrum was raised with steps leading up. It looked like a stage. In the middle, at the front of the rostrum, was a pulpit equipped with a microphone for a public address system. On each side of the pulpit, were three rows of benches. On the left-hand side was an organ. Up and behind the pulpit were six very long rows of benches, and behind them was a huge stained glass window, in the shape of the Star of David. A picture of Jesse and Irene hung on the wall close to the window.

Behind the pulpit and benches and on the left were two huge dining rooms with lots of tables and chairs. Past the dining room was a restaurant-style kitchen. At the right of the steps was a door leading to the church offices and the council room. Outside, there were exit doors with a carport overhead where the Pratt family parked, and the parking lot was paved.[13]

3

Early in the 1960s, Jesse made several property transactions which proved beneficial for the church but ended up proving to be even more beneficial for the Pratt family. In 1961 Jesse bought a 1,000-acre ranch in Bouse, Arizona, for 1.1 million dollars for the Church.[14] The original owner was from San Francisco.[15] It was supposed to be a money-maker for the Church, and Jesse said that he planned to build a retirement home on the ranch. A group of members were sent to work on this ranch to grow and pick cotton and soybeans, as well as taking care of the cattle. The members lived in small, poorly built sheds made of wood. Jesse's brother Herbert ran the ranch and served as the Union Assembly pastor.[16] At one point, Jesse and his brother Herbert took out a loan to buy cattle. This act would later cause major problems for Herbert of which will be discussed in a later chapter.

On April 11, 1961, the Church of God of the Union Assembly transferred eleven tracts of land—4,000 total acres—to Jesse F. Pratt.[17] Then on February 17, 1962, the same eleven tracts were transferred from Jesse Pratt back to the Church.[18] On September 28, 1962, the Church of God of the Union Assembly transferred the same property to Ranches Inc.[19] The president of Ranches Inc. was Harold Sowder, who was the financial adviser for the Church. The secretary who signed the deed for Ranches Inc. was an attorney from Summerville, Georgia. In a rather convoluted way, the Church transferred its own property to Ranches Inc., which was owned by members of the Church of God of the Union Assembly—and specifically the Pratt family. Records show the property was transferred intact the last time from

Ranches Inc. to Jesse F. Pratt Sr. and Archie Winkler on January 28, 1963.[20] A summation of those properties conveyed in Whitfield and Murray Counties, Georgia can be found in the endnotes.[21]

A grand total of 4,000 acres of property in Whitfield and Murray Counties, Georgia, owned by the Church of God of the Union Assembly free and clear of any debt, were transferred to Jesse and Archie Winkler in 1962. This was not all the property that the Church owned in Whitfield County and Murray County at that time. They owned property and businesses around Union City. Moreover, interviews suggest that the Church was the largest land holder in Whitfield County at this time other than the United States Government. But it did not stop here. As stated by former members, there were even more farms and home-places to be turned over to the Church by the membership.

Informants said that Jesse continued along the path of his father by reminding his poor followers that they needed to give all they had to the Lord. If the poor were going to inherit the earth, as Jesse always argued in his sermons, then the parishioners of the Church of God of the Union Assembly were going to get their share.[22] What about the Pratt family? One man interviewed said, "I guess the Pratts were God's bankers."

On March 21, 1963, Jesse Pratt deeded three tracts of land, including businesses, to the church that were on 41 Highway. These included Pearl's Truck Stop and Restaurant, the Union City Oil Company, Bulk Plant Division, and Nix's Truck Stop. The IRS may have noticed these property movements inside the Union Assembly, because in April 11, 1963 the IRS came down hard on the Church of God of the Union Assembly.[23] The IRS determined that the church had not reported the property given to them during 1959, 1960, and 1961 as income; in addition, the profit made in all the Church-owned businesses had not been reported as income. The IRS assessed the church $58,066.11 for 1959, $67,035.78 for 1960, and $83,797.88 for 1961 for unpaid back taxes. The total amount of the assessments owed to the IRS by the Church of God of the Union Assembly came to $208,899.77. Therefore the IRS put a tax lien against several tracts of land owned by the Church. Much of this land had been donated by Lawrence H. Underwood, as well as P. Parsons and Owen Hill. The Church of God of the Union Assembly settled with the IRS, but the Church lost some of the property it had acquired through gifts.[24]

On December 13, 1965, Jesse borrowed $262,874.00 from Oregon-based company, Continental Service Corporation. The properties on 41 Highway in Whitfield County were given as collateral. The Church's monthly payment on the loan was $1,840.12. It was reported by two men interviewed that sometime during the mid-1960s, a representative for the Church approached a group of wealthy businessmen in Dalton and offered to sell them a number of farms owned by the Church of God of the Union Assembly. One person interviewed said the deal included 3 farms, while another said 5 farms. The businessmen told the Union Assembly representative that they would discuss the offer and get back to the Church, and that they needed to see all of the property. But the representative told these men that the deal was only for that day. The asking price is not known, but it must have been way below the estimated value or appraisal. They rented a helicopter and flew over the property on Friday. One farm was partly in Murray County and partly in Whitfield County, Georgia. One piece of property was the Prater's Mill Farm in North Whitfield County, which is now owned by Whitfield County and is used for the well-known Prater's Mill Crafts Fair.

The men decided to buy the property that day, but both the Whitfield and Murray County courthouses, where the deeds would have to be transferred, had closed. They arranged to open the courthouses on a Saturday, and the property was transferred to different businessmen. In a few transactions, the buyers had to pay off the loan that was on the property and county back taxes, but the Union Assembly did receive some cash. It was reported that, before the sale, officials at the IRS had informed the Church that they would seize this property for nonpayment of federal income taxes. On the following Monday, representatives from the IRS came to Dalton to seize the Union Assembly property, but they were too late. Nothing was particularly illegal about these land sales, but the Church still owed the back taxes.[25]

This transaction likely happened on Friday, April 26, 1966, because Deed Book 44, page 293, in Whitfield County, Georgia, Court House shows where three wealth businessmen in Dalton bought 444 acres from Jesse Pratt Sr. and Archie Winkler for ten dollars plus assuming the indebtedness on the property.[26] Also, about this same time, Jesse sold the Prater's Mill property of 410 acres to a wealthy Dalton business.

Jesse's wide-ranging property transactions continued in other parts of the country. In 1966 Jesse expanded the Arizona property to 12,400 acres, and he also bought a huge cattle ranch near Texarkana, Texas. Those interviewed said he talked thousands of members into payments of $2,000 each toward the Arizona property. Some members gave more. Jesse also invested almost 3 million dollars in improvements to irrigate the desert farm property.[27] To raise all of this capital, Jesse again went among the members selling them on the idea that the church would build a retirement home on this ranch in Arizona so that aging members would have a place to retire plus a place to attend conventions.[28]

When Jesse needed refinancing of 1.3 million dollars, he again sought the money from Continental Service Corporation in Portland, Oregon. To achieve this refinancing in 1966, the church members needed to provide roughly $600,000 cash. Church members were to subscribe to a twenty-five-year certificate through the Church Service Program and members contributing their hard-earned money or borrowed funds who died were to be repaid by the Church to their estates. Unfortunately, the Continental Service Corporation went bankrupt after taking over the ranch financing. The Oregon financing was arranged based on selling $1,000 certificates that would pay back $1,500 upon maturity to a member holding one.[29] Few would ever get a return on their investment.

4

During the mid-1960s, to earn additional income, Jesse would visit other churches outside of Dalton to hold revivals. Former members interviewed said he always had a group of men around him, and that it would be hard for a common member to get close to Jesse. They identified the majority of these men who protected Jesse as his relatives, such as his nephew Jesse W. Hughes—called J. W.—who was well over six feet tall and weighed about 300 pounds. J. W. was the son of Jesse's sister, Flora, who had married Winston "Tobe" Hughes. It was stated by interviewees that during Jesse's time as moderator there were members severely rebuked inside the Church—some almost died because of these thrashings.[30]

Everyone in church knew there were stories of how Jesse could cast spells on a person and they would die. Once, before C. T. was kicked out of the Church, he sold a house on Dug Gap Road, which is in South Whitfield County, Georgia. Tobe Hughes, C. T. Pratt's son-in-law who dealt in real estate, told C. T. that he had sold the house way too cheap. Jesse was there with them when Tobe said he "didn't get near enough money for that." C. T. told Tobe "well in the long run with this other property, I'm selling it for that price to set up selling the other." Tobe repeated, "No, you sold that way too cheap." Jesse intervened against his own brother-in-law and said, "Bless God, you're gonna die for what you did—crossing my daddy." It was only a short time after this incident when Tobe died of stomach cancer.[31]

According to Pitner and also confirmed by Brenda Moore, Jesse was both insulated and protected from the Church's most common members, which allowed him to commit violent acts that would otherwise go unpunished. Following is a story told by Pitner to the author and confirmed by his brother, Otha Pitner Jr., during an interview: "Well—Jesse came up here right after Dad was removed as pastor in North Carolina for a revival and he was telling everybody that my dad had been telling lies. So I had heard about all I could stand, so after church I went to talk to Jesse. I figured they'd be a fight, so I had my brother Joe with me. With Jesse were Herbert, Wayman, Wesley Crider, and J. W. Hughes. They stood around us as me and Jesse talked. Once I disagreed with Jesse about my daddy being a liar, Wesley Crider got a hold of me before I could move. J. W. knocked me off the porch, and I hit the chain link fence that went around the church. I hit that fence so hard that it bent the top railing. J. W. Hughes threw my brother, Joe, over the fence. They started beating the hell out of me and Joe. I had a big belt on with a big buckle, and I had just enough room to get that belt off, and when I did, there in front of me was Herbert, so I whopped him a good one. Now, I like old Herbert. Well, they was backing us down Albertson Way. A neighbor over there yelled, 'Them holy rollers about to kill you?' I said, 'Yeah, call the law before they kill me.' They knocked my brother on his ass out in the middle of Albertson Way.

"We went home that night to our wives, and one said, 'I thought you'n were going to church.' We had our shirts torn off of us, we were bloody. I said, "We went to church." I want to tell you something, if there is a God in heaven, what I've told you is the truth. It is the truth. I'd take a lie detector test."[32]

Former member Charles Roberts said he even saw knives pulled on people in church. He also claimed to have witnessed several men beaten unconscious in church by ministers and family members of the Pratts. Roberts said that he has seen grown men picked up and thrown against walls so hard that they could not walk for days, and that he has seen men thrown out the door of the Church and told to never come back. During his interview, he added this observation: "There was a woman at the Church who use to sit back there in the back and pull her hair and beat herself in the neck and say, 'Kill 'em Lord, kill 'em, kill 'em Lord, kill' em.' She was talking about the Pratts. But she kept going to church there."

In addition to the beatings, Jesse engaged in ritual humiliation. Former members stated that it was awful once Jesse started the "confession train," when members would march in front of Jesse to confess their sins. The members were scared to death because they didn't know what Jesse might already know. Members started telling on one another when they knew someone had sinned or broken a church rule. Jesse acted like God was the one who told him about these people's transgressions. If a person had broken a rule and not confessed this to Jesse, then they would be rebuked severely—and no one wanted to be rebuked. Sometimes Jesse would rebuke someone for no known reason other than he had upset Jesse in some trivial way. One person said she had urinated in her pants standing in line because she was so frightened she would be rebuked, although she was not aware of breaking any church rules.[33]

These confessions took place in front of everyone present.. On one occasion, a young man confessed to Jesse that he'd had sex with someone out of wedlock. Jesse asked him if it was with someone outside of the Chruch or another member. The young man said he'd had sex with both—outside members and inside members. Jesse asked with whom had he fornicated with and the young man started pointing at women in the congregation and saying, "Her, her, and her, and that one hiding over there behind the bench." It was reported that some of these women were married women who were rebuked and then soon divorced.[34]

As mentioned previously, if a person was thrown out of the Church for some unknown reason, they were cut off from their family members and shunned. For example, one member's grandfather had been expelled from the Church at a tent revival in 1968. The member's grandmother left with her husband. The remaining family members were warned by Jesse that if they contacted their own grandparents they would be turned out and never allowed back. The poor grandfather lived for thirteen more years without ever seeing his son or grandchildren again. They did not go to the grandfather's funeral. The grandson, who is in his sixties now, still holds guilt in his heart for never seeing his grandfather or even his grandmother before they died. He is still extremely bitter about what was allowed to happen.

Fighting back tears in an interview, he said, "You cannot go back and relive life once the times has gone."[35]

By the 1960s and through the 1970s, Jesse controlled his community so thoroughly that interviewees reported that Jesse would dissolve marriages from the pulpit by simply pointing at a couple and saying, "This woman is no longer your wife." Then Jesse would point to another woman and say, "This woman is your wife now." To the man who had lost his wife, Jesse would occasionally give him another man's wife. Inevitably, during all this movement of spouses, some poor man or woman would be left without a spouse. If anyone refused to follow Jesse's orders, they would be rebuked. If the rebuking didn't work, they would be thrown out of the Church and that meant going to hell. The only way spouses could stay together after being ordered to divorce would be for both man and wife to leave the church. This happened occasionally, but according to the Church's eschatological precepts, if they wanted to stay out of hell, they had to follow Jesse's demands. Occasionally when the split-up of a family occurred, the Church gained the individual's property that was left behind.[36]

Occasionally, a spouse left the Church because he or she didn't follow Jesse's demands. As a result, Jesse would tell the remaining spouse who had not yet gotten a divorce, "I'd rather be in a bed with a rattlesnake, than in one with a dismissed member." It wasn't long until the ministers at the other Union Assembly Churches were doing and saying the same thing about dismissed members.[37]

Eric Smithey, whose grandparents had been members of the Union Assembly Church in Center, Georgia, said in an interview, "I can remember hearing my grandmother's baby sister telling how her Uncle Claud Knight, once he had left the Church, would stand outside the front door to the church in Center and say to the men as they walked inside, 'You better put your wife in your pocket or you're gonna lose her.'"

In 1959, one husband sued Johnny Burnett, a Union Assembly minister in Knoxville, Tennessee. According to the *Kokomo Tribune* newspaper, testimony at the divorce hearing revealed that the man's wife and children had been taken from the Knoxville Church to the church of Kokomo on one occasion when the trouble with the couple started. The husband testified that the minister, Burnett, from the Church of God of the Union Assembly in Knoxville, had broken up his home by encouraging his wife not to live with him after he had been "turned out of the church." The husband was awarded a divorce, and he later brought an alienation of affections suit against Minister Johnny Burnett and was awarded $12,000.[38]

A nonmember, who worked at a local funeral home and helped conduct services for deceased members of the Union Assembly, had this to report: "Many times during a funeral service, the preacher—usually Jesse or Jesse Junior—would verbally belittle and demean former members who had come to the funeral in the Church. They would try to force them into rejoining the church or leave. Some left, some stayed, and some rejoined the Church. A few stayed and took the verbal abuse.

Most of these former members were family members of the deceased. Many of these people would cry and bawl while being disparaged. It would not be uncommon for pushing and shoving between former members and members to happen after the service."

5

Jesse and Irene had six children together. In birth order, their names are Jesse Franklin Junior, Pamela Rena, Charlie Thomas III, Margaret Elizabeth, Johnnie Herbert, and Marty Lane. Jesse Junior had already become an ordained minister and learned to play the steel guitar—some said he played it better than his father, Jesse Senior. Jesse Junior started his own gospel singing group, called the Trailblazers Quartet. They traveled all over the United States singing and playing religious music.[39]

Late in 1966, the Vietnam conflict had escalated into a full-scale war. On August 7 of that year, seven U.S. planes were shot down, the most lost in one day to date in the Vietnam War. Some young men of the Church were drafted into the army and sent to Southeast Asia. More would follow.

Eight of C. T. Pratt's children. *Left to right, front*: Herbert, Wayman, Jesse; *middle*: Leola, Tiny, Flora; back: Edmond, Estle. Courtesy of Nell Belcher.

In August of that same year, C. T. Pratt fell ill. He had turned eighty-seven that month. Brother Pratt could no longer get out of bed. Jesse and his family went to visit him, and Jesse held him in his arms. C. T. was so weak he could not speak above a whisper, but he got to see his children, grandchildren, and great-grandchildren before he passed away.[40] One of C. T.'s old buddies and fellow founder of the Union Assembly, Rev. J. Willie Burnett, came to visit Reverend Pratt at his home. Burnett clasped hands with the feeble, elderly church founder, embraced him, and exchanged pleasant greetings. On September 12, 1966, C. T. Pratt—the man who would never die—died. Jesse asked Rev. Willie Burnett to say the last words over Brother Pratt.[41] Charlie Thomas "C. T." Pratt was buried in West Hill Cemetery next to Emory Street in Dalton, Georgia.[42] The lot was in the lowest section of the cemetery. C. T. had never purchased a burial plot for himself because he never planned on using one. There is no epitaph on his tombstone other than his name and his date of birth and death. Brother Pratt's wife, Minnie, would stay in their home at 219 Pine Hill Road in Dalton and have her daughter Flora Hughes move in with her. On December 4, 1971, Minnie died at the age of eighty-two.[43] She was buried next to the man she had married sixty-eight years before.

12

The Boss

"Nobody likes for a brother to act like he is a boss."

JESSE PRATT,
"Jesse Pratt Says," *The Southerner,* Jan. 1956, 3

1

After the death of C. T. in 1966, Jesse set himself up to be the only true God to his people. As the young men of America were sent to fight in the Vietnam War, Jesse took more control over the lives of his members. Interviews confirm that he demanded much more from members, and he made sure he received it—whether it was praise, worship, saluting him and his picture, or money. He and Irene dressed in the finest clothes and drove the finest cars. One pilot from the airport where some of the Church airplanes were located reported that Jesse came in sometimes wearing a fur coat. The title of National Moderator was changed to General Overseer. Two synonyms for OVERSEER are BOSS and SUPERVISOR. Ironically, Jesse F. Pratt was quoted in an article printed by *The Southerner: Voice of the People* in 1956: "Nobody likes for a brother to act like he is a boss."[1]

After C. T.'s death, Jesse did pay some respect to his father and mother by having a picture of them put up on the wall of all the Union Assembly Churches in the back, which faced the members as they entered the churches. In death C. T. and Minnie were able to rejoin the church. Of course, Jesse had his own picture with Irene placed on the same walls of the churches. In the picture, Jesse is holding an open Bible while a smiling Irene is on his right. In the Dalton Church, these pictures were placed on either side of a stained-glass window in the shape of the Star of David. It wasn't long until each sermon in all the churches was started by having the members stand and do military-type salutes to these pictures, and it wasn't long until C. T. and Minnie's picture was removed.

When interviewing former members Robert and Marie Anderson, they were asked if there were any pictures of Jesus in the Church. "No there were never any pictures of Jesus," said Robert. "They didn't even allow you to have a cross or to wear a cross or have a cross anywhere in the building. They preached against this and made fun of churches who had a steeple with a cross on it." Added Marie:, "We could not even take our Bible to church. I didn't even have my own Bible until 1997."[2] Both Robert and Marie were born in 1957.

Regarding the actual church service, another member, Johnnie Haney Butler, reported:

This portrait of Irene and Jesse was placed on the wall of every Union Assembly Church to be saluted by the membership at each service. Courtesy of Teresa Howard Coker.

As Brother Jesse and his family walked into the church, everyone stood up and began clapping. Brother Pratt stepped onto the rostrum with several men following behind. He sat at the end of the first bench on the right side of the pulpit. Brother Pratt was a tall, thin man with salt-and-pepper hair and dressed in a dark suit with a white shirt and a tie. He sat there quietly looking over the congregation. Then he nodded his head to the woman at the piano and she started playing. After everyone sang a few songs, Brother Pratt stood, went to the rostrum, and began speaking. He spoke slowly and quietly at first then built to a faster, louder, almost hollering sermon. By this point in the sermon the people began throwing their arms up and shouting loudly. Within minutes the shouting became so loud and continuous that I could only hear a word or two from Brother Pratt's preaching. I wondered how anyone knew what the preacher had said.[3]

Jesse expanded his father's pledge idea by having members of the Church commit to giving a certain amount of money—usually more than they could afford—and then Jesse would give them thirty days to come up with the cash. If necessary, the people were expected to go to a bank or a finance company and borrow the money on ninety-day notes. They preferred ninety-day notes because members might have to get another loan again soon. Jesse would tell the congregations the names of some of the people who had pledged a great deal of money and would ask them why they couldn't do the same. He created competition out of the pledges. If someone was unable to pay, Jesse would say that he had made this pledge to God, and if he didn't pay it, he was taking money from God. If a minister, who was expected to make the biggest pledges, didn't pay, he was dropped down to a deacon. If a deacon didn't pay, he was dropped to a mere member. If a member didn't pay, he or she were kicked out of the Church.[4] There were no women ministers so this only applied to men.

In addition, every time Jesse Senior, Irene, or one of their children had a birthday, they received money from every church that had taken up a "birthday collection" for them. This money was mailed to whichever person had a birthday. As one member said, "Pretty nice birthday gifts, wouldn't you say?"[5]

In 1964, while they were building the new church on Highway 41, Jesse pulled a ruse on some of his people. As interviews reveal, the Church owned eight to ten houses on Ezzard Avenue in Dalton, which were sold to members. The Church held the deeds to these houses because they had financed them for their members. The members made payments directly to the church office. Jesse announced to these people, "Don't come back down here to the office and pay any more house payments." Jesse said they had too much going on to mess with it now. A deacon by the name of Frank went to the bank and borrowed money to pay his house off. His wife was a secretary at the Church and kept up with some of the finances. Another man by the name of Clint kept going down to the office and making his house payments. The rest of the members didn't, and the Church foreclosed on all these houses. Frank proved he owned his house, and Clint had receipts indicating he had made his house payments, so these two men could not be moved out of their homes. But Jesse kicked them out of the Church because they had gone against Jesse's instructions—and had avoided foreclosure.[6] In other words, those who did follow Jesse's orders to not pay lost their homes, and those who did not and made their payments saved their homes but were kicked out of the Church.

It was reported that another fear tactic Jesse used involved enforcing punctuality. A former member reported: "If the Sunday night service was supposed to start at seven o'clock and Jesse decided to start preaching at six o'clock, then the doors were locked and no one was allowed inside. Anytime a member was late to any service, they were locked out of the building. Jesse didn't give them a five-minute window to get inside. Once he started preaching the doors were locked and stayed locked until he dismissed everyone. A late person who missed the service would probably find himself rebuked at the next service he or she attended. If anyone missed too much, they were kicked out of the Church."[7]

As a result, many members arrived very early to the services, in case Jesse wanted to begin before the announced hour. Robert Anderson reported the following: "People would be sitting there [in church] two or three hours before the service started so they could get them a seat. And they would just be sitting there crying—fearful—just scared to death. They would start crying just to show tears—so help me God. . . . That's the way they did him [Jesse]. It's like—if you did not have that fearful spirit they could detect you and call you out. They would scan the crowd, and they would know, and they would pick you out, and they would make a beeline toward you and you would become their victim. You had to show tears. Everyone was scared to death."[8]

Other preachers at other Union Assembly churches expected the same thing from their members, but if these ministers were in front of Jesse, they were also fearful. There was a pecking order, even in the Church.[9]

Jesse had other ways to intimidate his parishioners. One odd technique occurred in 1969 when a married man and his wife had gone on vacation and someone told Jesse that they had broken a church rule by swimming and lying out in the sun together. On a Sunday morning in front of a packed house at the Church, Jesse called this man and his wife to the front of the congregation and had them lie down together on their backs on the floor. Jesse then preached to them and belittled them for their sin against the Church and made them ask him and the entire church for forgiveness.[10] By having members directly ask the Church for forgiveness, was Jesse moving himself closer to the status of God?

Otherworldly powers were also bestowed on Jesse's sister Leola, who would speak in tongues. Jesse would stand next to her during services and say, "Speak on, Sister." She would then call someone's name and say they were not living right with the Lord, and Jesse would rebuke them. In some cases, Jesse would throw these men or women around, severely injuring them. While rebuking one particular woman at a service, Jesse's hands stuck to her head because she wore so much hairspray. Jesse actually yanked some of her hair out trying to get his hands free. After that, Jesse made women stop wearing hairspray and men hair tonic because it got all over his hands when he rebuked them.[11]

The rebuking was severe enough for members to seek revenge, even if it meant expulsion from the church. According to one member, a man who owned a fruit stand carried a knife with him and was going to kill Jesse if the latter rebuked him again on Sunday morning. (Jesse had rebuked him at Saturday night's service.) Brother Johnny Burnett, the pilot and good friend to Jesse who married Jesse to his first wife Ethel, got into an altercation with Jesse at a revival at the Knoxville church. When Jesse put his hands on Burnett's head to rebuke him, Burnett pushed Jesse away. Jesse said, "The revival is over." Then he left the building.[12]

A former minister, who believed Jesse to be bipolar, offered this unsolicited observation about his erratic behavior: "I didn't know Jesse was bipolar at the time, but I figured it out later. If we were sitting right here with him [Jesse], he'd think it was your fault the way he felt. He could be a 'Wildman' at times. He'd scream and holler at those poor people like he was about to kill them. They were scared to death of him. He was a wild man, abusive. He didn't have the spirit of love. He had a disease. Sometimes Jesse would be so kind you'd want to kiss his feet—the nicest guy you'd ever want to meet. But when that came over him, he'd think it was your fault—he'd be a WILD MAN—a wild man supposedly a man of God."[13]

Jesse would even rebuke his own son, at least according to an anonymous source who did business with Pratt and witnessed the event:

> It was about 1970 when I was building a house. I knew most of the Pratts because I flew in and out of the airport as a pilot, so when I told Jesse about my building, he asked me to use some of his members. One of the workers who did the sheet-rocking was his bastard son—a guy name Jimmy. [It was actually Jesse's son by his first wife.[14]]
>
> Jesse had vouched for Jimmy and told me that if he didn't do a good job to call him. Well, I had some 20-foot high ceilings and Jimmy made a mess, plus he left one of the bathtubs full of sheet rock mud—ruined the tub. So, I called Jesse and told him. The next thing I know Jesse comes to the house. He looks around and sees the mess made, and then he and some of the other workers take Jimmy over behind some trees and Jesse starts shaking him by the head and the other men started hitting him with rolled up paper. Jesse was screaming at Jimmy. Jimmy was a grown man, but his daddy rebuked him. At least that's what the other workers said was happening.[15]

Oddly, outside of church, Jesse could be a very pleasant person to be around and usually fit in with whomever his companions were, such as the group of pilots who "hung-out" at the airport. Even former member Don Pitner, who had lots of trouble with Jesse and the Church after his dad was kicked out, had this to say about

Jesse: "Back when I drank real heavy and I'd be at a bar and call him [Jesse], Irene would answer the phone and say, 'Who is this?' and I'd say, 'This is Don Pitner.' Then she'd say, 'He's eating supper.' Then Jesse would say, 'Irene, give me that phone.' Then he'd say, 'Son, what can I do for you?' He'd always talk to me—he never did not talk to me. You can't help but like them people. And, it's like you lost part of your family—that's all we knew—that's all we knew in the way of religion."[16]

2

Some former members remarked that Irene was able to manipulate Jesse for a while, thus curbing his destructive tendencies and behaviors. One member commented that "Irene was not only smarter than Jesse; she was extremely good at finessing people to get what she wanted."[17] It was presumed and reported in interviews that Jesse had control over Irene and she obeyed his orders, and, outwardly, no one saw her defying him, but former members stated that she was able to finagle what she wanted from Jesse, and later from her children, through her intelligent shrewdness. They believed she was much smarter than her husband and would provoke certain thoughts or ideas in his mind by planting her beliefs in his head.[18] However, some reported that although she worked behind the scenes to influence Jesse, he would sometimes grow tired of her manipulation. It is important to remember that Irene did give up her first three children to be Jesse's wife.

Not long after Jesse officially took over as general overseer and Dalton's minister, he told the people that the only way they could get to heaven was go to the Church of God of the Union Assembly. He didn't talk about salvation or believing in the resurrection of Jesus or the profession of faith as the way to heaven. It was all about going to the Church. Once someone asked Jesse if people who went to other churches had a chance on going to heaven, and he said yes, "but once you have heard us preach, you can't go anywhere else and go to heaven."[19] Jesse did mention Jesus, but he did not talk about Jesus being the way to heaven. One member said, "He [Jesse] was in competition with Jesus. He didn't want to talk much about Jesus. He wanted the members to believe in him."[20] This view was shared by others, including a former member, who believed Jesse's Holiness brand of religion was entirely self-serving. She sent the following email to the author: "My father and mother, as many THOUSANDS of churchgoers, worked until their fingers bled and GAVE, GAVE, GAVE to the church—gave so much they could barely feed their own families or pay for their home. While all this money went to 'the church,' it was actually going straight to THE PRATT family's pockets. They were the ones dressed in the finest clothes, wearing diamond rings, driving Cadillacs and Mercedes and living high-on-the-hog. All because of a multitude of poor, hungry, brainwashed people, thinking that was the way they were going to Heaven. We were taught there was NO other way. This was it. They worshipped Jesse Pratt as if he were Jesus himself. He could do no wrong."[21]

Evidence for membership devotion, even with the rebukings and ostracizing, was the size of the weekly offerings. It was reported that there may be several money offerings performed at a single service. They'd have a "good-will" offering on a particular project—building a new church in some town, or improvement to a particular church. They would even have an offering for the Pratt family. Jesse knew how much everyone was giving, because he sat there and watched the people put their money on the Bible or in the guitar case. If he felt like someone was not giving enough, Jesse would call them out in church. One former long-time member said this about the offering: "They stood my daddy up in 1970 and [Pratt] said he ain't giving any money in 1969 to that church. My daddy made $32,800.00 that year and gave $16,400 of it to the Church, and they stood him up and said he didn't give any money to the Church." The IRS called this person's father in for an audit for that year's taxes and when the IRS saw his proof of donations to the Church, they couldn't believe it.[22]

When certain members didn't give all they had to the Lord, Jesse might employ even more draconian methods of chastisement. A non-member reported that in the early 1970s he was working for Shaw Carpet in Dallas, Texas, selling carpet. He had a good customer from Denton, Texas, who had a wholesale outlet, and the company was doing well, selling lots of carpet. The owner and employees of the store in Denton were members of the Church of God of the Union Assembly. "A big fat man came to pick up the carpet and he would always sit on the desks of the good-looking women at our office and flirt with them. One day the fat man came in and said the outlet store was closing because Jesse Pratt was sending the owner to Fort Myers, Florida. The fat man said Jesse thought they were making too much money and not sending enough to the Church." That was the last time the Shaw salesman saw anyone from the outlet store.[23]

Some informants reported that Jesse would often take the entire check of some of the members and give them back what he thought they needed, which was usually barely enough to eliminate hunger. Not all members were made to participate in this—only the common members. The more elite members who had their own businesses were expected to share their profits with the Church.[24] After asking one of the former members how Jesse Pratt was able to collect so much money, he responded after a long pause:

> Huh, I got five or six different answers—I don't know which one to go with. But the whole thing was built on fear . . . not necessarily fear of God . . . huh . . . fear of Jesse. Because you can't get to God—forget Jesus Christ—he's not the intermediate, Jesse is. That's the way it was, you know—if it's me staying in good with Jesse or whatever it takes . . . huh . . . that's what they [members] are going to do. We are talking about airplanes too . . . you name it, you know. I've seen people give every dime they had and wonder how they were going to buy lunch for their kids . . . and the rest of the people . . . the Pratts . . . you know . . . are running around in

a Coupe Deville Cadillac, and that's their second car. You know, there is no psychiatrist in the world that can fumble through this. It would blow his mind in about 30 minutes.[25]

Although all Union Assembly churches had their own operating expenses, most of the money collected by the Union Assembly churches, no matter how far away, traveled to Dalton, Georgia during the 1960s and 70s. Indeed, it was the ministers' job at all fifty-plus churches to keep the money coming in and flowing to the Dalton Church—really directly to the Pratts. They were judged by the family on how much money they could produce and send to Dalton. Saving souls for the Lord seemed to be secondary in the mind of Jesse Pratt. He would even remove one of his own brothers from a church if he didn't make his weekly or monthly allotment. This happened with his brother Wayman, who was the pastor of the Atlanta church around 1972. "They might have told everybody they were dropped as minister for other reasons but it was for the money or the lack of money," recalled one member. "This happened to my daddy when he was a pastor."[26]

3

Female members of the church fared no better than the men under Jesse, as they, too, were singled out and treated poorly. As one informant put it, "The women who were members of the Church were treated like second-class citizens.[27] Although they were certainly not treated well under C. T., under Jesse their lives grew yet harsher. The women in all Union Assembly churches, not just the one in Dalton, were also forced to raise money for the Church. One particular idea arose that brought in the money. No one seems to know who came up with this "money-maker," but Irene's name came up often during interviews. Under Jesse, many women and children sold donuts on Saturdays from six in the morning until church services that night. The donuts were purchased from the Krispy Kreme Bakery in Chattanooga, and brought to Dalton in station wagons for the children and women to sell.

Another female member had this to say about growing up as a woman in the Church:

> Being raised where you cannot wear normal clothes like your other friends at school, cannot cut your hair, wear makeup, do normal things like going to a ballgame or a movie—was an awful way to grow up. You were made fun of, ridiculed, bullied at school. Women WERE treated badly at that church. They were supposed to keep silent in the church and be obedient to their husbands, SLAVES if you will. Women could not even go outside of their home without pantyhose on. If you were caught not wearing pantyhose in town, you would be rebuked and brought out before all at the next church service. It was a pretty hard life, but again, everyone was taught that THIS was THE WAY; the only way to Heaven. We were the chosen ones, and Jesse Pratt was the MAN OF GOD that would lead us all to heaven.[28]

The Pratt family also used women as servants in their home. These women lived in the home with the family and were not paid, but expected to clean, cook, and be there waiting on the family. A former Dalton member reported that she was brought to live with the Pratt family as a young girl and worked and lived with Irene.[29] Another member recalled that two women lived with Irene for years and "did all the laundry, housecleaning, cooking, and ironing—everything hand and foot for the Pratts."[30] "Of course, the women of the Pratt family were treated like royalty—most of them," added another informant.[31]

Some members said that some Union Assembly women were little more than slaves as Jesse drove them deeper and deeper towards being totally under his control. Former member Sue Haney Johnson told the following story about her life growing up in the church during that period: "I was young when we moved from Center to Dalton. In Dalton, we lived behind the A & W Root Beer stand on Goodwill Drive. They call that area 'Union City' because many of the Union Assembly Church businesses were in that area. Also, a lot of members lived in that neighborhood." Although I seldom ask my informants leading questions, with Sue I made an exception, as I knew her mother had died while a member of the Church.

"Sue," I asked bluntly, "can you tell me the story of how your mother died?"

Sue thought a minute and then said, "First there was something else that happened before she died that took me years, years, and years to get over. I'm not sure that I'm over it yet."

I waited in silence for a long moment and finally said to Sue, "Do you want to tell me about it?"

"Yes I do. I was—I was—maybe—maybe fourteen-years-old when I quit school and started working at the church laundry—right next to the slaughterhouse."

"How much did the Church pay you to work for them?"

"Nothing! We were just supposed to do it for the Church. On Saturdays I worked twelve to fourteen hours at Pratt's grocery store and never got a dime—and that's after working at the dry cleaners all week. Our house was only a few feet from the slaughterhouse. One day when I went home to get a break from the dry cleaners and laundry—of course the cleaners belonged to the Pratts, too. I went home to get me some water and take a break. So this one time, well, to start with I found this big old black spider—plastic spider in the yard that the kids had been playing with. So when I went in to get a drink of water I put the plastic black spider on the sink. Then my mother came along, and all of a sudden she started screaming. And I went into the kitchen to see what was wrong, and she screamed, 'That spider right there! Who put that spider right there? Did you put it there?' I said 'I did. I was playing with it and just put it on the sink there, why?' After I told her that, she slapped my face so hard I almost fell down, and she said, 'You get back to work!'"

Sue took a long breath and continued, "Well, about a month later, I came home to take a break and there were people in the house. And my Aunt Jesse Bee—Aunt

Johnnie and Sue Haney's mother,
Margie Lewis Haney.
Courtesy of Johnnie Haney Butler.

Bee was my mother's sister—I said to her, 'What's going on— what's going on?'
Aunt Bee said, 'You just go back to work.' And I said, No, what is it?' And Aunt Bee
said, 'Your mama just had a [stillborn] baby.' And I said, 'What! I didn't know she
was pregnant.' And Aunt Bee said, 'You marked that baby with that black spider. It
was born black. It didn't even have no bones inside its body or nothing.' You know,
I never did see that baby—never seen it, so I don't know what it looked like."

Tears formed in Sue's eyes and ran down her cheek. "You know, I never got
over that. I am seventy-three and I still ain't got over what I did to my momma or
happened to me because of that church."

I asked, "When did you stop going to the Union Assembly?"

Sue said, "I left the church when I got married at age fifteen. We were not allowed to marry anyone who was not a member of the Church, so I had to leave
when I married an outsider. I went years without seeing my family."

13

The Root of All Evil

"The trouble with a lot of men is that they love money—
even as a bunch of hogs—more than they love people."

JESSE PRATT
"Jesse Pratt Says," *The Southerner,* 4

1

Evidence shows that Jesse loved to spend money—other people's money—God's money, as his daddy had called it. Of course, all the Pratt leaders called it the Church's money and that everything, including the money, belonged to the Church. However, a human had to be in control. How can a building spend money? Jesse had expensive hobbies. He liked to buy and fly airplanes. At one point in the late 1960s the Church—really Jesse—owned between 8 and 10 airplanes. The two largest were a DC-3 and a Convair, which held up to 52 passengers. These larger planes could have been bought relatively cheap, going for a couple of hundred thousand back in the '70s, because there was a surplus of them. The DC-3 and Convair were being replaced by faster jets. Nevertheless, these large airplanes were very expensive to operate, especially the Convair, which burned 80 to 90 gallons of fuel per hour in each engine. That would be a total of 160 to 180 gallons burned per hour of flight. In 1970 that would be about $1.70 per gallon for aviation fuel at 160 g/h equals $270 per hour to fly and that is if it is only 80 gallons and not 90 gallons per hour. Further, the round engines on the Convair required expensive maintenance just to keep them flying. The smallest airplane the Church owned was a Luscombe. The Church also operated two Cessna 152s, one Cessna 172, and two Cessna 182s. The Church had two Cessna Skymasters as well, the so-called push-pull airplane. It also owned three twin-engine Aero Commanders, a 680, a 560, and later they traded one of the Aero Commanders for a Turbo Commander.[1]

The Pratts were known to have had all of these airplanes during the late 1960s through the 1980s. They may not have had them all at one time, but they may also have had more. Most of these airplanes were kept in Gaston, Alabama, even though the Church owned a large hangar at the north end of the Dalton Airport. The Aero Commander stayed in Dalton, along with the smaller Cessna 152s, 172, and 182s, and occasionally the Skymaster. The big DC-3 only came to Dalton a few times in order to pick up a large group of people. No Church pilot interviewed remembered seeing the Convair in Dalton. It flew into nearby Chattanooga, Tennessee—30 miles north of Dalton.

Once in the early 1970s as college students started protesting the Vietnam War, Jesse informed his parishioners that he had to have a new Aero Commander. This was a very expensive airplane that used two gas turbine engines. According to one of the church pilots, and several former members, Jesse had about a hundred of the Church members come to the airport in Dalton to see it while it was for sale. Then he asked them and the other members of the Church during services to donate $1,000 each to buy the airplane. He told them they could ride on it anytime they wished. He received lots of money, but it was not enough to buy the plane, so he borrowed the rest of the money from the bank and got his Aero Commander.[2]

The pilots at the Dalton Airport called Jesse's collection of planes "God's Air Force."[3] Of course, these airplanes were utilized. Almost every Monday morning, some of these planes came into Dalton from some of the 54 churches, some as far away as Ohio, Indiana, and Texas, to bring the money collected at Saturday and Sunday services and other services during that week. A bag man waited at the airport to take the money directly to a bank in Dalton to be counted and deposited.[4]

In addition to flying planes, Jesse also liked other more mundane activities, but the airplanes were usually involved in these activities. At the ranch near Bouse, Arizona, Jesse would ride in the back of a pickup truck and hunt jackrabbits and rattlesnakes with pistols. Jesse hunted all kinds of wild game there too, and had hunting trophies scattered around in his home, office, and other buildings. He loved to form hunting parties with members and non-members, including bankers with whom he dealt with in business affairs. In the bigger airplanes, Jesse would fly non-members whom he did business with to the Arizona ranch to hunt.[5]

2

Why did these Church of God of the Union Assembly members allow this man and his family to take so much from them and create a life of hardship all in the name of God? This question may ultimately be unfathomable to outside observers of this community, but some aspects can be explored, if not partially answered. By the time Jesse and then Jesse Jr. assumed leadership, during the mid-1960s and early 1970s, 99 percent of these members were third-generation members of the Church. Among groups that are commonly referred to as cults or sects, it is unusual for the community to outlast the death of its original leader. Imagine a child being brought up to believe that the Pratt family knew all the answers regarding the route to heaven. And many members saw the Pratts as Gods themselves. Moreover, independent thinking and even a remote dissent from what Jesse taught were met with force. Members were taught that if they did not follow the Church rules, they would be driven out of the Church and essentially out of the only family they had known. Many former members interviewed reported that when they were called to come forward to the altar to face Jesse's wrath, they would break out into uncontrollable sobbing, and become disoriented, a feeling of being completely lost and alone. Of course they were certainly lost and alone at the altar.

Some members never accepted the fact that their religious views were the result of socialization, indoctrination, or that they might simply be wrong. Most refuse to accept it even today. Former member Robert Anderson used the following metaphor to explain why he had not left the Union Assembly earlier: "If you hold a book up close to your face—say two inches—you can't read a word of that book—you don't know what's going on. But if you hold that book away from you so your eyes can focus on it, you can see the words, and you know what's going on. That's the same way with the Church. If you're in it, you are too close and can't see what is really going on."

Another member explained there was and may still be a hierarchy in the Church with some followers considered commoners and others considered the higher echelon, but none outside the Pratt family were part of the "seed" or "seed-seed."[6] The Pratts called it the "seed" because C. T. Pratt taught that he came from the seed of Abraham. The "seed-seed" were C. T.'s daughters and their families because once the daughters married they lost the Pratt name.[7] There was never a good explanation to explain why the Pratt family used this connotation other than to separate the Pratt family from all other members. This set the hierarchy of the Church into four distinct levels—"seed," "seed-seed," "higher echelon," members, and "commoner" members. According to interviews, the commoners and the higher echelon were used in one way or the other by the Pratt family. According to a former member interviewed who said his family came from the higher echelon: "A member's status in the Church was all about the money and how much they gave to God—or the

Jesse and Irene Pratt.
Courtesy of Nell Belcher.

family of God."[8] The Church's strata is similar to a pyramid in that the majority of the members—commoners—were at the bottom, the higher echelon were even fewer but never as few as the members of the Pratt family—seed-seed—who did not have the Pratt name, and then on top of the pyramid were the very few Pratt family members who carried the family name. Each group had its own function in the Church.

A great example of how Jesse controlled his membership through fear took place during his sermon on Sunday, November 24, 1963—two days after President John F. Kennedy was gunned down in Dallas, Texas. Jesse had always preached against President Kennedy because JFK was a Catholic, and Jesse had a hatred for the Catholic religion. Former member Charles Roberts added, "Jesse hated any religion that wasn't the Church of God of the Union Assembly." But on that Sunday while the United States mourned the death of its president, Jesse said this about the horrible tragedy: "I cut off his head with the sword of the spirit." In other words, Jesse claimed to have killed John F. Kennedy by the power of his prayers. "But," according to Roberts, who related this story, "that is not the worst of it—the worst of it took place when the people, believing that Jesse had this godly power, rejoiced over the death of their president with shouts of 'amen.' I thought, if Jesse has this much power to kill the President of the United States, then what can he do to me?"[9]

3

Once fear was implanted in the members' minds, it was almost impossible to be fully eliminated no matter how much time passed. A few former members flatly refused to be interviewed on the grounds that it was too horrifying for them to go back to those times in their mind. Some of the people who agreed to be interviewed had been out of the Church for thirty, forty, even fifty years, but still had trouble talking about what they experienced. Some even broke down and cried. They often said their mental state would swing from extreme sadness to extreme anger, which sometimes included screaming about the abuse by the authorities of the Church. On several occasions, former members interviewed showed signs of guilt when I contacted them for a follow-up interview or asked them to answer a few additional questions. The tension and worry that came after they reflected upon what they had said earlier was clear. However, when I asked if what they had professed in their earlier interview was true, they emphatically said that it was and then usually added more information.

It seems clear that these Union Assembly members who felt guilt during interviews were programmed not to discuss the happenings in the Church, so when they were kicked out or just left on their own, they had internalized the Church commandment—keep your mouth shut or suffer hell's fire. Some of these former members were still afraid for their real names to be used, even though they had been out of the Church for decades and had no family members still in the group. One sixty-nine-year-old informant has this to say about the permanent impact of the Church on its members, particularly those who left: "The funny thing about it—I was never part of the Church and the people I knew were in the church because we lived in the same neighborhood. I don't like going down there to the Church, but for a funeral, if I have to, I'll go. But my wife, she grew up there, and she's terrified when she walks in there. She hangs on to me, and we went in there because I was friends with all those boys and walked straight out of that church down there. And my wife says, 'Get me out of here.'"[10]

A Kokomo, Indiana resident, who was in his mid-seventies, said this about leaving the Church: "At age twenty-five, I moved out to California with my wife and two sons for a while, and then moved back here. We were in and out of different churches. I just could not get over what happened while I was a member of the Union Assembly. I got to drinking pretty heavy . . . and the end results, was we got a divorce. We had three children during that time. Then I moved to Texas and got involved with a Baptist church out there, and I talked to the minister a lot about what had happened at the Church. That minister spent a lot of time with me and helped me see the way of the Lord, and God opened my eyes. It was like you turned a light switch on and off. I moved back to Kokomo. My wife and I are still divorced but we see each other a least once a week."[11]

A woman who went to the Hamilton, Ohio, Union Assembly Church during the 1980s said this about the power of its minister, Dan Helmick: "Dan's control even stretched to everyone's life as far as imposing a curfew on us. He would call around to our houses and make sure we were home. If any of the church people were at our house, they would have to be quiet when you were on the phone with Dan so that he wouldn't know they were there. He would get very jealous if you visited any church member other than him. If he found out you did, you would get in trouble for not wanting to go to the 'man of God's' house. That is what he called himself.

"He went so far as forcing all the women to wear a hat on Easter whether you wanted to or not because 'Mother' [Irene Pratt] did. Vivian [Dan's wife] brought a bunch of ugly hats for women to put on if they weren't wearing one. If you didn't put one on, then you got rebuked by Dan—your head shaken—for not being obedient ... I have put things out of my mind for a long time. I have had to go to therapy to try to come to terms with what my life was like. It is hard to not have that fear in the back of your mind all the time and worry that everything you do is wrong."[12]

It is easy to see how these former members became psychiatric casualties. From what I have heard, they lived through hell much of the time while members of the Church, especially from the 1960s through 1995. Every former member interviewed stated that being a member of the Union Assembly damaged them mentally—every single one.

An interview with a former Union Assembly minister's wife in her sixties summed up this damage succinctly: "There is still that little bit of fear because we were raised to be careful of what you think—you better be careful what you say—you better not say anything about the family—the Pratts—they were called 'the Family.' There is still that little bit of fear when I talk, you know what I mean. But I've been gone twenty years and it was pretty much a horror story. At the time you thought you had to live that way because I was raised that way—raised that way until I got out at age 39."[13]

14

The Wages of Sin Is Death

"You are not worth a dime to any church or union
until you get to where you can stand the fire."

JESSE PRATT
"Jesse Pratt Says," *The Southerner,* 4

1

The late 1960s and early 1970s were turbulent times for the world, the United States, and the Pratt family. The Vietnam conflict became visible, if not relevant, to most Americans by 1965. Martin Luther King Jr., led the Selma to Montgomery Voting Rights marches in the spring of 1965, when violence erupted and the savagery was shown on national TV. Race riots raged in Watts, a Los Angeles neighborhood for five days in August of 1965, leaving 34 dead. And Bob Dylan's hit song "The Times They Are A-Changing" became the protest anthem that stirred the conscience of millions of Americans.

By 1967, the Vietnam conflict had escalated into a full-blown war with American soldiers dying daily. The local draft boards had cranked up, causing many more young men to be called to serve their country in a cause that many questioned.

Many young men who belonged to the Church of God of the Union Assembly found themselves drafted or about to be drafted into the military, and one of them was Jesse F. Pratt, Junior, the oldest son between the union of Jesse and Irene Pratt. Jesse Junior had quit high school before graduating and had begun his career to become an ordained minister like his daddy, uncles, half-brothers, and about every other grown man in his family.

The rules of the Church forbade all members from taking up arms and going to war because the commandment of God, "Thou Shalt Not Kill" was taken literally. However, members were allowed to serve their country as a soldier any way they could except by doing violence to any man.[1] But Jesse Pratt Jr., who had run away from home several times while in his teens, talked his father, Jesse Pratt Sr., into signing the paper allowing him to serve in the US Army. After training, Jesse Junior was sent to serve in Germany even though the war was raging in Vietnam. It wasn't long after his arrival there that rumors started spreading like a tidal wave throughout the congregation that Jesse Junior was in trouble. Some members heard that he had killed and robbed a man and was on the run—even found hiding in a local barn to escape capture. The consistent rumor was that Jesse Junior had taken a sock and filled it with rocks and used it to hit a sleeping man in the head and then stole twenty dollars from his victim. Some said the man had died, but one of Jesse Junior's cousins reported in an interview that Jesse had only mugged the man and stole his money.[2]

Jesse F. Pratt Jr.'s service record, which was obtained by the author under the Freedom of Information Act, lists his duty status as simply discharged. He was a private when he was dismissed from Fort Dix, New Jersey, on January 4, 1968—two years and nine months after entering the Army on April 28, 1965. Fort Dix was and is still the largest Federal Correctional Institute in the United States housing military personnel.[3] Also, Jesse Junior's Record of Assignments shows his actual duties. He was a Security Guard for six months, and an Ammo Helper until July 27, 1967. During this time Jesse Junior was stationed in Europe. After the July 27, 1967, date, Jesse F. Pratt Jr. had no Duty MOS (Military Occupational Specialty Code) listed, which is highly unusual. He also had no Principal Duty listed on his records during this time, but had been transferred back to the United States as his station and theater chart reads: Sp Proc Det Sp TRPS USAG. (The USAG stands for United States Army Garrison). He was released from Fort Dix on January 4, 1968. This report had "blacked-out" or redacted his conduct and efficiency records for some unknown reason.[4] Even though this is not proof of Jesse's actions, it does show that Jesse could have been in Fort Dix's Federal Prison. The service record indicates that there is certainly some evidence that, at the very least, Jesse Jr. had an unusual time in the military because of the redacted conduct and efficiency records, no mention of his duties for four months, and his discharge not being listed as Honorable or anyway other than simply "discharged." Too many people

US Army photograph of Jesse F. Pratt Jr.
Courtesy of US Army.

who were interviewed reported on this incident for there not to be some truth to Jesse Junior's misconduct.

2

Between the 1960s and 1970s, the Church of God of the Union Assembly sent approximately fifty families from their different churches to Bouse, Arizona, to live and work on their 2,000-acre ranch and farm there. At one time, there were around four hundred people present—although no one remembers the exact head count because it was always changing. The farm or ranch was situated a few miles south of Bouse in a little crossroads called Utting, which was not far from the Colorado River and less than thirty miles east of the California state line[5]

The landscape surrounding Bouse, Arizona is basically flat with sparse, low-growing vegetation, but deep canyons cut through the dry, arid terrain closer to the river. Like most desert environments, the area vegetation is dominated by cacti and chaparral, with few trees or arable land. Nevertheless, the ranch created a great location for one of Jesse's favorite sporting activities, riding with a group in the back of a truck and shooting jackrabbits with a pistol. When traveling to Bouse, the members would fly into either Parker's Avi Suquilla Airport or Phoenix's PHX Airport in Union Assembly's large-passenger Convair or DC-3 airplane.

The alfalfa produced on the ranch was sold to dairy farms in Arizona and California, and they were able to make three or four cuttings annually. The first three cuttings—a green chop—went to a dairy, while summer hay from June through August went to the horse market. September and October cuttings were also bound for dairies. By using church members for labor, the Church saw a profit from their Arizona ranch.

On the Arizona ranch the one large building was used for church services and other gatherings. The families lived in tiny wooden homes made out of redwood. They were poorly constructed and not much better than shanties. The redwood houses were described by a person living there at the time, "They were not nice. You could see the chickens through the cracks in the floor or the birds flying through the holes in the ceiling."[6] Common visitors included tarantulas and scorpions, which crawled through the cracks in the floor. Western Diamondback and Sidewinder rattlesnakes occasionally slithered through the gaps in the floor for a short stop-over. Since the members were not allowed to use medical services, a bite could be deadly. It was reported by a woman who lived on the ranch for several years that a member's boy between seven and ten was killed from the bite of a rattlesnake.[7]

Everyone worked—men, women, and children. Since they were paid fifty cents an hour and then had to give their wages back to the Church, and some men worked at other jobs as far away as California to make ends meet. Some of that outside money was also given to the Church. "It was slave labor, pure and simple," said one former workhand at the ranch. They called their way of living a "communal life" because they shared everything collectively, including labor, chores, food, expenses, trucks, equipment, and childrearing. "You name it we shared it," said the member.[8] It was rumored that even some of the women were shared by husbands. Fact, rumor or gossip, the allegations of wife-swapping reached all the way back to Dalton and to other Union Assembly churches. The speculation is still talked about even today—forty-five years later.[9] The swapping of spouses in Arizona may have been similar to what was reported in the other Union Assembly churches when pastors, especially Jesse, directed the exchanging of spouses.

Herbert Hoover Pratt, Jesse's younger brother, also lived on the ranch and served as the pastor, general overseer, and on-site family member. A former member who lived on the ranch in Arizona reported Herbert Pratt was the main instigator and participant in the wife-swapping activities. "Many women felt it an honor to sleep with one of the Pratt men," said one former member, "and a woman that wouldn't normally do that with someone other than her husband would be led to having this adulterous sex with one of the Pratts, and sometimes their husbands would also consent to this happening."[10] One interviewee indicated that a male member even lost his arm in an accident at the ranch. Herbert apparently told the man not to worry about his incapacitating injury, for he would take care of the man's wife for him, which seemed to ultimately resolve the matter. As a former member reported, "Herbert was good to his word."[11]

Herbert Pratt was in his mid-forties when he ran the ranch in Arizona. He was considered a good-looking man by some of the women interviewed. He stood about five-ten and was slim as a young man, but became thicker and heavier as he aged. He had sharp features with a thin nose and square jaw. His hands were thick and callused from laying block and brick as a young man. While at the ranch, however, Herbert did not do manual labor. He sent the money produced on the ranch back to his brother, Jesse, in Dalton. Herbert Pratt's roles were preaching, singing, and simply being the Pratt in charge at the ranch. Several people interviewed said that Herbert was as honest as the day was long when it came to taking care of money. "You could count on him paying off his debts," said a cousin and present member. Another relative added that "My uncle [Herbert] was a fine man, he just got done wrong by Irene and Jesse Junior." Others were less complimentary, particularly former Church members, who stated, "Herbert was honest with money, but I wouldn't trust him around my wife."[12]

At this time the Church also had a 790-acre farm in east Texas for growing cotton. The farm, which located near Texarkana, also used church members as laborers. In both places, members were told they were working for God, and all profits would supposedly go into a communal fund to be given back out to the workers in the form of housing and food. The rest of the money was sent back to Dalton, reportedly to go into the Church of God of the Union Assembly's communal fund.

Paul Hughes with Jesse Pratt. Courtesy of an anonymous family member.

Under Jesse's direction, most of the money was put into bank security deposits, but he also purchased more land and paid down bank loans. By the beginning of the 1970s, the Church had millions of dollars in liquid assets and still owned almost one-fourth of Whitfield County in Georgia.[13] The Union Assembly had obtained 133 deeds to property by 1970 just in Whitfield and Murray Counties.[14]

On May 18, 1970, National Guardsmen fired into a crowd of Kent State University students protesting the Vietnam War, killing two women and two men and wounding eight others. This event angered the majority of Americans who tried to comprehend the cause of such a tragedy. Soon protest against the war sprang up across the country and even in Europe. The Union Assembly still had sons serving in Vietnam. Those interviewed said that Jesse Sr. appeared to be upset with Jesse Junior for abandoning his duties and even belittled him at times during sermons.[15]

In the early 1970s, Jesse and Herbert bought a large herd of cattle—at least a thousand. The brothers took out a loan on the cattle for their purchase—the cattle being the collateral. They were engaging in a risky financial transaction called speculation, and they hoped to profit from the fluctuations in the price of cattle. Jesse planned to sell the cattle when the prices rose to a favorable level, and with that money he would pay off the loan. In just a few years, through bizarre circumstances in the Pratt family, this financial deal would cause Herbert to spend time in prison.

3

It is not unusual for a funeral home to receive a phone call during the middle of the night. Death comes at any hour, so when the phone rang at the Smith's Funeral Home[16] in Dalton, Georgia, about one in the morning, no one thought much about it. It was March 15, 1972. The caller identified himself as an employee of the Chattanooga airport. He said they had received a message from the pilot of a twin-engine Convair airplane, which had departed from Bouse, Arizona, and was in route to Chattanooga Metropolitan Airport, also known as Lovell Field. The man on the phone said the pilot had contacted them while he was over Arkansas and asked them to call this particular funeral home. The pilot instructed the airport to have a hearse from their funeral home come to the Church of God Union Assembly's hangar between four and five o'clock that morning.

Tim and Ralph,[17] who were on call at the funeral home that night, left Dalton on Interstate 75, drove the twenty-five miles to the Georgia–Tennessee state line, crossed over into Tennessee, and then drove the remaining few miles to Lovell Field. They arrived early and went to the designated hangar but only had to wait a short time before the fifty-passenger Convair belonging to the Union Assembly Church landed and taxied up to the hangar. The roaring engines revved a few seconds and then settled into a purr until finally falling silent as the big three-prong props came to a halt. Tim looked at his watch. It was five-thirty.

After a short few minutes, the airplane's door, located on the left side of the fuselage not far from the cockpit windows, opened by lifting up. A set of stairs descended to the ground at the same time. Tim and Ralph recognized the first person to exit the plane. It was Jesse Pratt, who was wearing a black coat and a black hat. "A black hat and coat like those gangsters wear in the movies," commented Ralph forty years later. About four or five men wearing similar attire streamed down the stairs and stood around Jesse as if they were body guards.

Jesse walked straight to Tim and told him that Brother Paul Hughes was on the plane and that he had passed—meaning died. Jesse and the other men with him turned and hurried toward a Cadillac parked near the hangar.

"Wait," said Tim. "We can't take a dead body across the state line. You're going to have to call the coroner."

Jesse stopped and turned back. He told Tim to take Brother Hughes to their funeral home and when Tim said "no" again, Jesse said, "Call Phil Smith[18] and get this squared away and take the body to Smith's Funeral Home in Dalton, Georgia."

Tim asked Jesse to wait, and then he and Ralph rushed up the Convair's steps. Ralph went into the cockpit. Tim wandered back along the seats toward the rear of the plane. His heart picked up its pace when the faint odor of death grew stronger as he moved along the aisle. He could smell Brother Hughes even before he saw him slumped in one of the rear seats. Tim was accustomed to death. He had worked around dead bodies his entire adult life, for he also was an embalmer, but what Tim saw when he stooped down next to Paul, made Tim's racing heart hit a higher gear. "Calm down," he told himself, but Tim knew this wasn't right.

Tim pulled back Paul's shirt. A red soaked bandage covered the abdomen between his rib cage and umbilicus. Tim realized Paul Hughes had been gut-shot. Gasses of decaying human flesh filled Tim's nostrils.

"Been dead awhile?" asked Ralph, who had moved behind Tim.

The two men left the plane and went up to Jesse, who was still surrounded by his entourage. Tim told Jesse again he couldn't take a dead body across the state line; especially one who had been shot.

Again, Jesse told Tim to call Phil Smith because they didn't want to deal with this.

Tim replied, "I'm going to call Phil because I don't want to do it either."

Jesse's face turned angry. He moved from the circle of men surrounding him and walked close to Tim, getting into his personal space. With his good right eye glaring into Tim's face and his useless left eye looking up and to his left, Jesse said with piercing words, "We been doing business with Smith's for years, and if you want to keep our business, you'll take care of this for us." After making this threat, Jesse moved back amongst his entourage and walked toward the Cadillac.

Tim told Jesse not to leave. He said he would call Phil and, once he saw Jesse and his men stop at the car, Tim hurried toward the terminal to find a phone booth.

Once there, Tim called Phil Smith and reported what had just transpired including Jesse's threat about taking the Church's business away from Smith's Funeral Home if they didn't take care of this.

After Tim finished, Phil said, "Did Jesse say that to YOU?"

"Yes! We can't drive him across the state line—him being shot. Phil, he's been dead awhile, maybe several days. I'm not going to do it, and I don't think we should."

"NO! Of course not, we can't do that—they'd put both of us in jail," said Phil. "I'll call the Chattanooga coroner."

Tim took his time going back to meet Jesse, hoping the coroner would hurry. When Tim got back to the Convair, Ralph was talking to several men who had flown in on the airplane with Jesse. For a minute, Tim thought Jesse had left, but Jesse came out of the airplane when he saw Tim arrive. Several airport personnel had also gathered, creating a small crowd.

Jesse asked Tim what Phil said.

"The coroner is on his way," said Tim.

Jesse's face turned to an angry red, and he was about to berate Tim when a new black Ford drove up and a man in a black suit got out with a black bag in his hand. Tim knew it was one of the Chattanooga coroners and not the nice one. They had sent the coroner who did his job and asked questions and was always in a sour mood, especially this early in the morning.

The coroner marched straight up to Tim, whom he knew. With a grumpy, why-the-hell-did-you-wake-me-up, voice, said, "Where's this body?"

"You the coroner?" asked Tim even though he knew the answer.

"Yeah!" he growled, "You know who I am. Where's the BODY?"

Tim looked at the airplane's door and nodded his head while he started walking toward the Convair's steps. Once inside, the coroner examined the body, took out his stethoscope, placed in on Brother Hughes's chest, and said "What in the name of Jesus happened here? He's been dead a while."[19]

Tim started telling the coroner the story from their arrival to the present.

The coroner stood up and went to the door and down the stairs. He hurried to the airport personnel and told them to call an ambulance. The coroner's mood had changed—it had degraded to horrible. He proceeded to chew-out every one of the men around the Convair's steps, including Jesse. He talked to Tim as if Tim was the pilot, gunman, and next-of-kin to the dead man all rolled into one. Ralph had gone back to the Smith Funeral Home hearse for a smoke.

Calmly, Jesse stepped forward and introduced himself to the coroner as J. F. Pratt of Dalton, Georgia, and said he would answer any questions the coroner had. Also another man came forward and introduced himself as Charles E. Carson of Calhoun, Georgia. About that time another car pulled next to the hangar. Out jumped Detective Charles Gregory of the Chattanooga Police Department, who went straight to the coroner. After a brief discussion, they went up the steps and disappeared inside the airplane.

As the sky turned light, an ambulance from Erlanger Hospital arrived and emergency personnel took their gurney up the airplane steps. After what seemed like fifteen minutes, Detective Charles Gregory and the coroner got off the plane and went straight to Jesse Pratt and Charles Carson.

Detective Gregory, standing beside the coroner, wanted to know what had happened.

Pratt answered, "Brother Hughes was wounded at Bouse, Arizona, when he tripped and fell and a .22-caliber pistol in his hand discharged."[20]

The detective asked where this happened, and Pratt or Charles Carson answered "that the shooting incident happened in the desert near Bouse."[21]

Detective Gregory asked why they didn't take him to the hospital near Bouse, and Jesse answered that "Paul Hughes was a member of the Church of God of the Union Assembly at Dalton, and his religious beliefs would not allow him to accept medical treatment." Jesse Pratt then reported that "Hughes was taken back to the airplane and the flight to Chattanooga started."[22]

The Detective got Jesse and Charles Carson's addresses and told them they could go because no charges were to be filed at the moment, but that he was going to have to contact the Arizona authorities about the incident.

Jesse and his entourage got into the big Cadillac and left. Tim and Ralph drove back to the funeral home without Brother Hughes. The ambulance took Paul Hughes's body to Erlanger Hospital. The next day, someone from Smith's Funeral Home picked up Hughes's body from Erlanger and took it back to Dalton. His body was embalmed but that did not negate the signs or odor of decaying flesh, so the funeral home had to place the body in an air-tight, glass-covered coffin after cleaning Hughes up and getting his swollen body into a suit.[23] After that, forty-year-old Paul Hughes, pastor of the Church of God of the Union Assembly of Glencoe, Alabama, and son of Flora Pratt Hughes, C. T. and Minnie Pratt's oldest daughter, was ready for viewing that Thursday night at Smith's Funeral Home.[24]

Many years later, I inspected Paul Hughes's death certificate issued by the Tennessee Department of Public Health. One oddity was immediately apparent: it was never signed by a coroner. There is no cause of death listed. It does not say if an autopsy was done. There is no physician listed, but only that the decedent died in Chattanooga, Tennessee, at Erlanger Hospital. In fact, the entire bottom portion of the death certificate is blank except his place of burial and the name of the funeral home. Probably, the Chattanooga coroner refused to sign the certificate because the death did not happen in Tennessee—that will remain a mystery. Also, if Arizona failed to send anyone to investigate, there was no one to sign the certificate. This was not the first nor would it be the last bizarre death of a high-ranking family member of the Church.

4

According to those interviewed, Paul Hughes had been a rising star as a minister in the Church of God of the Union Assembly. Those interviewed stated that Hughes was well-liked, even loved, by not only the members of his church in Glencoe, Alabama, but also the members in his hometown of Dalton. His movement up the Church hierarchy escalated at a phenomenal rate, and members thought he was destined to climb all the way to the top if anything should happen to Jesse. Even Jesse showed fondness for his nephew, admiring his abilities as a preacher and his proficiency at bringing in money for the organization. More importantly, it was reported in interviews that Paul had been one of Minnie Pratt's favorite grandsons before her death on December 4, 1971, just three months before Hughes's own death.[25]

Paul was married to the sister of Irene Pratt, Margaret McClure, and they had two sons. Thus, Paul was Jesse's nephew as well as his brother-in-law. Paul was only fourteen years younger than Jesse and about the same age as his uncles Herbert and Wayman. He was better-educated than his uncles, especially Jesse, who only went to the fourth grade. Paul was an eloquent speaker who could hold his audiences spellbound. He was a handsome man with dark, wavy hair and a receding hairline. He stood a little over six-feet tall and had a muscular build.

After conducting numerous interviews, I heard several different stories about how Paul Hughes was fatally wounded at the Church's ranch in Arizona. Other than Jesse Pratt and Paul Hughes, it seems that Jesse's two sons, Jesse Junior and Charlie Thomas III, were also present. Jesse Junior would have been twenty-five-years-old, and Charles would have been eighteen-years-old in March of 1972. When questioned about Paul's accident, Jesse told the Chattanooga detective that Paul had tripped and his .22 caliber pistol discharged.[26] Several people interviewed for this narrative stated that Jesse, Paul, Jesse Junior, and Charlie were riding in the back of a pickup truck—one family relative said it was a dump truck—and they were hunting the long-eared jack rabbit. The majority of the time the group hunted at night while using spotlights and small handguns. They would also kill sidewinder rattlesnakes if they spotted any.[27]

As reported by those interviewed who were present at Paul's funeral, Jesse said that Paul was holding his pistol when the truck hit a bump, and that when Paul saw the 22 pistol was going to discharge and shoot Jesse's son, Charlie, Paul turned the gun on himself.[28] This made Paul a hero in the eyes of Church members. Charles Roberts said, "Paul must have been a super-fast individual to pull that off. He would have had to been faster than a speeding bullet."[29]

Obviously, there are still unanswered questions about Paul Hughes's death. As stated earlier, when Paul Hughes's body was viewed at the funeral home, it was in an airtight copper casket, which had a thick piece of gasket-sealed glass covering the front of his body, so he could be seen. The Church of God of the Union Assembly had always used the same simple metal casket for its deceased, even in the cases of C. T. and Minnie Pratt, so the use of this newer expensive casket was unusual. Church members were told that they used the glass covering over his casket because his body was full of toxic lead that was dangerous to everyone else.[30] No one mentioned that he was in an airtight casket to keep the decaying stench inside. Those interviewed said that the members believed everything they were told by the Pratt family. They may have wondered, but they did not question why Brother Paul's body was so swollen and out of proportion. Every former member interviewed stated they knew that if they asked too many questions about the death of Paul Hughes, Jesse and the family would chastise and rebuke them, possibly even dismissing them from the Church—or worse.

But how could these men get away with a crime? For it is a crime to bring a dead body across a state line. How could Jesse tell the authorities that Paul died on the airplane while they were in the skies between Bouse, Arizona, and Chattanooga, Tennessee, when Hughes's body was so decomposed it was already decaying? No person arriving on the airplane told the authorities anything that morning but what had been ordered by Jesse F. Pratt—members and nonmembers alike. (Only Jesse later told the story to a detective about Paul shooting himself with a .22.) It was reported that some men on the hunting trip were not church members but business associates whom Jesse had invited.[31] Next, witnesses to the condition of Hughes's body were never interviewed by the authorities. The fear created by Jesse Pratt was profound and had traveled across an entire continent. The people who lived on the ranch in Arizona may or may not have been questioned, but if they were, they all stuck to the same story.

According to either eyewitnesses or individuals who heard first-hand accounts of the incident, possible causes of Hughes's death included the following: Paul had accidently shot himself when the truck hit a bump. One of Jesse's sons had accidentally shot Paul while in the back of the truck. Hughes stepped in between Jesse and one of Jesse's brothers and was shot. One of Paul Hughes's brothers told one member interviewed that when the gun went off in the back of the truck, Paul said, "Uncle Jesse, somebody shot me."[32]

Several days after Hughes's funeral, the Georgia Bureau of Alcohol, Tobacco, Firearms, and Explosives (ATF) sent several agents to question Jesse about the incident because the authorities were told that illegal firearms had crossed the state line on the Church's airplane. One of the ATF agents interviewed for this book, George Farmer, reported that they went to the Church of God of the Union Assembly on 41 Highway in Dalton, Georgia, to investigate the allegations. Farmer and two other ATF agents met with Harold Sowder at the church. The ATF agents told Sowder that they needed to talk to Jesse Pratt, but Sowder said Jesse was out-of-state. Added Farmer: "Mr. Sowder was able to provide us with all the information we needed, and we determined that we didn't have enough information about them transporting any illegal firearms across the state line. Since Hughes's death was out of our jurisdiction, we could not pursue it. That was left to Tennessee and Arizona."[33]

Farmer also reported that he didn't think the Arizona authorities had ever sent anyone to Chattanooga to investigate the death of Hughes. Bill Phillips of the Chattanooga Police Department, cold case section, stated in July 2015 that the Paul

Hughes case files were lost in a Chattanooga flood during the 1980s. In 1989 the Tennessee River overflowed its banks and flooded a major portion of Chattanooga, including the Chattanooga Police warehouse, where old case files were stored.[34] Moreover, the Church Ranch had been in Yuma County, Arizona, but the county was divided on January 1, 1983. The ranch, which was sold in the early 1980s, is now in La Paz County. Both Sheriff's Departments in Yuma and La Paz were contacted for this book in June 2015. Curiously, they had no records of the incident, as the Yuma County Sheriff's Department had purged all the paper files going back to the 1970s.[35]

Little did Jesse F. Pratt Sr., or anyone else know that exactly two years later in 1974 and on the same date, March 15, Jesse Senior would be found dead, and his death would seem even stranger than that of his nephew and brother-in-law, Paul Hughes.

15

A Prudent Wife

"I will be the ruler of my house if I have to take a skillet
or a ball bat to my wife."

JESSE F. PRATT

1

The women were not well-respected by many of the men in the Church,[1] including those women in positions of leadership. Men and women alike were taught by
Jesse in his sermons that women were on earth to please men. He once told the
pastors in a minister's meeting to take a ball bat to a woman if she didn't do what
she's supposed to do. "Us women at the Church were not treated any better than
cattle," added another former female member.[2]

A sermon preached by Jesse Pratt, and captured on live radio in the early 1970s,
further elucidates his negative view of women (italics indicate words from the
KJV Bible): "All right, First Timothy, chapter five, verse one: *Rebuke not an elder,*
but intreat HIM as a father: and the younger men as brethren. Now, can a woman
be an elder? If she can, she can be a father. Rebuke not an elder, but intreat him

as a father. So, that cut Agnes out, didn't it—Aunt Jemima, too, and Aunt Jenny because they cannot be fathers, therefore they can't be elders." Jesse expanded on this topic for almost five minutes and then near the end of the sermon Jesse said that the Bible calls women cows: "Then when Sampson, you know, they got the secret over there from his girlfriend there, they called it you know. He (Sampson) said, he told them, 'you would have guessed not the riddle there had you not been plowing with my heifer.' So you see that God illustrates them (women) as that (cows) sometimes."[3]

By the end of 1973, the people of the United States—really the entire world—had become convinced that the highest political office in the world was corrupt. All eyes were on President Richard Nixon as one after another of his enter staff members were implemented in a cover-up called Watergate. By 1974 President Nixon fought alone to save his presidency and his name by telling America that he was not a crook. But as the White House tapes would prove, Nixon had covered up the scandal and lied to the world about his participation in the Watergate break-in.

By contrast, as 1973 turned into 1974, Jesse F. Pratt Sr. seemed to be at the height of his powers. He had total control of the fifty-four churches of the Church of God of the Union Assembly. Most of the Church membership at the time thought him to be a prophet of God. Others thought he was even equal to God. Jesse expected everyone to obey his teaching and demands. His control was overwhelming and covered all aspects of his followers' lives, including activities, finances, possessions, dress codes, and personal relationships. Those interviewed said that Jesse expected unyielding obedience from his members, a power which only continued to fuel his fire.

During the early 1970s, members also started making note of the power his wife Irene possessed. Nearly everyone said Irene could talk Jesse into about anything she wanted done. She had taken on the role of prophesying, which was not common among the female members. Jesse's sister, Alma, had also done some prophesying during Jesse's time as the Church ruler, but she had not done anything comparable. Several informants pointed out that it was not uncommon for mothers to ask Irene to name their newborn babies, and Irene named lots of them using names of former and present Pratts. Not everyone held her in such high regards. One man who married a former Union Assembly member said this, "The mean and spiteful things that happened down there went through Irene. She was the meanest woman who ever lived."[4] Former member Charles Roberts, who was also present at the interview, responded, "You got that right. She was vindictive. She ran that church."

Irene also started money drives to enrich the Church financially. One of Irene's methods of obtaining money was through candy sales, which will be discussed later. Irene usually started a goal of raising one million dollars for a particular church project. Unfortunately, the majority of these projects never materialized, and no one questioned where the money went. Former members said they were afraid to question her authority, as they feared being rebuked, prophesied against, or even turned out of the Church. As a result, very little information about the group reached nonmembers.[5]

Of course, no one questioned Jesse's authority, or even offered praise to other ministers. Charles Roberts and several others reported that if someone bragged on another minister for preaching a good sermon, that minister would soon be rebuked by Jesse. Roberts said, "This was Jesse's way of either keeping the man humble, or it was pure jealousy and envy on Jesse's part." In fact, when Jesse flew out of Dalton, he usually told everyone what time he would arrive back at the Dalton airport because he expected members who were not working to meet and welcome him home. It was not uncommon for over a hundred members to welcome and cheer Jesse when he stepped off the airplane. Often the people present at the airport when he arrived would form two lines facing one another that stretched fifty to a hundred feet. Jesse and his group would disembark and walk between the two lines of admirers who were often applauding. Some even bowed their heads. One pilot—not a church member—claimed, "Some of the people actually kissed a ring Jesse wore like they do the Pope."[6] Charles Roberts added, "We [the members] created this hell. We let it happen. We could have said no. We didn't have to let him treat us this way. But . . . But when you're there—in the middle of all of it—you don't see it. I would have died for him."[7]

During the early 1970s if members wanted to make a large purchase, such as a car, refrigerator, stove, or furniture, they had to go to Jesse for permission to buy it. If he agreed, Jesse usually had them purchase the item in places owned by members. At other times he plainly refused to allow members to buy these things, saying that they didn't need to spend that much money as they had an obligation to the Church. If a couple in the Union Assembly Church wanted to marry, they had to get Jesse's or Irene's permission first. Already, Irene had started match-making and setting up marriages between couples. If they failed to follow through with the wedding, there was hell to pay, and these members could be subject to being rebuked, having prophesies of doom cast on them, or being expulsed from the Church. If a member wanted to wed a nonmember, that nonmember had to first join the Church of God of the Union Assembly and be a member for six months before given permission to marry.

Those interviewed confirmed that when a member was dismissed from the Union Assembly Church, the rest of his family was not dismissed unless they, too, had displeased Jesse. Since Jesse and Irene had removed the rule of divorce, Jesse encouraged, even demanded, that the spouse of a dismissed member file for a divorce, and they were ordered to never have any—none whatsoever—contact with the dismissed member.[8]

On one occasion, a dismissed man by the name of Clayton who had displeased Jesse came home from work to find his wife and children moved out of his home. Charles Roberts said, "They didn't even leave Clayton any dust in his house. They'd cleaned him out, dust and all."[9] Another man, whose name will remain anonymous, came home and found not only his wife and family gone but also all the furniture, all the wife's and children's clothes, and, unbelievably, all the man's own clothes had been taken from the house, too.

Following is a recorded story from Rita Gazaway, daughter to Bob and Clara Gazaway. Clara's parents, Louis Taylor and Viola Taylor, had lost a 180-acre farm located in Ringgold, Georgia. "Once my mamma put on a pair of pants—or something after Daddy got back into the Church. Daddy had been kicked out earlier because he'd failed to cry while Brother Jesse was playing the steel guitar. Anyway, Brother Jesse, Jesse Senior, told my daddy to leave my mamma. He [Jesse] was always telling one spouse to leave the other one for different reasons—trimming their hair—go out of their house without stockings—shaving their legs—swimming without their skirt pinned together at the legs or anything like that.

"So, she (Clara) went over to Brother Jesse's house looking for my daddy. Irene told Mamma, 'You can't go in there.' Mamma walked in anyway just in time to see daddy down at Brother Jesse's feet begging him to let him stay in the Church. Brother Jesse was telling daddy to stay away from his wife and that he didn't need her.

"I don't know what Mamma did wrong, nothing much really, but she heard what Jesse told daddy. Mamma grabbed Daddy and she stomped out of there. Of course, they never went back to church there after that. Mamma told me this story many times over the years."[10]

One member reported that his grandfather, who lived in Cleveland, Tennessee, thirty miles northeast of Dalton, was turned out of the Union Assembly Church. Jesse told the entire family that if they let the grandfather in their house, talked to him on the phone, visited him, wrote him a letter, or had anything to do with him, they would refer charges against his family and turn all of them out of the Church. This member never saw his grandfather or grandmother again. When asked what he meant by "refer charges," the man said, "the Church was the law—the ruler of your life. It wasn't like government laws; it was church laws they were referring to when they said 'refer charges.'"[11]

2

Another tactic used by Jesse and the Family was prophesying doom and death to the members. Other than prophesying a particular disease, Jesse began to forecast car wrecks as well.[12] One former member said that his father, Junior Roberts, was a minister in White, Georgia, about forty-five miles south of Dalton, and once Jesse came to that church during a revival and stood his father up in front of the entire congregation. Jesse charged that he was allowing his members to break rules, and his church wasn't earning enough money. That night as Junior Roberts was being chastised before his own congregation, Irene prophesied that Junior Roberts and his family would have a car wreck sometime that week as they drove home to Dalton. Jesse also added that their bodies would be scattered all over the highway. Junior must have been convinced of their pending disaster because his son said,

"Dad drove about thirty miles per hour every night to the church and back. We were all terrified on the way home. Dad would almost come to a stop when we met an approaching car."[13]

Flora Hughes and Leola Crider, daughters to C. T. and Minnie Pratt, and Dimple Sneed delivered most of the members' babies in North Georgia and the surrounding states at the Church maternity ward in Spring Place, Georgia, about fifteen miles due east of Dalton. At Spring Place, the Church also had apartments that had been converted into a maternity ward. Other apartments there were occupied by older women, usually widows who had given their homes or farms to the Church.[14]

Johnnie Haney Butler, who gave birth at the maternity ward, described her first visit to the facilities. "The maternity center was a large building that the church had bought and remodeled," recalled Butler. "It had a large living room and large kitchen and lots of bedrooms. There were a few rooms set aside for expectant mothers. It was a maternity center and an old folks-home, in one. They [midwives] told me that I needed to bring some pads with me when I came to have the baby—big pads made out of newspaper and old, white sheets to use on the bed."[15] Months later, when Johnnie's baby was born at the maternity center she said, "Sister Hughes left the room. In a moment Sister Hughes walked back into the room with an axe in her hand. 'What is that for?' I asked. 'This is to put under your bed to cut the after-birth pains in half.' Sister Hughes stuck the axe underneath my bed and I wondered how these people could be so superstitious."[16]

The Union Assembly's Maternity Center located in Spring Place, Georgia.
Photo by the author.

Another way Jesse intimidated his followers, reported former members interviewed, was to call one of them up to the podium during services and announce to the entire group a sin this person had committed. Then Jesse would have the person confess the sin and ask for forgiveness from Jesse—not forgiveness from Jesus Christ or God but from Jesse and then the Church looked to Jesse for forgiveness. Usually this person would get rebuked by Jesse or by one of his family members. Some former members said that the membership believed Jesse had some spiritual discernment from a higher being in order to tell who had been sinful and who had not. But, according to a few members, in this atmosphere of high suspicion, members would tell on one another to deflect attention from themselves or to please Jesse. If a member knew that a man was having an affair with another man's wife, he would go to see Jesse and let him know. Jesse would pick the opportune time to call the man up to announce the man's sins in front of his wife and children. Then there would be a rebuking. This also happened to women.[17] Even trivial gossip—women seen without stockings, men seen smoking or drinking, women seen wearing slacks—might end in a public shaming and rebuking.[18] Jesse could even turn the tears on himself during his sermons and often did while pulling out a handkerchief to wipe his eyes. The congregation had better start crying too or there would be hell to pay.

Jesse's elevation far above his flock resulted in another peculiar understanding within the Church. Jesse, his wife, and children were "untouchables." Common members were not allowed to lay a finger on any of them, or they might be beaten up very quickly—physically beaten up. Even family members were not immune to the do-not-touch-Jesse rule; at least they had to be careful in how they laid their hands on Jesse.

One interview revealed one rare instance when Jesse's tactics were turned against him. In late 1972 or early 1973, not long after Jesse's brother Wayman had been expelled as minister of the Union Assembly Church in Atlanta, he preached a sermon at the Dalton church. Despite being expelled as a minister, at this time Wayman still held an administrative post in the Church as the assistant general overseer—second in command to Jesse. During the sermon, Wayman belittled Irene for having too much control, for interfering in church affairs, and for casting spells on people with her prophesying. After calling her out, Wayman shocked everyone by going over to Jesse, grabbing him by the head, and rebuking him just like Jesse had done to other members. That was a mistake. No one rebuked Brother Jesse, but astoundingly nothing was done to Wayman at the service. He was not beaten up or even reprimanded by Jesse that night.[19] His punishment would come later.

It was also during the early 1970s, that Irene seemed to be losing control over Jesse. The membership could sense trouble brewing. Only weeks after being rebuked by his brother, Jesse kicked Wayman out as assistant overseer and replaced him with his nineteen-year-old son, Charlie T. Pratt III. This appointment raised more questions. Why did Jesse Junior, who was older at twenty-six, not become assistant overseer? Former members and a few nonmembers said Jesse Junior had an alcohol problem and a drug problem. They indicated that he had been caught several times high on drugs or drunk on alcohol and had even been charged with a DUI. Jesse Junior's gospel singing group, the Trailblazers, began traveling on the gospel singing circuit. He was also a very talented steel guitar player, and he had great aptitude for singing. Once, Jesse Senior had preached a sermon to his son Jesse Junior, warning him of the family's problem with alcoholism and told him he had to stop drinking or he would die an alcoholic's death.[20] Junior stopped for a while, or at least he kept his drinking hidden, but a few former members said his father was not happy with Jesse Junior during this time.[21]

Everyone interviewed who was old enough to remember said Jesse became even more paranoid about people getting close to him. When Jesse was with his inner circle, he always had a group surrounding him who acted as his bodyguards. Often a fight would occur.

These fights also happened outside the Church, even with nonmembers if the situation presented itself. Once, during a funeral inside the church building, a funeral home attendant who was not a member of the Union Assembly stood at the foot of the coffin. When a woman stopped in front of the body for what he thought was too long, he lightly touched her on the shoulder and told her she needed to keep moving. Immediately two men came after the attendant but were stopped by one of the deacons. During the service that deacon stood up and announced what had happened and, while pointing at the attendant, said, "You men need to take care of that man after the service." The owner of the funeral home, who was present, sent his assistant back to the funeral home and told him not to come back. The attendant, who had the often solitary job of delivering flowers to graves after funerals, reportedly carried a baseball bat around with him for nearly a year.[22]

By March of 1974, Jesse was at the top of his world. Through the Church, Jesse had accumulated more power, money, and property than his father, C. T. Pratt, ever had. Jesse added new churches in Florida, Georgia, Tennessee, Alabama, Mississippi, Arkansas, and Texas. Of course, every time a new Church of God of the Union Assembly was built, a fund was formed and the money was raised with a special offering. Jesse therefore got praise for the new openings, while the members raised the money—and lots of it. Jesse had built an empire in the name of God. When Jesse took over from his father, C. T. Pratt, in 1961, the net worth of the Church of God of the Union Assembly was approximately one million dollars. In thirteen years, 1974, the Union Assembly's net worth had risen to ten million dollars. Charles Roberts recalled, "The talk at the church was that the total was more like twelve million dollars, and that's not counting the ton of money given by the members at each service plus the candy sales at all the churches. Man, I'll tell you, it was unbelievable what went on down there."[23]

Despite all this wealth, or because of it, changes and troubles were already starting to surface within the Pratt family when 1974 arrived, and Jesse would have to make some critical decisions—decisions that could fragment the family. However, no one anticipated that Jesse Franklin Pratt, at age fifty-six, had only a few months to live.

3

Late in 1973 and early 1974, the nation and the world became captivated by the Watergate scandal. On March 15, 1974, a federal grand jury had concluded that President Richard Nixon had joined in a conspiracy to cover up White House involvement in the break-in of Democratic Party offices at the Watergate Hotel in Washington, DC. On that same day, an enormous event transpired inside the Union Assembly community that would change them forever.

In late 1973 or early 1974, Jesse left Irene and moved to one of the Church farms fifteen miles away in Murray County, Georgia. Everyone in the Union Assembly Church soon knew of their separation. Rumors had spread throughout the congregation that Jesse and Irene's marriage was on rocky ground and a divorce was possible. Some said Jesse was having an affair, but no evidence of this has ever surfaced. In fact, a man and his wife who lived at the farm at that time reported that Jesse never had another woman visit him on the farm.[24]

During church services, just prior to the separation, Jesse started rebuking Irene physically—shaking her by the head. Irene was no longer in good standing with the leadership of the Church. When Jesse's brother, Wayman Pratt, came to Dalton during early March 1974, Wayman even rebuked Irene for witchcraft. According to one of his sons, Wayman was in the process of establishing a mission for the Union Assembly Church in Colorado City, Texas, and was traveling between there and Dalton. A former member reported that Wayman told him that he'd had a long talk with Jesse about Irene in March. It was reported by several interviewed that Wayman advised Jesse to go home to his wife and get everything straightened out with her one way or another because this separation did not look good for anyone connected to the Church.[25]

In March 1974, Irene had a house full of permanent guests. Living in the house were two of her unmarried sons, one unmarried daughter, and two women who were not part of the Pratt family but were friends of Irene. Irene's son Charlie and his wife, Joy, stayed with Irene at this time. For at least a year, Irene was constantly surrounded by these people and was almost never alone.[26]

Jesse Junior and his second wife, Wanda Jean Poole Pratt, would drop by to see Irene often. Jesse Junior had married Mary Sue Burkett soon after leaving the army in 1967, but divorced her sometime before 1969, because early in 1969 he had married his second wife, Wanda. Charles Roberts reported that he remembered this happening in either January or February 1969 because that is when he and his father went to Fort Worth, Texas, and Jesse Senior preached a sermon that lasted five hours. No one ever knew how long Jesse Senior's sermons would last or, sometimes, when they would start. By 1974 Jesse Junior and Wanda Jean had children of their own and visited Irene often.

During one memorable service on Sunday March 10, 1974, Jesse preached on the sin of homosexuality and women sleeping with other women. Three men interviewed said that during this service, Jesse rebuked his wife, Irene, along with two unmarried women living in the house with Irene.[27] Rumors spread that Irene and the women living in her house were lovers, but nothing has been found to substantiate this accusation. In fact, one of the women who was not a member of the family but lived in Irene's house cooked, did all the washing and cleaning, and waited on everyone who lived there. She was, ostensibly, a live-in maid. A few individuals called her "Irene's slave," but none doubted her dedication to Irene and her family.

No matter the reality of the situation, Jesse Senior and Irene had been arguing for months. For those who had first-hand knowledge of the relationship, the situation was clear: Irene could no longer control Jesse, and he was a violent man when he became angry. Although she still had control over her children, including Jesse Junior, who turned twenty-seven-years-old in December, her world was falling apart. She was a very intelligent woman and former members interviewed felt she knew that losing Jesse meant the loss of her position as virtually a queen, the loss of access to millions of dollars, and possibly her excommunication from the Church. Desperate people can do desperate things, and numerous interviews indicate that Irene Pratt had become desperate.[28]

But if anything happened to Jesse—especially if he should die unexpectedly— Irene had a world of other problems. First, Jesse's brother Wayman still had power in the Church and could be expected to take Jesse's place. Wayman had also previously demonstrated he believed Irene to be a witch.[29] Another of Jesse's brothers, Herbert, had already been told by Irene or Jesse to sell the cattle in Arizona and Texas that had been purchased through a bank loan that had not been paid—an act of criminal fraud. Irene or Jesse (some interviewees said it was Irene while some reported that it was Jesse) told Herbert that the money from the sale would be used to pay the loan off on the cattle, but Herbert had already committed fraud by selling the cattle that the bank held a loan against, and had already sent the money to the Church. Herbert was frantic to get the loan paid off before the bank learned of this.[30] Jesse was reported to have told Herbert that he would take care of the problem, but Herbert was now neutralized.

Jesse also had three other sons by his first wife, Ethel, who were ordained ministers in the Union Assembly, and, in the event of Jesse's passing, they could possibly take over—or at least they might support Wayman. But basically, no one knew where their loyalties rested, especially Irene. Her only hope to remain in power rested in Jesse F. Pratt Jr. Irene's next oldest son, Charlie, was only twenty years old. The one other person who could have possibly been accepted as the head of the Union

Assembly Church was Paul Hughes, but, as chronicled earlier, he had accidentally been shot under mysterious circumstances and had died exactly two years before.

During the morning of Thursday March 14, 1974, Jesse was at the Church farm in Murray County, Georgia, where he had been staying for months. A young man in his twenties came to the farm that day and ended up talking to Jesse, who informed this person that he was living on the farm and separated from Irene.[31] But it was stated that everyone at the Church knew that their preacher, leader, and God was separated from his wife. This young man who reported this had a father who was one of the twelve Elders of the Union Assembly Church and both the son and father were very well respected by Jesse and the family. The next time this young man would see Jesse, the church leader would be lying in a copper casket.

4

Jesse was a licensed pilot and had passed a mandatory pilot's physical on March 1, 1974, by Doctor Felker. It was and still is standard procedure during these physicals for the pilot's heart to be examined, but often only superficially.[32] How well a doctor may have done this in 1974 was up to the doctor, of course. Taking an electrocardiogram, also known as an EKG, was not a standard procedure for keeping a private pilot's license. Moreover, Jesse had no outward signs of having heart problems, and they did not run in his family.

There are a few different stories about what happened that Thursday night when Jesse went home to talk to Irene. The most reliable evidence was provided by several sources, including a family member of one the people present that night, one of the funeral home attendants who picked up Jesse's body, a person who arrived at the house just a short time after Jesse had been picked up, and what Irene reported to friends, family, and the congregation of the Church. As we will see, Jesse's death certificate also provides some clues.

When Jesse first arrived at his and Irene's house that night, only a son, Herbie, was present. Irene and the other people who lived there had earlier been at the Thursday night service at the Union Assembly Church in Dalton. It was reported by those interviewed that Jesse had not attended that meeting, and everyone was told that he was working at the Church farm.[33] When Irene and the others arrived at the house, Herbie was playing "What a Friend We Have in Jesus" on the piano while Jesse stood there crying. The ones present that night other than Jesse, Herbie, and Irene were their son Charlie Pratt III and his wife, Joy, their son Marty Pratt, daughter Margaret Pratt; and two female friends who worked for Irene as servants.

After the song finished, Jesse, who was still crying, went into his and Irene's bedroom. Irene followed Jesse. In just a short time the others went to their rooms and went to sleep. Close to four o'clock on Friday morning, Irene started crying and screaming, which woke everyone and brought them running to her room. When the others arrived at Irene's bedroom, Jesse was lying in the floor with his head and face covered in blood. Irene was yelling that Jesse had fallen and hit his head on the window sill. Blood was coming from a gash in Jesse's forehead. A huge amount of blood covered the carpet around Jesse's prone, lifeless body. Blood covered the sink in Irene's bathroom, but that could have come from the towels she was using on his head.

According to informants, Jesse's body was moved to the bed and the women started cleaning the blood off of him and out of the carpet. No one reported that Jesse ever regained consciousness, except one former member, who stated that one of the women in the house that night had told him that Jesse was moaning and asking to be taken to the hospital.[34] No one else reported this, however. Jesse had always preached that wherever he fell, he would lie there and die. He said he would never go to the hospital, so, if he was not yet dead, his family stood there and watched him die. They may have prayed for his recovery or even tried to staunch the flow of blood if Jesse had not yet bled out.

It appears that the Whitfield County Coroner, Lebron Houston, came to the house to pronounce Jesse dead, because he signed Jesse's death certificate and designated the time of death as 4:10 a.m. on March 15, 1974. The writing on the death certificate is consistent with his handwriting and signature. Oddly, there is no evidence that Dalton Police Chief Robert Lankford ever investigated Jesse's death or even sent anyone to the home before Jesse was removed. There is also no evidence that any member of the police department ever questioned those present at Jesse's death about what happened. Of course, the coroner may not have called and reported this to the Dalton Police. One informant said that the Dalton Police did send an investigator over but believed what Irene told him.[35] Nothing was in Dalton's newspaper about Jesse's death except his obituary, which stated that he suffered a sudden heart attack. The Dalton Police chief is not an elected official but is appointed by the City Council. The City Council at that time was comprised of Union Assembly "enablers," so individual council members could have been involved in a cover-up—or at least did not encourage a more thorough investigation—especially if they thought it might bring unwanted attention to the city of Dalton.

Jesse was taken directly to the funeral home for embalming and no autopsy was performed.[36] True, the coroner did not ask for an autopsy and the death certificate indicates this as the box for AUTOPSY is checked with a "No." In any event, since the Union Assembly did not believe in using medical doctors, they would not have allowed an autopsy if they were given that option. Mr. Houston, the coroner, listed Jesse's cause of death on the death certificate as a sudden heart attack, and it is in the coroner's own handwriting.[37]

5

Jesse Junior, who lived on one of the Church farms in Murray County, was called early that morning and was compelled to come to his mother's house because his father had died. As soon as he arrived, Irene sent Jesse Junior to the home of Dennis

Smith, who was married to Irene's sister Ruth. Irene instructed Dennis, a mere member of the Supreme Council, to swear Jesse Junior in as the General Overseer of the Church of God of the Union Assembly. Within four hours of his father's death, Jesse F. Pratt Jr. became the third General Overseer of the Union Assembly.[38] This was done before the Supreme Council could meet to vote on Jesse Senior's successor. Jesse Junior's brother, Charlie, was the assistant general overseer, but he was only twenty years old and did not question his mother's decision. After Jesse Senior's death, no one in the family was willing to question Irene's decree, except perhaps Jesse Senior's brother, Wayman.

How could the coroner determine that a heart attack had caused Jesse's death without an autopsy? That very morning, Irene had called one of the Union Assembly pastors, Kenneth Bailey, and asked him to preach at Jesse's funeral, telling him that he was the only one qualified to take on the job. Bailey and other members, including the young man who had spoken to Jesse the day before at the Church farm, also came to Jesse and Irene's house that morning, just hours after his body had been moved to the funeral home. The same young man later reported he witnessed blood on the carpet in Irene's bedroom and blood covering the sink and floor in Irene's bathroom. Two individuals, he added, were still at work trying to clean the blood out of the carpet where Jesse fell.[39]

Wayman was one of the last family members to learn of Jesse's death, even though he was in Dalton.[40] It was reported by former members present that Wayman came to the house and did not say much to anyone. It wasn't until later when he learned that Jesse Junior had been sworn in as the leader of the Church. He thought the Supreme Council had made the decision even though he was a member of that group. According to former members interviewed, Irene had acted so fast during the traumatic situation that most of the Supreme Council members, church elders, and general membership did not realize what she had done.[41] Evidence suggests that Irene made countless rational decisions in a short time. "Not bad for a wife in shock," reported Charles Roberts.

Whereas Irene had seemingly lost control of Jesse Senior before his death, interviewees said she had complete control over her twenty-seven-year-old son, Jesse Junior. She instructed him how to take charge and what needed to be done. The majority of the men on the Supreme Council were children and grandchildren to C. T. and Minnie Pratt. Several of Flora and Tobe Hughes's sons were on the council and would do as they were instructed by Jesse Junior.[42]

All of Jesse Senior's siblings who made it to adulthood were still alive except Lloyd, who had died in 1951. Herbert Pratt was still responsible for the outstanding debt to the bank for the loan on the cattle he and Jesse had bought. Herbert had sold them and sent the money to his brother who was now dead. Soon after the death of his brother, Herbert asked Jesse Junior to give him the money Jesse Senior owed him for the loan. It was reported Jesse Junior told his Uncle Herbert that he was not responsible for his father's debts. It wasn't long until Herbert Pratt was locked away in prison for larceny for selling property—the cattle—which still had a loan against it. Jesse or Irene had told Herbert to sell the cattle and now Jesse was dead.[43]

Jesse was brought from the funeral home to lie in state at the Dalton Union Assembly Church. Some members of the Church stayed up all night on Sunday and sat with their dead leader. It was reported that a number of members expected him to rise from the dead. His own son, Jesse Junior, was convinced that his father would rise up from the casket and told people that he would. It has been stated that at one point Jesse Junior told some people that he would bring his father back from the land of the dead.[44]

The funeral home used makeup on Jesse's face trying to hide the dark red spot on his forehead. It was in the shape of the letter J and very noticeable to the people who saw him in the casket. Irene had told the people in the house the night Jesse died that he fell and hit his head on the window frame. However, by the time of the funeral, she was telling members that he fell and hit his head on the door jam. When people started talking about all the blood in the bathroom, Irene said that while Jesse was in the bathroom he hit his head on the toilet seat. At the funeral, Irene even told several people that Jesse had been in the bathroom and jumped up hitting his head on the door facing. The various members, who told all these differing explanations from Irene for his death, all swore she said what she had said to each of them, no matter how contradictory the stories seem. Much later it was reported that Irene claimed Jesse fell and hit his head on the fireplace hearth, but that was in a different room, and she would not have been foolish enough to say that, surely, for Irene was far from stupid. Rumors spread through the congregation about Jesse's death. Even some of the family members said that they thought Irene killed Jesse, but no one outside of the eight other people present in that home at 305 Robinwood Drive knew much about what really happened that night, and it is very possible that only Irene knew for sure specifically how Jesse met his fate.[45]

Needless to say, there are several unanswered questions about Jesse's true cause of death. And some of the accusations are supported by more than a few witnesses. Jesse Senior and Irene were having marital problems. He had moved out of the house. Jesse had rebuked Irene and preached against her rumored activities. Irene's influence with Jesse was slipping. In all appearances, Jesse was a healthy fifty-six-year-old who had never complained of having any chest pains. Although this does not rule out him having a heart attack, it makes it less likely. He went home to see Irene on Thursday evening and was dead by 4:10 am in the morning on Friday.

One common theme among all the witnesses was that there was a tremendous amount of blood at the scene, which means we can assume these things: One, Jesse either fell and struck his head on something that could penetrate his skull, or he was struck by someone with enough force to penetrate his skull. A fall usually will not cause a penetrating or skull fracture wound unless it is from very high—unless they were shoved very hard. Two, his heart continued to pump blood until almost all of it was out of his body, which cannot happen if a person's heart suddenly stops due to a heart attack. Three, Irene apparently did not try to stop the bleeding with direct pressure before he had lost so much blood. And four, to have fallen so hard to create so much blood, Jesse may have broken his neck, but if Jesse had, the heart would have to keep pumping in order to almost empty his body of blood. Moreover, it was reported by a member of the funeral home that Jesse had very little blood still left in his body. Robert Anderson, who was present at the funeral, said, "They told us at church that Jesse was so full of the Holy Ghost that he only had one pint of blood left in his body after he died. They could tell he bled to death."[46] And, as already noted, the coroner also did not ask for an autopsy to be performed. He took the word of Irene that he was having chest pains prior to falling over, and there was never an investigation by any authorities concerning Jesse's death.

Wayman Pratt, Jesse Pratt, and Estle Pratt. Note the picture behind them—
the one of Jesse and Irene saluted at every service by the members.
Courtesy of an anonymous family member.

There are always rumors when the exact incident, especially a death, is surrounded by unanswered questions. Almost all of the former members willing to discuss the event reported that Jesse was going to see Irene that night to ask for a divorce. Several men claimed they spoke to Archie Winkler and his wife, who lived on the farm in Murray County where Jesse was living the day of his death, and said that Jesse had told them he was going into Dalton to split up with Irene. Archie and his wife told members that Jesse was moving to Arizona and taking them and others with him. The rumor about Jesse wishing to divorce Irene had even spread through the Dalton Church before Jesse's death.[47]

It was also reported by several former members interviewed that they had heard that Irene had told Jesse Junior, "The meal ticket was about to come to an end."[48]

At least two informants said that after Jesse's death it was rumored that Irene hit Jesse in the head with a "blue boy'" brass candle holder. Another person said Irene hit him in the head with a violin, which is hard to imagine, since it seems unlikely that a fiddle could do that kind of damage. Another said she had heard it was a frying pan. The only reason the brass candle holder was mentioned as a weapon is that it was the only object in Irene's bedroom that could have caused such a wound, but it was never tested by forensic experts because there was never an investigation. Of course, if he had been hit with anything, it could have been removed.[49] There was one other event that took place several weeks later that added more fuel to the rumor-fire about Jesse's sudden death.

6

Jesse Franklin Pratt's funeral was scheduled for Monday, March 18, 1974, at two o'clock in the afternoon at the Church of God of the Union Assembly in Dalton, Georgia. Jesse's body lay in state from Saturday thru Monday at the church. The Reverend Kenneth Bailey was scheduled to preach Brother Jesse's funeral. Thousands of church members from all fifty-four Union Assembly churches came to the funeral, including entire congregations from Kokomo, Indiana; St. Petersburg, Florida; Corinth, Mississippi; Fort Smith, Arkansas; Rock Hill, South Carolina; Hamilton, Ohio; three churches in Texas; nine churches in Tennessee; three churches from Kentucky; five churches from Alabama; two churches from North Carolina; and ten from Georgia.

The line of people to view Brother Jesse's body stretched out the hall and around the church. When the time for the funeral came at two o'clock, the people were still lined up outside the church and coming in to see their Jesse for the last time. Everyone wept and moaned. Some women fell on the floor in front of the casket and bawled. Funeral directors stood at each end of the casket and tried to move people along, but they knew better than to touch any of the women. After about three hours, one of the funeral directors said that he had to sit and rest because he felt as if he was about to pass out.[50] People who had been scheduled to sing during the funeral started singing and sang for a long time. At one point, Brother Kenneth

Bailey got up to preach but stopped after a few minutes because no one was listening to him; they were either bawling or talking to one another. Some said they heard him preach, and some said they never heard a sermon. The lines continued to file before Jesse's casket and time kept dragging on.

Finally, about dusk, Jesse's casket was closed and taken to the burial grounds at West Hill Cemetery in Dalton, and there Kenneth Bailey preached the last words at Jesse Franklin Pratt's gravesite. For years after this day, members from the Church bought burial plots on this hill and buried their loved ones as close to Jesse as they could until the little hillside became known as Pratt Hill. This is one of the highest spots in West Hill Cemetery. As noted in Chapter 11, buried way down at the lowest spot in this cemetery are C. T. and Minnie Pratt, the founders of the Church.

The members then went home. Wayman Pratt took his family back to Colorado Springs, Texas, and word got back to Irene that Wayman was not happy having Jesse Junior as the general overseer. Some of the other family members did not trust Junior either, but only Wayman voiced a negative opinion.

Some former members reported that Jesse Junior took members of the Supreme Council, mostly his family members, and flew to Texas to confront Wayman. Once there, they took Wayman into a back room and started questioning him. It wasn't long until Jesse Junior sucker-punched his uncle in the side of the head, and Wayman went to the floor. Every time he tried to get up, one of the council members would hit Wayman in the face or stomach again until he went down. Wayman started shouting for them to leave him alone. Jesse Junior screamed and reminded Wayman of how he had rebuked his mother Irene. Jesse also accused him of not preaching the prescribed doctrine of the Church. One of the council members bent Wayman's thumb back until it broke or was dislocated.[51]

Wayman's son, Steve Pratt, agreed to be interviewed about these events. At the time, he was outside the room and heard the commotion and thought they were preaching or shouting, like they might in church services. When he went into the room, he saw his daddy bleeding and on the floor, screaming in pain. Jesse Junior and the Supreme Council picked Wayman up, sat him in a chair, and told him to get back to the basics of the Church. Junior and the council members left a battered Wayman and went back to Dalton.[52] Robert Anderson reported that at the next ministers' meeting, "Charlie [Pratt III] stood up and said, 'I think brother Wayman owes the church an apology.' And he was the one that got beat up. I was there that night. I know this for a fact."[53]

When questioned directly about the event, Steve Pratt responded by stating: "They asked for forgiveness before he [his father] died—before they died. You know, they kind of roughed him up a little bit, but, you know, it ain't no personal thing with us. My dad took a stand on principle really. Some people thought it was a power struggle, but it was more a principle of the Bible with my daddy. It wasn't a power struggle with my daddy. It may have been with them. My daddy always taught us to love them . . . years later they asked my dad for forgiveness."[54]

A number of prominent church leaders were neutralized before and soon after Jesse's death. Herbert would soon be in prison for selling cattle with a bank loan against them. Wayman had certainly been sent a message by Jesse Junior and the Supreme Council when they beat him bloody. Paul Hughes's shooting in an apparent hunting accident exactly two years to the day before Jesse's death also ensured that he could not become a leader in the Church. Jesse's three sons by Ethel had never been revered as part of the sacred family, even though they were ministers in the Church—but not in Dalton. Jesse's surviving brothers were never very dominant in the Union Assembly Church, even though they were ministers. Jesse's oldest brother, Edmond, who was sixty-nine at the time of Jesse's death, was on the Supreme Council in 1942 but had been removed by 1961. He had been demoted to a mere deacon. Estle was sixty-four and on the Supreme Council, and those interviewed who were old enough to remember said Estle was scared to death of Jesse and Irene. Perhaps the members' grumbling about the appointment of Jesse Junior as the general overseer ceased because Wayman's beating became common knowledge in the Church.

Wayman and Herbert Pratt left the Union Assembly Church shortly after Jesse Senior's death. The two brothers formed their own Church of God, which was not affiliated with the Union Assembly. It was reported that during sermons, Jesse Junior derisively called Wayman and Herbert's new church "The Goat Pin." Of course, Herbert still had to spend some time in prison, which left Wayman to put their new church on its feet.[55]

One also must not forget that a powerful potential leader, Cash Carmical, had been forced out of the Union Assembly Church earlier. That left only Jesse Junior and his twenty-year-old brother, Charlie T. Pratt III, to head the Church of God of the Union Assembly. But was Jesse Junior the right man to continue the family's control over the membership and the Church's money? Was Jesse Junior a man of God? Would Irene run the Church and control the money? Who was left to stop her?

PART III

A Dutiful Son, 1974–1996

"My late father, Rev. Jesse F. Pratt Sr., did not pass among the
faithful members of the church of God of the Union Assembly
seeking money."

JESSE F. PRATT JR.
"Rev. Pratt Replies to More Articles," *Dalton Daily Citizen-
News*, July 11, 1980, 1

16

A New Level of Hell

"... and as concerning the policies of The Church of God
of the Union Assembly, our policies are just and good.
We have lived by them this long, and thank God we'll
continue to live by them: they suit us just fine."

JESSE F. PRATT JR.
"Rev. Pratt Blasts News Articles," *Dalton Daily Citizen-News*,
July 9, 1980, 1

1

During the spring of 1974, just after the death of Jesse and the takeover by Jesse
Junior, Hank Aaron hit his 715th homerun to surpass Babe Ruth as the home run
king. On April 30, 1974, President Richard Nixon released edited transcripts of
the Nixon tapes to the House Judiciary Committee. Three months later, Nixon
became the first U. S. president in history to resign from office, and Gerald Ford,
who was appointed vice president by Nixon, was sworn in as the 38th President of
the United States. Spiro Agnew had left the vice presidency in disgrace following
a bribery scandal a year earlier.

Jesse Junior had started preaching at the age of seventeen. He had dropped out
of high school at sixteen without graduating and started preparing himself for the
ministry. When he was eighteen, in 1965, he held a revival in the Atlanta Union

Assembly Church. After the services in Atlanta, he had sex with three different single girls and got all three of them pregnant. One of the girls, a sixteen-year-old, was from Center, now often called White, Georgia, and the other two girls were from Atlanta. Irene paid for abortions for the two girls from Atlanta and sent the one from Center to one of the Church midwives in Dalton for her abortion. The girl from Center is dead now, but she told her best friend about it and swore her to secrecy. Her best friend, to whom she had confided, did not tell anyone until she left the church years later. This friend reported this to the author and the name of the girl from Center in a recorded interview.[1]

Consequently, Jesse Pratt Jr., the same man who may have taken a sock full of rocks and beat a man nearly to death for twenty dollars while serving an undistinguished stint in the U.S. Army, took over the Union Assembly Church the same day his father died. However, former members reported that Irene really did gained control of the Church after her husband's death. Older members and several older nonmembers interviewed reported that Jesse Junior was terrified of his mother and would do anything she asked. Irene took even a bigger part in the activities of the Church and created more money drives. It was stated that she had to raise money because Jesse Junior knew how to spend it. Once given this godlike power and wealth, Jesse Junior started his own rampage of terror that created a new level of hell.[2] A former friend reported that he and Jesse Junior were drinking beer at The El-Rancho restaurant in downtown Dalton on South Hamilton Street when Jesse got up and said, "Let's go down to the church and spend some of the church's money."[3] Junior went through all of the Union Assembly's millions of dollars in just a short period of time.

His mother had to create projects so the poor members could raise more cash for her son and family. Also, after Jesse Senior died they continued to take up a love offering for him in the name of Irene. Each of the 54 churches would have an offering for Jesse Junior in which each member would come to the front of the congregation and lay money on a Bible or in a guitar case. The Bible was on a long table in front of the pulpit or rostrum. After Jesse Junior got his offering and all the money was removed and put in a container, they would have one for Jesse Senior, who was dead. The members would all line up again and put some more money on the Bible. That money was then given to Irene. It is not clear how she conveyed that money to her dead husband. After one of Jesse and Irene's daughters lost her husband, a Vietnam veteran, to cancer, they started a collection for her, so the poor hard-working members would get up again and put more money on the Bible or in a guitar case.[4]

If one of Irene's children had a birthday, each church would have an offering for that family member. Once, Jesse Junior told the membership that he wanted a new Corvette for either his birthday or Christmas, and the faithful raised the money and got him the new sports car. Whatever he wanted, he got it. If Jesse noticed that someone was not giving enough money he would rebuke them violently. Former members said he would spare no one; he threw people around, knocking over chairs or whatever was in the way. On occasion the victims would vomit or urinate on themselves.[5]

More than half the people interviewed indicated that Jesse Junior started spending money so fast that the Church did, in fact, have to come up with new ways to raise more money. One former minister's wife said, "We were all the time giving money and making all kinds of pledges. I mean they were always coming up with: 'You need to pledge on this project, on that project.' We would give by the month, you know. My husband tried to give on everything because he was a minister, and he would get in trouble if he didn't give— him being a minister. They would openly reprove a lot of them if they didn't think they were paying their pledges—if they didn't think they were giving enough."[6]

Four times a year, once a quarter, the Union Assembly had a ministers' meeting in Dalton. During C. T.'s time, these meetings were held to go over church doctrines, but Jesse Senior soon added money pledging by the ministers during these quarterly meetings, and Jesse Junior upped the ante by demanding bigger pledges—which they called special drives— that could be paid to the Church monthly or weekly. During these ministers' meetings, Junior would rule with vengeance and retribution. No one was immune to his wrath. Fear and anxiety became so prevalent people reported they could smell it and feel it like needles pricking their skin. "It had a smell all its own," one member remembered. "It was the smell of panic that most animals seem to detect while living in the wild."[7]

Even though these quarterly gatherings were called ministers' meetings, they wanted all the deacons and members from the Dalton area to attend. Along with their ministers and assistant pastors, each of the fifty-four churches sent their deacons and all the wives of these men. One minister's wife said, "If you didn't go to these meetings, you would get into a lot of trouble." People had to attend even if they were sick—no excuses were accepted other than death. The minister's wife continued, "I've seen members get into trouble about everything and anything. I've seen people shook to the floor— off of the rostrum—over the pews. I've seen people chased out the door if Jesse told them to leave and they didn't leave fast enough. There would be a hoard of women and men come after them to chase them out the door. I had a friend that this happened to and he swore that one of the council members, Wesley Crider, hit him in the head so hard that it almost knocked him out, and he was so dazed he couldn't find his car, which made them mad at him. They screamed at him, 'What's the matter with you, can't you find your car?' And they ran over there and hit him and knocked him to the ground before he could get in his car." When asked if running members out of church happened often, the minister's wife replied, "Oh yeah, I've seen quite a few people get herded out the door. If they didn't get out of there fast enough, you know when one of the Pratts ordered them to leave, there would be lots of people there to chase them out and physically grab them—they were bombarded—honest to God—they were bombarded with the people coming at them. I've seen this happen to men and women alike."[8]

Jesse Junior was also described by former members as having what they called, "fits of rage," and he would point a finger at someone and scream for them to get out of the building. The same minister's wife described in a recorded interview: "Jesse Junior would get up in front of the church and if things were not going his way, he would pitch a tantrum and say, 'I'm going to resign.' Everyone would start crying and boo-hooing and shaking, and everyone would be terrified. He would just walk out the door and leave everybody hanging. And when he walked out the door, people would start yelling, 'Please forgive us! Oh please forgive us!' And everyone would start crying and going on. Now that I look back on it, it was sickening."[9] As those interviewed reveal, he began to expect this God-like treatment from his members.[10]

When asked to describe Jesse Junior's fits, the same minister's wife said, "If people didn't do what he wanted them to do, he would mistreat them, rebuke them, and— huh— I can't really describe it – he would just get mad! And when he walked out of the door and left people hanging, we thought we were not pleasing God by not pleasing him, and we knew we were wrong or at least thought we were. We were terrified all the time."[11] Almost all former members old enough to remember, said that when C. T. Pratt started the Church, he created a show that attracted new members, but Jesse Junior had turned the service into a horror show. As reported in interviews, there were lots of times when Jesse Junior told the ministers at their meeting that they needed to go to the bank at once and borrow $500 or more and give it to the Church. Once he told all the ministers to pay off all their own debts because they were about to have to borrow more money for the Church. If anyone failed to do as they were told and get the money turned in on time, then Jesse would have them rebuked, or in some cases, he would have them beaten up by some of the Supreme Council members. There was always some type of punishment for ministers who failed to do what Jesse ordered. There were penalties for the members, too, which usually included some type of mistreatment.

On the other hand, several former members stated that pastors who made money for the Church could do almost anything they wanted and create any kind of hell necessary to get more cash and send it back to Dalton. For example, Dan Helmick, a pastor in Harlan, Kentucky, between 1978 and 1981 impregnated a fifteen-year-old girl. Jesse Junior found out about this, and he took Brother Helmick off the Board of Elders and put him on the Supreme Council. Jesse then sent him to one of the Union Assembly churches in Hamilton, Ohio.[12] In Ohio, Helmick ruled with impunity over his church, as one former member recalled in an email:

> After getting caught molesting his stepdaughter, they moved Dan Helmick to our church in Hamilton, Ohio, and, boy, we endured four-and-a-half years of living HELL from him. He treated people badly—he acted like

a mini-Hitler. You couldn't do anything without checking with him first, not even attending a wedding in Kentucky. He was kept as pastor so long because he was a BIG MONEY GENERATOR for Jesse Junior and the Church. He made everyone sell homemade candy and give all proceeds to the church. Force, force, force, forced the people to sell candy—forced the people to give, give, give. Every family was forced to sell and raise money. It was unreal the amount of money that was going to Dalton, Georgia, from Dan's church. So when news traveled back to the church leaders about how badly Dan was treating people, it was shoved under the rug because they didn't want that stream of money stopped. Anyway, the teenage girl thing started again there in Hamilton, this time with a girl named ——— who was underage. Again, he was caught and found out and they moved him to Odessa, Texas. (After that, I don't know what he did in Texas) But about four or five years later he left the Church and went back to drinking and they found him dead in his house trailer [in Dalton], which had caught on fire. He was drunk when the trailer burned.[13]

Another member of the Hamilton Union Assembly Church shared similar views, adding:

> Dan Helmick was pure evil. He was sent up here to Ohio to be pastor because he enjoyed molesting little girls in Harlan, Kentucky. The reason he wasn't dropped from being a preacher is because he brought too much money into the church by forcing the members to give beyond their means. We could barely make ends meet so my father and my husband's mother would bring us groceries. Dan made the Hamilton church take up offerings for Jesse Junior, Charlie, and Irene every week. An offering was also taken from everyone each time one of the Family including all the grandchildren had birthdays.
>
> Dan also made everyone bring a dish to every service to share after the service. His wife would tell us what to bring. Then when we all had to go to the dining hall to eat, we had to donate money to eat it! You were forced to stay. If you went home without going back and eating, you knew you were going to be in trouble the next service. These dinners were one of the reasons why we barely had money to put food on our own tables.[14]

In 1993—the same year Bill Clinton was inaugurated as our forty-second president—Jesse Junior told all of his ministers in all the churches to have their members turn in a financial statement that included their monthly incomes. Those interviewed said that the members would then be told how much money they were expected to give monthly to the Church. If they failed to do this, there would be retribution. The ministers who failed to complete this task were demoted to deacons or to common members. This money did not include the offerings that were taken up at the services held on Sunday and throughout the week or during a revival, and the Church had lots of revivals, which lasted seven days a week for two or three weeks. Interviewees noted that a few people started leaving the Union Assembly during this period.[15]

In March of 1993 a rare blizzard hit the southeastern United States. It was called the storm of the century because of its rarity. Dalton was struck with almost two feet of snow, while high winds toppled trees, knocking out power throughout the county. People even lost water because the utilities had no power to pump water to towers. The power was not restored for weeks in some areas of Whitfield County. Water was unavailable for almost a week. A handful of people who died of natural causes in homes were left in back rooms for days until roads were cleared, allowing funeral homes to pick up the dead.

That same year and in the midst of this calamity, Jesse Junior told Junior Roberts, pastor of the Union Assembly Church in Summerville, Georgia, that Roberts's church had to sell more candy, or he was out. He also told him that year to find out how much money the members made and how much they owed, or the Church was going to drop him as a minister or kick him out completely. Roberts refused to do this, so he resigned his position and later left the Union Assembly. His son, Charles Roberts, left the Church that year also.[16]

2

There are lots of ways to spend millions of dollars quickly, but there is usually some type of self-abusive behavior involved. Some interviewees, including family members, reveal that Jesse Junior had three habits that may have caused him to go through large amounts of money in a short period of time—alcohol dependence, drug addiction, and gambling. On top of this, Jesse Junior lived extravagantly. He bought new cars and airplanes, and he built an extravagant mansion with an Olympic size pool, large pool house complete with hot tub, sauna and exercise room. His house also had a private tennis court and an eight-stall barn for horses, five miles south of Dalton, Georgia.

Another money-maker for the Pratt family was family portraits. Charles Roberts related how a lifetime friend and live-in companion of Irene, who had sold pictures of the Pratt family members to people as they left church services, started selling them as people came in and left the building. Several other women also started selling these pictures, and all the money went to Irene. They would have different pictures of the Family to sell almost weekly. The members felt obligated to buy these pictures. If a person had any money left in his pockets or her pocketbook when they went home after attending church, they were lucky. The Family found ingenious ways to get more and more money from its members. One former member had this to say about the sale of Pratt pictures, "It was nuts."[17] These pictures found their way into members' homes, framed and on their walls. Jesse Junior would remind members that Irene may visit their homes, and did they want to let "Mother," as everyone started calling her, see a dirty house? Of course, this was Jesse's way of reminding people to have lots of shrines displayed of the "Family of God" if Irene actually visited. She did visit homes occasionally, and she would criticize members if their homes were not clean enough or if they didn't have the new pictures of the Family displayed.[18]

Charles Roberts also reported that Union Assembly preacher Burton Frank in Albertville, Alabama, started selling pictures of himself and his family to his congregation. When Jesse Senior found out about it, he had him brought to Dalton and told Burton during a service that he was "high-minded" for selling his pictures. Jesse told Brother Frank that he needed to stop or be thrown out of the Church.[19] Several former female members talked about how, during the 1970s and 1980s, women would make home-made fudge and peanut brittle and sell it all over town— even in the schools. Starting at the age of six, members' children, mostly girls, were picked up each Saturday morning by four o'clock and given hundreds of bags of peanut brittle or fudge to sell. These children sold the candy on the street corners either in the hot, boiling Southern sun or in the bitter winter winds of winter. They were not taken home until all the bags of candy were gone or it turned dark. The Saturday candy sales lasted until the girls married and had children of their own.[20] All of the proceeds were turned in to Irene and she said it all went to the Church.[21] Former members reported that they questioned silently how much went into the Pratts' pockets. This did not only happen in Dalton, but it happened in each community where a Church of God of the Union Assembly was located. The candy sales became really big in the 1980s.

In Hamilton, Ohio under the leadership of Minister Dan Helmick, an anonymous former member reported on the hardships of selling candy door-to-door. "It was such a miserable time. At the time I had a baby girl and one of the things that Dan started having us sell was candy bars that were called Twookie's. Each person had to sell 22 per week, which means my family had to turn in $264 a month for them—this was in addition to all the pledges we had to make and pay, our Sunday School money we had to give every week, plus all the offerings they took up at every service. This meant I had to go door-to-door every night after work and sell them. I had to sell 66 per week because I was also forced to sell 22 for my baby who wasn't even walking yet as well as mine and my husband's. If you didn't sell them, you still had to turn in the money out of your own pocket."[22]

Even family members, excluding Jesse and Irene's children, had to give or make money for the Church. Leola Crider, one of C. T. and Minnie Pratt's daughters and sister to Jesse Senior, was expected to come up with money from candy sales. Leola's first marriage had been to Homer Brown, and they had children. Later she divorced Brown and married Minister and Supreme Council member Wesley Crider and they had children together. Wesley was a big man—standing about six-foot-two and powerfully built. Those interviewed said, "Wesley didn't mind hitting members."[23] He was one of the enforcers for his brother-in-law Jesse and then his nephew, Jesse Junior. In the mid-1950s, Leola, who was still married to Wesley, apparently had an affair with Jim Brewer, who was also on the Supreme Council. Of course, he was also married at the time. During the affair, Leola had a child whom several former members believed was the result of their affair because of its appearance. Wesley according to former members, also disregarded the sanctity of the marriage, and was known as a "ladies-man' who chased skirts around like a cat after a mouse."[24] Wesley divorced Leola and married a beautiful younger woman—much younger than himself—but later divorced the new wife to remarry Leola. It was reported that one time Wesley caught a man's wife (whose name will remain anonymous) coming out of the restroom and told her that she needed to learn what it was like to be with a real man. It was also reported that once Wesley said the same thing to Jesse Junior's second wife, Wanda, and Jesse Junior did nothing about it until he got Wesley in church in front of everyone. Then Junior gave Wesley a verbal thrashing about it and said in the service, "What do you mean by hitting on my wife?" Jesse Junior did not rebuke Wesley that day, and he did not confront Wesley one-on-one, man-to-man.[25]

Leola Pratt Crider had her own method of getting money for herself and the Church. One former minister's wife reported that during 1984, Leola would have her husband, who was crippled from a stroke, drive an hour from their home to Mableton, Georgia, to pick up Leola's allotment of candy to take back to his home-town and sell for her. He also had to sell his own allotment. After the candy was sold, the minister would drive the one-hour back to Leola's home and give her the money. She never asked him to come inside her house or even offered him a glass of water. She always met him at the door to give him the candy or take the money from him. Leola never gave the minister one cent for gas money."

She went on to add that Leola also borrowed money from her husband, which resulted in hardships for her entire family. "When we lived in Cedartown, Georgia," added Coker, Leola talked my husband into borrowing money for her. And over and over we would make the trip down there to borrow money in Mableton, and she would just take the money. [Mableton is about 40 miles southeast of Cedartown and not far from Atlanta.] I think just one time we were invited inside, but the rest of the time she would meet us at the door and take the money and not give us any gas money or nothing. Then one time Leola didn't pay us back and we ended up having to pay back the loan. And then Leola's husband, Wesley, found out about us borrowing money for her, and he told my husband not to do it—borrow money—for her anymore. And then Leola would treat us like a bunch of crap after my husband would not borrow money for her."[26]

3

Jesse Pratt Jr. continued the "confession train" or line that his father devised; how-ever, like everything else he did, Jesse contrived to create higher levels of terror. Since the beginning of the Union Assembly, the Church hosted an annual assembly in

Dalton when all the church members from all the Union Assembly churches came for a week-long gathering. There would be between five to ten thousand people attending from all the different states. As noted in an email by a former member and a family member:

> At the 1982 assembly meeting, Jesse Junior announced he wanted to have Communion and foot-washing at the end of the week, but first, he said, everyone had to be "cleansed" by confessing all their sins, and anything else they needed to admit. During that annual assembly meeting in 1982, Jesse Junior proceeded to have the entire congregation, between five and six thousand, form a line that reached from outside the building, around the walls, and up the aisles to him as he remained at the pulpit waiting to hear their transgressions. This event took almost three full days to complete. When Jesse Junior marched everyone in front of him, he looked in our faces, and he would supposedly see into our hearts whether we were right or not and that was terrifying to us—terrifying. The closer you got to him, the more frightened you became because you didn't know if he was going to say you were wrong, or you were going to hell, or if he was going to shake you, and you didn't know what he was going to do because you really thought he had that power to know your wrongdoings.[27]

Sometimes during this confession train, Jesse Junior would grab some people by the head and shake them down to the floor, all the while prodding them to confess more. He would scream, "Spit up the devils inside you." One woman, who was in her teens when this happened, reported in an interview, "I was so nervous and shaking so badly. It was the most fearful and scary time I've ever had at that Church."[28] Another member said, "It would take hours and hours to get through that line, and the closer you got the more afraid you became. Jesse [Junior] wanted people to confess their sins, and a lot of times you didn't know what you had done; you know you tried to live a good life. If you didn't know anything you had done, you tried to think of something to tell him to stay out of trouble because you thought they knew what they were talking about. It was awful."[29] Added Johnnie Haney Butler, "Sometimes I made up stuff to tell Jesse and Jesse Junior that I really hadn't done just because I thought that would please them."[30]

After three days of "cleansing," via "the confession train," Jesse Junior had Communion, and everyone had to come before him and take the unleavened bread and drink grape juice. That took an entire day, but the day in church was not finished. After Communion, everyone went back to the two dining halls—one for men, one for women—to wash each other's feet. The men had to be separated from the women because they were not permitted to see women's legs without pantyhose. One woman said, "I've never seen such nasty water in those buckets in my entire life. So many people had put their feet in them, by the time it was my turn to put my feet in it, that water was nasty and filthy."[31]

Once during communion at a ministers meeting, Jesse Junior called for the confessions line to form. He had the people come forward and place their hand on a Bible and swear they were without sin. Robert Anderson told this story about that particular day:

> A friend of mine's mother—her name was Mildred—she was a little frail lady—weighed about 95 pounds or so—I saw this with my own eyes. The church was full. She marched around there and, for some reason, Jesse Junior just turned on her like a vicious wild animal—immediately—she's a little old lady and he's a big grown, strong man—and he beats her all over the floor up there—and had the deacons drag her out the backdoor. She was crying, "Please forgive me. I don't know what I've done." Jesse Junior said, "Get her out of here." Later Jesse said she had a spirit against him.[32]

Those interviewed said that after each service the members ran to the carport where the Pratt family members parked their cars and waved to Brother Jesse Junior and his mother, Sister Irene. Jesse and Irene started having more and more young unmarried girls come to their homes to work for them—cooking, cleaning, ironing, or whatever needed to be done for them.

Soon after Jesse Junior took over, the membership started calling Irene "mother" because Jesse Junior referred to her as "mother" when he spoke about her during his services. They asked mother what soap she liked and if it was Dove Soap, then everyone used Dove Soap—or claimed they did. One member, Teresa Coker, said, "Mother liked Tetley Tea so everybody used Tetley Tea whether you like it or not." Some of those interviewed believed that Irene had become one of the gods to be worshiped, as her husband had been before, and her son had become.

Irene would also have "socials" at the Church fellowship hall. Members called these taco suppers, because that is what was usually prepared. A group of church women would do the cooking, serving, and cleaning and, of course, Irene did no labor. As one member who served at these events said, "Irene didn't get up and do anything, anytime. She'd sit there and talk to people while they gathered around her in the Fellowship Hall . . . A lot of members thought they had to hang around 'mother' to talk to her about everything."[33] Irene would have these events at the fellowship hall for special occasions such as Valentine's Day, or for a special group such as the Church band. "Of course Irene charged everyone who came and ate, even the ones who cooked and cleaned. And if a member was invited, they had better be there or all hell would come down upon them."[34]

One young woman reported that after she had married someone Irene didn't approve of, Irene prophesied at church that she would die before her child was born or during childbirth. This young wife, then in her eighth month of pregnancy, was told to make sure to be at church one particular night, and she suspected what was going to happen but she went anyway. That night she was rebuked by Jesse Junior for over an hour. She was thrown around so much that chairs were knocked over.

Robert Anderson at age seventeen.   Marie Hoskins at age sixteen.
Courtesy of Marie Hoskins Anderson.   Courtesy of Marie Hoskins Anderson.

It almost killed the young wife, but she didn't lose her baby or her life and lived to tell this story.[35]

According to Marie Anderson, "After Jesse Senior died, those boys [Irene's sons] took over. They did pretty much whatever Irene said." To prove her point, she recounted the following story that took place in 1976—the same year Georgia's Jimmy Carter was elected President. Marie was in love with another member, Robert Anderson, and she asked Irene if she could marry him. Irene told her that she could do better than that, and that God was going to send her someone special. "Well," said Marie, "it just broke my heart because you had to do what Irene said. So I broke up with him."[36]

Robert added, "It tore me up that you were not allowed to say anything. That's just the way it was. But that was Irene Pratt, and you couldn't go against what she said."[37]

Marie married someone else and so did Robert. He lived in Tennessee, and she moved to Florida. Both had families with children. As the years went by and their children grew into adults, they lived their separated lives. For all those years, they never talked to each other. During annual church assembly meetings in Dalton, Robert said he would see Marie from a distance as she sat with the women in the audience. Eventually, both their marriages fell apart, and they both divorced. And so, as fate would have it, almost forty years after Irene had refused Marie and Robert the right to wed, they were able to renew their love for one another. Accordingly, on June 6, 2015, they finally became man and wife.[38]

For a few years after Junior's takeover, his father and mother's picture still hung on the wall behind the pulpit. They would also stand, salute, and then applaud Junior, his wife, and his brothers and sisters as they came in to have a seat in the front or on the stage with the Supreme Council. But in time the picture of Jesse Senior came off the wall. It was not replaced by anyone else, but the saluting and standing ovation for the Pratt family continued. The worship of the Family and its image went forward without interruption.

Those interviewed said that the rebuking or reproving increased in all the Union Assembly churches. Jesse Junior would grab somebody during almost every service and shake them until they were almost unconscious. It is worth repeating what Charles Roberts said about going to the Church during Jesse Junior's time, "We were afraid to go to church, and we were afraid not to go."[39]

4

In January of 1986 the world mourned the loss of seven astronauts when the space shuttle *Challenger* exploded 74 seconds after liftoff. By that time, Jesse Junior had spent a huge amount of the Union Assembly churches' money, though luckily for him he had access to the continuous flow of money coming into the Church through pledges, offerings, and candy sales. To boost the candy sales and pledges, Jesse announced his plan for a campground in Catoosa County, the county just northwest of Whitfield. Members became ecstatic with joy about the prospects, since none of them were allowed to attend any "worldly events," such as movies, swimming pools, and the like, and the promise of a campground inspired the congregation to work harder and pledge even more. Jesse ended up buying 407 acres of property in Catoosa County. Almost half of the property was open land, but there were also two lakes, which together totaled six acres. He also told his parishioners that he had purchased land in Gordon County, the county south of Whitfield, to build a church park.[40]

Jesse told the membership during the annual assembly that he was creating the campground and park because a few young people had started leaving the Church. On the campgrounds, Jesse told his congregations that they could park their campers or place a tent there, because he planned to have electrical hookups. He said there would be two enclosed swimming pools, one for the men and one for the women, two tennis courts, restrooms, and separate shower stalls. There would be buildings where the kids could play various games. He even mentioned building a golf course later. He told his followers that the project would cost several million dollars to build, so pledges were encouraged—actually demanded—but after a time there still were no signs of a campground being built. Nevertheless, no one dared ask Jesse Junior why the campground was not developed. The members thought their man of God knew what he was doing.[41]

At the same time, Jesse Junior did not tell his members that he had joined the most expensive golf club in Whitfield County, called the Farm, during the 1990s, and had begun playing golf regularly with a group—even playing in shorts, which was against the Church's rules.[42]

While he began mixing with the wealthy elite in Dalton, his reign of terror continued inside the Church's walls. Former members stated that during the 1980s and early 1990s, Jesse Junior continued to have members beaten up in church services. He would start preaching about the sins of a particular member—no one ever knew who it would be—but Junior would "rant and rave" about the person, male or female, and spend the entire service belittling that individual. Then he would order that person out, and she would have to run quickly to get away from the ones coming after her.[43]

> Troy Overby witnessed one particularly fearful event of this kind when Rev. George W. Redwine was almost killed at a service. "Jesse started preaching to Brother Redwine telling him he had the wrong spirit. Anyway, they just ran and grabbed him, picked him up, and ran him down the steps—the steps leading to the double doors the Pratts used to park their cars. They were going to throw him out the door but they were locked. When they threw him up against the door he just bounced off them like a piece of stove wood.[44] Brother G. W. Redwine's son, Gaylon, had married Jesse Junior's sister—Jesse Senior's daughter—but that didn't matter, . . . Jesse Junior accused Redwine of saying he was tired of preaching about the [Pratt] family and was going to preach about Jesus."[45]

Although the incident did not involve Jesse Junior directly, another memorable beating was witnessed by Charles Roberts. "It was on Mother's Day, May 13, 1994," recalled Roberts, "When J. W. Hughes hit Rodney Brown [his own cousin and Jesse Junior's cousin] with an upper-cut, causing him to come completely off the ground and falling head first onto the sidewalk in the church parking lot. Rodney had gotten between his own father and Cousin Hughes, who were arguing with one another." According to another cousin who apparently witnessed the event, "Rodney smarted off to J. W. then he 'cold-cocked' him. Rodney almost died. Rodney was at home in a coma for a week."[46] [J. W. Hughes contacted the author through his grandson in 2019 and said that he fully regrets this incident, and that he was reprimanded by the Church.]

> One other incident worth mentioning is the Sunday Jesse Junior ran a man by the name of Ronnie Crider (not related to Wesley Crider) out of the services. Charles Roberts witnessed this and said, "Jesse told Ronnie Crider to get out of church. Ronnie got up to leave but before he could get out the door, [Jesse's cousin] and Wesley Crider grabbed Ronnie and

Jesse Junior and "Mother" Irene.
Courtesy of an anonymous
family member.

hit him a few times and ran him out the door. Ronnie tried to run but staggered to his car—Wesley grabbed Ronnie and started slamming his head against a Dodge van putting a dent in the van. [The cousin] said to Wesley, "You're not doing that right." Then [the cousin] grabbed Ronnie and put a bigger dent in the van. Ronnie sued the Union Assembly and they settled out of court. The judge told Jesse that he'd shut the Union Assembly down if anything like this happened again. Ronnie's cousin Chester Van Meter said Ronnie settled out of court for thirty thousand dollars."[47]

But by now, according to former members, the dam had sprung a leak—maybe a tiny leak—but, unlike the little Dutch boy who stuck his finger in the dyke to stop the leak and save the town, the Pratt family knew that a trickle of uncertainty about their leadership was spreading through their midst and could erupt at any moment, and no one knew how to plug this leak.

17

Dying in the Faith

"We're not ashamed of how we live. A lot of people talk about
this church, about us being silly for believing in faith and not
going to the doctor. But you see what happens. If they had had
as much power in their medicine, well she'd still be living."

JESSE PRATT JR.
at the funeral of Pamela Hamilton, 1985[1]

1

Since the beginning of the Church created and developed by C. T. Pratt until 1995, the members were not allowed to go to doctors or use medication. Instead of sprinkling the many unnecessary deaths and their cases chronologically into the past narrative, a few of those recorded by those interviewed and found in print are combined into this one chapter. This story would not be complete without giving examples of how these members "died with the faith." In fact, the Union Assembly's health practice is the chief contributor that led to the Church's major change to come in 1995.

Some former church members who had had family members die when they may have lived by seeing a doctor refused to be interviewed. Some of those individuals had been out of the Church for thirty or forty years, but they were still afraid to speak about their experiences. A few brave people did talk, and much more was discovered in print about this abusive acceptance of faith healing by the Union Assembly Church membership. Although there are many examples, this chapter summarizes the well-documented cases.

It would be almost impossible to compare the average number of deaths in the Church of God of the Union Assembly to the average number of deaths in the general population of Dalton and Whitfield County. A student from the University of Georgia came to one of the Dalton funeral homes to try to make some calculations, but he gave up after realizing there were too many variables involved.[2] Another thing that makes such an analysis unreliable involves the non-reporting of infants born dead and those who died soon after birth. There are two reasons for this. One, there is no consolidation of the records—except death certificates—that can be traced, and these death certificates do not identify a place of worship. Two, not all babies of Union Assembly members who died were taken to funeral homes where a death certificate would be filled out and recorded. Some members said babies were buried in shoeboxes, tool chests, or plastic bags without anyone except the person doing the burying knowing where this might be. Several former members who actually lost a child during childbirth at the Union Assembly's maternity ward in Spring Place, Georgia, were never showed the dead infant. They were told it was taken care of—no funeral—and there was no mention of the dead infant again or were told later that Flora buried them behind the maternity ward.[3]

Almost every former member interviewed had lost a member of the family— brother, sister, mother, or father—before the departed reached the age of fifty. Some lost young siblings or young children. Four older funeral directors from Whitfield County told the author on separate occasions that before the Union Assembly allowed doctor visits they picked up an inordinate number of dead children and young adults from the Church's membership as compared to children and young adults who died in the general population of Whitfield County.[4] When C. T. Pratt first threw away his medicine at the turn of the twentieth century and said he would never take it again, he was not necessarily being too rash, because the state of medical care at the time, for many conditions, did not necessarily improve one's chances of survival. But over the course of the twentieth century, spurred on particularly by advances made in the wake of two devastating world wars, medicine improved dramatically, becoming a lifesaver beyond imagination, especially when compared to what it was like just fifty or a hundred years before.

Although modern medicine has always recognized the "placebo effect," some Union Assembly members did testify to the healing power of Brother C. T. Pratt and Jesse Pratt Sr. Their testimony suggests strongly that sometimes healing did take place, even though, for whatever reason, they did get well without seeking medical care or taking medication. But it is also likely that a significant number of members from Church of God of the Union Assembly died as a direct result of not receiving blood pressure medicine, a vaccination, an antibiotic, regular insulin injection, or other medications.

For example, on Sunday, November 16, 1958, an article in the *Marietta Daily Journal* detailed how twelve children from the Church of God of the Union Assembly had died of pneumonia in and around Dalton, Georgia. In the article, Dr. Cecil Jacobs said, "I am sure all of them could have been saved. Children just don't die of pneumonia in this day and time." Regarding this incident, C. T. Pratt was quoted that week in the Atlanta newspaper that he did not tell parents to turn down medical assistance. However, Pratt did not mention the Church's strict rule on healing by faith only.[5]

The majority of clergy say that God gave us disease and early death, but he also gave us doctors and medication to use. In fact, Rev. Billy Graham said the following in a syndicated newspaper article that was also published in the *Dalton Daily Citizen* in 1970. The advice was in direct response to a woman asking him about his views on faith healing: "You should not hesitate to seek professional help if it is needed. The Bible tells us not to bear our burdens alone, but to 'carry each other's burdens.' At the same time, let this be a time when you draw closer to God."[6]

2

On March 7, 1962, Esther Roberts gave birth to a son who was born jaundiced, but, because she and her husband were members of the Union Assembly Church in Dalton, she did not seek medical help for her baby. On March 12, five days after his birth, the infant died. Esther's husband, Junior Roberts, did not have a car at the time. Jesse spoke with a local funeral home, which agreed to finance the funeral for the child. Junior and Esther's other children had nothing suitable to wear—the Church required a particular type of clothes to be worn to a funeral—so Junior walked his family on a cold March day to and from the Economy Department Store in Dalton, a distance of about three miles, to get the proper clothing for their children. Junior carried the two girls and Esther held the two boys' hands as they walked. Esther, still weak from the ordeal of giving birth and caring for the sick child, fell on the way home and her sons had to help their mother finish the trip. On the day of the funeral, the Roberts family walked to the funeral home, which was about two miles from their house on Ezzard Avenue. The oldest son, Charles Roberts, remembers that either J. C. Teems or C. U. Lyons gave them a ride home after the funeral. "Personally, I don't feel that one should have to ask the pastor for help," said Roberts. "The pastor should know the circumstances of his members and Jesse did. The first true Christians that I met in my life were J. C. Teems and C. U. Lyons."[7]

In 1974 on a Sunday, two weeks after the death of Jesse Senior, Jesse Bee, a mother of three girls and one son, went into labor. She was taken by her husband to the church's maternity ward at Spring Place, a distance of about ten miles from

Charles Roberts with his father, William "Junior" Roberts. Courtesy of Charles Roberts.

their home in Union City. Jesse Bee told her eighteen-year-old daughter, Teresa, who was traveling with them that she was glad to finally have this child because she had felt so flush and dizzy prior to delivery. Jesse Bee kept rubbing her swollen hands, and she complained about how much her feet had swollen during the last few weeks. Within hours after reaching the maternity ward, Jesse Bee had a new baby boy and all was fine for a few hours. Then Jesse Bee, who would turn forty-two the next day, became delirious. Her eyes rolled back in her head as her neck stiffened, which caused her chin to point to the ceiling as her head flew back. Soon after this, she began to shake, and the shaking became an uncontrollable jerking, which lasted several minutes, according to Teresa. She would realize years later that her mother had been having convulsions. Before daybreak Jesse Bee had several more convulsions and thick slobbering foam rolled out of her mouth. Her hands, feet, and face continued to swell until it was hard for her daughter to recognize her.

The midwife, Flora Hughes, started praying and sent word to the Church to ask for more prayers. The next morning, Teresa's father went after his other two daughters—one was thirteen and the other five. He brought them to see their mother, who had become blind during the night. Jesse Bee's one-year-old son was left in the care of a relative. Teresa, already married at the age of sixteen, stayed with her mother all night, wiping saliva from Jesse Bee's mouth and face. Jesse Bee had had five convulsions that Monday and did not recognize anyone by lunchtime. The thirteen-year-old daughter sat with Jesse Bee and cried when she realized her mother couldn't see. The daughter, Teresa, recalled that her mother wore a pink nightgown, which was covered with specks of blood. She recalled how her momma moaned and jerked around on the bed. By mid-morning, Jesse Bee's drool turned crimson—a sign of internal bleeding, or she could have bitten her tongue, cheek, or lip.

Ministers and some members from the Church arrived and took a position just outside the dying woman's door where they prayed openly—all at the same time creating a muffled staccato noise. Jesse Bee's daughter, who was five-years-old at the time, later recalled the horrific scene:

> "I just remember being in a lobby. I can't remember anybody being in there with me, there could've been. I was just on a couch, and didn't know where my momma and daddy were. I knew my momma was sick and something was wrong with her, so I went around looking for my momma. And I went in this room and my daddy was standing there with a handkerchief and blood was coming out of momma's mouth, and there was blood all over the handkerchief, and she was making this noise. She was having convulsions, I learned later, but I didn't know it at the time. And daddy screamed at me to get out of the room, and it terrified me to see my momma like that, so I went back to the lobby.
>
> "At some point, the midwives, or somebody, brought me into Momma's room. And my mother was lying there, and my sister, Teresa, asked momma if she knew me. And she moved—just her eyes moved. Momma just cut her eyes at me and stared at me, and she never said anything. Only her eyes moved. (I didn't learn until later that mamma was blind.) It was real scary the way she looked at me. I would dream about that—Momma in that bed looking at me—until I went to therapy 24 years later and talked about it in psychoanalysis sessions. After a long time in therapy, I just let go of something and stopped having that dream of Momma looking at me with blood on her mouth."[8]

After lunchtime Jesse Bee fell into a coma. This mother of five children, counting her new baby son, died just before nightfall.[9] If this woman had been under a physician's or registered midwife's care they would likely have noticed her symptoms of preeclampsia weeks before, and she most likely would have lived. She had classic symptoms of what was once called Toxemia of Pregnancy.[10]

This family's woes were not finished. Teresa's daddy, the father of five with three children still living at home, remarried in 1977, three years after the death of his first wife. In February 1978, his second wife awoke one morning and could not get out of bed and complained of back problems. The new wife thought she had broken her back, because when Teresa's father tried to stand his wife on her feet, she fell. The wife called her two older daughters, who were not members of the Church, and they came after their mother while her husband was at work and took her to the hospital. She learned that she had stage four breast cancer, which had already metastasized and spread to her vertebrae, causing them to weaken until breaking. Teresa's father was dropped as a preacher from the Union Assembly immediately— before nightfall—because his wife had gone to the hospital. He remained a member, nonetheless. His wife lived in agony for eight more months before she died.

Teresa's father, who was now a double widower, had applied for a job at one of the North Georgia carpet manufacturers. After having the required physical, he learned that he had extremely high blood pressure, which needed to be controlled with medication. Of course, because he belonged to the Union Assembly Church, the young widower refused to take medicine. He had already bought his and his first wife's tombstone, which was inscribed *Dying in the Faith*. That was what the majority of the Union Assembly members had on their tombstones, supposedly to let passersby know they had not sought medication. The author walked Dalton's graveyards to see this for himself.

In 1979 the man fell ill. He called his oldest daughter, Teresa, who by now was twenty-four years old with children of her own. He asked her if he and his three younger children could stay a few days until he got to feeling better. He was only forty-nine and would turn fifty in a few days. His hands and feet were very swollen. Also, he had trouble breathing; he grew very weak and had trouble walking. His youngest daughter remembers having to help him take his wedding ring off. He gave it to her to keep, and she kept it until 2013 when she gave it to one of her brothers. A few days later, Teresa's father said he felt better and wanted to go home for his fiftieth birthday. Teresa took her father and the children back to his house and planned to stay one night before going back home to her own family. Her father, who had typical signs of heart failure caused by long-term high blood pressure, turned fifty and died just after midnight. The youngest daughter, who would later have to have therapy for her reoccurring dreams, remembered hearing her older sister screaming, and when she ran into the kitchen, she saw her father slumped over in the chair. The youngest sister of Teresa said she recalled seeing her father being placed on a stretcher and men pulling a sheet over his face.[11]

The three parentless children went to live with their oldest sister, Teresa, and her children. Teresa's husband, who had a stroke at the age of twenty-eight, was unable to work. A few years after the death of her father, she went to visit her husband's sister Brenda, who was fifty and had been ill and bedridden for a couple of months. Teresa arrived at her sister-in-law's home early one morning. Brenda, while lying in bed, was throwing up pus and blood. She begged someone to take her to the hospital and said she didn't want to die. She begged Teresa to call an ambulance, but Teresa refused saying she didn't want to send this woman to hell by calling for medical help. Brenda died a horrible death without ever being able to get out of bed.

Teresa would leave the Church of God of the Union Assembly at the age of thirty-nine, but she carries guilt about these deaths on her shoulders to the present day. She commented that she doesn't hate the people (members of the Church)—she loves the people—and she thinks there are lots of good people in the Union Assembly, but Teresa thinks blood should be on someone's hands. "I believe that 100 percent," she commented tearfully in an interview.[12]

3

In the 1980s, several occurrences led to unwelcome publicity for the Church of God of the Union Assembly. Once the Union Assembly's secrets surfaced, it was impossible for some of the stories to be denied. The Jonestown Massacre in Guyana on November 18, 1978, when 912 members freely took their own lives when told by their leader Jim Jones to "drink the Kool-Aid" created a renewed awareness of dangerous religious cults and how, under extreme circumstances, they could control and destroy lives.

So the stage had been set for the general public to form an opinion regarding any cult-like behaviors within religious groups that were not conventional. All that was required was an event that might receive worldwide coverage, and that event occurred in 1983 when a twelve-year-old girl—small for her age—complained of pain in her left leg. Her father, a minister for the LaFollette, Tennessee, Church of God of the Union Assembly, took her to a chiropractor. By now, Church rules had changed to allow members to use dentists or have broken bones set, as well as receive general first aid, which included wound suturing. However, they still did not allow members to use any medications or receive standard medical treatment. According to Rule 23 in the *Minutes of the Church of God of the Union Assembly*, "all members of the church are forbidden to use medicine, vaccinations or shots of any kind but are taught by the church to live by faith."

Pamela Hamilton, the daughter of Larry and Deborah Hamilton, had complained about pain in her left leg for a month before her parents took her to a chiropractor. The chiropractor saw that her femur bone was broken and a growth had developed. He immediately sent her to an orthopedic surgeon, who set a small fracture and, being suspicious, took tissue samples of her leg. Pamela was diagnosed as having Ewing's sarcoma, a rare form of bone cancer that strikes young people and, if untreated, spreads quickly to the lungs and brain, killing its victim within months.

Dr. Frank Haraf, a cancer specialist, explained to Pamela's parents that the disease had a good cure rate if caught early and that chemotherapy meant a potential cure, not just buying more time. He told the parents that if the condition was left untreated, Pamela only had six months to live. The father said that he and the child would discuss it. The father did not mention any religious beliefs at that time, but later told Dr. Haraf that their daughter would not be getting the treatment because taking medication was against their religious beliefs. They believed that God could heal their daughter on his own. If he did not, then it was God's will that she die.

Dr. Haraf contacted the Tennessee Department of Human Services and, on

August 26, they sued for custody of the girl in Campbell County Juvenile Court. Facing charges of child neglect, Larry Hamilton hired attorney James Alexander Hamilton Bell and then fled his home to elude sheriff's deputies, who had come to take custody of Pamela. Bell worked with her parents to delay Pamela's treatment as long as he could. Bell said, "What Pamela wants is to let her father in heaven dictate her fate."[13] By now this had become a national story, and journalists from around the United States flocked to East Tennessee.

On September 17, a juvenile court judge called Pamela "the most courageous person I've ever been in contact with—child or adult. To allow her to die would constitute a very public wrong."[14] He ordered chemotherapy to begin and ordered ambulance attendants to take her to the appointed hospital. Pamela, wearing a blue-and-white gingham dress throughout the ten-hour hearing, broke into tears and resisted the attendants. Earlier in the trial, Pamela had said, "I do not want . . . chemotherapy because I do not want my hair to fall out. I do not want to be sick. I want to be home with my mama and daddy."[15]

At the end of the trial, the nationally televised news program *Nightline* ran an episode about Pamela Hamilton's case. Not one Pratt member agreed to be interviewed for the show, but the entire outside world was beginning to learn about the Church of God of the Union Assembly.

Nevertheless, attorney Bell and Larry Hamilton maneuvered to delay the start of Pamela's treatment for two more weeks by petitioning the Campbell County Circuit Court on November 8.[16] This act, initiated by Pamela's father, prolonged her cancer treatment. Dr. Frank Haraf, Pamela's cancer specialist, said that the ten weeks wasted in the legal battle over high principles reduced Pamela's chance of survival from 75 to 25 percent, and the tumor had grown from the size of a baseball to the size of a watermelon. By the start of treatment Pamela's weight had dropped to 86 pounds.[17]

As a result of the national media attention, the Church of God of the Union Assembly was known throughout much of the United States. Pamela's tumor did shrink after treatment. Her parents and Jesse Pratt Jr. insisted the improvements were caused by their prayers and had nothing to do with the medicine she had received. Pamela's family dropped its fight against her treatment in January 1984 after the Tennessee Court of Appeals upheld a juvenile court judge's ruling that, if treatments were withdrawn, she would be considered neglected by her parents and could be placed in state custody.

In the fall of 1984, doctors discontinued Pamela's chemotherapy. The cancer in her left leg had stopped growing, and signs of it had almost disappeared, except for scar tissue. However, a checkup in January 1985 revealed that tumors had spread to her lungs and back. Only a few months later, on the morning of March 28, 1985, Pamela lapsed into a coma and died that afternoon. The fourteen-year-old child, who had been taught by her Holiness religion to put her life in God's hands, lost her battle with cancer and died.

Three hundred mourners attended her funeral on Saturday at the Dalton Church of God of the Union Assembly. Jesse Pratt Jr. preached her funeral. "I never heard her grumble," said Pratt. "I never heard that little girl grumble one iota. She didn't want nothing but God." Jesse blamed her death on the chemotherapy and the burden of publicity. He went on to say in the one-and-a-half-hour funeral oration, "We're not ashamed of how we live. A lot of people talk about this church, about us being silly for believing in faith and not going to the doctor. But you see what happens. If they had had as much power in their medicine, well, she'd still be living."[18]

Between the publicity of Pamela's trial and her death, another Union Assembly child died from lack of medical treatment. On February 20, 1984, in Trion, Georgia, thirty-six miles southwest of Dalton, C. D. Long, a member of the Church of God of the Union Assembly, was arrested for manslaughter after his teen-aged foster son died of appendicitis. The foster son, Tommy Glenn Hester, sixteen, had died in September 1983, but his death was not reported to authorities for another five months. Tommy's aunt, Glenda Eden, complained to the sheriff and county coroner, which prompted an investigation and the subsequent arrest. Mrs. Eden also reported that another Hester child, Karen, had died six years earlier of appendicitis when she was seven years old. Former member Tammy Magill, recalled how her and other illnesses were handled in the Church: "I grew up in the Dalton Church. I saw numerous kids and adults die. I feel sorry for the adults that died, but the kids that died had absolutely no legal rights and no choice in the matter. I will never forget what happened to the Hester family. Glenda had three kids. The father had been accidently electrocuted and died a few years prior. Glenda eventually remarried D. Butler. Glenda's child, Karen had become extremely ill with appendicitis. One night Glenda came running into the church during the middle of a service carrying a very limp body of her little girl. Karen was seven years old at the time. Glenda had not attended the service that night because her child was so ill. Glenda was crying and asking for prayers. I'll never forget Jesse Junior's response to her. He told her that God had laid his hand on her child because she did not attend service that night. Jesse said God would probably take her child from her. He began to yell and scream at her, and all the members began to yell and scream at her. Meanwhile, there was a sad and desperate mom in the middle of the room crying and begging for her daughter's life. Everyone just stood there and watched Karen die that evening. This image will never leave me."[19]

Tammy also remembered that Glenda (Hester) Butler got pregnant not long after this and died from complications after giving birth. Her children were left with their foster parents, C. D. and Judy Long. After his arrest, C. D. Long commented to a *Rome News Tribune* reporter, "You may say, 'why wasn't Tommy healed? That's God's business.'" Mr. Long also said in the same article that Tommy did not want to go to the doctor. "We loved our son." Long said. "But if anyone thinks he can make me hang my head and deny the blood of Jesus that cleansed me, he's got another thing coming." Mr. Long accused Hester's aunt of trying to make trouble by reporting

Tommy's death. He defended faith healing by saying, "You ever read the Bible? Did Christ ever send anyone to the doctor?" C. D. Long also claimed that his diabetes was healed by faith. "Through the power of prayer, I was completely healed."[20]

However blessed C. D. Long may have been, there are accounts of other members dying from untreated diabetes. A former member related a story about a diabetic woman on insulin who joined the Knoxville Union Assembly Church during a revival. Because of the Church rules she stopped taking her insulin. Within weeks she developed diabetic ketoacidosis, known as DKA, and died.[21]

The publicity surrounding the Union Assembly also caused mainstream religious leaders to publically respond to the Union Assembly's faith healing practices, including the Reverend Lee Jessup, a pastor of the First United Church of Christ in Lexington, Kentucky. In an article entitled "God Expects Us To Use Our Minds," published in the *Lexington Dispatch* on March 16, 1984, Jessup discussed the Tommy and Karen Hester case. The Reverend Jessup stated that Tommy and Karen, foster children of C. D. Long, who died from appendicitis, "lived with a man and his wife, who most would say were sincere in their Christian faith—sincere to the point of fanaticism, perhaps, but sincere nonetheless." Jessup then revealed that C.D. Long and his wife were members of the Church of God of the Union Assembly.

"You see," Jessup said in his article, "the Longs and others belong to a church which believes that only God can heal, and the work of physicians is an unnecessary evil in the world. They view doctors as performing work best left to the Lord. Man's medicine is of 'this earth,' they might say, suggesting that God's magical powers of healing are the only powers which work." Jessup also quoted their foster father, C. D. Long, who told the *Atlanta Constitution*, "You may say, 'why wasn't Tommy healed?' That's God's business. In response, Jessup replied : "Does this mean that God created us as idiots? Did He not give human beings the gift of knowledge? Are we not the only creatures in the universe with the powers of perception? Are we supposed to rid our minds of all knowledge of the human body, and its own recuperative powers?" In analyzing this statement, Reverend Jessup argued that this means that God did not, in fact, create us as idiots.

Jessup added that "God gave us the ability to think, to learn about ourselves and how to perform the medical miracles we see daily. If we believe God is a magician with superpowers, and He sends them down from heaven like Zeus would through a lightning bolt, then we completely and utterly deny that He is also present in the hands and minds and hearts of men and women. Physicians are like all the rest of us. They have been called by God to perform a task in the world." He concluded the article by saying, "To deny physicians the opportunity to use their God-given abilities, is in my mind to deny the existence of God."[22]

4

Newspaper articles, as well as former members, described other stories of needless deaths in the Church of God of the Union Assembly—such as five-year-old Tory

Beeler's story. In 1987 Conley Ray Beeler's twin sons, Tory and Cory, were jumping on the bed when Tory fell and struck his head on the wooden bedframe. Because they were members of the LaFollette, Tennessee, Union Assembly Church, the parents refused to take Tory to the doctor even though he remained lethargic and listless. Then two days after the accident, the child's head swelled and he started to vomit. The parents still did not seek medical help. As taught by their religion, the Beelers prayed and left the life of their child in the hands of God. Tory, moaning in pain, finally lost consciousness and, two days later, died.[23]

An anonymous former member at the Church of God of the Union Assembly in Hamilton, Ohio, reported the following death to the author via email. "In January of 1978 Wallace White died because he had refused to take his insulin for 'sugar' diabetes after joining the Church. The diabetes ate him to death slowly and painfully. One foot almost rotted off before he died. It turned black and smelled like decaying meat as the flesh on his foot rotted away."[24] One other former member confirmed the event.[25]

In 1973, Marie Hoskins Anderson's thirty-two-year-old mother, Donna, was attending the Union Assembly Church in St. Petersburg, Florida. Marie's mother and father had divorced when Marie was six, and her mom had remarried. Marie, now living in Knoxville, described what happened when she was sixteen: "We lived in Florida and it had rained. We had concrete steps coming out of the house and they (steps) had this real slick paint—so when they were wet they were very slippery. Well, she [her mother, Donna] came out of the house one day and slipped and fell right on her bottom. Well, not long after that—a few weeks, maybe—she comes down sick. I didn't know it at the time, but now I think she was pregnant. And the reason I'm saying that is because when she would lie down in the bed, something would try to come out of her—down there—[her private parts]. And when that would happen they—these women from the church, Leola Crider, and mother's sisters—would take her out in the hallway where they would get around her, and they would all stand her up on her head and hold her upside down and jostle her trying to get that thing back up in her. The odor was awful when this would happen, and it got really bad before she died."

She and her maternal grandfather, Estle Richardson, who was on the Supreme Council and a pastor in the Church would sit up with her mother during the night. Marie continued: "Going back to my mother—just before she died—she would scream for an ambulance until she passed out. And no one ever called her an ambulance. At one point my mother got the rattles just before she died, and my grandfather—mother's father—asked Donna if she was afraid of dying. And she said, 'No, I'm worried what's going to happen to Marie and Mike.' And then my grandfather said, 'Don't worry about that; I'll take care of them. At that point, I thought my life was over. Finally mom passed away at the age of 32. And that has haunted me for years that I didn't do anything about it. And me and my brother went to live with my grandfather and grandmother." Marie's grandfather, Estle

Marie Hoskins with her mother, Donna, 1973. Courtesy of Marie Anderson

Richardson, had sexually abused Marie since she was ten years old. When she brought his abuse to the Union Assembly Church's hierarchy, they told her not to report it to the authorities. The Church moved Estle off the Supreme Council but allowed him to continue preaching at his church. Marie and her brother ran away from their grandparents' home within a year.[26] Marie had to spend years in counseling as an adult.

In 1978, fifty-one-year-old Illyne Blackwood, the mother of Joy Pratt who is the wife of Charlie T. Pratt III, developed a tumor in her breast that proved to be cancerous. She declined medical treatment and refused to go to the hospital. According to friends, she suffered in pain for months before she died at home on October 1, 1978.[27]

In 1982, Zella Moore died from an undetermined disease. Before death, she suffered for months, reportedly coughing up a black bile which could have been blood. She became so weak she could not get out of bed even to go to the bathroom. The Church's minister, Dan Helmick (mentioned in Chapter 16), went to visit Zella. Did he console her and pray for her healing? No! It was reported that Dan *rebuked* her in her bed by shaking her head with his hands. "I don't know how she could stand this," reported a witness to the event. Zella lived in constant pain for another week before dying.[28]

Charles Roberts, who suffered dearly as a result of the Union Assembly church, believes countless needless deaths occurred to members through the years. When I told him recently I was working on this very chapter, Charles laughed ruefully and said, "There will be a lot of deaths in that chapter because there have been so many."

Then he turned serious and said, "If you do, it will take an entire book to list them, much less tell their story."

I replied, "Well, I'm not going to tell them all because I don't know them all."

"Listen," he said with a sad face while shaking his head. "If you write about all the crazy, insane, awful stuff that went on in that church, well, you would have three books—maybe more. It's so unbelievable what all went on down there. It ruined many lives . . . including mine." He stared out his window, deep in thought and fighting back tears.

And Ye Shall Know the Truth

"You're not forced to give nothing but what you feel like giving.
I know everyone of you fellows that's saying these things.
I could write your name down in this paper
and you know I could."

JESSE PRATT JR.
"Rev. Pratt Blasts News Articles,"
Daily Citizen-News, July 11, 1980, 1

1

The collapse of Jesse Junior's reign was not swift or, at the least, not as swift as it should have been. His dynasty lasted a little over twenty years, but during the last few years he wielded power. Jesse Junior's control dissolved into a heap because of his own self-destruction. This transformation of the Church of God of the Union Assembly might have happened regardless of who became the general overseer after the death of his father, Jesse F. Pratt, in 1974, but the power placed on the young Pratt's shoulders was probably too much for a man with limited education and lack of experience. His grandfather, C. T., and father, Jesse, came up during a different era when at least a high school education was not yet the norm, but by 1974 when Junior took over, 74.9 percent of students entering the ninth grade in the United States received a high school diploma.[1] Jesse F. Pratt Jr. did not finish high school. Therefore, Jesse may not have been mentally capable of handling an organization of between five and seven thousand members spread across twelve states. The number of members and churches had dropped during his reign even though he denied this repeatedly to his membership and to the public.

As one former member said, "Junior could talk the talk, but he couldn't walk the walk." In other words, he could not and did not live by example. At least his grandfather and father appeared to live somewhat modestly and presented an image of righteousness and virtue (even though, as this work documents, especially in Jesse Senior's case, this was largely a façade). However, Jesse Junior failed even to try to conceal his transgressions. For a long time the congregation refused to believe the rumors that often spread like wildfire through dry grass concerning the misconduct of their new god. Later, when his indiscretions mounted to an astronomical quantity, the dam fractured, and the flood of resentment became impossible to restrain.

The beginning of the end for Jesse Junior began in 1980 when a television station from Atlanta, *WXIA 11 Alive*, investigated the Church of God of the Union Assembly and ran a series of programs about the Church on its newscast. It was entitled, "Religion Based on Fear." The program was very negative towards Jesse Junior and the Union Assembly Church. A female reporter from *11 Alive* tried to enter the church building, but she was stopped at the door and told to stay out. She asked why and was simply told she could not come into the church wearing pants. A picture captured this event as she was being ordered to depart and ran in the local paper, the *Daily Citizen-News*. Since the 1960s the Union Assembly had allowed their members to own and watch television. Therefore, they were exposed to television news programs which may have opened a few members' eyes to the outside world. A level of doubt about the Church doctrine may have started creeping into the membership as they gained new access to other opinions.

Jesse Junior was distraught with frustration to the point of being hysterical. Every sermon he preached became a lambasting of the publicity the Church received. Of course, Jesse would take no blame. To him, it was everyone else's fault. Then the news turned away from the Union Assembly Church when a string of child and young adult male murders in Atlanta turned into a hunt for a serial killer called the Atlanta Child Killer. One Sunday, soon after the television station stopped investigating Jesse and the Church, Jesse Junior preached a sermon about the child murders in Atlanta. About these murders, Jesse was quoted by former members as saying something to the effect, "Well, that's what God has done to make them leave his people alone."[2] Did Jesse really believe God kills children? Did the members really believe that, too? By making such statements, Jesse Junior was insulting the intelligence of his membership, and some of them obviously noticed it.

By 1980, controversy followed Jesse Junior around like a shadow he couldn't escape. For six years, Jesse Junior had depleted the church's coffers on bad investments and to subsidize his own lavish lifestyle. One member reported that "Jesse Junior would buy these big tractors and pay $200,000 or more for them with the Church's money. He'd turn around and sell them—see—he would sell everything for $70,000. Jesse Junior would get these super tractors for $250,000 and keep them a week or two and then sell them for $70,000. He'd buy a bus and pay several hundred thousand and turn around and sell it for $70,000. Of course we know he kept the money."[3]

Jesse Junior also drained the important assets away from the Church by selling its fleet of airplanes. It was reported by a nonmember that he sold five or six of them to Ed Weaver, who owned Diamond Carpet Mills in Chatsworth, Georgia, eleven miles from Dalton. Jesse himself would later set up a carpet store off of Exit 228, I-75 and sell carpet from Ed Weaver's carpet mill. Jesse traded the Church of God of the Union Assembly assets to Weaver for carpet at a ridiculous price—pennies on the dollar.[4] During all of this extravagant spending by Jesse Junior, the membership was still making and selling candy to bring in hundreds of thousands of dollars to the Church. In addition, the collections taken up from the different Union Assembly churches added up to a considerable amount of money, but all of this was apparently not enough.

Soon afterwards, Jesse started requiring members to turn in statements about their weekly or monthly income. He then set amounts that working members had to contribute back to the Union Assembly. Those working as contract laborers had to report what they intended to make on a particular job site. An example of this involved Allen Ward who was not a member nor had ever been a member of the Union Assembly. When Ward decided to re-carpet his home, he hired a carpet-laying group to install it. The installers happened to belong to the Church of God of the Union Assembly, but that made no difference to this man. He just wanted his carpet laid.

The two young men first picked up the carpet where Ward had bought it, which is customary procedure. The two installers took the entire day to lay all the rooms and did a great job according to Ward, but they had not finished installing carpet on the stairs when they came to him and wanted to be paid—not just for what they had done, but for what they still needed to finish. He told them he would pay them when they finished the steps and asked how long before they could come back. They said they could probably come back to finish in two or three weeks because they were booked up until then. Ward told them he would wait until they finished before writing them a check. They told him they had to have the money then because they had to take it to their church by 6:30 that afternoon. One of them said Jesse Junior was expecting it that night, and they would get into trouble if they didn't take the money to their church. Allen realized that Jesse Junior was the minister at the Church of God of the Union Assembly, but he still refused to pay for a contract job that wasn't finished. They said they would make a call to Jesse and did so. In a few minutes, they came back to Ward and told him that they had permission to stay and finish the steps which would complete their contract. Within two hours they had completed the steps, so he gave them a check. They left, and Ward was pleased with their work but found the entire interaction to be an ordeal.[5]

In addition to money troubles, the Church was suffering from a leader whose poor personal habits were becoming too obvious to ignore. There had always been rumors about Jesse Junior's alcohol and drug problem within the membership, but as he made more and more demands on his followers, some began to question his ability to lead at all. He craved friends to associate with, and these friends started telling their friends about their escapades, and soon the dam sprung a leak that couldn't be stopped.[6]

Jesse Junior also continued to tour with his gospel singing group the Trailblazers, which caused him to spend more and more time away from home and his flock. A few members interviewed said Wanda Jean accused Jesse of sleeping with other women, and one interviewee reported that he had.[7] Charles Roberts said that Wanda's father, who lived with Jesse Junior and Wanda, told him that Jesse would hit Wanda on the side of the head during their arguments about his infidelity.[8] Several former members said Jesse could and would not hide his corrupt habits; he drank, he partied, he gambled, and he started using cocaine. His gambling included high stakes poker, and the more he drank and doped himself, the more Union Assembly money he lost.[9]

More controversy was on the way after Jesse Junior sold the church ranch in Bouse, Arizona, in January 1980. Jesse Senior had bought the first 1,000 acres in November of 1961 and presented it as retirement home and farming community for the church's elders. In 1966 Jesse Senior needed $1.3 million to refinance the Arizona property which was then called Arizona Western Ranches. So, Reverend Jesse Pratt Sr. went among his ministers and church members and asked them to bring him cash for the ranch. As mentioned earlier, quite a few Church members subscribed to a twenty-five-year certificate through the Church Service Program, and members contributed their hard-earned money or borrowed funds that were to be repaid to their estate if they died. The certificates were based on $1,000 units that would pay back $1,500 upon maturity to a certificate holding member. While Jesse Senior was still alive the church invested $2 or $3 million in improvements to irrigate the desert farm property and to grow crops.[10]

Then the staggering news came that Jesse Junior had sold their future retirement home in Arizona plus other church properties for $6.6 million. The members, who had given thousands of dollars towards its purchase and development, wondered what had become of their investment. Some certificate holders, who had been guaranteed a return on a significant investment, were no longer members, so questions were asked. Some hired lawyers, and the news spread that the Union Assembly may be an unethical, corrupt organization—and this rumor spread far beyond the walls of the Church. It wasn't long before the Dalton newspaper, the *Daily Citizen-News*, started its own investigation into the reports.[11]

2

The first article from the *Daily Citizen-News* about the Church of God of the Union Assembly came out on June 17, 1980. It was written by *Citizen-News* staff writer Moody Connell. Jesse Junior's picture, showing him on the phone in the church office, was in the article, even though Jesse himself was not quoted. The church's general secretary, Harold Sowder, was quoted in the interview. Sowder told how the Union Assembly began and stated that they followed the same general rules in a church covenant written in 1921. When asked why the three former leaders were all from the Pratt family, Sowder stated: "It is not an inherited job. They [church leaders] were put in by a total vote of all the membership." He also said they had 54 churches in 15 states, and at one time they were in 16 states. Sowder claimed that the membership had not decreased during Jesse Junior's tenure. At the end of the article, reporter Connell asked Sowder if their members were taught to avoid doctors and medical facilities. Sowder stated: "We believe in faith. We preach faith, but it is up to the individual on what to do." Sowder, however, did not report the rebuking or bodies being slammed to the floor.[12]

Two days later, on June 19, another article by Connell appeared on the front page of the *Daily Citizen-News*. It was titled: "Church of God Doctrine Said Strict." The *Daily Citizen* had been presented a copy of Minnie Pratt's book, *We Walked Alone*, and Connell spent the first half of the article talking about the founding of "The Church" as it was called by the members. Then Connell turned to one of the church's general rules listed then, which states: "Members of the Church are forbidden to use medicine, vaccinations or shots of any kind but are taught by the Church to live by faith."[13]

Connell described other rules, including the dress code that applied to female members and injunctions against members not to attend worldly events, such as movies and ballgames. Then he hit the Church with the following statement: "But one rule which has caused shock waves that still divides even family members is a church rule that commands church members 'to stay away from any dismissed members.'"[14]

Four days later, on June 23, Connell came out with his third in a series on the Union Assembly Church titled "Former Church Ministers 'Disillusioned,'" which was also found on the *Daily Citizen*'s front page. Connell started the article by reporting how founder C. T. Pratt had members sell their homes and move to Dalton "to await the last days, but instead many found their own faith ending here." Connell said ex-members and present members were talking to him. He stated: "They speak of separated families, they speak of their own fears that they would be cut off from God."[15]

Connell goes on to say: "Disappointed in the late '60s when the end of time didn't come about as predicted, some members turned back to their own home states after having sold homes or businesses to support the church." He quoted former members about "rebuking" and being cast out of the church. One ex-member quoted talked about having to give much more money than the standard 10 percent. Another former member said he almost starved to death while in the church working for "nothing." Connell said he listened to both sides and quoted members who talked about Jesse Senior being a quick-draw gun-handler. Connell also described the Pratt male family members as "well-dressed, driving nice cars and living in modest homes."[16]

"Whether it was an airplane or an Arizona farm to buy," noted Connell, "they [members] learned to dig deeply into their pockets." After reporting about church rules against medicine, TV, and insisting on natural childbirth, Connell added: "Now these same people who molded and shaped their entire life around this faith say they are told they are outcasts and to be shunned by church members." Finally, Connell wrote that he was still listening to hear the church leaders speak because that is the way this project had begun. Connell wanted to hear the church leadership's version of events.[17]

Connell's fourth article in the series, which came out on June 27, related how properties were bought and sold. He revealed how a total of 12,400 acres—which the ranch property was a major part of—was sold for $6.6 million. He closed the article by saying "former members are still trying to secure a return from the thousands of dollars they put into a desert ranch which in a few years may become an electric power-producing plant instead of a retirement home."[18]

Moody Connell hit Jesse Junior and its leadership even harder with his fifth article, which was published on Monday June 30. He quoted a former member as saying: "I was never paid and you can tell the lawyer that." The man also produced documentation that indicated repayment is still being anticipated. Allen Bickert, the Union Assembly lawyer, said "he thought ex-church members should be refunded, and he speculated that only a few unpaid claims might remain because he was advised the church had paid back the exact amount paid into the venture by individuals holding church certificates." However, a former member produced a letter for Mr. Connell's article that showed that a group term life insurance policy on the life of the lender provided benefits in case of the death of the lender. The letter also showed that upon the lender's death, the full face value of their certificate would be immediately payable. But, the church lawyer said, "They [the Church] let the insurance coverage lapse and never did notified us what they had done." Connell closed his article by saying: "A letter furnished the *Daily Citizen-News* that was dated Aug. 3, 1971, said that monthly payments made on that venture were to be sent directly to the church office in Dalton, although formerly paid in Arizona."[19]

The next day, Tuesday July 1, a prepared reply by Jesse Junior was printed on the front page of the *Daily Citizen-News*. Pratt referred to the first article by Connell that ran on June 17 and called the accusations against the Church of God of the Union Assembly idle and false. And then he confidently stated that the Church was here to stay. Jesse Junior went on to explain how his father had been unanimously elected the general overseer of the Church of God of the Union Assembly on October 12, 1961, when the church "owed an indebtedness of well over a million dollars for various properties and businesses." He reported that his father had to raise for the church in excess of $60,000 per month for a period of twenty-seven months.[20]

Jesse Junior then reported on the "places that his father prepared for people to live in rent-free, and in most places, utilities included." Among these properties, he listed the following: the retirement center in Spring Place with 17 residents, which added up to a total monthly cost of $2,823.75, including utilities; a motel in Spring Place where four people lived, which added up to a total monthly cost of $2,123.75, including utilities; forty-five houses and apartments across the United States, which added up to a total monthly cost for the Church of $8,611.50.[21]

Jesse Junior went on to write: "I think the church people have a great influence. The governor has come to see me both times during his campaigns, and a lot of local politicians come and talk to me, asking for the church's support. Yes, I would say we must have some influence." Pratt went on to say that "We don't try to force what we believe on anyone; Law is force and grace is favor. And we don't try to interpret what the Bible says either."[22]

In analyzing Jesse F. Pratt Jr.'s reply, one can see great inconsistencies. First, where did his father, Jesse Senior, come up with the $60,000 a month for twenty-seven months? He did not go back to painting houses. He raised it two ways—he sold property, such as the cannery, slaughterhouse, etc., and of course the membership had to dig deep in its pocket for the money. Second, the seventeen widow women living in the Spring Place maternity ward—yes, he failed to mention that detail—had given the Church their homes or farms in exchange for living there.[23] Third, the four people living in the Spring Place motel at a cost of $2,123.75 a month just does not make sense. Was the motel not in operation for a profit? Did the Church have an entire motel for four people? Fourth, the people living in the forty-five houses and apartments across the United States with a monthly rent of over eleven-thousand dollars must have been paying rent to the Church. Numerous former members have come forth and stated, on the record, they were given nothing but much was taken away. Where did these forty-five houses and apartments come from in the first place? Could they have been given to the Church? Well over a hundred members' homes and farms were gifted to the Church, as court records show.

On Wednesday, July 2, the sixth article in the series appeared in the Dalton newspaper, and Moody Connell reported about other damning incidents that had taken place in the Church. In the article, Moody also succinctly stated what many thought, but few, if any, had ever said in print: "A closed society which exerts power and influence over its followers, the Church of God of the Union Assembly has been dominated by the general overseer who tightens control by preaching fear of God's wrath."[24] Later in article, Connell also quoted the damaging rule about current members being commanded to stay away from dismissed ministers and dismissed members. He described the 1961 decree which gave the general overseer full authority to control the Church and its membership. After listing a half-dozen of the Union Assembly rules, Connell ended the article with a quote from a former member: "The wrath of God falling on church members has been expounded on frequently in the church."[25]

The following day, Thursday, July 3, an article written by Jesse Junior appeared in the *Daily Citizen-News* on page 1. In the rebuttal, Pratt talked about his grandfather and his father and how they formed this great church. He then attacked Connell's citations of the Church rules. Pratt stated that the rules have not changed since the founding of the Union Assembly, but that his father, Jesse Senior, updated the minutes in 1965. He argued that Connell's June 19 article, which stated: "Our rule which has caused shock waves that still divides even family members is a church rule that commands church members to stay away from any dismissed member was incorrect." In response, Jesse Junior said, "That's another false statement," and then he quoted the rule in full, which read: "All members are forbidden to attend meetings that are held by a dismissed preacher, or to go around him. They are commanded to stay away from any dismissed member who is against the church as stated in II Thessalonians, Chapter 3, verses 11 and 14."[26]

As a rebuttal, this made very little sense. Junior was supposedly talking about the final words of the rule, namely, "who is against the church. . . ." However, after more than six years of research and conducting almost a thousand interviews, it is clear all dismissed members were considered "against the church." Either way, the act of shunning tore families apart—mothers from their children, brothers from brothers, sisters from sisters, and so forth.

On Wednesday, July 9, the same paper printed another reply by Reverend Pratt. This time it was in response to the article by Connell published on June 23. Jesse Junior, among other things, directly called Moody Connell a liar in his response, stating: "My grandfather never forced anyone to move anywhere, and as concerning their faith ending, it ended when they departed the church that was preaching faith."[27] Of course, the operative word is "forced." Interviews reveal that members did have a choice about whether to accept a directive to move, but not accepting meant leaving the Church, and leaving the Church meant losing your family, friends, maybe a job, and, according to the Church's theology, going to hell. If threatening to send someone to hell is not using force with fear, then what is?[28]

Pratt went on to say all the statements in the June 23 article were false. Specifically, he took issue with Connell's claim that "The Church requesting more than 10 percent . . . Whether it was an airplane, or an Arizona farm to buy, they learned to dig deep in their pockets." Perhaps surprisingly, Pratt also publicly took on his accusers, if not directly threatened them: "Our offerings are free will, it always has been and always will be. You're not forced to give nothing but what you feel like giving. I know every one of you fellows that's saying these things. I could write your names down in this paper and you know I could. I don't have to name you[,] God knows you too." Then Pratt called out those members who would not let the paper use their names because they still had family members in the Church. In doing so, he quoted his father, Jesse Senior, who once said "It's a might sorry character that's ashamed of his name."[29]

In the last paragraph, Jesse Junior concluded his response by adding, "Last but not least, Mr. Connell said he was still listening to hear from the leaders of the church. You needn't wait any longer. We didn't come here running, and we won't be leaving. We're in Dalton to stay."[30]

However, at the beginning of this article, a *Daily Citizen-News* editor had reminded the readers that Mr. Connell was just reporting events related to him by news sources—and that Connell did not fabricate the statements in the article.

Two days later, on July 11, another rejoinder by Jesse Junior was printed on the front page. In this piece, Jesse assured the public that the certificates issued on the Arizona Ranch were still valid, and the Church would pay their face amount in full if anyone wanted to come forward and ask. Pratt did state that the twenty-five-year certificates were not scheduled to come due, however, until 1991. He said that even though the property was sold, the certificates were good and that the dream of a retirement home for the elderly that his late father had "still lives on."[31]

In the days that followed, the Church of God of the Union Assembly lived up to Jesse's pledge and refunded the money for the certificates. Former members were able to get their checks from the certificates at a local hotel in Dalton if they brought them there in person. Present members were presented a check in the church office. It was reported that some members—how many is not known—endorsed the check and handed it back to the Church.[32] Charles Roberts said that he learned later that his father had also done this, and that it truly broke his heart.

The seventh and final article came out on July 16, also under Moody Connell's byline. However, the article was, more accurately, an interview with the Reverend J. Willie (J. W.) Burnett, who said he had helped shape the Church of God of the Union Assembly with the man he called "a natural brother," C. T. Pratt, until Burnett fell in disfavor and his lifetime church membership was revoked. He also called C. T. Pratt "one of the greatest men I ever knew." Burnett said that he and Jesse Senior had married sisters and that this marriage was Jesse Senior's second one, and he had challenged Jesse's second marriage to Irene for being against the church rules. Burnett said he sought to bring this matter before the Supreme Council of the church but was himself removed from the council that he had organized.[33]

Reverend Burnett said that years later Jesse Senior called him to tell him that Brother C. T. was dying and asked him to preach his father's funeral. He then related a touching scene when he visited his sinking friend at his home. "I recall clasping the hand of the feeble, elderly church founder, embracing him and exchanging pleasant greetings."[34]

Burnett also recalled church members being encouraged to move to Dalton from other states to join the "Camp of the Saints" and the approaching end of time forecast by Brother C. T. Pratt. He confirmed that people were selling out and moving to Dalton. He believed that C. T. was correct about the end of times, but had just missed the date.[35]

Burnett said, years ago, he was warned that he would soon die when he broke off relationships with the church. Someone had a vision that Burnett would die tragically on Thanksgiving Day. He said that he had become concerned about interpretation of church doctrine and about the all-consuming emphasis placed on getting money for the church. He said he also opposed "rebuking" of church members, which he described as physically shaking that individual.[36]

Reverend Burnett added that he left the church once in 1945 and returned. He said he was upset when his parents deeded their home to the church, as other members had, but Jesse Senior reversed that by sending money to his parents. Burnett went on to explain how Brother Jesse became general overseer and Brother C. T. lost his ruling status and how they were confronted by large holdings of church property and financial problems when the church lost a lengthy court battle and had to begin paying property taxes. He said he had come back to the church in the 1960s when the Union Assembly reversed itself and got away from the "money thing." But this change did not last, as he stated, "When I came back, everyone was coming back, but a year later they [the Church] went back to the money thing." Burnett also expressed opposition to pregnant women going to midwives instead of doctors.[37] There were no more rebuttals from Jesse Junior printed in the newspaper.

3

On the heels of the negative publicity about the Church in the Dalton newspaper came the unwanted national exposure of the Pamela Hamilton case and the deaths of the Hester children, which showed that the membership was, in fact, commanded to rely on faith healing and to stay away from medicine and medical treatment. Jesse also continued to lose enormous amounts of money for the Union Assembly. Some members started speculating among themselves that their general overseer may be involved in acts unbecoming a man of God, but the majority of the church followers continued to support their leader.

In 1983, Jesse Junior announced that the Church would be purchasing a large quantity of cattle for the members of the Union Assembly. He told his people in all 54 churches that if they wanted to buy a half-cow or a whole cow, they should send in their money to the Dalton Church office, and arrangements would be made to get their beef to them., Many members (about half) even went out and purchased freezers for $300 to $400 so they would have some way to store the beef. They then paid for the beef and waited... and waited. Months turned into more months, and soon not another word was heard about the beef. A few people in Dalton did receive their beef, but that was it. Where did this money go?[38]

One former member elaborated on the cattle scandal: "One time at a ministers meeting, Jesse Junior got up and wanted us to buy cattle. We could buy a whole one or go in halves with someone and buy a half of one. So we went in with another man to buy half. The way it was to work was that when they were ready to kill and process, we would get the meat from our cows. So that never happened. We paid for them and then he [Jesse] sent men around to the different churches with checks to give us for our cows we never got, so we could sign the checks back over to the church and then they would be justified so to speak because they supposedly offered us our money back. We knew better than to not sign the checks back to them. That was the whole idea and reason for them coming around with the check books. It was made clear to us what we were to do. . . . He [Jesse] knew how to work us. They called special meetings in our churches for these men to come around and have us sign those checks back over to the church."[39]

Jesse fooled them at a 1987 Ministers Meeting in Dalton, when he announced that he would like to renovate the Dalton Church and build balconies. Hence, a "Balcony Fund" was initiated and money for the balcony was collected for years and turned in to the Church. To this day, there is not a balcony in the Dalton Church of God of the Union Assembly. Charles Roberts has been quoted as saying that if anyone will bring him a picture of the balcony in the Dalton Church, he would give him his Corvette and $1,000 in cash.[40]

While Union Assembly members could hardly afford to buy groceries for their families—almost all were on food stamps and welfare—in 1988, Jesse Junior built a 6,283-square-foot home on 5.6 acres of land. The home was located in the southwest portion of Whitfield County on Dug Gap Road, about five miles south of downtown Dalton. There were countless talented people who went to the Union Assembly Church, and these members gave their time to construct the all-brick, two-story home with four bedrooms, five bathrooms, a paneled study, a huge bonus room, a massive main-level master suite, a modern kitchen with all built-in appliances, a separate three-car garage, an Olympic-sized pool, a 1,400-square-foot pool house, and an eight-stall barn. In the master suite, the ceiling was covered with mirrors. There were secret passageways leading to rooms with two-way mirrors spying on the bedrooms. The main grounds—about two acres—where the home sat was surrounded by a seven-foot high wall made of brick and wrought iron. The floors were hardwood, tile, and plush carpeting.[41] Former member Robert Anderson stated that he often drove down from the Knoxville Church to work on Jesse Junior's house which, he added was built and paid for by the church members.

Several former members reported that Jesse's second wife, Wanda Jean Poole, once went to the church office to obtain thousands of dollars to buy furniture and curtains that went into their new home. Jesse also had Cadillacs, Mercedes, motorcycles, RVs, and a huge, top-of-the-line tour bus to carry his singing group from city to city. He even had a separate garage built on the property for the large bus.[42]

With the balcony fund campaign over and his new home completed, Jesse did not wait much longer before creating another fund raiser. In 1989, he announced a "Beautification Fund" to raise money to go toward improving the churches and their properties, including planting trees, landscaping, painting, and remodeling. Nothing was beautified except at the Dalton Church, but even there, not as much as promised was spent. But through pledges, special offerings, candy sales, and the taking of some of the members' paychecks, the money kept pouring into someone's pockets—most likely Jesse's, but others could have been taking a share.[43] Jesse's brother, Charlie T. Pratt III, was the assistant general overseer and also often preached at different Union Assembly churches, thus earned a paycheck from the Church. Still, Charlie lived modestly and in a modest home, was never known to drink alcohol, take drugs, or gamble. None of my interviewees alleged that Charlie Pratt III ever had affairs outside his marriage, and he is presently married to his only wife—a childhood sweetheart.[44] Both of Jesse Junior's sisters and youngest brother graduated from high school and all are currently working for a living.

On July 28, 1989, Jesse and Wanda's home on Dug Gap Road was deeded back to the Church of God of the Union Assembly.[45] The reason for this is not definitely known. Some of those interviewed speculated that it had something to do with property taxes Jesse had to pay, and by putting the house back into the name of the Church, these taxes could be avoided. However, Jesse and his family still resided in the home, and this is obvious from what happened four month later.

It was November 19, 1989—a Sunday night about nine—when a lone white man with a shotgun and a pistol forced his way into Jesse and Wanda Pratt's new home on Dug Gap Road. The gunman ordered the occupants of the house into the rear bedroom and told them not to leave. Somehow, he locked the family in the room, and then he took an undisclosed amount of cash from a pocketbook. The only description of the home invader appeared in the *Calhoun Times and Gordon County News*, who identified the robber as a white male. According to the Whitfield County Sheriff's Department the suspect was believed to be driving a light-colored (brown or beige) minivan with dark stripes as a getaway vehicle.

The deputies refused to disclose the number of people in the house or their identities. No one was injured during the robbery, which lasted about ninety minutes. That is a long time for no one to get a description, and a long time for someone to rob a pocketbook. The story also reported that the Pratts resided on a 5.6-acre estate appraised at more than a half-million dollars and that the estate was transferred to the name of the Church of God of the Union Assembly in September.[46] However, court records show it was transferred back to the Church on July 28.[47]

The following Sunday after the robbery, Jesse told the Dalton Union Assembly congregation that it was Clinton Dukes who robbed his family. Clinton was a former member who had had trouble with Irene's son, who was Jesse Junior's brother. "Herbie and Clinton had a falling out, so they were mad at him," reported Charles Roberts, "but Clinton must have been 'the man of steel' and faster than a speeding bullet because it was later determined that Clinton was in Knoxville, Tennessee, that night." Dalton and Knoxville are about two hours apart.

By 1989 Jesse's estate of 5.6 acres on Dug Gap Road had grown in value and was worth much more.[48] The value of half a million dollars in today's market would be almost one million dollars. In October 2014, Kinard Realty had it on the market for $1.5million. It was sold within months but for less than that.

4

In 1991, as the world watched Desert Storm launch the First Gulf War, rumors about Jesse Junior's transgressions started spreading to the entire membership. Many members resisted believing the stories, but as the stories kept coming, more than a few members began to have doubts about the Church's doctrine they had been taught their entire lives. Jesse must have recognized the change in attitude, because more and more of his elite members were speaking out against his immoral behavior. Some informants said they could smell alcohol on his breath at church. He was seen at bars by some of the younger members who themselves visited the same bars in Atlanta and Chattanooga. But Jesse Junior met this new situation head-on with the only method he understood—FEAR. So fear he created.

Interviews reveal that by this time, Jesse F. Pratt Jr. had almost financially wrecked the Church of God of the Union Assembly. Much more money was going out than coming in but few members realized it at the time. The situation was on a downhill slide that couldn't be slowed as long as Junior was the general overseer. How many members realized exactly how much money was leaving the Union Assembly's treasury is not known—probably few, because the word had not reached far outside the family circle about his expansive spending habit.[49] Every Sunday airplanes belonging to the Church flew into the Dalton Airport loaded with cash from some of the 54 churches scattered across 15 states, while money from the churches close to Dalton arrived by car.[50] The weekly offerings taken up at church services in guitar cases must have been huge, and put an enormous burden on the membership, but Jesse Junior told them to keep sacrificing for the Lord. "We need this money for new churches and to spread the word of God," he reminded his members.[51] When discussing the period of the early 1990s, one member said, "It is almost unbelievable how much money was coming into the Church during these times."[52]

After Jesse spent the bulk of the church's savings and determined that the cash that was coming in weekly from the members was not enough, he started borrowing money, or, more correctly, the Church started borrowing money, using its property as collateral. It was just a matter of time until much of the property would be sold.

On September 3, 1991, the Church of God of the Union Assembly under the leadership of Jesse F. Pratt Jr. acquired a loan from Fidelity Federal Savings Bank of Dalton, Georgia, for $1,032,417.44. The loan required using the 407-acre tract of land in Catoosa County, Georgia, as security.[53] This was the same land the Church had purchased in 1986 for the purpose of building a campground with swimming pools and other entertainment. This is the same land the members and their children had worked so hard to acquire. Irene had given them a goal to raise two million dollars for this campground. This was the land members were so excited about—so excited that they went far and above to raise the money for their campground. Former members said that some of the membership even borrowed money to cover their pledges for this campground. This money was not only raised in Dalton, but also in fifty-four other towns scattered across the United States where the Union Assembly Churches were located. But only Jesse and a few closes allies knew the money was borrowed against property bought during the 1980s and 1990s. It would be a few more years before the members knew they had worked so hard only to provide collateral to back up a debt.

In addition to stacking up enormous financial losses, Jesse Junior began to show signs of instability and arbitrariness, which lead to some dramatic changes in the rules Union Assembly members lived under. One of the most difficult to accept was with regard to clothing. Although some former members believed Jesse's brother, Charlie T. Pratt III, convinced Jesse to make the male and female dress code changes—two former members, as well as Jesse Junior's former banker, had a different story.

According to former Union Assembly member Robert Anderson, who played guitar for a singing group called the Georgia Sound. (This group traveled with Jesse's group, The Trailblazers.) The dress code changes were made suddenly with very little fanfare:

> Well, there was this weekend and we were doing a show at the Tivoli Theater in Chattanooga, and we were scheduled to sing and so were The Trailblazers. Now we heard through the grapevine that there was going to be some changes made about what we could do or not do. While I was standing in the foyer with a guy named Paul Thomas Hughes—and Charlie Pratt [III] was standing there too—we were having a conversation and greeting people as they came by. In about fifteen minutes, Jesse Junior walked in—he was talking to somebody else—his singing partner—I think—and Jesse ignored us. He had jet black hair—he had just dyed his hair, and low and behold Jesse had on a pair of shorts. And when Charlie saw him, Charlie's eyes looked like Superman's eyes—you know—like he could pierce a piece of steel. That's the way Charlie looked when he didn't like something—even today. Charlie followed his brother and went up and confronted Jesse. . . .
>
> Jesse wanted everybody to be able to wear shorts, and women to cut their hair, and to wear makeup—stuff we couldn't do before because it was a sin, and if you did that you were going to hell.

Robert's wife, Marie, who was also interviewed with Robert, agreed: "That's when things started to change—when The Trailblazers started really traveling on the Southern Gospel Tour. Jesse had told Wanda [Jesse's wife], 'we got to do some-thing our—women are so embarrassing with their hair and long dresses.' Because if they were in your area, you had better be there—and lots of women came, and Jesse was embarrassed."

Continued Robert: "After Charlie confronted Jesse, he took Charlie out to the bus and rebuked him all over the bus for not accepting these changes. I saw this first hand, and later one of the boys, Tray Starnes, who was in Jesse's group told us that Jesse really let Charlie have it. I mean he did that to his own brother—that just put fear in all of us."[54]

Jesse Junior's friend and personal banker—not a member of the Church—said in an interview that Jesse told him he was thinking about changing the dress code for the women."[55]

Changes regarding the membership's use of medicine came on the heels of the changes in the dress code, but were partly instituted as a result of the measles outbreak of the late 1980s and 1990s. According to the CDC, by May 10, 1991, local and state health departments had reported "a provisional total of 27,672 measles cases in the United States for 1990—a 52.1% increase over the 18,193 cases reported for 1989—and 89 suspected measles-associated deaths." The 89 deaths documented in 1990 were the "largest number reported in a single year since 1971 (90 deaths and 75,290 reported cases) and the highest death-to-case ratio documented in the past 30 years."[56]

Indeed, between 1989 and 1991, measles accounted for more than 11,000 hospi-talizations and 123 deaths nationwide. These hospitalizations and deaths occurred predominantly among unvaccinated preschoolers.[57] Although the *1990 Minutes of the Church of God of the Union Assembly, Inc.*, stated that members' children were allowed to get required vaccination shots, most members did not believe in them. Of course, state laws required these vaccinations before a child entered public schools, but the children of the Union Assembly churches were not expected to get vaccinations until they actually enrolled in a school system.

Dr. Luis Viamonte, a pediatrician in Dalton, had reason to believe that Union Assembly members actually were responsible for spreading the disease across North Georgia after hosting another religious group "from Texas that brought Rubeola (Measles) to our area." According to Viamonte, "due to their belief that immu-nizations were not necessary they spread this serious illness among themselves and forced an aggressive immunization booster campaign in our area. There was a least one death as a result and some required hospitalization."[58] And one of the most severe cases of measles hit the son of the assistant general overseer, Charlie T. Pratt III, brother to Jesse Junior.

When Charlie and Joy Pratt's young seven-year-old son, Johnny Franklin Pratt, contracted measles in 1990, the family was expecting the virus to run its course, but the young preschool child turned deathly sick instead of getting better. Charlie loved his son so much that he took him to the Dalton hospital where he was diagnosed with pneumonia. The sick child was put on antibiotics, which probably saved his life. Several former members reported that Charlie then went to his brother, Jesse Junior, and, since he had violated the Church's rules regarding seeking medical help, offered to resign as assistant moderator. Jesse refused to accept his brother's resignation and told him that maybe God was trying to tell them something.[59]

Immediately after Charlie had his son treated medically, Jesse had the rule of not using doctors and medication brought before the Supreme Council and Board of Elders who voted to eliminate the rule from the Church doctrine. Members were told that it was not against God's wishes for them to use doctors and medication, and if they did, they would not be rebuked, dismissed, or go to hell. Jesse Junior did tell them to continue using prayer and faith in God for their healing, and it was up to the individual to make their own decision regarding medical attention.

It took some time for the membership to acknowledge this new freedom. They had been indoctrinated against it all their lives, and the rule had been a cornerstone of the Union Assembly since C. T. Pratt, who likely had been sickened by some remedy he had been taking, had tossed his bottle of medicine away and sworn off doctors forever. It was reported by some members as well as former members that the changing of these church laws during the 1990s created a paradox for the older generation, who had been members for a long time, sometimes decades into the past. Half the people I interviewed said their parents would ask themselves, "When was I wrong—back during the time when the former strict rules of the Church, such as not seeing doctors and not wearing makeup, were enforced? Or, am I wrong now, with the Church's new doctrines, which are absent of these former regulations?"[60] A few chose to cling to the old doctrines with regard to their clothing, but all of them began to accept medical intervention when they needed to. Breaking through socialization and indoctrination of the young can be extremely difficult if not impossible. More than half the former members interviewed also said that, at times, they had needed professional help to overcome the worries and fears instilled in their subconscious and conscious minds after their long experiences with the Church.[61]

On the heels of this change came other rule modifications. Jesse, with the guidance of his brother Charlie, had made another remarkable claim in the *Minutes of the Church of God of the Union Assembly, 1990* edition which stated: 9 (a) "There had never been a rule in the history of the Church against the women wearing earrings. The Supreme Council and the Elders of the Church agreed to permit the wearing of earrings, as long as the sisters wore small ones rather than large, gawky-looking earrings."[62]

In the new section entitled "Moral Christian Guidelines," (which replaced "The Rules to Govern the Church of God of the Union Assembly,"), Jesse and the ruling body made the following changes: members were allowed to rent video movies, but the rules warned them to be very selective in the material they rented. He advised against videos that contained abusive language, vulgarity, or nudity. Jesse was giving new freedom but only a little at a time. The dress code was also changed. Women were permitted to wear slacks as long as they were not tight fitting and not at church functions.[63]

Perhaps even more astounding, members were suddenly given permission to marry someone who was a member of another Christian faith without having to leave the Church. They still had to get approval from the general or assistant overseer for permission to marry. Jesse explained through Bible verses that a person was saved by faith in Christ Jesus, and through him, they could enjoy eternal life.[64]

Besides being able to wear pants, women were allowed to use makeup but only lightly. All members were allowed to attend and participate in sporting events. They were also allowed to wear attire appropriate to the sporting event, such as shorts and knickers, sweat pants, and boat pants, but clothing must fall below the knee and never be worn to town or church events. If they wanted to swim, women were allowed to wear swimming suits, as long as the suit was worn over a full leotard. Nothing was said about boys and girls using separate swimming pools.[65]

Once these church rule changes started, others were adopted soon afterwards. Almost all of the high school girls at Dalton High and Southeast Whitfield High started bringing more modern and stylish clothes to school in their book bags and changing into them either in the locker room or a restroom. After this, the girls dressed like other high school girls and wore jeans, T-shirts, and dresses above the knee. However, their hair was still long and not cut, so they were still slightly different in appearance. The Union Assembly students also started dressing out in gym shorts during physical education classes.[66] One former member Marie Anderson, recalled: "The rule changes—dress code and hairstyle—came about gradually. First our hair could only be cut to a specified length, and the shorts had to be to our knees. However, once these modest changes were made by the Union Assembly, it wasn't long until we pushed the rules to the limit. Very soon—I mean within a year—all the younger girls and women could not be recognized from the general public."[67]

But the one rule that bound members to the Church and kept them from leaving still had not been removed. This rule that caused families to be separated from dismissed members or members who had left the Church, including family members, remained in the Union Assembly's General Rules and was enforced up until the mid-1990s.[68]

6

Despite loosening his grip somewhat, Jesse just could not stop his spending or losing the Church's money. His mismanagement of the Church of God of the Union Assembly's vast empire had him reaching deeper and deeper into its reserve. Former members said that it was inconceivable to imagine how someone could spend, lose, or mislay just the amount of money coming into the Dalton Church, much less squander the assets the Church had when Jesse took over from his father just twenty years before, which he claimed in the 1990 Church minutes to be 10 million dollars.[69]

On top of all that, the IRS audited Jesse Junior during the early 1990s. The IRS had learned that he had failed to declare all his earnings when filing his federal and state income taxes during those years—the IRS has not made known the exact number of years. In addition to not reporting all the income he was receiving from the Church, Jesse Junior had failed to file other taxes, such as capital gains on some of the property like airplanes and land. He was audited, and the IRS issued an order indicating the amount of money he would need to pay on back taxes by the end of 1992—or the IRS would seize some of the land he had put in the name of the Church of God of the Union Assembly, including the big home he still occupied on Dug Gap Road. Jesse not only owed the IRS back taxes, but also owed the interest on those taxes—again the exact amount was never known by the public.[70] During this time, Jesse announced in Church that he wanted everyone to quit reporting they were giving money directly to him—that the IRS was after him—and they needed to report that they were giving it to somebody else because of the IRS.[71]

On December 7, 1991, the Union Assembly sold Jesse Junior's home on Dug Gap Road to Zach Norville. The exact amount that he paid for this home is not fully known, but in 2011, prior to his death, Norville reported that he traded property for Jesse's home. Norville had earlier purchased the old Ryman Pontiac-Cadillac dealership, which was located next to the Church of God of the Union Assembly. Milton Ryman had sold this property to Norville for $378,400.[72] Zach Norville told me that he was looking for property with Charlie Cofield when Charlie took him to see Jesse's house on Dug Gap Road. Cofield was never a member of the Church of God of the Union Assembly, but he did check with the Church about the sale of the property.

When Cofield described the arrangement to Norville, the latter took it. Norville went on to say that he met with Harold Sowder, and Sowder agreed to the offer but said Jesse Junior would have to approve it first. Jesse approved, and Zach said he got a great deal.[73] One final twist to this story shows up in the property record in the Whitfield County Clerk's office. Norville acquired the house and property, but the amount of the property listed as 5.62 acres was crossed out and 46.45 acres was written below it. The value of the property alone was listed as $226,696 in the December 1992 tax assessor's records, and the value of the home and other buildings was listed as $887,908.[74] It could not be determined if any other money was exchanged between Norville and the Union Assembly Church.

In the meantime, Jesse Junior's singing group, the Trailblazers, continued to tour. Sometime during the early 1990s, Jesse told his parishioners at the Dalton Union Assembly Church that he needed $55,000 to buy a bus, so all the churches made a pledge and came up with the money. They gave Jesse Junior the money. Within a few days, he came back to report that the money had been lost. He said that he and his family had looked everywhere but could not find any of it. The ministers of all the Union Assembly churches asked their members at their specific churches to help them raise another $55,000 to replace the money Jesse had lost. The money was soon raised, but informants said that Jesse began to seem more like a very fallible man rather than a god.[75]

On July 2, 1993, the Church of God of the Union Assembly borrowed $53,147 against the church's maternity ward and the land around it at Spring Place, Georgia. Also, the plot of land adjacent to the Union Assembly Church on 41 Highway south of Dalton that had come from Norville was used to secure the loan. The principal and interest came due on December 29, 1993.[76] At that time, the prime interest rate was 6 percent. Most banks charge 1 to 2 percent above prime, though customers with exceptionally high credit scores sometimes could get prime rates. If the lending bank gave the Church an interest rate of 6 percent for a six month loan, it would make the amount of money due in December to be roughly $54,741.41.

Six weeks after this July loan, on August 18, 1993, Fidelity Federal Savings Bank of Dalton, Georgia, loaned the Church of God of the Union Assembly $100,017 on the same property plus an additional tract of land in Murray County, Georgia.[77] Now, there are two possibilities concerning this loan. On the one hand, the loan might have been a new, independent loan, which would have brought the total amount of money loaned up to $153,164. On the other hand, the Church may have decided it needed more money and had a new loan agreement drawn up, which would be a total of the $100,017—combining the $53,147 with an additional $46,870 borrowed. A banker interviewed stated that accruing the loans is the more common way these types of loans are made.

Ten weeks later, on October 28, 1993, Fidelity Federal Savings Bank loaned the Church of God of the Union Assembly another $500,692—over a half-million dollars on the same property plus new church properties in Whitfield County added as collateral.[78] Again, this could have been an additional loan bringing the total up to $653,856, or the bank combined the other loans to a grand total of the half-million dollars—the more likely scenario. But the Church, or Jesse, was not finished. They, or he, needed more money. So, ten weeks later, on January 5, 1994, Fidelity Federal Savings Bank of Dalton loaned the Union Assembly Church $1,738,515.67 on all the combined properties plus a huge property in Catoosa County, Georgia.[79] If these were separate loans, then Fidelity had loaned the Church of God of the Union Assembly $3,434,789; however, it is inconceivable for a bank to loan that much money against that amount of property. The numbers just don't add up. Court documents show that the Union Assembly borrowed $1,738,515.67 from Fidelity Federal and all the previous loans were combined into that amount. The bank loaned the Church the money on the properties because they were valued at much higher than the loan. The president of Fidelity Federal Bank was one of Jesse Junior's best friends at the time. Nevertheless, all five loans, going all the way back to the $1,032,417.44 loan in 1991, were all signed by only one person from the Union Assembly Church: Jesse F. Pratt Jr. What did he do with this money?

This money was to be paid back to Fidelity Federal in monthly installments over a period of three years at approximately 6 percent, but the rate was flexible after this three-year period. That would mean that the Union Assembly would have to come up with $12,455 per month as a payment for the first three years and could possibly have to make larger payments later. Why did the Church of God of the Union Assembly need so much money? Why would Jesse F. Pratt Jr. need so much money?

These questions may never be fully answerable, but they do raise additional important questions: First, who knew that Jesse Junior had even borrowed this large amount of money? Second, who knew that Jesse had bled the Church's assets dry? If Irene knew, surely she would have stopped him, and if Charlie knew, what could he have done to stop his older brother? Somebody had to know and that somebody had to be the person handling the Church's money—the person who had absolute control over all church affairs—Jesse F. Pratt Jr. After all, the Supreme Council and the Board of Elders had given this power to C. T. Pratt, Jesse Pratt, and then Jesse Pratt Jr.

The endless rumors about Jesse Junior's lack of good judgment were just too much for some members to bear, causing several to leave the Church entirely. A former member explained why she left the Church in 1994 after being a lifetime member:

> My sister had left the church at the time and that gave me courage to leave. But I think the final straw for me, was when I was sitting in church, and I had already been bothered and confused about a lot of things, and the pastor read a letter from Charlie [Charles Pratt III]. He had sent it out to all the churches because we were not in Dalton at the time. The letter was about [why] people needed to stop talking about Jesse Junior. There were a lot of rumors floating around that things were not right, and I can't remember exactly what all it said, but at the time, there were things pretty well-known about Jesse Junior. I just remember getting up and walking out of the church and my pastor's wife followed me out and sat in the car with me, and she said, 'He had to read that letter, and we are confused about a lot of things, too, but he has to read that letter. We don't understand it ourselves.' She and her husband left the Church later. That was the last straw for me.[80]

A former member who had become irate about what was happening at the Union Assembly even called the IRS and reported what she knew about Jesse Junior's "Pastor's offering" and other money-making schemes she was sure he was not paying taxes on. She also reported that the Church of God of the Union Assembly had been selling candy for profit with the intention of spending the money on a balcony and a campground, which was never even started years after the money was raised. The IRS took her complaint seriously and called her regularly for eight months to get more information.[81]

Jesse Junior had gone through the money his father had banked and all the millions of dollars the members had raised for the Church. He had borrowed a great sum of money from a bank against the property owned by the Church. His status as a god on Earth had dwindled down to being a mere man. He tried to create more fear, but the fear soon turned inward. About the time Jesse Junior thought his troubles could not get worse, they did—for waiting in his immediate future were still bigger problems—mostly of his own making.

And the Truth Shall Make You Free

"It's like a man that told my father once that the church is
going down. My father told him, if you think the church is
going down, mister you're standing on your head."

JESSE PRATT JR.
"Rev. Pratt Blasts News Articles," *Daily Citizen–News*

1

When C. T. Pratt made Dalton, Georgia, his national headquarters in 1922, the
world's population was 2 billion people. By 1994 the population had almost tripled to
a population of 5.6 billion people. At the same time, the rules of the Church of God
of the Union Assembly had disappeared, or the members, especially the younger
adults, had stopped following them. The younger adult women were having their
hair cut shorter and styled—they were wearing stylish clothing, using makeup,
wearing pants and shorts, and wearing regular bathing suits and swimming with
the opposite sex. Old customs were also starting to change. Physical rebuking by the
ministers had almost vanished and did so entirely by the following year. A member
might be verbally rebuked, but Jesse and the other pastors stopped shaking their
followers. Jesse's brother, Charlie, had insisted in a ministers' meeting that physical

rebuking had to be stopped and it was. In fact, some members interviewed said that Charlie Pratt III was the driving force behind the Church relaxing of rules and less-violent atmosphere.

Additionally, the law prohibiting the visitation of dismissed members was no longer strictly enforced. For example, when a son of Irene Pratt, who had been a minister, left the Union Assembly in the early 1990s, she continued to visit him, and he visited her.[1] Therefore, the rule of staying away from dismissed members no longer applied, even though some people continued to observe it. Such changes were not easy for all the members of the Church, especially the older members. A total reversal in a person's mind when they have been conditioned to obey blindly the rules set forth by an authoritarian leader doesn't just go away overnight.

Also, tragedy struck in Jesse Junior's life on September 17, 1994, when his wife and the mother of his six children died at the age of forty-two, after complaining of headaches and weakness of the arms and legs. After a seizure, she was taken to the hospital in Dalton, and a tumor was found in her brain. She was then sent to Emory Hospital in Atlanta and diagnosed with Meningioma, a slowly growing, usually benign, tumor. The doctors at Emory removed the growth that had formed on the covering (the meninges) of Wanda's brain and believed the operation to be a successful one. Most patients recover quickly from these surgeries, but something

Jesse Pratt Jr. with second wife, Wanda Poole, after women in the Church were allowed to cut and style their hair. Courtesy of an anonymous family member.

went wrong in this case. Twenty-four hours after the surgery, Wanda went into a coma. Her vital signs showed that she was brain dead, and her condition was irreversible. The doctors diagnosed the cause as a cerebral infarction, which is a type of ischemic stroke resulting from a blockage in the blood vessels supplying blood to the brain. Wanda's death certificate stated that she was brain dead for six hours before she was pronounced dead. She had been a beautiful young woman, loving wife, and a mother. Wanda's funeral was on Monday, September 18, 1994 with her brother-in-law, Charlie T. Pratt III, officiating. Former members interviewed observed this to be the turning point in Jesse Junior's life—a turning point for the worse—a turning point that hastened his own demise.

2

Before Wanda's death, she and Jesse Junior had moved to a very nice but smaller home in a subdivision not far from the home that they had given back to the Church and that was eventually sold to Zach Norville. Not long after Wanda's death, Jesse Junior treated one of his female neighbors to a weekend in Gatlinburg, Tennessee, and then married her. This angered some of his grown children who started spreading the news—so much news that Jesse had the marriage dissolved.

Although Wanda's death occurred in September 1994, the following year Jesse was married for the fourth time, and this time to a woman named Darlene. The couple married at the main Church in Dalton and held a reception at the Northwest Georgia Trade Center, a large convention hall in Dalton. Jesse's mother, Irene, made the arrangements and invited not only church members but also nonmembers who were business associates with the family and church.

The guests drove from the Union Assembly Church to the Trade Center, where refreshments and a huge wedding cake were offered. A problem arose when Jesse and his new bride did not arrive on time. The guests and family waited and waited until the situation began to anger Irene. Finally, after close to two hours, Jesse and Darlene arrived in a limousine. Irene went out to see what the problem had been and came back very upset because Jesse was intoxicated. Some interviewed believed that they had been driving around while Jesse drank because when he came into the reception center, Jesse was extremely intoxicated on either alcohol or drugs. Some interviewees reported that they smelled alcohol on his breath.[2]

One person present, who was not a member of the Union Assembly but attended the wedding because she was the wife of a business associate and friend of the groom, said that Jesse was dressed in a tuxedo with real diamond studs on his shirt front and cuff links. She thought the diamonds were at least three carats in size.[3] Jesse played the part well even though he had to know his performance was nearing its end. Yes, Jesse F. Pratt Junior's time as general overseer and leader was swiftly coming to an end, and none too soon—the Church of God of the Union Assembly had not only lost its assets, it was now deep in debt.[4] Within weeks of the wedding, Jesse was defrocked by the Union Assembly's Supreme Council and

Board of Elders, and his younger brother, Charlie Thomas Pratt III, was elected as general overseer. The young Charlie, grandson of C. T. Pratt and son of Jesse F. Pratt Sr., was left with a church on the brink of financial collapse. It is not known if Charlie knew the mess he inherited, but, if he didn't, he quickly learned. Jesse had borrowed millions of dollars from banks against church property. To try to meet the financial needs of the Church, Charlie had little choice but to sell off most of the Union Assembly's assets. The problem, however, was that the property they owned at the time was little more than the land the churches were occupying. Therefore, some of the smaller unproductive Union Assembly churches were closed and sold in towns across the United States. In the end, the number of Union Assembly churches dropped from 54 down to the present number of 38. Instead of being in sixteen states, the Church had branches in only twelve.

The Church was also unable to raise large amounts of money. The membership gave, but not like they had contributed during the past when their parents and grandparents gave almost everything they had. And Charlie did not demand this extravagant giving. He wanted to modernize the Church of God of the Union Assembly, and he did. The cloak of fear, which had once enveloped the members of the Church, and been used as a cudgel to extract money from members was beginning to vanish like a bad dream. But like a bad dream, that cloak of fear was embedded in the members' minds, and for most, it would stay with them until they died.

3

The state of Georgia also put tax liens on Jesse Junior for failing to pay his 1994 and 1995 state income taxes. For 1994 his unpaid taxes were $8,500; for 1995 they were $11,800. The IRS was also placing liens against him for failure to pay federal taxes, but the amounts remained confidential. One person said that Jesse Junior drove a truck to earn money for a short period of time, and another member said he thought Jesse started laying carpet. It is not known if his mother funneled him money, but he had received money from someone, because he continued to be seen drinking and carousing in both Dalton and in Atlanta.

Some of those interviewed said that Jesse Junior never recovered after his wife, Wanda, died and that his drinking and use of drugs worsened. Others thought that Jesse Junior was terrified of his mother and this led to his drinking. Still others mentioned that he didn't like the way the Church had been treating its members, and he felt guilty. The latter reason seems unlikely, since Jesse F. Pratt Jr. himself was responsible for mistreating members during his long twenty-one-year reign.

One episode actually occurred around 1995, as recalled by an anonymous family member: "I saw Jesse not long after he married Darlene [about a year after Wanda died] and he was moving into a home near Cartersville, Georgia. I heard that he was going to be some sort of charter bus driver, but I am not sure if he did that.

After the church stopped his payroll and he had to face the real world is when he completely toppled into poverty and alcoholism."[5]

On Tuesday, February 6, 1996, the Church of God of the Union Assembly sold the 407 acres of property in Catoosa County—the property originally intended for a campground. They sold it to pay off the loan Jesse Junior had against it, and that money that had already been spent. The Warranty Deed was signed by the new general overseer, Charlie T. Pratt III, and secretary, Harold Sowder.[6]

A plan was then put in place by Charlie and the Supreme Council to take all the restrictions off of the Church's members and to raise the money needed to pay off their debts. A general accounting of the Church's finances was presented to the members, but no pressure was placed on them to go beyond their capabilities in addressing them. The Church of God of the Union Assembly unlocked its doors and invited anyone to enter their services.

The Church also invited former members who had been expelled to return— some did and some did not. More than half of the former members interviewed for this work said they could never enter another church of any denomination. It is regrettable that these members still bear deep scars—scars that former members carry around in their minds—scars that reach the depths of their soul—scars that will never heal.

Some families who were torn apart reunited, but others did not because they could not. They did not because their differences could not be acknowledged, but as reported in several interviews some families could not because death had separated them from one another. One of the most touching interviews explains so much about the heartbreak caused by the Union Assembly church. It is a heartbreak that cannot be changed or denied. Johnnie Haney Butler, after recalling the death of her mother, who was only 34 at the time, said this to me on August 16, 2015: "My dad started drinking and quit church a few years later. He became an alcoholic, but before he got to drinking heavy and quit the Union Assembly, he remarried a woman with a three-year-old daughter. He married her not long after mom died. His drinking got worse and worse until he left the Church."

I then asked Johnnie, "Who did you live with after your dad quit going?"

She replied, "After he left the Church, I lived with my step-mom and continued going to the Union Assembly Church. So I could not have contact with my dad again because he had quit going to church, and we were not allowed to have contact with a former member—even a family member. And my sister, Sue, stopped going soon after that, and I couldn't see her. It was awful, just awful."

Then Johnnie broke down and cried openly for at least a minute before going on with her thoughts, "I thought I was going to the right church. I went on for years and years believing in their crap." Johnnie cried and could not talk for several more minutes.

And then sounding angry, she said, "I am so sorry for breaking down like this. It is a hurt that is never ever going to leave me." On January 6, 2018, I received a call from Johnnie's daughter, Margie, that Johnnie, who was looking so forward to reading this book, had died at 9:34 that morning.

Charles Roberts, whose words grace much of this book, summed up his own thoughts about the Church's shortcomings and those of its leadership. He made the following statement in a phone conversation on Sunday, January 29, 2017. "While I was a member of the Church we were never told about a loving God. I just found a verse that I want you to read. I never heard this in church—John, chapter 4, verse 18." We talked a few minutes more, and after hanging up, I looked the verse up. This is what it says in the KJV: "There is no fear in love; but perfect love casteth out fear; because fear hath torment. He that feareth is not made perfect in love."

I believe the human troubles and fears brought about by some religious sects is not the wrath of God, but created by men and sometimes women who believe they can speak for God until they become convinced they are God.

EPILOGUE

In June 2005, Jesse Pratt Jr., now only fifty-eight years old, was admitted to Hamilton Medical Center in Dalton. He was in the last stages of cirrhosis of the liver. Divorced and alone, he had come home to die. He did not live in a mansion like the one he'd lost in 1991 but in an apartment in Calhoun, Georgia, only 22 miles south of Dalton. His mother, Irene, was still living at eighty-seven. His brother, Charlie, was still the general overseer of the Union Assembly.

While he was in the hospital in Dalton, a childhood friend, Curtis F. Belcher, who was a former member of the Church, came to visit Jesse Junior. The men had grown up together in the Union Assembly Church. The visitor's father had been a minister with Jesse Junior's grandfather, C. T. Pratt. The childhood friend, also fifty-eight, was a minister at another Church of God but not in the Union Assembly organization.

Jesse Junior had a yellow tint to his normally dark complexion, and his body was swollen and bloated because the liver had shut down, thus allowing the toxins to accumulate in his blood and tissue. Belcher described Jesse's legs as swollen and looking like stovepipes. Jesse's youngest sister sat with them. The doctors had told Pastor Belcher that Jesse would never be able to leave the hospital—meaning Jesse Junior would die there.

This is Pastor Belcher's account of this event in his own words:

> I went to visit Jesse Pratt Jr., in the hospital at Dalton, Georgia. He was in Intensive Care. We reminisced about elementary school, and he asked me about several of our old classmates and if I had heard from them over the years. I told him I had not. We talked about several other things. I spent quite a bit of time with him and another family member. He told me his health was deteriorating.
>
> I then asked him, "Is everything right between you and the Lord?"
>
> He closed his eyes, and I said, "I'm not going to leave here until you tell me that you're saved and ready to meet the Lord."
>
> He didn't say a word to me. I repeated myself and said, "I'm not leaving until you answer me."
>
> He said, "You don't know what I've done."
>
> I said, "It doesn't matter what you've done, the Blood of Jesus will cleanse you from all sin and unrighteousness."
>
> I asked him again and again, "Is everything all right between you and the Lord?"
>
> He closed his eyes and never answered me. I revisited him several times, but he had slipped into a coma. A few days later, he passed away.[1]

Jesse Senior's tombstone in Dalton. Photo by the author.

On June 21, 2005, at 10:45 p.m., Jesse Franklin Pratt Jr. died as his father had warned he might—a drunkard's death. The cause of death on his death certificate was listed as "liver failure and respiratory failure due to, or as consequence of ETOH." ETOH is an acronym for ethyl alcohol—the type of alcohol found in all alcoholic beverages. On the death certificate his occupation was listed as a minister, and his youngest sister provided the information.[2] He was survived by four sons and two daughters. Jesse Junior was laid to rest on the same hill with his father and next to his second wife and the mother of all his children, Wanda Jean Poole Pratt. The epitaph on their shared gravestone reads simply: "In loving memory of our dearest Mother, whose love was larger than life and whose bond was stronger than death."

Nothing was ever added to the gravestone about Jesse Junior other than his dates of birth and death.

On November 8, 2005, Johnny Franklin Pratt, the son of Charlie T. Pratt III, and the same son who had been saved from death by taking antibiotics in 1990, was leaving his job site while working for Dalton Utilities. It was a Friday, and all the workers wanted to get back to the maintenance building to start their weekend. The truck carrying a load of logs had room for only the driver, but Johnny jumped in and stood beside the driver. On the way down a hill, the truck slipped off the road and turned over. Johnny was thrown out, and the logs crushed his body, killing him. This was a heart-wrenching blow to Charlie and his wife Joy.

On July 7, 2008, Wayman Pratt, the youngest and only living child of Charlie (C. T.) and Minnie Pratt, died.

On March 26, 2011, Charles Thomas "Tom" Pratt, the son of Lloyd Pratt, died at the age of eighty-two. He had pastored the Union Assembly in Kokomo, Indiana, where he allowed a baby to die in the basement of his church while he preached. He had also been the pastor of the Hamilton, Ohio, Union Assembly Church, where witnesses said he worked members of his church sixteen hours a day for slave wages or none at all.

On November 23, 2011, at the age of ninety-three, Irene McClure Pratt died at her home. She had never remarried after Jesse Senior had died thirty-seven years before. They had been married for twenty-eight years and had had six children together—five of whom were still living. She had three children with Oscar Smith and her youngest child with Oscar, Janet Smith Purcell, died just six days before her mother. Irene was survived by forty-four grandchildren, many great-grandchildren, and a few great-great-grandchildren.

In 2014, Charlie Thomas Pratt III resigned as general overseer of the Church of God of the Union Assembly, but thanks to him, the church founded by his grandfather, C. T. Pratt, survived. Charlie Pratt III was replaced by Oley Wilson—the first general overseer who was not a Pratt, or was not related to the Pratts.

On February 21, 2016, James (Jimmy) L. Pratt, the last child between Jesse Senior and Ethel Pratt, died at the age of seventy-one. Jimmy had served as a minister of the Church of God of the Union Assembly. He had suffered from both Alzheimer's and Parkinson's disease for four years before his death.[3]

On August 8, 2015, I interviewed a woman from Tennessee for over two hours. She told me about her life in the Church. After we finished the interview, instead of feeling depressed, I felt good understanding that this story had purpose. The below quotation was extracted from the last minute and ten seconds of that interview:

I said, "You've had some heartache."

She replied, "I have, but it has made me a better person."

I asked, "The preacher who rebuked you and prophesied to you, was he related to the Pratts?"

"Lord, yes," she said then laughed. "I forgave them, but I'm glad I walked when I walked. I taught my children about God. You can go to God without going through hell. I learned that."

"Is there anything else you want to tell me?"

She laughed, "Oh, there is so much, but I'm a person who don't believe in worrying about the past, it can ruin your future. But I think people ought to know about this [the Church of God of the Union Assembly]."

Then she got a very serious tone in her voice, "I remember where I was and what I was doing when I heard about Jim Jones and all those people killing themselves. My first thought—I had the radio on—we would do that. That was my thought—we would do that. I felt compassion for those people."

I said, "People asked me why I'm writing this book, and I say, 'The truth has got to be told so it doesn't happen again.'"

She said, "The truth will always stand."

In March of 2017, my forty-year-old son was helping me videotape a former member's interview. As we were putting the equipment away, he said, "You know Dad, people have to understand evil in order to avoid it." I realized then that these seven years of research had been worth the countless hours that I, along with others, put into completing this book.

Today the Church of God of the Union Assembly has thirty-eight churches in twelve states and approximately six thousand members. The cross of Jesus, which was once forbidden, is on steeples over their churches as well as behind their pulpits. Men and women can now read their Bibles and bring them to church. The cloak of fear that once engulfed its members is only a memory and should stay that way because no one deserves to be intimidated in the name of God or allow themselves to be intimidated in the name of God.

In July 2018, as this book was set to go to press, general overseer Oley Wilson made this remark at the Union Assembly's 2018 national assembly in Dalton, Georgia. The remark was posted on YouTube and on the Union Assembly Facebook page. Oley Wilson said: "Over the years, some things have happened in our Churches that shouldn't have. There are people who have been hurt, treated unfairly, or dismissed from our fellowship for reasons that they feel were unwarranted. On behalf of our assembly, and all of our ministers, present and past, I would like to apologize and personally ask you to forgive us. If any of you would like to speak to me at some point in the future, feel free to contact me, Sincerely Oley Wilson, General Overseer of the Church of God of the Union Assembly."[4]

NOTES

INTRODUCTION

1. Rick Soll, "Fundamentalist Fear: Former Church Members Paint Picture of Intimidation," *Chicago Sun Times,* October 7, 1983.
2. Interviews by author with over fifty members and former members during a six-year period.

PROLOGUE

1. "U.S. Congress Votes to Enter the War," *Chronicle of the 20th Century,* (Liberty, MO: JL International Publishing, 1992), 217.
2. Earnest R. Sandeen, *Roots of Fundamentalism: British and American Millenarianism,* 1800–1930 (Chicago: University of Chicago Press, 1970), 59–61.
3. Mary Minnie Pratt, (Mrs. C. T. Pratt), *We Walked Alone: Part of The Story of My Life* (*The Southerner Press,* Dalton, Georgia, 1 July, 1955), 10.
4. *Minutes of the 24th Annual Meeting of the Union Assembly of the Church of God, Inc.* (Oct. 18, 19, 20, 1945), 28.
5. Harold Sowder, "History of the Church of God of the Union Assembly," http://www .thechurchofgodua.org/index_files/History.html accessed 2007, (website which has since been removed). The author has a hard copy.
6. Sandeen, *Roots of Fundamentalism,* 59–61.
7. Pratt, *We Walked Alone,* 1.
8. Sandeen, *Roots of Fundamentalism,* 56–62.
9. Moody Connell, "Former Church Leader Interviewed," *Daily Citizen-News,* July 16, 1980, 1.
10. Pratt, *We Walked Alone,* 10.

1. IN THE BEGINNING

1. United States Federal Census 1880, Monticello, Wayne County, Kentucky, p. 106.
2. "United States Civil War Solders Index, 1861–1865," index, *FamilySearch* https:// familysearch.org/pal:MM9.1.1/FS4C-FX7, accessed August 19, 2014.
3. http://files.usgwarchives.net/ky/wayne/military/roster001.txt.
4. Selected Records of the War Department relating to Confederate Prisoners of War. Roll: M 598_22.
5. Frederick H. Dyer, *A Compendium of the War of the Rebellion* (Des Moines, IA: Dyer Publishing Co., 1908), 1192–3.
6. United States Federal Census 1900, Parnell, Wayne County, Kentucky, District 0127.
7. United States Federal Census, 1900.
8. Jesse Pratt Jr., *Minutes of The Church of God of the Union Assembly, Inc.,* 1990 Edition, 6.
9. "Kentucky Death Records, 1911-1955." Index, FamilySearch https://familysearch.org /pal:MM9.1.1/NS26-X5B, accessed August 21, 2014.

10. Thomas E. Bonsall, *More Than They Promised: The Studebaker Story* (Stanford: Stanford University Press, 2000), 21.

11. "Wrights fly heavier-than-air plane," *Chronicle of the 20th Century*, 59.

12. "Mother Jones Must Get Out of Colorado," *Chronicle of the 20th Century*, 62.

13. "Kentucky Births and Christenings, 1839–1960," index, *FamilySearch* https://familysearch.org/pal:MM9.1.1/FWK7-Z8G, accessed Sept. 29, 2014.

14. Pratt, *We Walked Alone*, 1.

15. Marriage Bond, Whitley County, Kentucky, pages 614–15.

16. Pratt, *We Walked Alone*, 1.

17. Williamsburg, Kentucky, https://www.williamsburgky.com/about_us/index.php, accessed Oct. 2014.

18. David Beasley, *Without Mercy: The Stunning True Story of Race, Crime, and Corruption in the Deep South* (New York: St. Martin's Press, 2014), 126.

19. Pratt, *We Walked Alone*, 2.

20. Ibid.

21. Ibid.

22. Ibid, 3.

23. Ibid.

24. John M. Barry, *The Great Influenza: The Story of the Deadliest Pandemic in History* (New York: Penguin, 2009), 31.

25. Ibid., 6.

26. Pratt, *We Walked Alone*, 3.

27. Ibid.

28. Ken Warrington, *Pentecostal Theology: A Theology of Encounter* (New York: T and T Clark, 2008).

29. J. C. Furnas, *Great Times: An Informal Social History of the United States*, 1914–1929 (New York: Hill and Wang, 1995), 98.

30. Ernest R. Sandeen, "Toward a Historical Interpretation of the Origins of Fundamentalism," *Church History* 36 (1) (March 1967): 6.

31. George W. Marsden, *Fundamentalism and American Culture: The Shaping of Twentieth Century Evangelicalism* (New York: Oxford University Press, 1973), 5.

32. Vinson Synan, *The Holiness–Pentecostal Tradition: Charismatic Movements in the Twentieth Century* (Wm. B. Eerdmans Publishing Co., Grand Rapids, MI, 1997). x.

33. Eric Smithey, interview with the author, Atlanta, Georgia, Sept. 9, 2015.

34. Pratt, *We Walked Alone*, 4.

35. Ibid.

36. Ibid.

37. Ibid., 5.

38. Ibid.

39. Eric Smithey, interview with the author.

40. Pratt, *We Walked Alone*, 6.

41. Church of God Mountain Assembly, *Minutes of the Seventh Annual Session of the Churches of God* (Jellico, TN: Church of God Mountain Assembly, 1913), 5.

42. Pratt, *We Walked Alone*, 6.

43. Church of God Mountain Assembly, *Minutes of the Eleventh Annual Session of the*

Mountain Assembly of the Church of God (Jellico, TN: Church of God Mountain Assembly, 1917), 7–8.

44. Pratt, *We Walked Alone*, 7.
45. Church of God Mountain Assembly, *Minutes of the Eleventh Annual Session*, 7–8.
46. Pratt, *We Walked Alone*, 7.
47. Michael Padgett, "Fundamentalism and the Church of God Mountain Assembly," B.A. thesis, University of Kentucky, May 3, 2007.
48. Pratt, *We Walked Alone*, 10.
49. Catherine Wessinger, ed., *The Oxford Handbook of Millennialism* (Oxford: Oxford University Press, 2011).
50. Charles Roberts, Buddy Coiffeur, Don Pitner, interviews with the author, as well as other former members interview with author who did not want to be named.
51. Padgett, "Fundamentalism."
52. Harold Sowder, "History of the Church of God of the Union Assembly," CGUA website, which has been removed, but the author has a printed copy.

2. CREATION

1. "Virulent Flu is Killing Millions Worldwide," *Chronicle of the 20th Century*, 240.
2. Barry, *The Great Influenza*, 353.
3. Ibid., 353.
4. Ibid.
5. Ibid., 355.
6. Pratt, *We Walked Alone*, 7.
7. Ibid.
8. http://www.patheos.com/Library/Pentecostal.
9. "Growth of Economy to Depend on Roads," *Chronicle of the 20th Century*, 250.
10. Pratt, *We Walked Alone*, 7.
11. Ibid.
12. Ibid.
13. *Church of God of the Union Assembly Minutes*, 1990 edition, 8–9.
14. *Official History of Whitfield County, Georgia* (Dalton, GA: A. J. Showalter Company, 1932, reprint, 1981), 98.
15. Pratt, *We Walked Alone*, 8.
16. Ibid.
17. Ibid.
18. Charles Roberts, Charlie Carmical, and three others, interviews with the author.

3. CAMP OF THE SAINTS

1. *Official History of Whitfield County, Georgia*, 47–89.
2. Ibid., 42.
3. Ibid., 79–80.
4. Douglas Flamming, *Creating the Modern South: Millhands and Managers in Dalton, Georgia, 1884–1984* (Chapel Hill: University of North Carolina Press, 1992), xxi, xxii.
5. Ibid., 47.
6. Ibid., 48.

7. Ibid., 49, 50.

8. Ibid., 164.

9. Walter S. Bogle, "William B. Is Introduced," in Bogle Clipping File, CGA; *North Georgia Citizen*, Oct. 26, 1899.

10. Flamming, *Creating the Modern South*, 101.

11. Ibid., xxii.

12. Ibid., 95, 96.

13. Ibid., 99–101.

14. Ibid., 113.

15. Ibid., 50.

16. *Official History of Whitfield County*, 95–98.

17. Flamming, *Creating the Modern South*, 113.

18. Ibid., 50.

19. *Official History of Whitfield County*, 95–98.

20. Charlie Carmical, interview with the author.

4. BRINGING IN THE SHEAVES

1. Flamming, *Creating the Modern South*, 151.

2. Ibid, 157.

3. Shouting in church involved members, either one or many, getting caught up in the moment, and starting to call out Bible verses or singing religious songs. Sometimes they shouted out nonsense words, flayed their arms wildly, and jumped up and down or over pews. [In Pentecostal churches, this behavior is referred to as testifying or being "slain in the (Holy) spirit." It is a common practice in all Holiness churches.]

4. Flamming, *Creating the Modern South*, 157.

5. Ibid.

6. George Weissman, "In The Face Of Persecution," *The Southerner: A Voice of the People*, May 1955, 5.

7. *Minutes of the 24 Annual Meeting of the Union Assembly of the Church of God*, Inc. 1945.

8. Flamming, *Creating the Modern South*, 166.

9. *Official History of Whitfield County*, 98; Dalton City Directory, 1936, 76; Robert Mapes Anderson, *Vision of the Disinherited: The Making of American Pentecostalism* (Peabody, MA: Hendrickson, 1992), chap. 7 (quotation on 136).

10. *Official History of Whitfield County*, 98: Dalton City Directory, 1936, 98.

11. Weissman, "In The Face of Persecution."

12. Pratt, "Three Classes of People," *The Southerner: A Voice of the People, July 1955*, 3.

13. Ibid., 4.

14. *Minutes of the 24th Annual Meeting of the Union Assembly*, 28.

15. Ibid., 25.

16. Charles Roberts, Libby Neighbors, Don Pitner, Brenda Pitner, interviews with the author.

17. *Minutes of the 7th Annual Meeting of the Union Assembly of the Church of God*.

18. "Black Thursday: Stock Market Crash," *Chronicle of the 20th Century*, 375.

19. Flamming, *Creating the Modern South*, 46, 188–89.

20. Ibid., 189–90.

21. Ibid., 190.

22. Ken Burns, *The Roosevelts: An Intimate History* (part 4, "The Storm," Aug. 16, 2014).

23. Rita Gazaway Woody, Varnel Schaeffner, interviews with the author. About 90 percent of those interviewed whom I asked about this confirmed details.

24. Flamming, *Creating the Modern South*, 193.

25. Ibid.

26. United States Federal Census 1930, Murray County, Georgia, Middle District 824, district 0005.

27. Ibid.

28. United States Federal Census 1940, Whitfield County, Georgia, Dalton, sheet number 3A.

5. LOVE THY NEIGHBOR

1. *Minutes of the 24th Annual Meeting of the Union Assembly*, 21, 22.

2. Ibid., 3.

3. Ibid., 5, 6.

4. Ibid., 40.

5. Ibid., 43.

6. Charles Roberts said he heard his parents talking about this practice. Curtis Belcher also reported hearing this from his parents, as did Charlie Carmical.

7. *Church of God of the Union Assembly minutes, 1990*, 12.

8. Charles Roberts, interview with the author.

9. Marriage License, State of Georgia, County of Whitfield, Book L, page 25.

10. Varnel Schaeffner, interview with the author, Luttrell, Tennessee, Nov. 17, 2014.

11. Jesse and Johnny Burnett were depicted together in an early picture donated by Nell Belcher.

12. Charlie Thomas Pratt III, interview with the author, Dalton, Georgia, Jan. 6, 2016.

13. Flamming, *Creating the Modern South*, 233.

14. Ibid., 234.

15. Sixteenth Census of the United States, 1940, S. D. No. 7; E. D. No. 155-13; sheet 6B.

16. Sixteenth Census of the United States, 1940, S. D. No. 7: E. D. No. 155-15A; sheets 3A, 3B.

17. United States Federal Census 1940, Whitfield County, Georgia, Dalton, Militia District 872, sheet 16A.

18. Grady Lance, interview by the author, Oct. 8, 2015; Raita Gazaway Woody interview from her mother.

19. The author's mother worked at Cabin Craft making parachutes and often talked about how much money was being made in Dalton during the War years. Also, it was reported in the *Minutes of the 24th Annual Meeting of the Union Assembly*.

20. Charlie Carmical, interview with the author.

21. *Minutes of the 24th Annual Meeting of the Union Assembly*.

22. Harvey Halman, interview with the author, Dalton, Georgia, Feb. 2, 2015; confirmed by two other anonymous former members interviewed.

23. Charlie Carmical, interviews by the author several times between 2011 and 2017, and told to the author by others who were interviewed.

24. This was told to me by my uncle, Virgil T. Smith, who was a member of the Georgia State House of Representative for sixteen years. I was also told by Marshal Mauldin whose father, Gerald Mauldin, was the sheriff of Whitfield County during the 1950s and 1960s.

25. *Minutes of the Church of God of the Union Assembly, 1990,* 13.

26. Copy of application of incorporation of the Union Assembly of the Church of God to the Superior Court of Whitfield County, Georgia; July 16, 1942.

27. Deed Books: 35, pages 194, 582, Book 36, page 30, Book 38, page 390, Book 53, pages 322–3, Clerk of Superior Court, and Whitfield County, Georgia Court House.

28. Deed Book 64, pages 53–4, Clerk of Superior Court, Whitfield County, Georgia Court House.

29. Deed Books in Clerk of Superior Court, Whitfield County, Georgia Court House.

30. William Lowe, anonymous former CGUA member, interview by the author in Dalton, Georgia, December 17, 2014. This informant would not allow me to use his real name because he was afraid for the lives of his children. This story was confirmed by six other members.

31. Jack Poston, interview with the author, Dalton, Georgia, Apr. 11, 2014.

32. 213 Ga. 76,97 S.E.2d 132, CHURCH OF GOD OF THE UNION ASSEMBLY, INC. et al. v. CITY OF DALTON et al. No 19612. Supreme Court of Georgia, Submitted March 11, 1957.

6. THOU SHALL NOT COVET THY NEIGHBOR'S WIFE

1. *Minutes of the Church of God of the Union Assembly,* 1990, 9–10.

2. Minnie Pratt, *We Walked Alone,* 12.

3. *Minutes of the Church of God of the Union Assembly,* 1990, 10.

4. Former member Charles Roberts provided a drawing that showed this design, and Charlie Carmical confirmed the basic layout.

5. Charlie Carmical, Buddy Coiffeur, interview with the author.

6. Scholar Paul Williamson made this observation when he reviewed this work for the University of Tennessee Press.

7. Sherry Cady, interview with the author, Dalton, Georgia, June 1, 2011.

8. Sherry Cady, Charlie Carmical, other eye witnesses reported on Jesse's prowess with guns in interviews with the author.

9. Charlie Carmical, interview with the author.

10. "Post WW II Strike," *Textile Labor* (newspaper), Sept. 1945, 2, 4.

11. Flamming, *Creating the Modern South,* 248.

12. Buddy Coiffeur, interview with the author.

13. Flora Cady, grandmother of the author who worked at C. T. Pratt Chenille Company in 1946, provided this detail to the author. Also, Julian Saul, interview with the author, Sept. 5, 2016.

14. Julian Saul, interview with the author in Dalton, Georgia, and a copy of the bill of sale.

15. Charlie Carmical, interview with the author.

16. *Minutes of the 24th Annual Meeting of the Union Assembly of the Church of God,* 20.

17. Charles Roberts; Charlie Carmical, interviews by the author.

18. Buddy Coiffeur, interview by the author. This is not this man's real name because he does lots of business with present members, but he had been a member of the Church since childhood until recently. His father was a minister for the Church. Irene's arrival was related to me by other people who were members of the Church at that time.

19. Varnell Schaeffner, interview with the author.

20. United States Federal Census 1940, Whitfield County, Georgia, Dalton, City Ward, sheet 4A.
21. A synopsis of interviews with the author. Informants included Charlie Carmical, Nell Belcher, and Charles Roberts.
22. Nell Belcher by way of her son in an interview with this author.
23. https://divorceseekers.wordpress.com/2013/06/16/nevada-as-a-place-to-split-is-a -legend-of-our-time/ accessed June, 2018.
24. Varnell Schaeffner, interview with the author.
25. Marriage licenses, Vital Records Marriage records for Washoe County, Nevada, book 110, p. 156.
26. The outlines of this story were confirmed in interviews with Charles Roberts, Buddy Coiffeur, and two other anonymous informants.
27. Nell Belcher interview by way of her son, Mar. 2015.
28. As years went forward, the Pratt family became more closed-mouth about this event to the point that they all but denied it happening and or tried to cover up the fact that Jesse and Irene had been married to other people previously. It was hard to repudiate the fact that Jesse had three sons by another marriage and Irene had one son and two daughters by another marriage.
29. Charles Roberts, interview with the author. Also confirmed by Charlie Carmical.
30. These details were confirmed in interviews with Charles Roberts, Buddy Coiffeur, and Varnell Schaeffner.
31. *Minutes of the Church of God of the Union Assembly,* 1990, 13.
32. Interviews with Charles Roberts, Buddy Coiffeur, Charlie Carmical, as well as with Nell Belcher through her son.
33. Charlie Carmical, interview with the author.
34. Ibid.
35. Ibid.
36. Buddy Coiffeur, interview with the author.
37. Shirley Lee Carmical, (1st cousin to Charlie Carmical) interview with the author Chattanooga, Tennessee, Nov. 17, 2014.
38. Charlie Carmical, interview with the author.
39. Ibid.
40. Buddy Coiffeur, interview with the author. When I asked Charles Roberts to confirm this story, he did so, and then added that this happened more than once and to other members.
41. Robert and Marie Anderson, interview with the author, Knoxville, Tennessee, May 1, 2016.
42. Charlie Carmical; Shirley Lee Carmical, interviews by the author.
43. Charles Roberts, Charlie Carmical, Chris Camp, Rita Gazaway Woody, interviews with the author.
44. Charles Roberts, interview with the author.
45. Buddy Coiffeur, interview with the author. Confirmed by Charles Roberts and several others.
46. Buddy Coiffeur, interview with the author.
47. Charles Roberts; Buddy Coiffeur; Charlie Carmical, interviews with the author.

7. AN ATTITUDE CHANGE

1. Charles Roberts, interviews with the author.
2. Charles Roberts, Billy Lowe, and Buddy Coiffeur, interviews with the author.
3. Ibid.
4. Moody Connell, "Former Church Leader Interviewed, *Daily Citizen-News*, July 16, 1980.
5. Charles Roberts, Curtis Belcher, interviews with the author.
6. Charles Roberts interviews with author.
7. Steve Hassan, *Combating Cult Mind Control* (Newton, MA: Freedom of Mind Press, 2015).
8. Ralph Hood Jr., Peter C. Hill, and Bernard Spilka, *Psychology of Religion: An Empirical Approach,* fourth edition, (Guilford Press, 2009), 395.
9. Ibid., 7.
10. Ibid., 395.
11. Buddy Coiffeur, interview with the author.

8. THOU SHALL NOT BEAR FALSE WITNESS

1. "National Affairs—Eggs in the Dust," *Time,* Sept. 13, 1948.
2. Ibid.
3. James J. Lorence, *A Hard Journey: The Life of Don West* (Urbana and Chicago: University of Illinois Press, 2007), 140.
4. Charlie Carmical, interview with the author.
5. Cited in Lorence, *A Hard Journey,* 140.
6. Petition filed in the Superior Court of Whitfield County, Georgia, to amend the original charter to change the name to "The Church of God of the Union Assembly, Inc.," dated Oct. 10, 1950.
7. Charlie Carmical, interview with the author.
8. Flamming, *Creating the Modern South,* 290.
9. Jim Gowin, interview with the author, Dalton, Georgia, May 18, 2011.
10. Rita Gazaway Woody, interview with the author, Rocky Face, Georgia, Sept. 30, 2014.
11. Flamming, *Creating the Modern South,* 290.
12. Lorence, *A Hard Journey,* 153.
13. Ibid., 155.
14. Flamming, *Creating the Modern South,* 290.
15. Lorence, *A Hard Journey,* 154–55.
16. Flamming, *Creating the Modern South,* 290.
17. Quotes from *The Southerner: Voice of the People,* May 1955, 1.
18. Quotes from *The Southerner, Voice of the People,* Apr. 1955.
19. *The Southerner, Voice of the People,* May 1955.
20. Ibid., and *The Southerner, Voice of the People,* Sept. 1955.
21. Flamming, *Creating the Modern South,* 291.
22. Ibid., 293–94, and Lorence, *A Hard Journey,* 156.
23. Ibid., and Lorence, *A Hard Journey,* 157–58.
24. Flamming, *Creating the Modern South,* 294–95, and Lorence, *A Hard Journey,* 158–59.
25. Lorence, *A Hard Journey,* 158.
26. Donald Davis left this note about West while reviewing this manuscript.

27. *Dalton News*, Aug. 28, 1955; *Dalton Citizen*, Sept. 1, 1955.

28. Lorence, *A Hard Journey*, 160–61.

29. *Dalton Citizen*, Sept. 1, 1955.

30. *Dalton Citizen*, Oct. 13, 1955, 6.

31. Lorence, *A Hard Journey*, 163.

32. Erwin Mitchell, interview with the author, Dalton, Georgia, June 25, 2011, and Mark Pace, interview with the author, July 2, 2011.

33. Flamming, *Creating the Modern South*, 303.

34. Ibid.,305.

35. Erwin Mitchell, interview with the author.

36. Constitution State News Service, "Church Puts Out Dalton's Don West," *Dalton Citizen-News*, Jan. 13, 1956, and Erwin Mitchell, interview with the author, June 25, 2011; Mark Pace, interview with the author, July 2, 2011.

37. "The Oath I Was Ready to Take" and "Why I Resigned from the Church of God," both in box 1, George Weissman Papers; "Resigned Prior to Ouster, West Says; Puts Blame of Pratt's Change of Mind on Mitchell," *Dalton Citizen*, Jan. 15, 1955, Lorence, *A Hard Journey*, 166.

9. THOU SHALL NOT COMMIT ADULTERY

1. Ken Atwell, "Phone Call From Bell Is Reported," *Kokomo Tribune*, Dec. 15, 1959. See also "Accused Pastor in Molesting of Young Girl," *Chicago Daily Tribune*, Dec. 16, 1959.

2. Ken Atwell, "Bell Reported En Route Here," *Kokomo Tribune*, Dec. 15, 1959. See also "Pastor in Sex Case Back to Face Charges," *Chicago Sunday Tribune*, Dec. 20, 1959.

3. Don Pitner, Brenda Moore, interviews with the author. Four other informants commented on Bell's preaching style.

4. Ken Atwell, "Local Minister Sought After Molesting Charge," *Kokomo Tribune*, Dec. 15, 1959.

5. Don Pitner, interview with the author, Kokomo, Indiana, Feb. 11, 2014.

6. Fred Odiet, "Pastor Says He Regrets His Actions," *Kokomo Tribune*, Dec. 19, 1959, in addition to interviews with former members of Bell's church.

7. Don Pitner, interview with the author.

8. Don Pitner, Buddy Coiffeur, interviews with the author. Two other informants confirmed these fears.

9. Dorothy Bliss, interview with the author, Logansport, Indiana, Jan. 15, 2014.

10. Don Pitner, Dorothy Bliss, interviews with the author.

11. Don Pitner, interview with the author.

12. Don Pitner, Charles Roberts, Brenda Moore, interviews with the author.

13. Don Pitner, Charles Roberts, and one anonymous woman from Kokomo, interviews with the author.

14. Dorothy Bliss, interview with the author.

15. Don Pitner, Dorothy Bliss, interviews with the author.

16. Dorothy Bliss, interview with the author.

17. Dorothy Bliss, Don Pitner, Charles Roberts, interviews with the author.

18. Dorothy Bliss, Don Pitner, Charles Roberts, Brenda Moore, Varnel Schaeffner, Charlie Carmical, and an anonymous member, interviews with the author.

19. Dorothy Bliss, interview with the author.

20. Dorothy Bliss, interview with the author.

21. Brenda Moore, interview with the author, and Fred Odiet, "Custody of Girl in Bell Case is Given Sister," *Kokomo Tribune*, Jan. 7, 1960.

22. Dorothy Bliss, interview with the author.

23. Brenda Moore, interview with the author.

24. Brenda Moore, Don Pitner, interviews with the author.

25. Don Pitner, interview with the author.

26. Don Pitner, Brenda Moore, interviews with the author.

27. *Anderson (Indiana) Daily Bulletin,* Jan. 13, 1960, 7. Available at http://www.newspapers .com/newspage/14648972/ >, accessed Oct. 2014.

28. Atwell, "Local Minister Sought After Molesting Charge."

29. Ibid.

30. Ibid.

31. Odiet, "Preacher Says He Regrets His Actions."

32. Atwell, "Local Minister Sought After Molesting Charge."

33. Don Pitner, Charles Roberts, Brenda Moore, interviews with the author.

34. Don Pitner, Charlie Carmical, Dorothy Bliss, Brenda Moore, Vernel Schaeffner, and Buddy Coiffeur, interviews with the author.

35. In an interview in January 2015, Don said that he should have forgiven his wife earlier because she was underage, only fifteen years old, when she had her encounter with Bell, and that it was Bell who had taken advantage of her. In their seventies now, Don drives his former wife every Saturday to her dialysis treatments.

36. Odiet, "Custody of Girl in Bell Case is Given Sister."

37. Atwell, "Local Minister Sought After Molesting Charge."

38. Odiet, "Custody of Girl in Bell Case is Given Sister."

39. "Girl Tells of Running Away from Home," *Kokomo Tribune*, Dec. 30, 1959.

40. Odiet, "Custody of Girl in Bell Case is Given Sister."

41. Don Pitner, interview with the author.

42. Fred Odiet, "Grand Jury: No Action Taken in Regard to Testimony in Clinton Bell Case," *Kokomo Tribune*, Jan. 7, 1960.

43. "Bell Facing Sex Charges," *Anderson Daily Bulletin*, Jan. 27, 1960, page 7.

44. Ibid.

45. Brenda Moore, Don Pitner, and Buddy Coiffeur, interviews with the author.

46. "Clinton Bell Case set for Trial May 16."

47. Don Pitner and Brenda Moore gave these numbers in interviews. C. T. was quoted in a newspaper article from the Dec. 15, 1959, edition of the *Kokomo Tribune*, stating that "about a dozen young girls and women had had something to do with Brother Bell." The deputy from the newspaper's same article quoted C. T. Pratt relating that he told the girls and women: "you will be forgiven, but the Lord will take care of Clinton Bell."

48. Varnell Schaeffner, interview with the author.

49. Charles Roberts, Don Pitner, and Buddy Coiffeur, interviews with the author.

10. HONOR THY FATHER AND THY MOTHER

1. *Minutes of the Church of God of the Union Assembly,* 1990, 13.

2. Petition in the Superior Court of Whitfield County, Georgia, to amend the original charter, Oct. 10, 1950. Also, Charlie Carmical, interview with the author.

3. Charlie Carmical, Charles Roberts, and Buddy Coiffeur, interviews with the author.

4. *Minutes of the 24th Annual Meeting of the Union Assembly of the Church of God*, 20.

5. J. W. Burnett, quoted in an article by Connell, "Former Church Leader Interviewed." Buddy Coiffeur, interview with the author. Coiffeur's father was one of the charter members.

6. Marie Hoskins Anderson, interviewed by the author in Dalton, Georgia, May 1, 2016. Other former members interviewed talked about this.

7. Johnnie Haney Butler, *Standing on the Edge of Sanity*, unpublished memoir, 1998, 126.

8. Paul Saylor, YouTube, March 25, 2014. https://www.youtube.com/watch?v=qh1AFrPjQoc.

9. Hattie Johnson (not her real name to protect her identity), interview with the author, Dalton, Georgia, Aug. 8, 2015.

10. Eric Smithey, interview with the author, Atlanta, Georgia, Sept. 15, 2015; Charles Roberts, Bobby Lowe, Robert Anderson, interviews with the author.

11. Charles Roberts, Teresa Howard Coker, interviews with the author.

12. Connell, "Former Church Leader Interviewed."

13. Charles Roberts, Buddy Coiffeur, interviews with the author; confirmed by other former members.

14. Buddy Coiffeur, interview with the author. I also remember hearing this personally at the Belcher home during the 1950s.

15. Brenda Moore, interview with the author.

16. Charles Roberts, interview with the author; Chris Camp, recorded interview with the author.

17. Charlie Carmical, interview with the author, and confirmed by other church members.

18. Buddy Coiffeur, interview with the author.

19. Charlie Carmical, interview with the author.

20. Buddy Coiffeur, interview with the author.

21. Charlie Carmical, Charles Roberts, interviews with the author, as well as an interview with an anonymous woman who still has family in the Church.

22. The Church of God of the Union Assembly, Inc., Et Al. v. H. D. Carmical. 214 Ga 243 (1958).

23. Charles Roberts, interview with the author, and *Minutes of the Church of God of the Union Assembly*, 1990, 10.

24. Charlie Carmical, Charles Roberts, and Libby Neighbors, interviews with the author.

25. Buddy Coiffeur, Charlie Carmical, and Charles Roberts, interviews with the author.

26. The Church of God of the Union Assembly, Inc., Et Al. v. H. D. Carmical.

27. Charles Roberts, interview with the author.

28. Charles Roberts, Robert Anderson, interviews with the author. Roughly half of the former and present members interviewed confirmed these details.

29. Campdvd email, (hereafter, "Campdvd" is used to refer to an anonymous source who will be identified as Campdvd because he/she is a former member); James Beeler from *Church Forum*.

30. Charlie Carmical, Charles Roberts, interviews with the author.

31. Church of God of the Union Assembly, Inc. Et Al. v. Isaacs. 23442, 222 GA 243 (1966).

32. Rita Gazaway Woody, interview with the author.

33. Campdvd email.

34. Bobby Barton, interview with the author, Dalton, Georgia, Oct. 30, 2014.

35. Billy Lowe (not his real name to protect his anonymity), recorded interview with the author, Dalton, Georgia, Dec. 17, 21, 2014; this person was a member of the Church of

God of the Union Assembly from birth (about 1950) until adulthood. His father was a minister of the Church for many years even after this person left. He said his family was part of the elite.

36. The preachers, usually a member of the Pratt family, would rebuke members by grabbing them by the head and shaking it violently.

37. This is an A & W Root Beer drive-in on East Morris Street—also called Highway 52 that the author could see from his front porch as a young boy.

38. The house was owned by the Church or the Pratts and her father rented it from them.

39. Libby Neighbors, interview with the author, Dalton, Georgia, May 21, 2014.

40. Charlie Carmical, Charles Roberts, interviews with the author.

41. C. T. Pratt's own great-grandson, who did not want to be identified, among other former members interviewed, recalled this detail.

42. Charles Roberts, Buddy Coiffeur, interviews with the author. These details were confirmed by several others.

43. Charles Roberts, Buddy Coiffeur, and Libby Neighbors, interviews with the author; confirmed by others.

44. Charles Roberts, Buddy Coiffeur, as well as two anonymous family members, interviews with the author.

45. Charles Roberts, Buddy Coiffeur, interviews with the author.

46. *Minutes of the Church of God of the Union Assembly,* 1990, 10.

47. This was told to me in a recorded interview by one of C. T. and Minnie's great-grandsons—grandson to Flora Hughes.

48. Connell, "Former Church Leader Interviewed."

49. Charles Roberts, Buddy Coiffeur, interviews with the author.

50. *Minutes of the Church of God of the Union Assembly,* 1990, 11.

51. Buddy Coiffeur, interview with the author.

52. Charles Roberts, interview with the author.

53. George Hobbs, great-grandson of C. T. Pratt, interview with the author, 2017.

11. BUILDING FEAR

1. Moody Connell, "Former Church Leader Interviewed, *Daily Citizen-News,* July 16, 1980, 1.

2. Charles Roberts, interview with the author. Confirmed by others interviewed.

3. Billy B. Lowe, interview with the author.

4. Charles Roberts, interview with the author.

5. Moody Connell, "Faithful Follow Rules of Church," *Daily Citizen-News,* July 6, 1980, 1.

6. *Minutes of the 24th Annual Meeting of the Union Assembly of the Church of God,* 18.

7. Ibid.

8. *Minutes of the Church of God of the Union Assembly,* 1990, 24, and told to the author in interviews with Charles Roberts, Robert Anderson, plus more former members. Also, Dorothy Pitner Bliss sent the author a copy of the 1954 General Rules and Guidelines handed out to the members in Kokomo, Indiana.

9. Campdvd email, Thursday, Apr. 24, 2014. This story about Tom Pratt was confirmed by an anonymous former member on Dec. 8, 2015.

10. Brenda Moore, interview with the author.

11. Robert and Marie Anderson, interview with the author, May 1, 2016.
12. *Minutes of the Church of God of the Union Assembly*, 1990, 15.
13. Butler, *Standing on the Edge of Sanity*, 40.
14. Jesse Pratt Jr., "Rev. Pratt Replies to More Articles," *Daily Citizen-News*, July 11, 1980, 1.
15. Bobby Lee Cook, interview with the author in Summerville, Georgia, Mar. 25, 2015.
16. An anonymous present member told me this and got mad at me when he realized who I was and hung up the phone even though I had identified myself earlier and told him the interview was for a book. Also, Billy B. Lowe, interview with the author.
17. Clerk of Superior Court, Whitfield County, Deed Book 38, p. 598.
18. Clerk of Superior Court, Whitfield County, Deed Book 40, p. 306.
19. Clerk of Superior Court, Whitfield County, Deed Book 41, p. 469.
20. Clerk of Superior Court, Whitfield County, Deed Book 42, p. 329.
21. Tract #1 = 27 acres in Whitfield County, part of land lot 131 (formerly owned by T. N. Hurst)

   Tract #2 = 20 acres in Whitfield County, part of land lot 168 (Formally owned by C. G. Weeks)

   Tract #3 = 410 acres in Whitfield County, part or all of land lots 202, 231, 232, 239, with 231 (formerly known as the Prater's Farm)

   Tract #4 = 265 acres in Whitfield County, part or all of land lots 165, 195, and 165 (formerly estate of John C. Anderson)

   Tract #5 = 73 acres in Whitfield County, part of land lot 160 (formerly owned by M. R. Tatum)

   Also = 30 acres in Whitfield County, part of land lot 165 (formerly owned by M. R. Tatum)

   Also = 12 acres in Whitfield County, part of land lots 165 and 166 (formerly owned by M. R. Tatum)

   Tract #6 = 168 acres in Whitfield County, part of land lots 201, 202, and 203 (on Prater's Mill Road, formerly owned by W. H. Harper)

   Tract #7 = 160 acres in Whitfield and Murray Counties, lot 246

   Also = 74.75 acres in Whitfield and Murray Counties, part of land lot 245 (formerly owned by W. P. Poteet)

   Also = 40 acres in Murray County, part of land lot 245

   Also = 20 acres in Murray County, part of land lot 224

   Also = 90 acres in Murray County, part of land lot 223

   Also = 400 acres in Whitfield County, part or all of land lots 223, 224, and 247

   Tract #8 = 433 acres in Whitfield County near Varnell, GA, land lots 194, 193 (formerly owned by the W. E. Bare family)

   Also = 160 acres in Whitfield County, land lot 204

   Also = 160 acres in Whitfield County, land lot 230

   Tract #9 = 444 acres in Murray County, part or all of land lots 19, 35, 36, 37, 38, and 54 (Conveyed to the First National Bank of Dalton by W. C. Martin and Mrs. Jesse River)

   Tract #10 = 210.09 acres in Murray County, part of land lots 30, 31, 32, and 43

   Tract #11 = 803.26 acres in Whitfield and Murray County, part or all of land lots 79, 101, 102, 114, 115, 116, 138, and 139.

22. Charles Roberts, Buddy Coiffeur, Billy Lowe, and others, interviews with the author.
23. Charles Roberts, interview with the author.
24. U.S. Treasury Department, Internal Revenue Service, Form 669-C, Book 169, pp. 544–45.
25. This story was reported to the author by several men from Dalton: Jack Freeman, LaVerne Damron, and others. Jack Freeman said he heard this story at a Christmas party at the beach home of one of the men who bought the property and the lawyer who arranged the deals.
26. Clerk of Superior Court, Whitfield County, Deed Book 44, p. 293.
27. Moody Connell, "Ex-Churchmen Seek Ranch Money," *Daily Citizen-News,* June 27, 1980, 1.
28. *Minutes of the Church of God of the Union Assembly,* 1990, 16, and Connell, "Ex-Churchmen Seek Ranch Money," 1.
29. Ibid.
30. Charles Roberts, two other former members, interviews with the author.
31. Buddy Coiffeur, interview with the author.
32. Don Pitner, Brenda Moore, interviews with the author.
33. An anonymous member of the family, Campdvd, and other members told me about the confession train.
34. Charles Roberts, Buddy Coiffeur, and Billy B. Lowe, interviews with the author.
35. Charles Roberts, interview with the author.
36. Varnel Schaeffner, Eric Smithey, interviews with the author. Also Charles Roberts, Billy Lowe, interviews with the author. Other former members confirmed these details.
37. Charles Roberts, Eric Smithey interviews with the author.
38. Atwell, "Phone Call from Bell Is Reported." See also Atwell, "Accused Pastor in Molesting of Young Girl."
39. Charles Roberts, Don Pitner, interviews with the author, and the Trailblazers Quartet were well-known in the Southern United States.
40. *Minutes of the Church of God of the Union Assembly,* 1990, 11.
41. Connell, "Former Church Leader Interviewed."
42. Certificate of Death, State of Georgia, Charlie Thomas Pratt, Sept. 12, 1966.
43. Certificate of Death, State of Georgia, Mary Minnie Pratt, Dec. 4, 1971.

12. THE BOSS

1. Jesse Pratt, "Jesse Pratt Says," *The Southerner,* Jan. 1956, 3.
2. Robert and Marie Anderson, interview by the author, Knoxville, Tennessee, May 1, 2016.
3. Butler, *Standing on the Edge of Sanity,* 40.
4. Buddy Coiffeur, Charles Roberts, and Libby Neighbors, interviews with the author.
5. Campdvd email.
6. Charles Roberts, Buddy Coiffeur, interviews with the author.
7. Charles Roberts, Billy B. Lowe, interviews with the author.
8. Robert Anderson, interview with the author.
9. Robert and Marie Anderson, Charles Roberts, interviews with the author, details confirmed by others.
10. Charles Roberts, interview, with the author, as well as an interview with an anonymous family member.

11. Buddy Coiffeur, Charles Roberts, interviews with the author.
12. Buddy Coiffeur, interview with the author.
13. Ibid.
14. It was actually Jesse's son by Ethel, but all the members called these children Jesse's bastards because they had been taught that they were. They did not acknowledge that Jesse and Ethel had ever been married. However, I found a copy of Jesse's and Ethel's marriage license.
15. Anonymous nonmember of Union Assembly who still does business with the Church, interview with the author, Dalton, Georgia, Oct. 25, 2014.
16. Don Pitner, interview with the author.
17. Billy Lowe, interview with the author.
18. Billy Lowe, Charles Roberts, Buddy Coiffeur, interviews with the author, Campdvd email.
19. Bubby Coiffeur, interview with the author.
20. Ibid.
21. Campdvd, anonymous former member and family member's email to author on Apr. 23, 2014.
22. Charles Roberts, interview with the author.
23. James Allen, interview by the author, Dalton, Georgia, Mar. 11, 2013.
24. Jim Gowin, interview with the author, along with other anonymous nonmembers. Also Billy Lowe, interview with the author.
25. Billy Lowe, interview with the author.
26. Charles Roberts, interview with the author.
27. Charles Roberts, interview with the author.
28. Campdvd email.
29. The woman I interviewed for this information asked to remain anonymous because she still fears the Church will harm her.
30. Campdvd email.
31. Charles Roberts, interview with the author.

13. THE ROOT OF ALL EVIL

1. Harvey Halman, interview with the author.
2. Ibid.
3. Joe Duncan, conversation with author, Harvey Halman, interview with the author, an interview with an anonymous pilot from Dalton.
4. Zac Norvill and Jim Gowin, interview with the author, Dalton, Georgia, May 18, 2011.
5. This information was obtained from interviews with an anonymous family member and an anonymous business associate of the Pratt family.
6. Descendants were called "Seed" if they are direct descendants of C. T. and Minnie down through Jesse. The "seed-seed" included other family members, such as Flora Pratt Hughes and her offspring.
7. Anonymous former member, interview with the author, Feb. 16, 2012.
8. Billy Lowe, interview with the author.
9. Charles Roberts, interview with the author; confirmed by two other sources.
10. Sherry Williams, interview with the author, Dalton, Georgia, Nov. 13, 2014.
11. Don Pitner, interview with the author.

12. Anonymous member sent this email to the author on December 6, 2015; however, the individual gave their actual name to the author.

13. Teresa Howard Coker, interview with the author, August 15, 2015.

14. THE WAGES OF SIN IS DEATH

1. *Minutes of the Church of God of the Union Assembly*, 1990, 70.

2. Anonymous family member whose great-grandfather was C. T. Pratt.

3. Robert Hanley, "Fort Dix May Become Federal Prison," *New York Times*, Aug. 30, 1992.

4. National Personnel Records Center, 1 Archives Drive, St. Louis, MO.

5. Rhettia, a member of the La Paz County Sheriff's Department, interview with the author, La Paz County, Arizona, July 27, 2015.

6. Recorded interview of an anonymous former member who lived on the ranch for twenty-one years. Interview with the author on Oct. 6, 2013.

7. Wanda Wright, the anonymous name of a woman who was a former member and lived on the Arizona Ranch for two years.

8. Billy Lowe, Wanda Wright, interviews with the author.

9. This story was told to me by Billy Lowe, who lived in Arizona during the summers while he was in high school. He didn't see wife-swapping happening, but he said everyone out there talked about it like it was a common practice. It was also told to me by Campdvd, who visited the ranch one time and heard people talking about it. It was also told to me by Wanda Wright, who lived there for two years. At least ten former members interviewed by the author confirmed that they had heard these stories.

10. Buddy Coiffeur, interview with the author.

11. Ibid.

12. Charles Roberts, interview with the author. Several other former members interviewed confirmed this, as well as one of Herbert's nephews.

13. *Minutes of the Church of God of the Union Assembly*, 1990, 15, and deed records recorded at the Whitfield Clerk of Superior Court.

14. Deed books from Whitfield County, Georgia Court House, Clerk of Superior Court.

15. Charles Roberts, interview with the author.

16. Not the real name of the funeral home because the funeral home is still in business.

17. Not their real names, but the interviews with Tim were tape-recorded.

18. Not his real name because revealing the correct name might implicate the funeral home.

19. Tim Pierce (anonymous name) interview with the author, Dalton, Georgia, Oct. 20, 2014, and July 3, 2015. Also Ralph Joyner (anonymous name) interview with the author, Dalton, Georgia, July 10, 2013.

20. "Wounded Hunter Dies on Airplane," *Chattanooga Times*, Mar. 16, 1972.

21. Ibid.

22. Ibid.

23. Ralph Joyner, interview with the author.

24. Obituaries appeared in the *Dalton Daily Citizen-News*, Mar. 17, 1972.

25. Charles Roberts and others interviewed told me this about Paul Hughes.

26. "Wounded Hunter Dies on Airplane," *Chattanooga Times*.

27. This version of the story was related to the author in a recorded interview by one of C. T. Pratt's grandsons and confirmed by one of Paul Hughes's nephews.

28. Charles Roberts, Buddy Coiffeur, interviews with the author. This version was related by a few other members as well.
29. Charles Roberts, interview with the author.
30. This was related to the author in a recorded interview by one of C. T. Pratt's grandsons and confirmed by one of Paul Hughes's nephews.
31. Buddy Coiffeur, interview with the author.
32. Buddy Coiffeur quoted Paul Hughes's brother; Charles Roberts, Billy Lowe, Don Pitner, interviews with the author. Several Pratt family members who wish to remain anonymous had their own versions of these stories.
33. George Farmer, interview with the author, Columbus, Georgia, June 24, 2015.
34. Bill Phillips, interview with the author, Chattanooga, Tennessee, July 7, 2015.
35. Yuma County Sheriff's Recorders Department, and La Paz Sheriff's Recorders Department, phone conversation with the author, July 17, 2015.

15. A PRUDENT WIFE

1. The epigraph that heads this chapter was reportedly included in many of Jesse's sermons about the family. Charles Roberts and Billy Lowe confirm this, and even his other preachers in other Union Assembly churches were saying similar things.
2. Charles Roberts, interview with the author. I was told this by more than one woman from the Church.
3. Paul Saylor, YouTube: Jesse F. Pratt Sermon on Women in Church, preached between 1972 and 1975, https://www.youtube.com/watch?v=G4IHb07YJY, viewed Mar. 13, 2015.
4. Sherry Williams, interview with the author. In this case, Sherry is a man's name.
5. Mary Joseph (anonymous name, because she was still afraid of the Pratt family), interview with the author, Tennessee, Aug. 8, 2015.
6. Harvey Halman, interview with the author.
7. Charles Roberts interview with the author.
8. Charles Roberts, Buddy Coiffeur, Don Pitner, Dorothy Bliss, and Brenda Moore, interviews with the author.
9. Charles Roberts, interview with the author.
10. Rita Gazaway Woody, interview with the author.
11. Charles Roberts, interview with the author.
12. Charles Roberts, Billy Lowe, and eight other people told similar stories in interviews with the author about the practice of prophesying car wrecks.
13. Charles Roberts, interview with the author.
14. Mary Joseph and Hattie Johnson, interviews with the author.
15. Butler, *Standing on the Edge of Sanity*, 100.
16. Ibid., 108.
17. Charles Roberts, interview with the author, also confirmed by other former members.
18. Billy Lowe, interview with the author.
19. Charles Roberts, interview with the author.
20. Charles Roberts, Buddy Coiffeur, interviews with the author.
21. Ibid.
22. Two directors of the funeral home and one of the owners told me this story several times.
23. Charles Roberts, interview with the author.

24. Charles Roberts, interview with the author, and the woman who lived on the farm.
25. Buddy Coiffeur, interview with the author.
26. Campdvd email, anonymous name.
27. Charles Roberts, Buddy Coiffeur, and Chris Camp, interviews with the author.
28. Charles Roberts, Sherry Williams, and Buddy Coiffeur, interviews with the author.
29. Charles Roberts, interview with the author. One of Jesse's nephews confirmed this story, too.
30. Buddy Coiffeur, Charles Roberts, interviews with the author. The cattle story was confirmed by one of Jesse's nephews; about ten others interviewed had some variant of this story.
31. Billy Lowe, interview with the author.
32. Buddy Coiffeur, interview with the author.
33. Buddy Coiffeur, Billy Lowe, and Teresa Howard Coker, interviews with the author.
34. Buddy Coiffeur, interview with the author.
35. Charles Roberts, interview with the author.
36. Coincidentally, the funeral home that had picked up Paul Hughes in Chattanooga exactly two years before to the day came after Jesse's body. One of the funeral home associates later told people that there was so much blood on the floor that his shoes squeaked when he walked across the carpet and that women were on the floor with towels trying to clean it up. However, this same associate refused to answer questions about the event and reported that he did not even remember being there. Later that carpet disappeared.
37. Georgia Department of Human Resources, Vital Records Unit, Certificate of Death, Jesse F. Pratt.
38. Charles Roberts, Buddy Coiffeur, interviews with the author.
39. Billy Lowe, interview with the author.
40. This claim was reported by one of Wayman Pratt's sons.
41. Charles Roberts, Billy Lowe, interviews with the author.
42. All of this section's information came from interviews with the author by Charles Roberts, Buddy Coiffeur, Billy Lowe, and one of Jesse's nephews, who will remain anonymous. More information came from an email from Campdvd, and an anonymous family member.
43. There were conflicting reports about who told Herbert to sell the cattle. Charles Roberts indicated it was Jesse, while Buddy Coiffeur thought it was Irene.
44. Buddy Coiffeur, Tim Pierce, interviews with the author.
45. All of this section's information came from interviews with the author by Charles Roberts, Buddy Coiffeur, and Billy Lowe, one of Jesse's nephews, who will remain anonymous, a funeral home director who spoke to many people and a Campdvd email.
46. Former members Robert Anderson and Marie Hoskins Anderson also told the author in an interview that they heard this at church.
47. Charles Roberts, Billy Lowe, and Buddy Coiffeur, interviews with the author.
48. Charles Roberts, Billy Lowe, interviews with the author.
49. Charles Roberts, Billy Lowe, Buddy Coiffeur, interviews with the author. A few others interviewed had similar suspicions.
50. Tim Pierce, interview with the author.
51. Charles Roberts, Buddy Coiffeur, and Tim Pierce, interviews with the author.
52. Steve Pratt, interview with the author, Knoxville, Tennessee, Jan. 8, 2014. These details were confirmed by Charles Roberts, Buddy Coiffeur, interviews with the author.

53. Robert Anderson, interview with the author.
54. Steve Pratt, interview with the author.
55. Johnnie Haney Butler, Charles Roberts, interviews with the author.

16. A NEW LEVEL OF HELL

1. Sue Johnson, interview with the author, Rydal, Georgia, Aug. 18, 2015; Teresa Howard Coker, interview with the author.
2. The number of people who reported this is too numerous to list here, but they include Junior Roberts, Sherry Williams, Sue Johnson, Johnnie Haney Butler, among others
3. Buddy Coiffeur, interview with the author.
4. Teresa Howard Coker, interview with the author.
5. Sue Johnson, interview with the author.
6. Teresa Howard Coker, interview with the author.
7. Charles Roberts, Johnnie Haney Butler, interviews with the author.
8. Charles Roberts, interview with the author.
9. Teresa Coker, interview with the author.
10. Junior Roberts, Johnnie Haney Butler, interviews with the author.
11. Junior Roberts, interview with the author.
12. Charles Roberts, interview with the author, Campdvd emails.
13. Campdvd email.
14. An anonymous family member sent this email to the author on Dec. 6, 2015.
15. Charles Roberts, Teresa Howard Coker, interviews with the author.
16. Charles Roberts, interview with the author.
17. Butler, *Standing on the Edge of Sanity,* 64.
18. Sue Johnson, Charles Roberts, interviews with the author. Stories about displaying pictures were confirmed by several others.
19. Charles Roberts, interview with the author.
20. Billy Lowe, interview with the author.
21. As a teacher at Dalton High School, the author often bought candy from the Union Assembly girls. It was really good candy.
22. Anonymous member sent this email to the author on Dec. 6, 2015.
23. Charles Roberts, interview with the author.
24. Buddy Coiffeur, interview with the author.
25. Teresa Coker; Charles Roberts; Buddy Coiffeur; and Billy Lowe, interviews with the author.
26. Teresa Coker, interview with the author.
27. Campdvd email.
28. Ibid.
29. Jesse Bee Howard's daughter, interview with the author. She did not want me to use her name because she still has family in the CGUA.
30. Johnnie Haney Butler, interview with the author.
31. This information came from an anonymous former member who left the Church in 1995 but was still afraid of the leaders of the Church.
32. Marie Hoskins Anderson, interview with the author.
33. Teresa Coker, interview with the author.
34. Ibid.
35. Recorded interview with author by an anonymous former member who did not want

to be identified because she still has family in the Church. This event was confirmed by Charles Roberts, who witnessed this abuse.

36. Robert and Marie Hoskins Anderson, interview with the author.

37. Ibid.

38. Charles Roberts, Marie Hoskins Anderson, interviews with the author.

39. Charles Roberts, Buddy Coiffeur, Johnnie Haney Butler, interviews with the author.

40. Catoosa County Records, Feb. 8, 1996, Deed Book 54, p. 6.

41. Johnnie Haney Butler, interview with the author.

42. This was reported to me by friends of mine who played golf with Jesse Junior at *The Farm*. Since this person's company still does business with the Union Assembly, he didn't want me to give his name.

43. Charles Roberts, Johnnie Haney Butler, Buddy Coiffeur, interviews with the author. Other informants confirm this behavior of Jesse Junior.

44. Troy Overby, interview with the author, Dalton, Georgia, Oct. 7, 2015.

45. Charles Roberts, Troy Overby, interviews with the author.

46. Charles Roberts, anonymous great grandson of C. T. and Minnie Pratt, interviews with the author, Sept. 2014. Victor Long, "Man Hospitalized After Fight at Church," *Daily Citizen-News*, May 10, 1994, 1.

47. Charles Roberts; Buddy Van Meter, interviews with the author.

17. DYING IN THE FAITH

1. Quoted in Dan George, Associated Press, Mar. 30, 1985, http://www.apnewsarchive .com/1985/Teen-Aged-Cancer-Patient-Mourned-At-Funeral-In-Church-That-Fought -Treatment/id.

2. Anonymous owner of a funeral home in Dalton told the author this story.

3. Don Pitner, Johnnie Haney Butler, Billy Lowe, interviews with the author. These observations have been confirmed by others.

4. The funeral directors wanted to remain anonymous.

5. "Death of 12 Children Laid to Refusal of Medical Aid," *Marietta Daily Journal*, Nov. 16, 1958.

6. Billy Graham, "Billy Graham Answers," *Dalton Daily Citizen-News*, 1970. This article was found in my deceased grandmother's bible and the exact date was missing. She had written 1970 and *Dalton Daily Citizen* above the article she had cut out of the newspaper.

7. Charles Roberts, interview with the author.

8. This interview was with one of Jesse Bee Howard's daughters who wanted to remain anonymous.

9. Johnnie Haney Butler, and this incident was reported to the author in interviews by three of this woman's children on Aug. 8, 2015.

10. M. B. Sibai, "Hypertension: Normal Problems of Pregnancy and Childbirth," *Obstetrics, Sixth Edition* (Philadelphia, W. B. Saunders Press, 2012).

11. This incident was reported to the author in interviews by three of this man's children, Aug. 8, 2015.

12. Ibid .

13. Rick Soll, "Pamela Faces Biggest Struggle," *Chicago Sun-Times*, Oct. 7, 1983.

14. Ibid.

15. Ibid.

16. Petition, Larry T. Hamilton, Circuit Court for Campbell County, Tennessee, Nov. 8, 1983.

17. Soll, "Pamela Faces Biggest Struggle."

18. Dan George, "Teen-Aged Cancer Patient Mourned at Funeral in Church That Fought Treatment," Associated Press, Mar. 30, 1985. See also Diane Fanning, *Her Deadly Web: The True Story of a Former Nurse and the Strange and Suspicious Deaths of Her Two Husbands* (New York: St. Martin's, 2012), 149–53.

19. Tammy Magill, email to the author, July 19, 2017.

20. "Trion Minister Sees Religious Basis in Arrest," *Rome News Tribune*, Feb. 21, 1984, 1.

21. Charlie Carmical, interview with the author.

22. Lee Jessup, "God Expects Us to Use Our Minds," (Lexington, NC) *Dispatch*, Mar. 16, 1984, 16.

23. Campdvd email to the author, Jan. 4, 2016.

24. Anonymous former member of the Union Assembly who is related the Pratt family.

25. Campdvd email.

26. Marie Hoskins Anderson, interview with the author.

27. Interview with the author by an anonymous former member of the Union Assembly in Hamilton, Ohio, who lived close to Illyne.

28. Campdvd email, and an anonymous former church member who witnessed these events.

18. AND YE SHALL KNOW THE TRUTH

1. National Center of Education Statistics. https://nces.ed.gov/programs/digest/d07/tables/dt07_100.asp

2. Charles Roberts, an anonymous woman who is related to the Pratt family, interviews with the author.

3. Buddy Coiffeur, interview with the author.

4. Harvey Halman, interview with the author, Feb. 2, 2015, Dalton, Georgia.

5. Allen Ward is a very good friend of the author and told me this story many times. Allen gave an official interview on Oct. 30, 2015, to the author.

6. Johnnie Haney Butler, Marie Anderson's interviews.

7. An anonymous family member told this to Charles Roberts, along with a former housekeeper for Jesse Junior.

8. Charles Roberts, interview with the author, confirmed by others.

9. Many reported these behaviors, including Charles Roberts, Charlie Carmical, Buddy Coiffeur, an anonymous great-grandson of C. T. and Minnie Pratt, and other family members.

10. Connell, "Ex-Churchmen Seek Ranch Money."

11. Ibid.

12. Moody Connell, "Things Change in Large Dalton-Based Church," *Daily Citizen-News*, June 17, 1980.

13. Moody Connell, "Church of God Doctrine Said Strict," *Daily Citizen-News*, June 19, 1980.

14. Ibid.

15. Ibid.

16. Ibid.

17. Ibid.

18. Connell, "Ex-Churchmen Seek Ranch Money."

19. Moody Connell, "Favors Refund to Ex-Church Members," *Daily Citizen-News*, June 30, 1980.

20. Jesse Pratt Jr., "Pratt Replies to Articles on Church," *Daily Citizen-News*, July 1, 1980.

21. Ibid.

22. Ibid.

23. Charles Roberts, Rita Gazaway, Johnnie Haney Butler, interviews with the author.

24. Connell, "Faithful Follow Rules of Church."

25. Ibid.

26. Jesse Pratt Jr., "Pratt Defends Church Doctrine," *Daily Citizen-News*, July 3, 1980.

27. Jesse Pratt Jr., "Rev. Pratt Blasts News Articles," *Daily Citizen-News*, July 9, 1980.

28. Charles Roberts, Don Pitner, Brenda Moore, interviews with the author. A host of other former members interviewed expressed similar views.

29. Pratt, "Rev. Pratt Blasts News Articles."

30. Ibid.

31. Jesse Pratt Jr., "Rev. Pratt Replies to More Articles," *Daily Citizen-News*, July 11, 1980.

32. Charles Roberts reported in an interview that his father along with other members did endorse their checks and returned them to the Church of God of the Union Assembly. He said his father's check was over $3,000.

33. Connell, "Former Church Leader Interviewed."

34. Ibid.

35. Ibid.

36. Ibid.

37. Ibid.

38. Campdvd email, Charles Roberts, Billy Lowe, interviews with the author. The beef story was confirmed by lots of other former members.

39. Campdvd email.

40. Campdvd email, and these details were confirmed by many former members.

41. Rita Norville, interview, also from personally viewing the estate by the author.

42. Teresa Howard Coker, interview with the author.

43. Charles Roberts, Teresa Howard Coker, interviews with the author, Campdvd emails. The author personally saw this property soon after it was sold to Zac Norville in 1992.

44. Charles Roberts, interview with the author, Campdvd email. These details were confirmed by other members.

45. Clerk of Superior Court, Whitfield County, Deed Book 2087, p. 203.

46. "Rev. Pratt Robbed at Home in Dalton," *Calhoun Times and Gordon County News*, Nov. 25, 1989.

47. Clerk of Superior Court, Whitfield County, Deed Book 2087, p. 203.

48. Residential Property Record Card, Whitfield County, Georgia, Tax Parcel Information, Whitfield County Deed Records, Book 2355, p. 121.

49. Charles Roberts, Robert Anderson, interviews with the author.

50. Harvey Halman, Joe Duncan, interviews with the author.

51. Charles Roberts, Billy Lowe; Teresa, Johnnie Haney Butler, interviews with the author. Also confirmed by Campdvd email.

52. Charles Roberts, interview with the author.

53. Clerk of Superior Court, of Whitfield County, Georgia, July 2, 1993, Deed Book 519, pp. 532–38. See also Clerk of Superior Court, Catoosa County, Georgia, July 26, 1993, Deed Book 411, pp. 264–70.

54. Robert and Marie Anderson, interview with the author.

55. A Dalton banker who wanted to remain anonymous because he still does business with members of CGUA had the following to say: "Jesse asked me one time what I thought about letting the church women dress like the general population. I told him, 'How would you like to have your hair tied up in a bun all the time and stand out like they do for being so different?' It wasn't long until he made the changes."

56. Centers for Disease Control, Morbidity and Mortality Weekly, Report, Measles—United States, 1989, and first 20 weeks 1990—accessed at http://www.cdc.gov/mmwr/preview /mmwrhtml/00001999.htm on Apr. 19, 2018.

57. Walter Orenstein, "The Role of Measles Elimination in Development of a National Immunization Program," *Pediatric Infectious Disease Journal* (2006): 12. Accessed at http://www.medscape.com/viewarticle/551272_5, subscription required.

58. Luis M. Viamonte, M.D., email to the author, Mar. 22, 2017.

59. This startling reversal was recounted by a close family member who does not want to be identified. The story is confirmed by Charles Roberts and others.

60. Billy Lowe, Buddy Coiffeur, interviews with the author, Campdvd email.

61. Marlene Winell, http://journeyfree.org/childhood-religious-indoctrination, accessed Feb. 2015.

62. *Minutes of the Church of God of the Union Assembly,* 1990, 31.

63. Ibid., 27.

64. Ibid., 28.

65. Ibid, 28–30.

66. The author, who taught at Dalton High School from 1969 through 2000, witnessed this happening. Several female teachers had seen the girls changing clothes and shared this with the staff. There were no objections from the staff about the girls changing.

67. Marie Anderson interview.

68. *Minutes of the Church of God of the Union Assembly,* 1990, 24; Charles Roberts, Robert and Marie Anderson, interviews with the author.

69. Robert and Marie Anderson, Charles Roberts, interviews with the author; confirmed by others interviewed.

70. Two anonymous local business men who bought property from the Church, interviewed together with the author in Dalton, Georgia, May 18, 2011.

71. Charles Roberts, interview with the author.

72. Whitfield County Deed Book 2475, p. 54.

73. Zack Norville, interview with the author, Dalton, Georgia, May 2011.

74. Property Record Card, Whitfield County, Georgia Tax Assessor's Office for 2400 Dug Gap RD, 12-7-92.

75. Robert and Marie Anderson interview. Also Charles Roberts interview.

76. Clerk of Superior Court, Whitfield County, Georgia, July 2, 1993, Warranty Deed to Secure Debt, Deed Book 2411, pp. 265–67. Also Clerk of Superior Court, Murray County, Georgia, July 26, 1993, Deed Book 217, pp. 793–95.

77. Clerk of Superior Court, Murray County, Georgia, Aug. 18, 1993, Warranty Deed to

Secure Debt, Deed Book 218, pp. 684–87. Also Clerk of Superior Court, Whitfield County, Georgia Court House, July 11, 1993, Deed Book 2421, p. 1.

78. Clerk of Superior Court, Whitfield County, Georgia, Oct. 28, 1993, Warranty Deed to Secure Debt, Deed Book 2446, pp. 9–12. Also Clerk of Superior Court, Murray County, Georgia, Nov. 5, 1993, Deed Book 221, p. 744.

79. Clerk of Superior Court, Whitfield County, Georgia, Jan. 4, 1994, Deed Book 2475, pp. 54–60. Also Deed Book 480, page 705, Clerk of Superior Court, Catoosa County, Georgia, February 4, 1994. Deed Book 225, page 66, Clerk of Superior Court, Murray County, Georgia, January 28, 1994.

80. This member would like to remain anonymous because she has family still in the Church, but allowed me to record and use her statements.

81. This former member would like to remain anonymous because she has family still in the Church but allowed me to record and use her statements.

19. AND THE TRUTH SHALL MAKE YOU FREE

1. Charles Roberts, the minister's wife who wants to remain anonymous, Teresa Howard Coker, interviews with the author.

2. This story was reported by a man and a woman who were witnesses, but do not want to be identified because they still do business with the Church. They were not nor had ever been members of the Union Assembly church.

3. This was told to the author by a woman he has known and trusted for many years.

4. Clerk of Superior Court, Whitfield County, Georgia, October 28, 1993, Warranty Deed to Secure Debt, Deed Book 2446, pp. 9–12. This loan was for $500,692.

5. Campdvd email.

6. Clerk of Superior Court, Catoosa County, Georgia, Feb. 8, 1996, Deed Book 541, p. 646.

EPILOGUE

1. Curtis F. Belcher, interview and a written statement presented to the author, Dalton, Georgia, March 21, 2016.

2. Certificate of Death/State of Georgia, Jesse Franklin Pratt Junior.

3. Certificate of Death/State of Georgia, James L Pratt.

4. Wilson's brief outreach speech can be found here: https://www.facebook.com/Dalton Services/videos/2185856638327876/UzpfSTEwMDAwMTE3NTU1MDM7NjoxNz E5OTkwODQoNzE2NzUx, accessed Aug. 16, 2018.

BIBLIOGRAPHY

STATE, FEDERAL, AND PRIMARY DOCUMENTS

Application of incorporation of the Union Assembly of the Church of God to the Superior Court of Whitfield County, Georgia; July 16, 1942.

CDC. Measles—United States, 1989, and first 20 weeks 1990. MMWR 1990; 39:353—5,361—3.

Certificate of Death, State of Georgia, Charlie Thomas Pratt, Sept. 12, 1966.

Certificate of Death, State of Georgia, Jesse F. Pratt, Sr., Mar. 15, 1974.

Certificate of Death, State of Georgia, Jesse F. Pratt, Jr., June 21, 2005.

Certificate of Death, State of Georgia, Paul L. Hughes, Mar. 15, 1972.

Certificate of Death, State of Georgia, Wanda P. Pratt, Sept. 17, 1994.

Church of God of the Union Assembly, Inc. et al. v. *City of Dalton et al.* No 19612. 213 Ga. 76,97 S.E.2d 132, Supreme Court of Georgia, Submitted Mar. 11, 1957.

Church of God of the Union Assembly, Inc., et al. v. *H. D. Carmical.* Supreme Court of Georgia on case No. 20138, September 5, 1958.

Church of God of the Union Assembly, Inc. et al. v. *Isaacs.* 23442, 222Ga. 243 (1966), 149 S.E.2d 466, Supreme Court of Georgia, Submitted May 9, 1966.

Marriage Bond, Whitley County, Kentucky, p. 614–15.

Marriage License, State of Georgia, County of Whitfield, Book L, p. 25.

Marriage Licenses, Vital Records Marriage records for Washoe County, Nevada; book 110, p. 156.

Minutes of the 24th Annual Meeting of the Union Assembly of the Church of God, Inc., Oct. 18, 19, 20, 1945, Dalton, GA.

Minutes of the Church of God of the Union Assembly, INC., 1990 edition, Dalton, GA.

Minutes of the Seventh Annual Session of the Church of God Mountain Assembly.

Minutes of the Eleventh Annual Session of the Church of God Mountain Assembly.

National Personnel Records Center, 1 Archives Drive, St Louis, MO 63138-1002. (Jesse Pratt Jr., Army Records).

National Center for Education Statistics, https://nces.ed.gov/programs/digest/d07/tables/dt07_100.asp

Petition, Larry T. Hamilton, In the Circuit Court for Campbell County, Tennessee, No. 7846. November 8, 1983.

Property Record Card, Whitfield County, Georgia Court House for 2400 Dug Gap RD, 12-7-92.

Selected Records of the War Department relating to Confederate Prisoners of war. Roll: M 598_22.

Sixteenth Census of the United States, 1940, S. D. No. 7; E. D. No. 155-13; sheet 6B.

Sixteenth Census of the United States, 1940, S. D. No. 7; E. D. No. 155-15A; sheets 3A, 3B.

United States Federal Census 1900, Wayne County Kentucky, Parnell, District 0127.

United States Federal Census 1930, Murray County, Georgia, Middle District 824, district 0005.

United States Federal Census 1940, Whitfield County, Georgia, Dalton, sheet number 3A.

United States Federal Census 1940, Whitfield County, Georgia, Dalton, Militia District 872, sheet 16A.

United States Federal Census 1940, Whitfield County, Georgia, Dalton, City Ward, sheet 4A.

U.S. Treasury Department – Internal Revenue Service, Form 669-C, Book 169, pages 544–45.

U.S. Treasury Department – Internal Revenue Service, Form 669-C: Certificate of Discharge of Property From Federal Tax Lien, the Church of God of the Union Assembly, Clerk of Superior Court, County of Whitfield, pages 93, 94, 95.

DEED BOOKS

Deed Book 35, pp. 194, 582, Book 36, p. 30, Book 38, p. 390, Book 53, pp. 322–33, Clerk of Superior Court, Whitfield County, Georgia.

Deed Book 64, pp. 53–54, Clerk of Superior Court, Whitfield County, Georgia.

Deed Book 38, p. 598, Clerk of Superior Court, Whitfield County, Georgia.

Deed Book 40, p. 306, Clerk of Superior Court, Whitfield County, Georgia.

Deed Book 42, p. 329, Clerk of Superior Court, Whitfield County, Georgia.

Deed Book 41, pp. 469–73, Clerk of Superior Court, Whitfield County, Georgia.

Deed Book 54, p. 6, Catoosa County Deed Records, Feb. 8, 1996.

Deed Book 217, pp. 793–95, Clerk of Superior Court, Murray County, Georgia, July 26, 1993.

Deed Book 242, pp. 684–85, Clerk of Superior Court, Whitfield County, Georgia, July 11, 1993.

Deed Book 242, pp. 684–85, Clerk of Superior Court, Whitfield County, Georgia, July 11, 1993.

Warranty Deed to Secure Debt, Deed Book 2411, pp. 265–67, Clerk of Superior Court, Whitfield County, Georgia, July 2, 1993.

Warranty Deed to Secure Debt, Deed Book 218, pp. 684–87, Clerk of Superior Court, Murray County, Georgia, Aug. 18, 1993.

Warranty Deed to Secure Debt, Deed Book 2446, pp. 9–12, Clerk of Superior Court, Whitfield Georgia, Oct. 28, 1993.

Warranty Deed to Secure Debt, Deed Book 2475, pp. 54–60, Clerk of Superior Court, Whitfield County, Georgia, Jan. 4, 1994.

Deed Book 221, p. 744, Clerk of Superior Court, Murray County, Georgia, County, Nov. 5, 1993.

Deed Book 480, p. 705, Clerk of Superior Court, Catoosa County, Georgia, Feb. 4, 1994.

Deed Book 225, p. 66, Clerk of Superior Court, Murray County, Georgia, Jan. 28, 1994.

Deed Book 541, p. 646, Clerk of Superior Court, Catoosa County, Georgia, Feb. 8, 1996.

INTERVIEWS AND EMAILS

Allen, James, interview with the author, Mar. 11, 2013.

Anderson, Marie, joint interview with Robert Anderson and the author, Apr. 3, 2016; emails, Jan. 19, 2017, March 28, 2017.

Anderson, Robert, joint interview with Marie Anderson and the author, Apr. 3, 2016; emails, Apr. 3, 2017, June 10, 2017.

Anonymous cousin of Jesse Junior, member of the Pratt family, interviews with the author, Oct. 10, 2013, Sept. 14, 2014, and Jan. 13, 2016.

Anonymous dentist from Dalton, Georgia, interview with the author, Oct. 30, 2013.

Anonymous employee of Fidelity Federal, interview by author, May 10, 2013.

Anonymous sister from Ohio, former member of the Church, related to the Pratt family, emails to the author, Dec. 3, 5, 6, 8, 2015.

Arizona deputy sheriff who works for the La Pas County Sheriff's Department, interview with the author, July 27, 2015.

Arizona worker at church ranch, interview by author, Oct. 6, 2013.

Ball, Jimmy "Jay," interviews with the author, Oct. 24, 2014, and Jan. 5, 2015.

Barton, Bobby, interview with the author, Oct. 30, 2014.

Belcher, Bobby, interview with the author, May 10, 2014.

Belcher, Curtis F., interview and a written statement presented to the author, Dalton, Georgia, Mar. 21, 2016.

Belcher, Donnie, interview with the author, May 10, 2014.

Bliss, Dorothy Pitner, interviews with the author Jan. 15, 2014, Apr. 28, 2014, and Jan. 5, 2015.

Bowling, Jim, interview with the author, June 8, 2016.

Butler, Johnnie Haney, interviews with the author, Aug. 16, 2015, Aug. 18, 2015, Sept. 30, 2015, and Oct. 5, 2015.

Cady, Flora, grandmother of author who worked for Queen Chenille owned by Harry Saul, who bought the Chenille business from C. T. Pratt.

Cady, Sherry, interviews with the author, Dalton, Georgia, June 1, 2011 and Oct. 21, 2011.

Camp, Chris, interview with the author, Dalton, Georgia, Dec. 29, 2012.

Campdvd [pseudonymous name for a former member], numerous emails, Apr. 23, 24, 25, 26, 27, 28, 29, 30, 2014, May 1, 4, 13, 15, 19, 2014, June 30, 2014, July 1, 8, 2014, Oct. 23, 2014, Nov. 6, 2014, Dec. 1, 2014, Apr. 17, 2015, May 5, 2015, July 1, 2015, Aug. 5, 13, 14, 2015, Oct. 25, 26, 2015, November 8, 17, 18, 2015, Dec. 1, 2, 3, 21, 2015.

Carmical, Charlie, interviews with the author, May 8, 2011, June 25, 2011, Nov. 14, 2011, Nov. 16, 2011, Oct. 15, 2013, Oct. 6, 2014.

Carmical, Shirley, interview with the author, Nov. 17, 2014.

Carson, Sandon, interview with the author, Sept. 30, 2015.

Carroll, Janette, interview with the author, Mar. 4, 2013.

Coiffeur, Buddy [pseudonym for a former member whose father was a minister at the Church], interviews with the author, Feb. 29, 2012, May 14, 2012, Mar. 25, 2013, Oct. 21, 2013, July 17, 2015, Aug. 4, 2017.

Coker, Teresa Howard, interviews with the author, Aug. 8, 15, 16, 2015, Sept. 2, 4, 8, 9, 11, 2015, Nov. 8, 9, 11, 2015, emails (5) on May 3, 2015.

Cook, Bobby Lee, interview with the author, Mar. 26, 2015, and email, Apr. 23, 2015.

Cross, Virginia, interview with the author, June 23, 2011.

Davis, Donald, added statement to manuscript while reviewing it, May 2018.

Doris [pseudonym for a former member] who is sister to Teresa and Hattie, also pseudonyms, interview with the author, Aug. 16, 2015.

Duke, Daniel, interview with the author, June 9, 2015.

Duncan, Joe, interview with the author, Apr. 1, 2013.

Farmer, George, interview with the author, June 24, 2015.

Freeman, Jack, interview with the author, Sept. 9, 2014.

Godwin, Meridian, email, Jan. 10, 2016.

Gowin, Jim, Interview with the author, May 18, 2011.

Greg [pseudonym for a former member of the Church who left it at an early age], interview with the author, Apr. 16, 2014.

Halman, Harvey, interviews with the author, Feb. 2, 2015, and Feb. 15, 2015.

Johnson, Al, interviews with the author, June 24, 2012, and June 10, 2012.

Johnson, Hattie [pseudonym for a former member and sister to Teresa and Doris], interview with the author, Aug. 8, 2015.

Johnson, Sue Haney, interview with the author, Aug. 18, 2015.

Joseph, Mary [pseudonym for a former member of the Church], interview with the author, Aug. 8, 2015.

La Paz Sherriff's Recorders Department, interview with the author, July 17, 2015.

Lance, Grady, interview with the author, Oct. 8, 2015.

Love, Harold Junior, interview with the author, Oct. 28, 2014.

Lowe, William (Billy) [pseudonym for a former member whose father was a minister and Supreme Council member for the Church], interviews with the author, Nov. 21, 2015, Dec. 17, 2015, Mar. 16, 17, 2015, Apr. 16, 2015, and June 16, 2015.

Magill, Tammy, email, July 19, 2017.

McDaniel, William MD, interview with the author, Mar. 11, 2013.

Mitchell, Erwin, interview with the author, June 25, 2011.

Moore, Brenda Pitner, interviews with the author, Mar. 16, 2014, Mar. 18, 2014, Apr. 18, 2014, Oct. 22, 2014, Dec. 1, 2014, and Jan. 3, 2015.

Nimmons, Billy, interview with the author, May 15, 2015.

Nonmember whose husband was a business associate to the Church, interview with the author, Oct. 5, 2015.

Norville, Rita, interview with the author, Sept. 10, 2014.

Overby, Troy, interview with the author, October 7, 2015.

Pace, Mark, interview with the author, July 2, 2011.

Percy, Jimmy, interviews with the author, Oct. 20, 2014, and July 3, 2015.

Phillips, Bill, Chattanooga detective for old case files, interview with the author, July 7, 2015.

Pierce, Tim, and his assistant, Ralph [pseudonyms for two individuals who once worked at local funeral home in Dalton, Georgia], interviews with the author, Oct. 20, 2014, and July 3, 2015.

Pitner, Donald W., interviews with the author, Feb. 11, 2014, Mar. 1, 2014, Dec. 27, 2014, and Jan. 2, 2015.

Poston, Jack, interviews with the author, Apr. 11, 2014, and Apr. 14, 2014.

Pratt, Charlie III, interviews with the author, Jan. 6, 2015, and Jan. 20, 2015.

Pratt, Marty, interview with the author, Sept. 26, 2011.

Pratt, Steve, interview with the author, Jan. 8, 2014.

Roberts, Charles, interviews with the author, Dec. 26, 2013, Jan. 16, 2014, Apr. 30, 2014, May 19, 2014, Oct. 6, 2014, Oct. 7, 2014, Nov. 3, 2014, Nov. 11, 2014, Mar. 22, 2015, May 15, 2015, July 25, 2015, Aug. 6, 2015, Sept. 8, 2015, Sept. 28, 2015, Oct. 4, 2015, Oct. 7, 2015, Oct. 23, 2015 [almost weekly during 2016 and 2017].

Roberts, Libby, interviews with the author, May 21, 2014, and Sept. 12, 2014.

Saul, Julian, interview with the author, Oct. 11, 2014.

Schaeffner, Varnell, interview with the author, Nov. 17, 2014.

Smith, Meredith, Facebook message to the author, Mar. 23, 2017.

Smithey, Eric, interview with the author, Sept. 13, 2015, and Sept. 9, 2015.

Viamonte, Luis M. MD, Facebook message to author, Mar. 22, 2017.

Wells, Dian Gentry, interview with the author, Aug. 14, 2017.

Williams, Sherry, interview with the author, Nov. 13, 2014.

Williams, Steve, interview with the author, Mar. 18, 2014.

Williamson, Paul W., added statement to manuscript while reviewing it, June 24, 2017.

Woody, Rita Gazaway, interviews with the author, June 24, 2014, Sept. 30, 2014, and email, Sept. 22, 2014.

Wright, Wanda [pseudonym for a former member who lived on the Ranch in Arizona]. Interview July 2016 and one email May 19, 2016.

Yuma County Sheriff's Recorders Department, interview with the author, July 17, 2015.

ARTICLES

"Accused Pastor in Molesting of Young Girl." *Chicago Daily Tribune,* Dec. 16, 1959.

Atwell, Ken. "Bell Reported En Route Here." *Kokomo Tribune,* Dec. 1959.

———. "Local Minister Sought After Molesting Charge." *Kokomo Tribune,* Dec. 1959.

———. "Phone Call from Bell is Reported." *Kokomo Tribune,* Dec. 15, 1959.

Blaising, Craig A. "Premillennialism." *Three Views of the Millennium and Beyond,* edited by Darrell L. Bock. Grand Rapids, MI: Zondervan Publishing House, 1999.

Bogle, Walter. "William B. Is Introduced." Bogles Clipping File, CGA; *North Georgia Citizen,* Dalton, Georgia, Oct. 26, 1899.

Cha, Arian Eunjung. "Researcher: Medical Errors Now Third Leading Cause of Death in United States," *Washington Post,* May 3, 2016.

"Clinton Bell Case Set for Trial May 16." *Kokomo Tribune,* Mar. 24, 1960.

Connell, Moody. "Church of God Doctrine Said Strict." *Dalton Daily Citizen-News,* June 19, 1980.

———. "Ex-Churchmen Seek Ranch Money." *Dalton Daily Citizen-News,* June 27, 1980.

———. "Faithful Follow Rules of Church." *Dalton Daily Citizen-News,* July 2, 1980.

———. "Favors Refund to Ex-Church Members." *Dalton Daily Citizen-News,* June 30, 1980.

———. "Former Church Leader Interviewed." *Dalton Daily Citizen-News,* July 16, 1980.

———. "Former Church Ministers 'Disillusioned.'" *Dalton Daily Citizen-News,* June 23, 1980.

———. "Things Change in Large Dalton-Based Church." *Dalton Daily Citizen-News,* June 17, 1980.

Constitution State News Service. "Church Puts Out Dalton's Don West." *Dalton Citizen,* Jan. 13, 1956.

Dalton Citizen, Oct. 16, 1947, 1, 9.

Dalton Citizen, Sept. 1, 1955.

Dalton News, Aug. 28, 1955.

"Death of 12 Children Laid to Refusal of Medical Aid." *Marietta Daily Journal,* Nov. 16, 1958.

George, Dan. "Teenaged Cancer Patient Mourned at Funeral in Church that Fought Treatment." Associated Press, Mar. 30, 1985.

Graham, Billy. "Billy Graham Answers," *Dalton Daily Citizen-News* [date unknown].

Jessup, Lee. "God Expects Us to Use Our Minds." (Lexington, N.C.) *The Dispatch*, Mar. 16, 1984.

Long, Victor, "Man Hospitalized After Fight at Church," *Daily Citizen-News*, May 10, 1994, 1.

McLeod, Saul. "Cognitive dissonance." *Simple Psychology* (updated 2018) http://www .simplypsychology.org/cognitive-dissonance.html, accessed Apr. 2, 2012.

"National Affairs—Eggs in the Dust." *Time*, Sept. 13, 1948.

"The Oath I Was Ready to Take" and "Why I Resigned from the Church of God." Both in box 1, George Weissman Papers.

Obituaries, *Dalton Daily Citizen-News*, Mar. 17, 1972.

Odiet, Fred. "Custody of Girl in Bell Case Is Given Sister." *Kokomo Tribune*, Jan. 7, 1960.

———. "Grand Jury: No Action Taken in Regard to Testimony in Clinton Bell Case." *Kokomo Tribune*, Jan. 7, 1960.

———. "Pastor Says He Regrets His Actions." *Kokomo Tribune*, Mar. 1960.

Orenstein, Walter, MD. "The Role of Measles Elimination in Development of a National Immunization Program," *Pediatric Infectious Disease Journal* (2006).

Padgett, Michael. "Fundamentalism Padgett and the Church of God Mountain Assembly." B.A. thesis, University of Kentucky, May 3, 2007.

"Pastor in Sex Case Back to Face Charges." *Chicago Sunday Tribune*, Dec. 20, 1959.

"Post WW II Strike." *Textile Labor* [Newspaper], Sept. 1945, 2.

Pratt, Charlie T. "Charlie Pratt Sayings." *The Southerner: Voice of the People*, Dalton, GA, Jan. 1956.

———. "Three Classes of People." *The Southerner: Voice of the People*, Dalton, GA, July 1955.

Pratt, Jesse Junior. "Pratt Defends Church Doctrine News Article." *Dalton Daily Citizen-News*, July 3, 1980.

———. "Pratt Replies to Articles on Church." *Dalton Daily Citizen-News*, July 1, 1980.

———. "Rev. Pratt Blasts News Articles." *Dalton Daily Citizen-News*, July 9, 1980.

"Resigned Prior to Ouster, Wes Says; Puts Blame of Pratt's Change of Mind on Mitchell." *Dalton Citizen*, Jan. 15, 1955.

"Rev. Pratt Robbed At Home In Dalton." *Calhoun Times and Gordon County News*, Nov. 25, 1989.

Russell, Bertrand. "The Essence of Religion (1912)." Reprinted in *Philosophy of Religion*. Leiden, Belgium: Martinus Nijhoff, 1987.

Sabai, B. M. "Hypertension: Normal Problems of Pregnancy and Childbirth." In *Obstetrics*, sixth edition. Philadelphia, W. B. Saunders Press, 2012.

"Seeking for the Truth." A Pentecostal History, http://www.seeking4thetruth.com /pentecostal_history.htm.

Singer, M. T., and R. Ofshe. "Thought Reform Programs and the Production of Psychiatric Casualties." *Psychiatric Annals*, 1990 (20): 188–93.

Soll, Rick. "Pamela Faces Biggest Struggle." *Chicago Sun-Times*, Oct. 7, 1983.

Sowder, Harold. "History of the Church of God of the Union Assembly." http://www .thechurchofgodua.org/index_files/History.html, accessed 2007.

Sternberg, Steve. "Medical Errors Are Third Leading Cause of Death in U.S." *U.S. New and World Report*, May 3, 2016.

"Trion Minister Sees Religious Basis in Arrest." *Rome New Tribune*, Feb. 21, 1984.

Weissman, George. "In the Face of Persecution." *The Southerner: Voice of the People*, Dalton, GA, May 1955.

"Wounded Hunter Dies on Airplane: Shot in Arizona, Alabama Man Was En Route Here Without Treatment." *Chattanooga Times*, Mar. 16, 1972.

Zukeran, Patrick. "Four Views of Revelation." http://www.probe.org/four-views-of -revelation/.

BOOKS AND PAMPHLETS

Anderson, Robert Mapes, *Vision of the Disinherited: The Making of American Pentecostalism*. New York: Oxford University Press, 1979.

Barry, John. *The Great Influenza: The Story of the Deadliest Pandemic in History*. New York: Penguin Books, 2009.

Baumgartner, Frederic J. *Longing for the End: A History of Millennialism in Western Civilization*. New York: Palgrave, 1999.

Beasley, David. *Without Mercy: The Stunning True Story of Race, Crime, and Corruption in the Deep South*. New York: St. Martin's Press, 2014.

Butler, Johnnie Haney. *Standing on the Edge of Sanity*. LaFayette, GA: unpublished personal memoir, 1998.

Clifton, D. *Chronicle of the 20th Century*. Yonkers, New York: Jacques Legrand, 2001.

Dyer, Frederick H. *A Compendium of the War of the Rebellion*. Des Moines, IA: Dyer Pub. Co., 1908.

Fanning, Diane. *Her Deadly Web*. New York: St. Martin's Paperbacks, 2012.

Festinger, L. *A Theory of Cognitive Dissonance*. Stanford: Stanford University Press, 1957.

Flamming, Douglas. *Creating the Modern South: Millhands and Managers in Dalton, Georgia, 1884–1984*. Chapel Hill: University of North Carolina Press, 1992.

Franklin, Robert. *Rediscovered Early Church Premillennialism: Teachings of Earliest Church Fathers on Prophecy*. Arlington, TX: Word Lamp Publications, LLC; 2014.

Furnas, J. C. *Great Times: An Informal Social History of the United States, 1914–1929*. New York: Hill and Wang, 1995.

Grusec, Joan E., and Paul D. Hastings, eds. *Handbook of Socialization: Theory and Research*, second edition. New York: Gulf Press, 2015.

Haram, K., E. Svendsen, and U. Abildgaard. "The HELLP Syndrome: Clinical Issues and Management. A Review," *BMC, Pregnancy and Childbirth*, February 26, 2009.

Hassan, Steve. *Combating Cult Mind Control*. Newton, MA: Freedom of Mind Press, 2015.

Hood, Ralph, Jr., Peter C. Hill, and Bernard Spilka. *The Psychology of Religion: An Empirical Approach*, fourth edition. New York: Guilford Press, 2009.

Jamison, Kay Redfield. *An Unquiet Mind*. New York: Alfred A. Knopf, 1996.

Kaplan, Harold I., and Benjamin J. Sudock. *Modern Group Book*, vol. 4: *Sensitivity through Encounter and Marathon*. New York: E. P. Dutton, 1972.

Le Bon, Gusstave. *The Crowd: A Study of the Popular Mind*. New York: Dove, 2002.

Lorence, James. *A Hard Journey: The Life of Don West*. Champaign, IL: University of Illinois Press, 2007.

Marsden, George W. *Fundamentalism and American Culture: The Shaping of Twentieth Century Evangelicalism*. New York: Oxford University Press, 1973.

McCulloch, Diarmaid. *Christianity: The First Three Thousand Years*, New York: Penguin Books, 2011.

Mounce, Robert. *The New International Commentary of the New Testament: The Book of Revelation*. Grand Rapids, MI: William Eerdmans Publishing Company, 1977.

Official History of Whitfield County, Georgia. Dalton, GA: A. J. Showalter Company, 1981.

Padgett, Michael. *A Goodly Heritage: A History of the Church of God Mountain Assembly, Inc.* Lexington, KY: self-published, 1958.

Pratt, Minnie. *We Walked Alone: Part of the Story of My Life.* Dalton, GA: The Southerner Press, 1955.

Quick Reference to the Diagnostic Criteria from DSM-IV-TR. Arlington, VA: American Psychiatric Association, 2000.

Reiterman, Tim, with John Jacobs. *Raven: The Untold Story of the Rev. Jim Jones and His People.* New York: Jeremy P. Tarcher/Penguin, 2008.

Rhodes, Ron. *The Challenge of the Cults and New Religions.* Grand Rapids, MI: Zondervan, 2001.

Sandeen, Earnest R. *Roots of Fundamentalism: British and American Millenarianism, 1880–1930.* Chicago, IL: University of Chicago Press, 1970.

Setright, L. J. K. *Drive On! A Social History of the Motor Car.* London: Granta Books.

Shapiro, E., "Destructive Cultism," *American Family Physician,* 1977, pages 80–83.

Spilka, Bernard, Ralph W. Hood Jr., Bruce Hunsberger, and Richard Gorsuch. *The Psychology of Religion,* third edition. New York: Guilford Press, 2003.

Synan, Vingon. *The Holiness-Pentecostal Tradition.* Grand Rapids, MI: Wm. B. Eerdmans, 1997.

Warrington, Ken, *Pentecostal Theology: A Theology of Encounter.* New York: T and T Clark, 2008.

Wessinger, Catherine, ed. *The Oxford Handbook of Millennialism.* Oxford: Oxford University Press, 2011.

West, Don. *No Lonesome Road: Selected Prose and Poems.* Champaign, IL: University of Illinois Press, 2004.

Wilson, J. *Aims in Education: The Philosophic Approach.* Manchester, U.K.: Manchester University Press, 1964.

Winell, Marlene. *Leaving the Fold: A Guide for Former Fundamentalists and Others Leaving Their Religion.* Berkeley, CA: Apocryphile Press, 2006.

Zimbardo, P. G. *The Lucifer Effect: Understanding How Good People Turn Evil.* New York, Random House, 2007.

Zukeran, Patrick, and Norman Geisler. *The Apologetics of Jesus.* Grand Rapids, MI: Baker Books: 2009.

ONLINE SOURCES

Ancestry.com. http://interactive.ancestry.com/1124/M598_530071/437586?backurl=; http:// person.ancestry.com/tree/7366860/person/-1104687620/facts/citation /580533977/edit/record.

Ancestry.com. http://person.ancestry.com/tree/7366860/person/-1104687620/facts.

"Average Life Expectancy," www.cdc.gov/nchs/data/lifetables/life1890-1910.pdf. "Average Life Expectancy," www.cdc.gov/nchs/data/lifetables/life1890-1910.pdf, accessed Oct. 10, 2014.

Beeler, James. http://wiki.answer.com/what_happed_to_the_dress_formally_practiced _by_theChurchofGodoftheUnionAssembly.com, accessed Feb. 22, 2013.

"Blue Letter Bible." https://www.blueletterbible.org/faq/mill.cfm, accessed Oct. 7, 2014.

Familysearch.org. http://familysearch.org/ark:61903/1:138ZC-3W2, accessed December 2014.

http://familysearch.org/ark:61903/1:1:3HM2-BT2, accessed December 2014.

http://familysearch.org/ark:/61903/1:1:K75Q-8/VB, accessed December 2014.

http://familysearch.org/ark:/61903/1:1:3F6F-9MM, accessed October 2014.

https://familysearch.org/ark:/61903/1:1:K4C9-IKR.

https://familysearch.org/pal:MM9.1.1/NS26-X5B, accessed 21 August 2014.

"Leading causes of death," www.cdc/gov/nchs/data/dvs/lead1900-98. And "leading causes of death," http://www.medicalnewstoday.com/articles/282929.php, accessed Sept. 3, 2014.

Newspapers.com http://www.newspapers.com/newspage/14648972/, accessed Oct. 2014.

Saylor, Paul, You Tube: Jesse F. Pratt Sermon on the Church, part 1. https://www.youtube.com/watch?v=u-AechOIC54, accessed Feb. 13, 2015.

Saylor, Paul, YouTube: Jesse F. Pratt Sermon on the Church part 2. https://www.youtube.com/watch?v=G4IHb07YJY, accessed Feb. 15, 2015.

Saylor, Paul, YouTube: Jesse F. Pratt Sermon on Women in Church, https://www.youtube.com/watch?v=G4IHb07YJY, accessed Mar. 13, 2015.

Truth12, http://wiki.answer.com/what_happed_to_the_dress_formally_practiced_by_the ChurchofGodoftheUnionAssembly.com, accessed July 15, 2008.

TELEVISION, MOVIES, AND DOCUMENTARIES

Burns, Ken, *The Roosevelts: An Intimate History*, Part 4, "The Storm," viewed Aug. 16, 2014.

INDEX

Page numbers in **boldface** refer to illustrations. Names in *italics* refer to nicknames or middle names by which a person was known.

A & W Root Beer, 76, 111, 135, 246n37
abortions, 176
African-Americans, 27–28, 74
airplanes, 9, **44**, 45, 47, **50**, 55, 133, 137–38, 148–51, 153, 157, 180, 205, 210, 215, 220
airports, 138, 148–50, 157, 215
Albertville, AL, Church in, 181
alcoholism, 9–11, 14, 91–94, 161, 176, 180, 206, 215, 227–29, 231
Alexander, Elsie *Jean* Pitner (daughter of Otha Pitner), 86, 90–91, 98
alfalfa, 145–46
Allen, Clifton, 75
Allen, Rufus, 75
amillennialism, 17
Amish, xviii
Anderson, Andy, 63–64
Anderson, Marie Hoskins, 118, 128, **185**, 185–86, 199–200, **200**, 216–17, 219
Anderson, Robert, 63–64, 103, 118, 128, 130, 139, 168, 170, 184, **185**, 185–86, 213, 216–17
Anderson, Robert Mapes, 35
anti-Catholicism, 77–78, 80, 140
anti-communism, 78–82
anti-Semitism, 80
appendicitis, 197
Aragon, GA, Church in, 21, 35
Archer Farm, 109
Arizona. *See* Bouse, AZ
Atlanta, GA, Church in, 101, 106, 134, 160, 175–76
Atlanta Child Killer, 204
Atlanta Constitution, 74, 77
Atwell, Ken, 97
automobiles. *See* cars

Bailey, Danny, 103
Bailey, Kenneth, 166, 169–70
Ball, Henry, 78
baptism of the Holy Spirit, 22
Baptists, 29, 141–42
Barton, Bobby, 110
Bartow County, GA, 13–15, 22–23; Church in, **17**
Bayliff, Edgar W., 99
Beards, Clarence, 40
Beeler, Conley Ray, 199
Beeler, Cory, 199
Beeler, Tory, 198–99
Belcher, Arlan, 61, 75, 107
Belcher, Curtis F., 231
Belcher, Nell, 60–61
Belcraft (company), 78, 80
Bell, Clinton M., xiv, 41–42, 48, 75, 83, 86, **88**, 90, **99**, 100, 117; blackmail of, 93; businesses of, 84; complaints against, 83–84, 93–99; drunkenness of, 91–94; and financial dishonesty, 95, 97; physical description of, 84, 96; preaching of, 84–85, 91, 98; scams by, 84–85; sexual activities of, 87–88, 91, 93–100; "training closet" of, 87–89, 92–94, 98; trial of, 98–99
Bell, Jackie, 83–84
Bell, James Alexander Hamilton, xxiii, 196
Bell, T. R., 23, 83
Bell Bargain Fair/Barn, 84–85, 87, 89, 95
Bible: interpretation of, 2, 22, 31, 36–37, 155–56, 209; King James Version, 15, 35; owning of by women prohibited, 87; persons permitted to have and use, 234; reading of discouraged, 43, 128
Bickert, Allen, 208
blackmail, 93
Blackwood, Illyne, 200
Bliss, Dorothy Pitner (daughter of Otha Pitner), 85–90, **90**, 91, 93–94, 97–98

Bohannon, Tom, 23, 41, 48, 70–71

Bolinger, L. Owen, 95–96, 99

Bonner, Wesley, 41

Bouse, AZ, 148, 151, 153; and Church ranch living conditions, 146; Church ranch sale, 206, 208; Church ranch site in, xxiv, 119, 121, 138, 145–47, 169, 208, 210–11, 250n9

Brenda (sister-in-law of Teresa), 194

Brewer, Jim, 42, 182

Brewer, M. O., 75

Brewer, Ollen, **107**

Brown, Harold (father of Rodney), 187

Brown, Homer (first husband of Leola Pratt), 181

Brown, Rodney (son of Harold), 187

Broyles, Lewis (father of Minnie Pratt), 9–10, 14

Broyles, Lucinda (grandmother of Minnie Pratt), 9

Broyles, Martha (*Tiny*) (mother of Minnie Pratt), 9–10, 14

Broyles, William (grandfather of Minnie Pratt), 9

Bundy, Edgar C., 80

Burgess, David S., 78

Burnett, Edna McClure (wife of Johnny, sister of Irene Pratt), 59, 61

Burnett, J. Willie (*J. W.*), xiv, 23, 41, 45, 48, 61, 70, 104, 115, 126, 211

Burnett, Johnny H., xiv, 41, **44**, 44–45, 47–48, 55, 59, 70, 75, **99**, 100, 124, 131; lawsuit against, 124

Butler, Glenda (Hester), 197

Butler, Johnnie Haney, 118–19, 128–29, 159, 183, 229–30

Butler, Margie (daughter of Johnnie), 230

C. T. Pratt Chenille Company, 57, **57**

Cadillacs, 62, 85, 91–94, 97, 132, 134, 149, 151, 213

Calhoun, Allston, Jr., 80

campground, 186–87, 215–16, 222, 229

cancer, treatment for refused, xxiii, xxv-xxvi, 195–96, 200

candy sales, 156, 161, 179–82, 186, 205, 214, 222, 253n21

Carmical, Charlie (son of Hugh), xiv, 29–31, 56, 62, 102, 105–6

Carmical, Clara F. (mother of Hugh), 61

Carmical, Hugh D. (*Cash*) (father of Charlie), xiv, 30, 61–64, 75, 81–82, 101, 105, **107**; as assistant moderator, 30, 64, 101–2, 105–6; business of, 62, 75, 106–8; departure from Church of, 105–7, 110, 171; lawsuit by, 107–8; as money-maker, 62–63, 75, 108; opposition to, 64, 75

Carmical, Lillian (*Bill*) (wife of Hugh), 61, 105–6

carpet industry, 57–58, 133, 205

cars, 9, 22, 62, 85, 127, 132, 176, 180, 191, 213. *See also* Cadillacs

Carson, Charles E., 150–51

Cass County Circuit Court (IN), 98–99

Cass Station, GA (Cassville), 14–15; Church in, 14–16; second Church in, **17**, 21, 33

Catholics, xvii-xviii, 77–78, 140

Catoosa County, GA, property in, 186, 215, 221, 229

cattle fraud, 212–13

cattle speculation, 148, 163, 166–67, 171

Cedartown, GA, Church in, 35

Center, GA, Church in, 35, 124, 176

Chandler, I. V., 58

Charlie Pratt College, 76–77

Chattanooga, TN, 26–28, 36; airport in, 148–49; Church in, 33, 35, 61; flood in, 154; police department of, 150–51, 153–54

chemotherapy, 196–97

Cherokee Indians, 25–26

Chicago Sun-Times, xxiii-xxiv

child labor, 28–29, 110–11, 135–36

children, deaths of, 146, 190–91, 196–99, 212

chiropractors, xxiii, 38, 195

Christian Scientists, xvii-xviii

Christianity, importance of in South, 30–31

Church of God, xvii; of Cleveland, TN, 16; Wayman and Herbert's, 171

Church of God of the Mountain Assembly, 1–2, 13, 15–16, 72; beliefs of, 15–18; expulsion of C. T. Pratt from, 2, 16–18

Church of God of the Union Assembly, xvii, 1, 29–30, 98; and abuse of members

by, xviii, xxv, 87–88, 91, 93–100, 104–5,
108–12, 117, 129–30, 133, 135, 141–42, 146,
176–79, 181, 194, 197, 200, 228; adultery
and fornication in, 84, 95–99, 146, 160,
176, 178–79, 182, 200, 206; airplane pilots
of, **44**, 44–45, 47, 55; and airplanes, **44**,
45, 47, **50**, 55, 133, 137–38, 148–51, 153, 205,
208, 210, 215; annual meeting of, 47–48,
58, 74, 102, 182–83, 185–86, 234; apartments owned by, 75–76, 109–10, 159, 209;
appeal of, 30–31, 34–37, 63; Arizona ranch
certificates redeemed, 211; Arizona ranch
of, xxiv, 119, 121, 138, 145–47, 152–53, 206,
208, 210–11, 250n9; and balcony fraud,
213, 222; beliefs of, 58, 84, 86–87, 207,
209; Board of Elders of, 54, 116, 178, 218,
222, 227; buildings of, 118–19; businesses
owned by, 75–76, 113, 118; and candy sales,
156, 161, 179–82, 186, 205, 214, 222, 253n21;
and cattle fraud, 212–13, 222; charter of,
75, 107; and child labor, 110–11, 135–36;
church government of, xxv; and Church
growth, 35–36, 40, 56, 58, 62, 116, 161–62;
and coercion, xviii, xxv, 81–82, 117, 179,
205; and communal living, 49, 146–47;
and Communion, 183; and Communism,
77, 79–82; and confession train, 123,
182–84; congregational characteristics of,
28, 33–38, 48, 72, 139–40; and control of
members, v, xxiv-xxv, 76, 90–91, 102–6,
115–18, 127, 129–30, 132, 139–42, 156–58,
177–79, 209–10; and crosses, 128, 234; as
cult, xxv, 71–72; death statistics in, 190;
deaths in due to lack of medical treatment, 189–201, 212; deaths in services of,
103–4, 117–18, 197; and divorce, 58–61,
157–58; and doubt by members, 215; and
dress code changes, 216–17, 219, 257n66;
expulsion of members from, 82, 106,
113–14, 116–18, 123–24, 129–30, 139, 153,
157–58, 177–78, 208, 211; false promises
made by, 108–10, 121, 212–14; and family
separations, xxv, 111–12, 117, 123–24, 136,
139, 157–58, 207, 210, 219, 229; farms
owned by, 109, 121, 162, 164–66, 169;
and fear, v, xix, xxiv-xxv, 31, 84–85, 91,

103–4, 106, 108–12, 114, 117, 123, 130, 133,
139–42, 153, 156–57, 177–78, 182–83, 186,
207, 209–10, 217, 228, 234; and financial corruption, 206, 208; and financial
problems of, 50–51, 78, 119–21, 209, 212,
215–16, 227–29; and financial records of
members, 179–80, 205; and fire at Dalton
Church, 53; and foot-washing, 64, 183;
and forgiveness, xxiv-xxv, 97, 102–3, 115,
130, 160, 170, 178, 233; and fundraising,
47–49, 55–57, 62–65, 84–85, 108, 121–22,
129, 176–81, 205, 209–10, 212–15, 220–21,
228–29; funerals at, 124–25, 141, 152–53,
161, 169–70; and giving everything to
Church, 37, 39, 42, 63–65, 75, 84–85,
108–12, 118, 120, 132–33, 207, 228; and
guilt, 141–42, 194, 199; hierarchy within,
110, 130, 139–40; homes owned by, 62, 105,
109–11, 129–30, 209, 246n38; influence of,
36, 47, 50, 53–54, 74–75, 209; and interior
Church design, 54–55, **55**; isolation of
members of, 35, 38; job loss by members
of, 78; labor conditions of members,
49, 110–11, 117–19, 132, 146–47, 208, 233;
leadership succession in, 62–63, 65, 101–2,
105–6, 112–14; and legal cases, xxiii, xxv-
xxvi, 98–99, 107–9, 124, 196–97; legal obstructionism by, 97–99, 196; and loans to,
120, 215–16, 221–23, 227–29; and marriage,
38, 42, 157–58, 211, 219; maternity ward of,
159, **159**, 190–92, 209, 221; medical beliefs
of criticized, 198, 212; medical treatment
permitted by, 195, 217–18; medical treatment rejected by, xxiii-xxvi, 12–13, 20, 38,
45, 76, 146, 151, 189–201, 207–8, 212, 218;
membership decline of, 113, 204, 207, 222,
228; membership return of, 115, 212, 229;
membership statistics of, xxiv, 76, 115–16,
134, 207, 215, 228, 234; and ministers'
meetings, 177, 184, 212–13, 225; ministers
of, 47–48, 60, 64, 81–82, 85–86, 88, 102–3,
105, 117, 129–30, 134, 157, 170–71, 177 (see
also names of individual ministers);
and money, xxiv, 46–49, 74, 85–86, 105,
108–13, 115, 117–18, 129, 132–34, 137–40,
147–48, 156, 161, 176–79, 186, 205, 208–10,

Church of God of the Union Assembly (*cont'd*), 212–13, 215, 219–20, 222; Moral Christian Guidelines of, 218–19; motel of, 76, 209; and net worth of, 161; and non-profit status, 50–51; as only way to heaven/ true church, 37, 49, 132, 134, 139; opposition to, 50–51, 53, 105–8; poor publicity about, xxiii–xxvi, 96–97, 195–98, 204, 206–12; poverty caused by, 49, 63–64, 105, 108–11, 118, 132–33, 139, 179, 182, 208, 213; property of, 118–21, 208–9; property acquisition by, 49, 53–54, 62, 65, 75–76, 105–6, 109, 112, 119–21, 124, 148, 208–9, 212, 214, 216; property of sold, 119–21, 209, 228–29; and prophesying doom against members, 69, 103–4, 122, 156–58; and psychological damage caused by, 141–43, 194–95, 199–201, 218, 226, 228–29, 233; and rebuking of ministers and members, 70, 102–6, 111, 118, 122–24, 130–31, 135, 153, 157–58, 160, 176, 186, 200, 207–8, 212, 217, 225, 233, 246n36; and rebuking physically stopped, 225–26; relocation of members to Dalton, 108–11, 207, 210–12; resource pooling by members of, 39, 49; and retaliation for seeking medical treatment, 194; and rules of, v, xxiv–xxv, 37–38, 42, 45, 47–48, 58, 60, 72, 76, 86–88, 102, 116–17, 123–24, 131, 139, 144, 157–58, 170, 175, 186–87, 191, 195, 207, 209–11, 219; and rules of changed, 115–17, 157, 195, 216–19, 225–26, 229; and rules of for women, 37–38, 47–48, 86–88, 110, 131, 134, 158, 183, 204, 207; and rumors in, 69–70, 87–89, 144, 146, 162, 167, 169, 204, 206, 212, 215, 222, 227; as sect, 72; services of described, xxv, 34, 129–30; sexual abuse by leaders of, 83–84, 87–88, 91, 93–100, 146, 160, 176, 178–79, 182, 200, 206; shunning of expelled members by, 38, 70, 72, 86, 113, 116–18, 124, 157–58, 207–10, 219, 226; and Studebaker trucks, 49–50; Supreme Council of, 48, 54, 70–72, 75, 83, 85–86, 96, 105, 109, 112–13, 116, 166, 170–71, 178, 181–82, 186, 199, 211, 218, 222, 227, 229; and taxes, 50–51, 78, 120–21, 212, 214;

violence in, 122–23, 170, 176–78, 181, 187, 225–26; and wife-swapping, 124, 146–47, 250n9; and women, 22, 37–38, 47–48, 86–88, 97, 102–3, 110–12, 123–24, 131, 134–36, 155–56, 158, 183, 191–93, 197, 199, 204, 206–7, 216–17, 225. *See also* Union Assembly of the Church of God

Church Service Program, 206

Church services, described, xxv, 34, 129–30

Cincinnati, OH, Church in, 35

Civil War, 8

class divisions, white, 27, 29, 34–36, 39

Claxton, TN, Church in, 23

Clayton (former member), 157–58

Cleveland, TN, Church in, 158

Cline, Virginia Jo (daughter of Lillian Carmical), 61

coercion, religious, xviii, xxiv–xxv, 81–82, 117, 179, 205

Cofield, Charlie, 220

Coker, L. L., 41, 48, 75

Coker, Teresa Howard, 182, 184, 192–95

Cold War, 76

Combating Cult Mind Control (Hassan), 71

communal living, 49, 146–47

communism, 73–74, 76–82

confession train, 123, 182–84

Congress of Industrial Organizations, 78

Connell, Moody, v, 207–11

Continental Service Corporation, 120–21

Cook, Bobby Lee, 51

Corinth, MS, Church in, 76

coroner, 149–51, 165–66, 168

cotton, 147

cotton mills, 26–27, 45

Crider, Leola. *See* Pratt (Crider), (Elva) *Leola*

Crider, Ronnie, 187–88

Crider, Wesley (second husband of Leola), xiv, 122, 177, 181–82, 187

crosses, 128, 234

Crown Cotton Mill, 27, **28**, 28–29, 34, 39–40, 45–46, 56, 78

Crown View Baptist Church (Dalton, GA), 29

cults, xvii–xviii, xxiii–xxv, 71–72, 139, 195

Cumberland, KY, Church in 23
curfew, 142

Daily Worker, 79
Dalton, GA, 16, 22–23, 25–27, 33–34; African-Americans in, 27–28; carpet industry in, 57–58, 63; cemetery in, 126, 170; Church construction in, 53–54, 75, 118, 213; Church fire in, 53; Church of God of the Union Assembly in, 16, 22–23, 29, 33–36, 40, 49, 53–54, 75–76, 104–5, 153, 160, 169–70, 177, 197, 213–14, 225, 227; churches (other) in, 28–29, 33–36; cotton mills in, 26–27, 39, 45, 56; funeral home in, 148–50; industrialization in 26–27, 39, 56–57; political campaigns in, 74–75; relocation of Church members to, 108–11; taxes Union Assembly church, 50–51; white economic classes in, 27, 29, 34–35, 39
Dalton, Mary, 26
Dalton Auction Company, 106
Dalton Citizen-News (and variant titles), 79–80, 115, 187, 191, 204, 206–11
Dalton Tourist Court, 76
Davidson, Judge, 96
Davis, Donald, 79
Dean, Paul, 40
deaths: of children, 146, 190–91, 196–99, 212; in church services, 103–4, 117–18, 197; due to lack of medical treatment, 189–201, 212; of infants, 117–18, 136, 190–91, 233; pregnancy-related, 135–36, 191–93, 197, 199
dentists, 38, 195
Denton, TX, Church in, 133
Detroit, MI, Church in, 61
diabetes, 191, 198–99
Diamond Carpet Mills, 205
Dieterly, Pete, 84, 97
Dispensationalism, 13
divorce, rules about, 38, 58, 60–61
Dixie Highway, 14, 33
donuts, 134
Dooley Chapel, TN, Church in, 35
Dukes, Clinton, 214

Dukes, Marshall, 92
Dyer, Mr., 104

earrings, wearing of permitted, 218
East Side Baptist Church (Dalton, GA), 29
Eden, Glenda, 197
Edwards, Cora Alma Pratt. *See* Pratt (Edwards), (Cora) *Alma*
Elizabethton, TN, Church in, 35
Erlanger Hospital (Chattanooga, TN), 151
Evans, W. R. 58
Everts, KY, Church in, 35

faith healing, xviii, xxiii, xxv-xxvi, 13, 20, 22, 35, 189–93, 195–99, 207, 212, 218; criticized, 198
farm economy, decline of, 26–27
Farmer, George, 153
Federal Bureau of Investigation (FBI), 96
Felker, Doctor, 164
Fidelity Federal Savings Bank, 215–16, 221
fights, 161, 187
fire, at Dalton Union Assembly Church, 53
firearms, illegal, 153
First Baptist Church (Dalton, GA), 29
First Methodist Church (Dalton, GA), 29
First Presbyterian Church (Dalton, GA), 29, 34
Flamming, Douglas, 34
foot-washing, 64, 183
forgiveness, xxiv-xxv, 97, 102–3, 115, 130, 160, 170, 178, 233
Fort Payne, AL, Church in, 35
Fort Smith, AR, Church in, 76
Foster, W. P., 41, 48, **50**, 57–58, 75
Frank, Burton, 181
full-preterism, 17
fundamentalists, 13, 35
funeral homes, 148–52, 180, 190–91, 252n36; employees of, 148–51, 161, 169, 190, 252n36
funerals, 124–25, 152–53, 161, 169–70, 191, 197

Gadsden, AL, Church in, 76
Gazaway, Bob, 158
Gazaway, Clara, 158

Gazaway, Rita, 158
George, Barbara Lou Pitner (daughter of Otha Pitner, wife of Ronnie), 86
George, Ronnie, 86
Georgia Bureau of Alcohol, Tobacco, Firearms, and Explosives, 153
Georgia Bureau of Investigation, 80
Georgia Sound (singing group), 216
Georgia State Industrial Union Council, 78
Georgia Supreme Court, 51, 108–9
Germany, 1, 22
gifts of the Holy Spirit, 22
Gillman, Charlie, 78
Gilsby, Oky, 92
Glencoe, AL, Church in, 151–52
glossolalia. See speaking in tongues
Gracie Lee (sister of Minnie Pratt), 14–15
Graham, Billy, 191
Great Depression, 38–40, 45
Gregory, Charles, 150–52
Griffin, Marvin, 80
guitars, 59, **107**, 125, 158, 161
gunshot wounds, 149–50
Guyton, A. K., 62
Guyton, Sam Jones, 13, 15
Guyton family, 13–15

Hamilton, Deborah, 195
Hamilton, Larry, xxiii, xxv, 195–96
Hamilton, OH, Church in, 35, 61, 86, 108–9, 142, 178–79, 181, 199, 233
Hamilton, Pamela, xxiii-xxvi, 189, 195–97, 212
Hamilton Street Methodist Church (Dalton, GA), 29
Haney, Margie Lewis, 135–36, **136**, 229
Haney, Mr., 229
Hannah, Brooks (husband of Gladys), 90–91
Hannah, Gladys Pitner (daughter of Otha Pitner), 86, 90
Haraf, Frank, xxvi, 195–96
Hardin, McCamy, and Minor, 107
Harlan, KY, Church in, 178–79
Harmonetts (singing group), **60**
Hassan, Steve, 71
hats, 142

heaven, Church as only way to, 132, 134, 139
Helmick, Dan, xiv, 142, 178–79, 181, 200
Helmick, Vivian, 142, 179
Hester, Karen, 197–98, 212
Hester, Tommy Glenn, 197–98, 212
high blood pressure, xxv, 191, 194
Hill, Owen, 120
Hill, Peter C., 71–72
Hobbs, George (great-grandson of C. T.), 114
Holiness groups, xvii, xxiv, 13, 15, 21–22, 35, 55; beliefs of, 22, 37, 196; prejudice against, 21–22, 35; worship practices of, 34, 238n3
Holy Rollers, 14, 35
"Homecoming" picnic, **54**
homosexuality, 163
Hood, Ralph W., Jr., 71–72; Foreword by, xvii-xix
Hoskins, Donna (mother of Marie Anderson), 199, **200**
Hoskins, Mike (brother of Marie Anderson), 199–200
House Un-American Activities Committee, 78–79, 81
Houston, Lebron, 165–66, 168
Howard, Dayton (brother of Floyd Pratt), 40
Howard, Jesse Bee, 135–36, 191–92
Howard, Junior, 41
Howard, Mr. (husband of Jesse Bee), 191–194
Howard, W. T., 41, 48, 75
Howard, Willie, 104
Howard County, IN, courts in, 96, 98–99
Hughes, Flora E. Pratt. *See* Pratt (Hughes), Flora E.
Hughes, George (son of Flora), 46
Hughes, Jesse (J. W.) (son of Flora), 46, 122, 187
Hughes, John E. (son of Flora), 40
Hughes, Margaret McClure (wife of Paul, sister of Irene Pratt), 152
Hughes, Minnie Kate (daughter of Flora), 46
Hughes, Paul L. (son of Flora), xiii, 46, **147**, 151–52; casket of, 151–52; death of 148–54, 164, 171

Hughes, Paul Thomas, 216
Hughes, Tobe. *See* Hughes, Winston (*Tobe*)
Hughes, Winston (*Tobe*) (husband of Flora), 40, 46, 122, 166

Icard, NC, Church in, 76
Illinois American Legion Americanism Committee, 80
industrialization, in Dalton, GA, 26–27, 39, 56–57; in South, 26–27
infants: deaths of, 117–18, 136, 190–91, 233; sick, 14–15
influenza: epidemic, 19–20; treatment of, 20–21
Internal Revenue Service (IRS), 51, 78, 120–21, 133, 220, 222
Isaacs, Chester F., 108–9

Jacobs, Cecil, 191
Jehovah's Witnesses, xvii
Jenkins, Earl, 92
Jessup, Lee, 198
Jesus Christ, 74, 132–33, 160, 187; millennial reign of, 16–17, 108, 112; return of, 1, 13, 16, 23, 37, 49, 108, 112–13; as savior, 219; as social revolutionary, 77
Johnson, Sue Haney, 135–36, 229
Jones, Claud, 23
Jones, Jim, and Jonestown Massacre, xxiii, 71, 195, 233

Kale (boy), 100
Keisling, Norman, 98–99
Kennedy, John F., 78, 140–41
Kennemer, Beulah, 40
Kennemer, Ulysess, 40
Kentucky, rural, 10
Knight, Claud, 124
Knight, Jim, 15–16
Knoxville, TN, xxiii-xxiv, xxvi, 15–16, 26–28, 214; Church in, xxiv, 15–16, 33, 35, 62–63, 86, 124, 131; street preaching in, 36, 64
Kokomo, IN, 83, 141–42; Church in, 76, 84, 86–87, 93–95, **96**, 97, 117–18, 233
Kokomo Tribune (IN), 83–84, 89, 95–97, 100, 124

labor activism, 76–79; opposition to, 78–80
labor disputes, 36
labor force, 28–29, 33–35, 37, 39–40, 45, 56–57, 63, 77; abuse of, 39–40, 49, 110–11, 117–19, 135, 146–47, 208, 233
labor strikes, 45, 80
labor unions, 36, 45, 77–80; opposition to, 79
LaFollette, TN, Church in, xxiii-xxiv, 195, 199
Lance, Grady, 46
Lanham, Henderson, 78–79
Lankford, Robert, 165
LaPaz County, AZ, 154
Lawtex Mill (company), 78, 80
Ledford, Alec, 23
Ledford, Mr., 75
legal obstructionism, by Church leaders and members, 97–99, 196
"Listen, I Am a Communist" (poem), 74, 79
Long, C. D., 197
Lovell Field (Chattanooga, TN), 148–49
Luttrell, TN, Church in, 35, 45, 100
Lynch, KY, Church in, 23
lynching threats, 79
Lyons, C. U., 191

Maddron, Hugh, 49
Magill, Tammy, 197
Malta, TX, Church in, 35
Manson cult, 71
marriage, restrictions on, 38, 42
Marsden, George, 13
Marshall, Betty Lou Pitner (daughter of Otha Pitner), 86
Maryville, TN, Church in, 63
McArthur, Hayes P., 75, 81–82
McCamy, Carlton, 51, 107
McCarthy, Joseph R., 76
McClure, Buddy (brother of Irene Pratt), 61
McClure, Irene. *See* Pratt, Irene McClure Smith
McClure, Margaret. *See* Hughes, Margaret McClure
McClure, Murray (father of Irene Pratt), 58
McClure, Naomi (mother of Irene Pratt), 58

McCollum, Frank, 41, 75
McGill, Ralph, 74, 77
measles, 217
medical treatment, use of forbidden,
    xxiii-xxvi, 12–13, 20, 38, 45, 76, 146, 151,
    189–201, 207–8, 212, 218
Meir, Golda, v
Methodists, 9, 11–13, 29
Middlesboro, KY, 1, 17, 23; Church in, 35
Middleton, OH, Church in, 35
midwives, 38, 40, 159, 176, 192–93, 212
Millennium, perspectives on, 1–2, 13, 16–17
ministers, death of, 103–4
*Minutes of the Church of God of the Union
    Assembly* (1990), 217–18
Minutes of the 24th Annual Meeting (1945),
    42, 58
Mitchell, Erwin, 80–82
Mitchell and Mitchell, 48, 55
mob violence, 79–80
Moonies, 71
Moore, Brenda Pitner (daughter of Otha
    Pitner), 85, 91, 93, 117, 122
Moore, Zella, 200
Morgan, Mr., 34
Mormons, xvii
Morris Street Methodist Episcopal Church
    (Dalton, GA), 29
Mount Rachel Baptist Church (Dalton,
    GA), 29
Mountain Assembly Church. *See* Church of
    God of the Mountain Assembly
Murray County, GA, 76, 148, 162, 164

Neighbors, Libby, 110–12
Neighbors family, 110–12
Nixon, Richard, 156, 160, 175
Norville, Zach, 220–21, 227

Oak Ridge, TN, 62
Odessa, TX, Church in, 179
Odiet, Fred, 83, 96
Official History of Whitfield County, Georgia,
    35–36
Oliver, Frank L., 98

O'Shea, James, 78
Overby, Troy, 187
Owens, Shady, 103

Pace, Mark, 79–82
Pam, and seizures, 103
Parsons, P., 120
Pat Craft Chenille Company, 57–58
Patsy (sister of Libby Neighbors), 111
Paul (brother of Libby Neighbors), 111
Paul, Estelle, xxv
Pentecostal movements, xvii, 13, 35
pew jumping, in church services, 34, 238n3
Phillips, Bill, 153–54
physical punishment, 70, 87, 91–92, 94, 98,
    102–8, 111, 122, 160–61
pilots, airplane, **44**, 45, 47
pistols, 55–56, 70, 79, 106, 138, 145, 151–53
Pitner, Don (son of Otha), 84–85, 91–94,
    97–98, 122–23, 131–32, 245n35
Pitner, Joe (son of Otha), 122
Pitner, Mary (wife of Don), 91, 93, 97,
    245n35
Pitner, Otha (father), xiv, 42, 86–94, 98, 122,
    131
Pitner, Otha, Jr. (son of Otha), 90, 122
Pitner, Richard (son of Otha), 90, 93
Pitner, Stella Mae (wife of Otha), 86, 90–91,
    98, 117
Pitner family, 86, 90–91. *See also* Alexander,
    Elsie *Jean* Pitner; Bliss, Dorothy Pitner;
    George, Barbara Lou Pitner; Hannah,
    Gladys Pitner; Marshall, Betty Lou
    Pitner; Moore, Brenda Pitner; Roberts,
    Esther Mae Pitner
Pittman, Kinney, and Pope, 107
pneumonia, 14, 191, 218
Poston, Claude, 49–50
Poston, Jack, 50
Prater's Mill (Farm), 76, 121
Pratt (Crider), (Elva) *Leola,* xi, xiii, 23, 40,
    43, **125**, 130, 159, 181–82, 199
Pratt (Edwards), (Cora) *Alma,* xi, xiii, 15,
    156
Pratt (Hughes), Flora E. (daughter of C. T.

and Minnie), xi, xiii, **3**, 14, 38, 40, 46, 93, 122, **125**, 126, 151, 159, 166, 190, 192

Pratt (Van Meter), Martha (*Tiny*) (daughter of C. T. and Minnie), xi, xiii, 23, 38, 40, 43, **60**, **125**

Pratt (Young), Polly (second wife of George W.), 9

Pratt, (Elmer) *Estle* (son of C. T. and Minnie), xi, xiii, **3**, 15, 40–41, 46, 48, 75, **125**, **168**, 171

Pratt, (Mary) *Minnie* Broyles (wife of C. T.), xi, xiii, 1–3, 9–11, 13–16, 21, 40, 60, 76, 105, 108, 112, 152; book by, 1, 9, 14, 207; as Church secretary/treasurer, 17, 46, 48–49, 55, 62, 85, 106, 113; death and burial of 126, 152, 170; expulsion of, 113, 116; marriage of, 10; and Methodist Church, 9, 11–13; as mother, 2–3, 11–16, 21, 23, 40, 43, 151, 159, 166, 181, 233; photos of, **3**, **95**, 128; physical description of, 10; support of C. T. by, 10–11, 13–15, 21–22

Pratt, Betty J. (daughter of Lloyd), 46, **60**

Pratt, Charles (father of George), 9

Pratt, Charles Thomas (*Tom*) (son of Lloyd), xiv, 40, 46, 117–18, 233

Pratt, Charles Thomas, I (*Charlie, C. T.*), xi, xiii–xiv, xvii–xviii, 1–3, 9, 40, 45, 48, 60, 70, 96, 104–6, 114, 151, 161, 177, 211, 228; on adultery, 97; aging of, 69, 71, 76, 101, 110, 112–14; and alcohol, 9–11, 14; anti-wealth preaching by, 36, 77; and appeal of his church, 30–31, 34–37, 63; as authoritarian, 36–37, 41, 43, 47, 49, 57; beliefs of, 1–2, 16–17, 20, 26, 31, 37, 42–43, 49, 58; Bible interpretation controlled by, 42–43, 47; Bible reading discouraged by, 43; businesses owned by, 57, 76; calling of to preach, 11–15; and Church control by, 47, 49, 55, 57, 62, 71–72, 75, 81–82, 106, 108–10, 116; Church control lost by, 43, 62, 65, 69, 71, 84, 102, 105–6, 112–13, 212; Church establishment by, 14–15, 20–23, 28–29, 210, 233; and Church growth, 14–18, 20–21, 23, 28–29, 34–36, 40, 42, 48, 54, 80; as Church treasurer, 41, 57; and college founding,

76–77; and communism, 74, 77–78, 80–82; conversion of, 10–11, 14–15; death and burial of, 126–28, 152, 170, 211; and devil, 2, 37, 42; and divorce attitude, 58, 60; and end times teachings, 37, 49, 72, 85, 108, 112, 207, 211–12; expulsion of from Church, 113–16; expulsion of from Mountain Assembly, 16–18; family tree of, xi; as farmer, 21, 26; as father, 3, 11, 14–15, 21, 23, 40, 43, 151, 159, 166, 181, 233; and fear, 31, 111; and financial problems of, 14–15, 43, 50–51; and fundraising, 37, 47, 49, 56–57, 62–63, 84–86, 92, 108; and giving everything to Church, 37, 39, 42, 56, 63–65, 75, 108–9, 111, 120; guilt used by, 36, 42, 63, 65, 97; and healing, 190; and Holiness ordination of, 13; illiteracy of, 2, 10, 13; illness of, 12, 126; image of, 204; jobs held by, 9–12, 15, 21; and labor support by, 34, 36, 56, 77, 80; and lawsuit against, 107–8; as manipulator, 30, 35–37, 42–43, 46, 49, 56–57, 63–65, 75, 81–82, 97, 109, 112; marriage of, 10; medical treatment rejected by, 12–13, 20, 38, 76, 189–91, 200, 218; mental problems of, 112, 114; and Methodist Church, 11–13; methods of, 30, 34–37, 42, 47, 49; ministers transferred by, 84; as moderator, 55, 75, 85, 96–97, 102, 109, 116; and money, 14–15, 37, 43, 47, 56–57, 62–63, 85–86, 92, 108, 137, 222; opponents of, 21, 78, 112–14; opposition to churches of, 15, 21, 50–51; paternalism by, 43, 46; photos of, **3**, **30**, **50**, **54**, **95**, 128; physical attacks on, 21; physical description of, 1, 10, 81; political influence of, 47, 50, 53–54; preaching by, 1–3, 14–15, 17, 20–22, 26, 29–31, 36–37, 42, 49, 58, 64–65, 72, 97, 101, 108, 114; relapses of, 11–12, 14; sayings of, 5, 7, 19, 25, 33, 41, 53, 67, 69, 73, 101, 115; showmanship of, 30, 36, 46, 63–65, 178; and singing, 30; and Studebaker trucks, 49–50; and taxes, 50–51; and teachings of, 102, 104, 112; and tithing, 42–43; and Wallace presidential campaign, 74; and women, 111–12, 134; youth of, 7–9

Pratt, Charlie Thomas, II (son of Jesse Sr. and Ethel), xi, xiv, 48, 59–60, 163, 171

Pratt, Charlie Thomas, III (aka Hughie Arlan Pratt; son of Jesse Sr. and Irene), xi, xiv, 103, 107, 125, 152–53, 162–64, 170–71, 179, 185, 216–18, 222, 225, 227, 232; as assistant overseer, 160, 166, 214, 218; as moderating influence, 216, 225–26; as overseer, 228–29, 231, 233; preaching by, 214; rebuke of by Jesse Jr., 217. *See also* Pratt, Hughie Arlan

Pratt, Cora. *See* Pratt (Edwards), (Cora) *Alma*

Pratt, Darlene (fourth wife of Jesse Jr.), 227–28

Pratt, David Ronald (son of Jesse Sr. and Ethel), xi, xiv, 48, 59–60, 163, 171

Pratt, Edmond L. (*Ed*) (son of C. T. and Minnie), xi, xiii, **3**, 10–12, 23, 40, **125**, 171

Pratt, Ethel B. Russell (first wife of Jesse Sr.), xi, xiv, 44–45, 47–48, 56, 58–60, 70, 131, 163, 171, 233, 249n14

Pratt, Faye (daughter of Lloyd), 46

Pratt, Floyd Howard (wife of Estle), 40

Pratt, Frances (daughter of Lloyd), 46

Pratt, George Washington (father of C. T.), xi, 7–9

Pratt, Herbert Hoover (son of C. T. and Minnie), xi, xiii, 23, 40, 43, 119, 122, **125**, 146–47, 152; and Arizona ranch, 146–47; and cattle speculation, 148, 163, 166–67, 171, 252n43; physical description of, 146–47

Pratt, Herbie. *See* Pratt, Johnnie Herbert

Pratt, Hughie Arlan (aka Charlie Thomas Pratt III, son of Jesse Sr. and Irene), 61, 106–7. *See also* Pratt, Charlie Thomas, III

Pratt, Irene McClure Smith (second wife of Jesse Sr.), xi, xiii-xv, 58–59, 70, 105–6, 108, 111, 119, 127, 129, 132, 134–35, 142, 147, 152, 171, 227; and cattle speculation, 163, 166–67, 252n43; character of, 156, 163; as Church treasurer, 113; and control of Church members by, 156–58, 176, 184–86; and control of Jesse Jr., 166, 176, 185; criticism of, 156, 160, 162; death of, 233; and death of Jesse Sr., 163–65, 167–69, 233; divorce of, 59–60, 241n28; and fundraising, 156–57, 176, 180–81, 184, 216; as manipulator, 132, 156, 160, 163, 165–66, 185–86; and marital problems with Jesse Sr., 162–64, 167, 169; marriages of, 59–61, 211; as match-maker, 157, 185–86; and money, 179–80, 222, 228; as mother (of children), 58–59, 61, 125, 132, 162, 226, 231, 233; as mother (title), 180, 184; photos of, **60**, 119, **128**, 128, **140**, 186, **188**; as pianist, 58–59, **60**; prophesying by, 156, 158, 160, 184; rebuking of, 160, 162, 170; servants of, 184; and social events, 184; and visits to members' homes by, 180–81

Pratt, Jesse Franklin, Jr. (son of Jesse Sr. and Irene), xi, xiv, xxv, 9, 43, 61, 124–25, 139, 152–53, 163, 165, 167; alcohol and drug use by, 161, 176, 180, 206, 215, 227–29; anger of, 177–78, 183, 197; army service of, 144, 148, 162, 176; and campground plan, 186–87; and Church control lost by, 203; and cirrhosis of the liver, 231–32; and confession train, 182–84; and country club membership, 187; death and burial of, 231–32; death of wife Wanda, 226–28; defense of Church by, 208–11; disadvantages of, 203; education of, 144, 203; emotional volatility of, 104, 170, 177–78, 204, 216; and extravagant spending by, 176–77, 180, 186, 204–6, 212, 219, 222–23, 227; and fear promoted by, 177–78, 182–83, 186, 209, 215, 217, 223; and gambling, 180, 206; and god-like treatment of, 178, 223; and golf, 186–87, 254n42; and guitar playing, 125, 161; home of, 180, 213–14, 220; and Internal Revenue Service, 220; and jobs of, 228–29; as manipulator, 178, 212–14, 220–21; marriages of, 162, 211, 227; as minister, 144, 175–76, 187–88; and misconduct by, 144–45, 161, 176, 204, 206, 212, 215, 220, 222–23, 228; and money, 176–80, 203, 205, 212–15, 220–22, 228–29; opposition to, 170–71, 206, 215; as overseer, 166, 170–71, 185, 209, 215; photos of, **145**, **188**, 207, **226**; physical description of, 231; and poverty, 229; preaching by, 187, 197, 204; and property sales, 204–6, 208; rebuking by, 176–77, 183–84, 186, 217, 225; and reign of terror by, 176–78, 182–83, 187; removal from power of, 227; rules changed by, 216–19, 225–26, 257n55; sayings of, 173, 175, 189, 203, 211; servants of, 184; and sexual activities of, 176, 206; and taxes, 220, 222, 228; and Trailblazers, 125, 161, 206, 213, 216–17, 220, 248n39; vengeance by, 177, 182; violence by, 144, 170–71, 176–78, 183–84, 186–87, 206, 217

Pratt, Jesse Franklin, Sr. (son of C. T. and Minnie, husband of Ethel and Irene), xi, xiii-xiv, 3, 16, 21, 23, 40–41, 43, 48, 55, 61, 75. 81, 83, 93–94, 96, 98, 114, 119, 125–26, 129, 144, 147, 181, 210, 228, 233; accomplishments of, 161; and acting like a god, 116, 127–28, 130, 132–34, 140–41, 157, 160; as airplane pilot, **44**, 45, 47, 55, 137–38, 164; and airplanes, 137–38, 149–51; as assistant moderator, 106; as Bible interpreter, 155–56; as bipolar, 104, 131; and blood at death scene, 164–68, 252n36; businesses owned by, 111; and Catholics, 140; and cattle speculation, 148, 163, 166–67, 252n43; and Church control by, 61, 69, 71, 84, 102, 104–5, 108–10, 113–14, 116, 123–24, 127, 129–30, 133, 135, 139–41, 156–57, 160; and Church growth, 116, 161; and communism, 77; and confession train, 123, 182; death and burial of, 154, 164–71, 175–76, 185, 191, 203; and death of Paul Hughes, 149–53; and devil, 103; divorce of, 59–60, 70, 104, 241n28; divorces ordered by, 124, 157–58; doctrinal changes by, 61, 71, 102, 104; education of, 43, 71, 152; emotional volatility of, 43–44, 70, 102, 104–5, 131–32, 163; eye injury of, 45; fatal spells cast by, 122; fear promoted by, 69–71, 102–4, 106, 111, 114, 117, 123, 130–31, 133, 140–41, 153,

160; and giving everything to Church, 109, 120; guards of, 122, 149, 161; and guitar playing, 59, 125, 158; and healing, 190; heart attack of alleged, 164–68; on homosexuality, 163; as house painter, 48, 55, 116, 118, 209; and humiliation of people by, 123–25, 130, 157, 160 ; and hunting, 138, 145, 152; image of, 204; jealousy by, 105, 157; kindness of, 131–32; lawsuit against, 107–8; as manipulator, 69–71, 102–3, 105–6, 113, 116–17, 122–23, 129–30, 149–52; and marital problems with Irene, 162–64; marriages of, xi, xiv, 44, 59–61, 70, 131, 249n14; as moderator/ overseer, 113, 115–16, 122, 127, 132, 208–9, 212; and money, 113, 117–18, 120–21, 129, 133–34, 137–38, 148, 161, 173, 209, 222; and obedience required by, 156–58; opposition to, 70; ordination of, 43; photos of, **44**, 119, **125**, **128**, 128, **140**, **147**, **168**, 186; physical description of, 45, 129; physical examination of, 45, 164; physical punishment by, 70, 102–5, 111, 131; and pistols, 55–56, 70, 106, 138, 145, 152, 208; preaching by, 44–45, 47–48, 58–61, 69, 77, 93, 101, 103–5, 108, 113, 120, 129–30, 132, 140, 148, 155, 161–63, 167; and property acquisition by, 119–20, 206; and property sales, 118–21, 209; prophesying of doom by, 69, 103–4, 122, 158; rebuked by Wayman, 160; and rebuking by, 70, 102–6, 111, 113, 122–24, 130–31, 153, 157–58, 160, 246n36; and rebuking of Irene by, 162–63, 167; regarded as God, 156; rules changed by, 61, 102, 115–17; sayings of, 73, 127, 137, 143, 155; and women, 124, 134, 155, 158, 160

Pratt, Jimmy L. (son of Jesse Sr. and Ethel), xi, xiv, 56, 58–60, 131, 163, 171, 233, 249n14

Pratt, Johnnie Herbert (*Herbie*) (son of Jesse Sr. and Irene), 125, 164, 214

Pratt, Johnny Franklin (son of Charlie III and Joy), 217–18, 232

Pratt, Joy (wife of Charlie III), 162, 164–66, 200, 214, 217, 232

Pratt, Juanita (daughter of Lloyd), 40
Pratt, Katie (wife of Lloyd), 40, 46
Pratt, Lewis, xiii, 11
Pratt, Lillian M. (daughter of Lloyd), 46
Pratt, Lloyd B. (son of C. T. and Minnie), xi, xiii-xiv, **3**, 11–12, 40–41, 46, 48, 117, 166
Pratt, Lula Mitchell, 23
Pratt, Margaret Elizabeth (daughter of Jesse Sr. and Irene), 125, 164–66, 214, 231–32
Pratt, Margaret Elizabeth Lair (mother of C. T.), xi, 7–8, **8**, 9
Pratt, Martha. *See* Pratt (Van Meter), Martha (*Tiny*)
Pratt, Marty Lane (son of Jesse Sr. and Irene), 125, 164, 214
Pratt, Mary Sue Burkett (first wife of Jesse Jr.), 162
Pratt, Minnie (daughter of Estle), 40
Pratt, Pamela Rena (daughter of Jesse Sr. and Irene), 125, 214
Pratt, Stephen (grandfather of George W.), 9
Pratt, Steve (son of Wayman), 170
Pratt, Virginia (sister of C. T.), 8–9
Pratt, Wanda Jean Poole (second wife of Jesse Jr.), xiv, 162–63, 182, 206, 213–14, 217, 226, **226**; death and burial of, 226–28, 232
Pratt, Wayman Paul, xi, 23, 40, 122, **125**, 134, 152, 160, 166, **168**; as assistant overseer, 160, 163; death of, 233; and physical assault on, 170–71; rebuking of Irene by, 160, 162, 170
"Pratt Church," 71
Pratt family, 85–86, 113, 129, 187, 208, 227; and airplanes, 137–38; businesses owned by, 76, 111; family tree of, xi; and fundraising, 181–82; as gods, 139, 181, 184, 186; and hierarchy in Church, 110, 139–40; leadership by, xxv, 137, 207; as ministers, 117–18, 163; and money, 132–34, 137, 139, 176, 179, 181, 215; and power struggles, 170; problems in, 161–62; sale of portraits of, 180; servants of, 135, 163–64, 184; as untouchable, 160
prayers, for healing, 20–21, 38, 192–93, 196–99

preeclampsia, 191–93
prejudice, against Holiness groups, 21–22, 35
prophecy, 22

Queen Chenille/Carpet, 57
quinine, 12, 20

radios, 87
Ranches Inc., 119–20
rattlesnakes, 146, 152
Redwine, Gaylon (son of George W.), 187
Redwine, George W., 187
revenge, for rebuking, 131
revivals, 11, 14, 21–23, 58, 93, 100, 102–3, 122, 131, 158, 180
Revolutionary War, 9
Richardson, Estle (grandfather of Marie Anderson), 199–200
riots, 143
Roberts, Charles, xv, 85, 89, 104, 114, 116, 123, 140–41, 156–57, 161–62, 166, 180–81, 186–87, 191, **192**, 201, 206, 211, 213–14, 230, 256n32
Roberts, Clarence, 41
Roberts, Esther Mae Pitner (daughter of Otha Pitner), 86, 191
Roberts, William (*Junior*) (father of Charles), xiv, 86, 158–59, 180, 191, **192**, 211, 256n32
Robertson, James, 104
Rock Hill, SC, Church in, 76
Rome, GA, Church in, 35
Roosevelt, Franklin D., 39, 73
Ross, Jack, 15
Ryman, Milton, 220

Sandeen, Ernest, 13
Saul, Harry, 57
Saunders, Barbara (sister of Libby Neighbors), 111–12
scabs, 77, 80
Scottsboro, AL, Church in, 76
sects, xvii-xviii, 72, 139
"seed" and Church hierarchy, 139–40
segregation, opposition to, 74

Sen-Sen, 92
Seventh-day Adventists, xvii
"Share-the-Work" plan, 39
Shaw Industries, 57–58
shorts, wearing of permitted, 216, 219, 225
shouting, in church services, 34, 238n3
shunning, xviii, 38, 70, 72, 86, 113, 116–18, 124, 157–58, 207–10, 219, 226
sin, confession of, 160
slacks, wearing of by women permitted, 219, 225
Smith (Purcell), Janet (youngest child of Irene and Oscar Smith), 58–61, 233
Smith, Betty (daughter of Irene and Oscar Smith), xi, 58–61
Smith, Cotton, xxiv
Smith, Dennis, xv, 42, 59, **107**, 165–66
Smith, Mae, xxv
Smith, Manuel, xxiv-xxv
Smith, Oscar (first husband of Irene Pratt), xi, xiv, 58, 61
Smith, Ruth (wife of Dennis, sister of Irene Pratt), 59, **60**, 61, 166
Smith, William (son of Irene and Oscar Smith), 58–61
Smithey, Eric, 124
Sneed, Dimple, 159
Soll, Rick, xxiv
South Dalton Baptist Church (Dalton, GA), 29
Southerner, The, xv, 76–80, 82
Sowder, Harold, 119, 153, 207, 220, 229
speaking in tongues, 22, 35, 130
Spilka, Bernard, 71–72
Spring Place, GA, maternity ward at, 159, **159**, 190–92, 209, 221
Springer, Frank, 34
St. Petersburg, FL, Church in, 76, 199
Stanley, Merton, 97–98
Starnes, Lonnie, 41
Starnes, Tray, 217
Staten, Lillie, 29
stock market crash (1929), 38
Studebaker trucks, 49–50
Summerville, GA, Church in, 35, 180

Tarver, Judge, 16
Taylor, Louis, 109, 158
Taylor, Viola (wife of Louis), 109, 158
Teems, J. C., 191
Teetersville, KY, Church in, 35
television, exposé of Church on, 204; ownership of permitted, 115, 204; use of restricted, 38, 76, 87, 208
Tennessee Department of Human Services, xxiii, 195–96
Texarkana, TX: Church in, 76; Church farm near, 121, 147
Textile Workers Union of America, 77–78, 80
Thurmond, Strom, 74
Trailblazers (singing group), 125, 161, 206, 213, 216–17, 220, 248n39
Trion, GA, Church in, 35, 103, 197
Truman, Harry, 73–74
Tufted Textile Manufacturer's Association, 78

Underwood, Lawrence H., 120
unemployed, 39–40; relief efforts for, 39, 46
Union Assembly of the Church of God, xiii, xvii-xviii, xxiv, 23, 35; charter of, xvii, 23; founding of, 18; incorporation of, 48; name change of, 75; 1943 meeting of, 41–42, 116. See also Church of God of the Union Assembly
Union City, GA, 75, 81, 109, 113, 120, 135
unionization, 33–34, 39–40, 45, 56, 79–80
unions, opposition to, 56
United Baptist Church, 13
United Textile Workers of America, 40, 45

vaccinations, 217
Van Meter, Chester, 188
Van Meter, Tiny. See Pratt (Van Meter), Martha (Tiny)
Vaughn, Joe, 23
Viamonte, Luis, 217
videos, rental of permitted, 218
Vietnam War, 125, 127, 138, 143–44, 148
Vinning, Louis, 50, 75
violence, 122–23, 125, 170, 176–78, 181, 187, 225–26

Wall Street, 38

Wallace, Henry, 73–74, 76–77, 79

Ward, Allen, 205

Watergate, 156, 162

Wayne, Cheryl, 94, 96

Wayne, Earl, 92, 94, 96

We Walked Alone (M. Pratt), 1, 9, 14, 207

Weaver, Ed, 205

welfare, provided by Church, 34

West, Don, xv, 73–74, 76–82

West Hill Cemetery (Dalton, GA), 126, 170

Whaley, Woodrow, 63

White, Edward, 26

White, GA, Church in, 158

White, L. B., 104

White, Wallace, 199

Whitfield County, GA, 23, 26, 48–49, 76, 109, 148; deaths in, 190–91; grand jury of, 80–82; Superior Court of, 51, 76, 109

Whitfield Milling Company, 75

Wiggs, George E., 41, 48, 62, 75

Wiggs, Jimmy, 108

Wilkesboro, NC, Church in, 76

Williamsburg, KY, Church in, 35

Williamson, Paul, 55

Wilson, Mildred, **60**

Wilson, Oley, 233–34

Wilson, Woodrow, 1

Winkler, Archie, 120–21, 169

women: abuse of, 87, 98, 105–6, 124, 134–35, 155, 184, 206; clothing of, 22, 37–38, 207; clothing regulations of changed, 216–17, 219, 225, 257n55; as cows, 156; disrespect for, 87–88, 97, 111–12, 134, 155–56; pregnancy-related deaths of, 135–36, 191–93, 197, 199; punishment of, 102–3, 123, 155, 158; restrictions on, 37–38, 47–48, 86–88, 110, 131, 134, 158, 183, 204, 207; as servants, 134–35

World War I, 1, 16, 19, 22, 27, 29

World War II, 41, 44–46, 48, 54, 56, 59, 61

worldly activities, rejection of, 22, 35, 37–38

worship practices, xxv, 34, 129–30, 238n3

Yuma County, AZ, 154